W9-DBR-585

Tosca's Rome

Susan Vandiver Nicassio

Tosca's Rome

THE PLAY AND THE OPERA
IN HISTORICAL PERSPECTIVE

With a new Appendix

THE UNIVERSITY OF CHICAGO PRESS Chicago and London

The University of Chicago Press, Chicago 60637
The University of Chicago Press, Ltd., London

© 1999, 2001 by The University of Chicago
All rights reserved. Published 1999
Paperback edition 2001

10 09 08 07 06 05 04 03 02 01   3 4 5 6 7

ISBN: 0-226-57971-9 (cloth)
ISBN: 0-226-57972-7 (paperback)

Library of Congress Cataloging-in-Publication Data

Nicassio, Susan Vandiver.
    Tosca's Rome : the play and the opera in historical perspective /
Susan Vandiver Nicassio.
        p.   cm.
    Includes bibliographical references and index.
    ISBN 0-226-57971-9 (alk. paper)
        1. Rome (Italy)—History—1798–1870.   2. Church and state—Italy—
Rome—History.   3. Sardou, Victorien, 1831–1908. Tosca.
    4. Puccini, Giacomo, 1858–1924. Tosca.   5. Rome (Italy—In
literature.   I. Title.
    DG812.4.N53   1999
    945′.63208—dc21   99-19417
                                                                  CIP

♾ The paper used in this publication meets the minimum
requirements of the American National Standard for
Information Sciences—Permanence of Paper for Printed
Library Materials, ANSI Z39.48-1992.

To My Family

My husband, who kept me going
My sister, who believed
My mother,
Sari Frances Chase Vandiver,
who started it all

Contents

List of Illustrations

MUSICAL EXAMPLES

Preface

On the afternoon of 13 December 1952 my mother, Sari Frances Chase Vandiver, had the radio tuned to the weekly broadcast from the Metropolitan Opera, as was her custom. My sister had recently married, leaving me the only plump little chick in the nest, and Dad's work had taken us away from New Orleans to Pensacola, Florida. It would have been difficult to get too much further from the glamour and sophistication that the Met then represented. The production of *Tosca* being broadcast on that day, as I discovered many years later, had a rather spectacular cast. The heroine was Dorothy Kirsten ("soprano from Montclair, N.J.," as the program noted in one of her first performances in the role). Kirsten, a slender, beautiful blonde and a protégée of Grace Moore, was one of those American opera singers of the 1940s and 1950s as much at home in the movies or on the Jack Benny Show as on the stage of the Met. Her Cavaradossi was Ferruccio Tagliavini ("tenor from Reggio Emilia"), a classic Italian tenor and at this time something of a matinee idol who performed with "reserves of energy and a great naturalness." His light voice and effortless charm made him a memorable hero. Scarpia was Paul Schoeffler ("baritone from Dresden, Germany"). The cast photograph shows a deeply lined, cynical face, arched eyebrows, a fastidious white wig, and cascades of lace at throat and cuffs. He holds a lorgnette with disdainfully arched fingers—no bellowing Scarpia here, and no Scarpia with moral qualms about his victims. In fact, a postwar Scarpia, and unambiguously evil, as Cavaradossi was unambiguously brave, and Tosca unambiguously loving. The 1950s did not lend themselves to shades of gray.

I'm not sure which of the three did the trick—I rather suspect it was Schoeffler—but mother must have been surprised mid-way through the second act to find her pre-pubescent daughter glued to the radio. I hadn't been consciously listening before that point; I have no memory of the mellifluous voice of Milton Cross delivering the plot summary. In fact, the details of the plot, as I winkled them out of mother, puzzled me: girls were more innocent in those days, and their mothers more reticent. No matter. I was obsessed. I would remain so.

My youthful politics were shaped as much by *Tosca* as by the Kennedy era. The revolutionaries were the good guys, the reactionaries were the bad guys: it was no stretch at all to see the entire twentieth century, and by extension the entire modern age, in terms of the vision presented by Puccini and by Sardou. Naïve, of course, but it meshed very nicely with the conventions of the day. It would be many years before I questioned any of these bedrock assumptions.

After a singing career too brief to be called undistinguished, I turned to history. Italian, of course. I dutifully explored the reforms of the eighteenth century in the North, the implications of the Napoleonic conquest, and the origins of Italian nationalism. I published monographs, delivered conference papers, and taught graduate students the intricacies of research and the stern, high demands of historiography. But all the while, of course, Tosca sang in my mind's ear.

It was not until my tenure as a post-doctoral Fellow at the American Academy in Rome in 1993–94—still researching a relatively prim mainstream topic—that it occurred to me that love and scholarship could coexist. And it took a broken leg to do the job. One false step descending from our apartment to the street changed everything. My left leg was very broken indeed. Then, after a week or ten days in a Roman hospital—an experience no philosopher should miss—I compounded the mess by falling out of my wheelchair and making a creditable though fortunately unsuccessful attempt to sever my right hand. (The awful joke, "She gave an arm and a leg for this book," was unavoidable.)

For most of the rest of my fellowship year, I was effectively confined to quarters. But these were not ordinary quarters. The American Academy in Rome nurtures in its ample bosom a select if eclectic crowd of researchers and academics—pre- and post-doctoral Fellows—in residence for the best part of a year, plus a constantly changing constellation of residents and visiting scholars. When the brew is right—and the 1993–94 brew was vintage—the results can be stimulating in the extreme. It is the ideal interdisciplinary context, with classicists, archeologists, artists, historians, musicians, poets, and the occasional stonemason gathering around the dinner table to discuss, debate, badger, and bait one another. Exciting enough when one goes out every day on one's individual quest; a real pressure cooker when one's horizons are narrowed to the Academy alone. During one of those sessions I must have been lamenting that my true love, *Tosca*, could hardly be considered an appropriate topic for a historian. And then the lights went on, illuminating the white hair of a senior scholar into a sort of halo as he made the casual comment that a book on *Tosca* would certainly be regarded as a valid historical topic at his university (Yale). The *Tosca* book was instantly transformed from the imaginary into the practical.

Confined by the combination of a wheelchair (later crutches) and Roman traffic, I set to work in the underground corridors of the Academy's ample library. I already knew enough about my subject to plunge directly into the material; and I was already familiar enough with the collections at venues like the Vatican, the Herziana, and the Archivio di Stato to deputize my husband for searches there. It quickly became apparent that this was definitely an exercise in historical research. But as the paths led deeper into the events of the summer of 1800, I couldn't help wondering, why do it this way? Why examine so minutely the historical context of *Tosca?* Why look at the Parthenopean disaster in Naples, the careers of long-dead opera singers, the perceptions of the castrati, the character of the executioner of Rome, or the hurried justice handed down by the special courts of 1799–1800?

Accurate historical knowledge is hardly essential to producing or performing the opera. A baritone singing Scarpia can do quite well without knowing the context within which an eighteenth-century police official worked, just as it is perfectly possible to perform Shakespeare without knowing anything about Tudor England, or even to go through life totally innocent of any understanding of history. But opera is deeply embedded in the historical-psychological-artistic-spiritual loam of our culture. (This fact may go some way toward explaining its enduring and frequently revitalized popularity.)

Tosca, like all opera, like all works of art, is an attempt to understand the human condition. The universality of *Tosca* includes not only the personal, the emotional, and the artistic, but also the greater world of political and religious struggle, and the titanic clash between revolutionary and traditional worldviews. What does the Parthenopean Republic have to do with *Tosca?* We might ask Sardou, who was certainly no fool. He made a major point of including it in the first act of his play, personalized by Angelotti's indignant recital of the sufferings of his revolutionary colleagues. Sardou did that because the account of the struggle in Naples immediately told his audience what was going to happen in Rome: the agents of tradition would mercilessly torture and destroy the agents of change. What does it matter that Puccini cut the verbiage and deleted any overt mention of Naples? When Angelotti staggers onto the stage, persecuted and in mortal danger, when Cavaradossi declaims that he will save him at the cost of his own life, the same message is conveyed. The fact that it is generalized only makes it more powerful. Modern audiences don't know about the Parthenopean Republic. But we do know a lot about tyranny, and we recognize heroism when we see it.

What does the world of eighteenth-century traditional theater have to do with *Tosca?* When Tosca sweeps into the church to the accompaniment of those elegant, Bellini-esque arpeggios, we know that she comes from a world characterized by stability and order, by elegance, and by an assumption that life makes sense. Sardou, using words where Puccini used music, makes it plain that in Floria Tosca's world, where traditional theater conveyed traditional values, a gentle pope could pat a young girl's cheek and tell her that "[her singing] is a way of praying to God." It is a quaint, old-fashioned, beautiful world—and it will be shattered and destroyed, because for us, as for Sardou and Puccini, it seems to be an illusion.

And yet if we look objectively at the Rome of the popes before 1800 we see that it was a coherent, secure state and relatively popular with its people, certainly when compared with the ones that immediately succeeded it. Why then were nineteenth-century liberals, Sardou and Puccini among them, determined to present the city, and the regime, as corrupt and repressive? In fact, in the context of 1798–1800, the Roman Republic fits this description far better than the papal state or the rule of the Allies. So, why not change the political allegiance of the characters? It could be done quite easily, with little change of venue or costume. It would not even require much of a time shift— moving it back a year and a half to November of 1798 would do the trick. The hero could be based on the nameless subdeacon who, according to the chronicler Fortunati, was shot in the Piazza del Popolo for replacing the Liberty Tree in his village with a crucifix. Laicize him, move him to Rome, and give him a wife or a lover who in her political naïveté supports the French. Floria Tosca would require little change. We would need only to pattern her on one of the women who really sang in Rome under the Republic. We could even take one of Sardou's characters and change him from victim to villain: Cesare Angelotti, if patterned more accurately on the real Liborio Angelucci, could take the place of Scarpia. All that the historical Angelucci would require would be the insertion of a bit of backbone, and a sexual appetite to match his appetite for money. Of course, the Te Deum would have to be changed to a Republican spectacle (the Feast of Regeneration, perhaps?), and Bonaparte as the victorious general named in the second act would have to become the decidedly less charismatic figure of Mélas.

And voilà! an Anti-Tosca.

Utterly unthinkable, of course. Certainly for Sardou or Puccini. Why?

My treatment of *Tosca* derives at least in part from a suspicion that, while all ages are in some sense pivotal, the one we have been tipped into at the end of the twentieth century has the potential to be the most cataclysmic since the French Revolution turned the world upside down. What does this have to do with *Tosca*, except for the apparently coincidental fact that the play and the opera are set during the era in which the French, led by Napoleon, were revolutionizing Europe? But is it only coincidence that *Tosca*, like our lives today, stands between centuries, the characters with one foot in the eighteenth, the other in the nineteenth century; the opera itself composed in the nineteenth and premiered in the twentieth (though purists will insist that January 1900 was the last year of the old century)? I have focused on the eighteenth-to-nineteenth transition, but one could as easily and as validly look more closely at the nineteenth-to-twentieth. Is it of only marginal interest that Sardou and Puccini, two late-nineteenth-century artists, based their melodramatic plots on this particular example of rather poor history? To say that it was "conventional" begs the question, but points toward a deeper issue: what was this theatrical convention, and why did it evoke the desired responses? And why does it continue to do so? These are some of the questions to which this book tries to suggest possible answers.

Tosca is a portmanteau of cultural icons. Sardou and Puccini must have instinctively understood the way it combines eternal themes (love, loyalty, betrayal) with the powerful political myth of Napoleon and the French Revolution. Now we seem to be on the edge of another massive shift of consciousness. If the French Revolution is finally over, where do we go from here? Tosca will not tell us. But by singing to us of the past, she may offer us hints for the future.

Acknowledgments

My thanks are due to my colleagues who were generous with their time and their talent, especially to Michele Girardi and Dexter Edge—with the usual emphatic disclaimer that any mistakes are mine alone. I would also like to thank the Fellows and staff at the American Academy in Rome, especially Norman M. Roberson; Maria Pia Ferraris at Ricordi; Deborah Burton; Kathleen Hansell for her faith in this project; and the librarians at Remington College, for service above and beyond the call of duty. Special thanks must go to my husband, Anthony R. Nicassio, and to our son, Alexander; to my sister Nancy; and to our mother, who on that fateful day in 1952 had the radio tuned to the Metropolitan Opera broadcast.

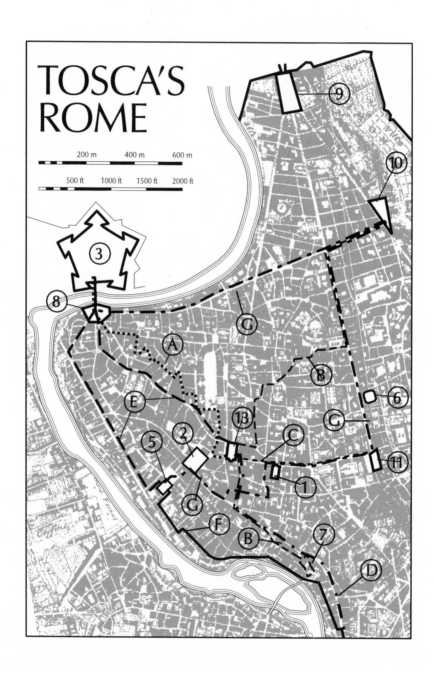

TOSCA'S ROME

200 m   400 m   600 m

500 ft   1000 ft   1500 ft   2000 ft

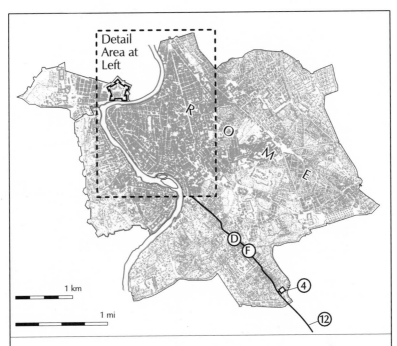

LEGEND

ROUTES

A *Angelotti:* Castel Sant'Angelo to Sant'Andrea della Valle, through the Piazza of the Angel

B *Cavaradossi:* Piazza di Spagna to Sant'Andrea della Valle, from there to the ghetto and back

C *Tosca:* Palazzo Venezia or the Argentina theater to Sant'Andrea della Valle

D *Cavaradossi and Angelotti:* Sant'Andrea della Valle to Cavaradossi's villa

E *Scarpia:* Farnese Palace to Sant'Angelo to Sant'Andrea della Valle

F *Spoletta:* Farnese Palace to Cavaradossi's villa and back

G *Tosca:* Farnese Palace to the Piazza di Spagna to the Castel Sant'Angelo

LOCATIONS

1. Argentina Theater
2. Campo dei Fiori
3. Castel Sant'Angelo
4. Cavaradossi's Villa
5. Farnese Palace
6. French Academy
7. Ghetto
8. Piazza of the Angel
9. Piazza del Popolo
10. Piazza di Spagna
11. Piazza Venezia
12. Appian Way
13. Sant'Andrea della Valle

Introduction

> . . . *Che lavoro d'orchestra e de violini,*
> *che motivi gustosi e origginali!*
> *Però li mezzi mejo, li più fini*
> *so' stati proprio quelli crericali.*
> *Puccini ch'è 'n artista, un bon'amico,*
> *pe' vede tutti quanti entusiasmati,*
> *ha dovuto ricorre ar tempo antico!*
> *Li pezzi ch'ânno fatto più impressione*
> *defatti, fijo mio, quali so' stati?!*
> *Tre: Campane, Te-Deum, e Pricissione!!*

> What a job for the orchestra and the violins!
> What delightful and original tunes!
> But the best methods, the finest,
> were precisely the clerical ones.
> Puccini, who is an artist and a good friend,
> In order to see everyone get enthusiastic
> had to go back to the old times!
> The pieces that made the biggest impression,
> In fact, my boy, what were they?!
> Three: Bells, Te Deum, and Procession!![1]

*F*irst impressions can be revealing. This dialect poem appeared in *La vera Roma* a few days after *Tosca*'s January 1900 premiere in Rome. In it the anonymous poet has put his finger on three themes that lie at the core of the opera: music, the Old Times (that is, papal Rome),[2] and the Roman Catholic Church. And these three themes—religion, history, and music—provide the scope of this interdisciplinary exploration of the times, places, and ideas of *Tosca*.

In his study of Puccini, Michele Girardi notes that religion gives both Sardou's play (on which the opera was based) and Puccini's opera their ideological framework.[3] While Puccini made skillful use of "local color" or atmosphere in all of his operas, nowhere is that atmosphere so important as in *Tosca*, where local color—that is, the re-creation of papal Rome—"not only provides a background for the action but motivates [the characters'] choices and their ideologies."[4] This ideological focus is not immediately obvious because almost all of the political detail that was so important in the play *La Tosca* has been cut from the opera. But one result of this cutting has been that the operatic drama is tied not to any specific historical or political events, but rather to the overpowering image of Rome as the center of Christianity. Victorien Sardou, the author of the play, used religion as a contrast to political liberalism; Puccini, who put no more faith in political liberalism than he put in the Church, presents both Church and State as hostile, and ultimately fatal, to the individual's futile struggle for happiness. How could he have done otherwise? Puccini the old "church mouse"—church musician and heir to church musicians; Puccini, the free thinker and libertine, living with another man's wife, seasoning his long-term adultery with short-term infidelities; Puccini, the favorite child of a pious widow, never quite losing his respect—or fear?—for "the faith of my mother"; Puccini, son of a troubled new Italy that had been born in conflict with the papacy; Puccini, the artist in a civilization that had traded tradition for progress and looked to Art as the language of the human spirit.

Religion in Rome, of course, is deeply embedded in history. And *Tosca* is by far the most obviously "historical" opera in the active repertoire, despite the fact that dozens of operas have plots that depend on more or less historical events and contexts.[5] Only *Tosca* is pinned, like a butterfly to a card, to a specific year, month, and day; it is even bracketed within a specific set of hours. The opera's libretto contents itself with setting the story in "June 1800" but the events (and the Sardou play on which the opera is based) narrow down the time of the action to just over sixteen hours from a few minutes before midday on 17 June (the bell for the Angelus rings shortly after the curtain rises on Act I) to a few minutes after dawn on 18 June (the firing squad arrives for the hero as the bells strike "the fourth hour" and Tosca, waiting, frets that "the sun is already rising" *(già sorge il sole)*.

The calendar and the clock are not the only things that tie *Tosca* to history. The plot revolves around historical events, from the fall of the Parthenopean Republic in Naples (June 1799—Angelotti, whose escape from prison sets the plot in motion, is a refugee from this debacle) to the battle of Marengo (14 June 1800—the hero Cavaradossi is so excited by news of this Napoleonic victory that he signs his own death warrant by shouting about it when the news reaches Rome on the night of 17 June). Sardou stuffed his play with enough historical and quasi-historical characters to create an illusion of authenticity that still deceives most commentators. Puccini and his librettists excised most of the supernumeraries (who include the real queen of Naples

and the real governor of Rome), but the commentator who does a bit of rudi-
mentary digging in the historical record discovers a tempting array of "real"
Toscas, Scarpias, Cavaradossis, and Angelottis.

It seems obvious, then, that an examination of the historical and religious
background of the events and ideas portrayed in this very historical and religious opera should provide useful insights into the work, its genesis, its
meaning, and its impact. But real history, like real life, is rarely simple. The
first thing the historian notices is that the opera, like the play, is only indi-
rectly concerned with the late eighteenth century or with Napoleonic Italy. If
the work can be seen as a historical document (and it can), that document
tells us less about 1800 than about the *perception* of 1800 that was current in
France in the late 1880s (Sardou's play was first produced in November 1887)
and in Italy a decade later (the opera *Tosca* was premiered in Rome in January 1900).

However, if Sardou's (and Puccini's) *(La) Tosca* taken at face value is not
very good history, we should note that in certain circumstances, "bad" history, distorted through the preoccupations and prejudices of its practitioners,
can tell us as much as "good" history. And when this bad history is embedded in a work of art, it can tell us a great deal indeed. A work of art such as
Tosca internalizes and expresses the images of history useful to the time in
which the art is created. This is especially clear in works that are below the
first rank in artistic terms—a category into which Sardou's play certainly
falls, and one to which not a few music critics would also consign the opera.
If we examine the realities of eighteenth-century Rome, and look at the ways
that Sardou and then Puccini and his librettists used those realities, we will
understand more about the creative process and about the relationship between the artist and the historical context within which she or he works. This
concept has taken hold during the past decade or so in the field of literary
criticism under the title of the New Historicism. The "new historicism" acknowledges this close relationship between the writer and the historical context within which the writer works.[6]

On the purely dramatic level, history fulfills a number of functions in both
the play and the opera: it provides a framework on which to display the sex,
self-sacrifice, and violent death that account for the visceral appeal of the
work; it offers a psychic distance that makes the horrors of the plot more
bearable; it elevates the sordid to the tragic. In terms of the creative process,
history gives both Sardou, and Puccini and his librettists, a shorthand way
of "plugging in" to powerful political, social, and cultural currents, allowing
them to connect directly with a set of assumptions and emotional responses

common to most members of their audience. This is true because both the play and the opera are built around one of the nodal points of Western self-definition: the myth of the French Revolution and Napoleon, a myth about liberty, individualism, and a militantly secular vision of the nature of the State. By attaching their plot(s) to this myth the creative artists have made connection with a set of ideas that remain sensitive in the popular subconscious. Sardou, a politicized Frenchman of the mid-nineteenth century, battered his audience with quasi-historical detail in order to make this connection. Puccini, appropriately for a turn-of-the-century Italian disillusioned with politics, savagely cut all the Sardovian verbiage, but the emotional punch that derives from the historical situation not only remains but is amplified: in the Te Deum, where the villain Scarpia's power and lust blend with the power of the Church; in the dark menace of state-sponsored torture and death; in the clarion heroism of Mario's "Vittoria!" outburst in Act II. The story about Floria Tosca, her lover, and their nemesis was written at the time of the first centennial of the French Revolution and Napoleon; the opera had its premiere almost precisely one hundred years after the story was supposed to have taken place. Now, a century later, it is remarkable how resonant the events of that time remain. Hardly a freshman enters university without a heavy load of mental baggage about the French Revolution, most of it wildly inaccurate. The archetypical vision of the revolution is almost identical to that espoused by Sardou and Puccini at the end of the nineteenth century, seeing it as a struggle between Good (the revolution) and Evil (the old-regime states).

Nineteenth-century Liberalism found its roots in the revolutionary and Napoleonic periods. The sort of history that we find in *Tosca* is a fairly typical popular redefinition of the earlier period that reflects nineteenth-century political and intellectual fashion: that is, late eighteenth-century history was seen as a dramatic demonstration of the futility (if not the villainy) of trying to halt the inevitable rise of secular liberalism. The subject of this book lies in the creative interaction between this "redefinition" and the period as scholars are now coming to understand it. This is by no means an argument that *Tosca* should be reinterpreted to bring it closer to historical reality, as if Puccini had somehow made a mistake that should or could be corrected by more dispassionate research. It is rather an argument that we can better understand the work of art, and the artist, when we gain as clear as possible an understanding of the soil in which they grew.

The primary, but not the exclusive, focus of this study is historical. But the book is a venture into that most dangerous and yet potentially most fruitful field—interdisciplinary studies. As such it draws not only on classical historical resources such as archival documents, but also on a range of other tools. These include musical analysis, textual analysis of the libretto, theater and religious studies, and the graphic arts.

In this multilayered structure we will first examine the genesis of the play and the opera in the late nineteenth century, paying particular attention to the anti-clericalism that was such an important element in the political and intellectual worlds of both Sardou and Puccini. Only then can we turn to the time and place in which the playwright and composer set their story: Rome, where the struggle between the Church and the State took on flesh and blood as secular powers, revolutionary and counter-revolutionary, attempted to rule the city without a pope for the first time since the fourteenth century.

The next three sections of the book deal with the eighteenth-century realities in which the fictional characters act out their drama. Each of the three sections is centered around one of the three central characters. Each explores the historical reality, and looks at figures, both real and not so real, on which the characters could have been modeled. "The Painter's Rome" was a center of world art rivaled only by Paris, and the culmination of the Grand Tour, which every European with pretensions of culture had to visit. "The Singer's Rome" serves as a gateway to the musical institutions of eighteenth-century Italy, in Rome and in Tosca's native Veneto. (She comes from Verona, a city that lies within the Veneto, that is, the territory ruled by Venice.) The chapter examines the Roman theatrical season of 1800 in some detail. "The Policeman's Rome" deals with the politics and law of this troubled period, and looks south to Naples, where Scarpia is supposed to have learned his trade.

The last four chapters offer a scene-by-scene examination of the opera, including an "entr'acte" section which considers the events that are assumed to take place between the first and second acts. These chapters look at the opera in terms of plot and character development, and examine the historical realities behind the theatrical representations. Although the present author makes no representations as to musical expertise, these chapters also include analysis of the musical content of key scenes of the opera.

Music, the Old Times, and the Church, then, give us the multifaceted lens with which to examine *Tosca*, and Tosca's Rome.

The reader may find it useful, before plunging into this account, to refresh his or her familiarity with the story of the opera (for a more detailed comparison between the opera and the play see appendix 1).

The first act of the opera is set in the church of Sant'Andrea della Valle in Rome. It is midday on the seventeenth of June 1800, seven months after the collapse of the short-lived Roman Republic and two weeks before the arrival of Pope Pius VII, the new pope who will assume rule of the city. Meanwhile Rome has been under the control of the Neapolitans, Austrians, and their allies against Republican France, whose armies, under the young General Bonaparte, are once again threatening Italy.

A political prisoner (Cesare Angelotti) has escaped from the Castel Sant' Angelo with the help of his sister, the marchesa Attavanti. She has left him the key to her family chapel and clothing and a fan with which to disguise himself as a woman. At the church Angelotti meets Mario Cavaradossi, an aristocratic painter with radical sympathies, who offers to help him. They are interrupted by the arrival of Cavaradossi's jealous lover, the singer Floria Tosca. Angelotti returns to his hiding place, and the lovers share an extended scene.

Cavaradossi avoids telling Tosca about the escape, as she shares none of his political liberalism or religious skepticism. When she leaves, Cavaradossi and Angelotti make hurried plans and, as a cannon shot announces the discovery of Angelotti's escape, both men hurry away, barely missing the arrival of the sacristan and the choir celebrating the (false) news of Bonaparte's defeat at Marengo. Baron Scarpia, the chief of police, arrives on the trail of the escaped prisoner. He connects the two men by their common political background and by the fact that Cavaradossi has, without realizing it, used Angelotti's sister as a model for Mary Magdalene. When Tosca returns, Scarpia plays on her ignorance and her jealous nature in order to find her lover and with him, the escaped prisoner. He produces a fan that was mislaid from Angelotti's disguise to convince her that Cavaradossi is betraying her with the marchesa. When she hurries to the secret villa, or country house, that she shares with the painter, she is followed by police agents. The first act of the opera ends here as an outwardly devout Scarpia kneels, secretly gloating over his coming conquest of the singer. Only later do we learn that at the villa Floria has learned the truth and then returned to Rome, where she is to sing that night for the queen of Naples; as soon as she leaves the villa the police arrest Cavaradossi, but are unable to find his hidden guest.

In Act II Cavaradossi is brought to Scarpia's quarters, which overlook the royal apartments at the Farnese palace. He denies any knowledge of Angelotti. Floria's voice is heard, singing at a gala reception given by the queen to celebrate a supposed victory over Bonaparte. Floria, summoned to the presence of the chief of police, arrives just as Cavaradossi is being taken into an adjoining room to be questioned under torture. As his groans become screams of pain she defies her lover's orders and reveals the hiding place, a well in their garden. He curses her for betraying him but is elated when a messenger hurries to inform Scarpia that Bonaparte, whom they had thought defeated, has in fact turned the tide and won the battle at Marengo. Mario is dragged away to be executed for treason and Floria pleads for his life. Scarpia agrees, on condition that she submit to his sexual pleasures. He gives orders for a sham execution and writes out a passport for the lovers. When he approaches her she stabs him and leaves his corpse on the floor, surrounded by candles, with a crucifix on his chest.

At the Castel Sant'Angelo Mario waits for daybreak, and death. He bribes a jailer to deliver a letter to Tosca, but is overcome with grief and cannot complete it. Floria arrives with the passport and news of Scarpia's death. She tells him that he has only to submit to the pretense of an execution, and then they will be free to slip away from the city. Whether or not Mario believes that he will be saved, he joins her in planning a new life far from Rome. But dawn comes and with it a genuine firing squad. As Tosca laments over her lover's bullet-riddled corpse, agents arrive with news of Scarpia's murder. Rather than be arrested, Floria throws herself from the battlements of the castle to death in the courtyard below.

The basic plot devices of the opera and the play are the same—political and religious repression as a background for the jealous singer, her lover, and the sadistic police chief; the portrait in the painting; the impulsive decision to help an escaped political prisoner; the arrest and torture of one of the lovers in order to force the other to betray the secret; the false offer of clemency in exchange for sex; and the culminating deaths of all the main characters by murder, execution, and suicide. Most of the differences between the play and the opera can be traced to Victorien Sardou's obsession with quasi-historical detail, to his French chauvinism, and to the shift in interest by Puccini and his librettists from the political to the personal. Sardou's "well-made play" is a cunningly detailed dramatic machine peopled with more or less cardboard characters. In Puccini's opera Tosca, Mario, and Scarpia are not much more convincing as individuals, but they have a profound emotional reality; they have sometimes been seen as images of the composer himself, obsessed with guilty sexual passion, romantic love, art, jealousy, and death.

The first act of the play closely parallels the first half of Act I of the opera, but in the play we are given massive amounts of biographical detail about Cavaradossi, Tosca, and Angelotti. We learn that Mario is Roman only through his father, having been born and raised in Paris, where he studied painting with Jacques-Louis David; he is in Rome on family business and intends to stay only until his new lover can leave for an engagement in Venice. We learn that Tosca is an orphan raised and trained in a convent in Verona, discovered by Cimarosa, and set free to sing in the theater by Pius VI. Angelotti recites a mini-novella on his own background in which he has a brief sexual encounter with Emma Hamilton, participates in the disastrous Parthenopean Republic, and flees to Rome only to be pursued by the menacing Sicilian baron Scarpia, who plans to send him back to Naples to hang for the entertainment of Angelotti's former whore, now Lady Hamilton, wife of the British ambassador and mistress of Lord Nelson.

In the play Tosca takes only a perfunctory interest in the portrait of the marchesa Attavanti, and instead establishes her character as kittenish, feather-headed, superstitious, and, above all, passionate, under the indulgent but controlling eye of her French lover. (Mario declines to tell her about Angelotti on the theory that "the only truly discrete woman is the one who knows nothing.") Both first acts close with a Te Deum sung in honor of the Austrian victory at the siege of Genoa, though of course in the opera the ceremony is much more effective.

The second half of Act I of the opera contains plot developments taken from Sardou's second act, which is set in the apartments of the queen of Naples at the Farnese Palace during a gala celebration attended by the court and nobility. This act is packed with minor characters and quaint Italian customs designed to show the charming decadence of the Romans in contrast to the bestial cruelty of the Neapolitans and the stalwart, forward-looking courage of the French (it ends with a French royalist émigré crying out, on hearing the news of Bonaparte's victory, "I am defeated but we are victorious: Vive la France!" to the sound of confused cheers offstage). The major plot advance of this act is the way in which Scarpia uses the fan he found in the Attavanti chapel to convince Tosca that her lover has taken the marchesa to the secret hideaway he usually shares with Tosca. The police have already searched for Cavaradossi and failed to find him, thus giving Scarpia the motive for his deception. Puccini's librettists rather unconvincingly moved this scene to the first act of the opera, where it sends the jealous singer to the villa, covertly pursued by police agents, long before anyone has even looked for the painter. In Sardou's Act II we see Scarpia as a courtier, afraid for his own safety. In an effectively dramatic closing scene, Queen Maria Carolina reads out what she thinks will be additional news from the victory at Marengo only to discover that it is news of Bonaparte's stunning surprise victory. This episode, moved to the second act of the opera (though without the presence of the queen), provokes Cavaradossi's "Vittoria!" outburst and serves as an all-too-visible patch to connect the two halves of that act.

Most of the material in the first half of Act II of the opera comes from the third act of the play, set at Cavaradossi's villa, where Angelotti takes refuge in the well (after we are treated to an extensive description and history of the hiding place). Floria arrives and discovers her mistake too late. She has been followed by Scarpia and his agents, and as in the opera she gives away the secret after a long and sadistically graphic (though offstage) torture scene. The third act of the play ends as Mario, bitterly disappointed by Floria's betrayal, pushes her aside and is dragged away to prison. There is no sudden message from Marengo, and no treasonable outburst. Tosca, having fainted, is also brought along to prison.

The events of the second half of the opera's second act take place in the play's Act IV, set in Scarpia's offices at the Castel Sant'Angelo. There is little difference between the action of the play and the opera here, except that the villain's sexual sadism is more graphic in the play.

The fifth and last act of the play consists of two very short scenes, which in terms of plot development are almost identical to the opera, but which are very different in tone and character. Where the operatic hero reviews his life in terms of sensory impressions and passions, and is overwhelmed by a yearning sense of loss, the stoic hero of the play brushes aside spiritual comfort of any sort, romantic or religious, in order to take a nap. The operatic heroine relives the trauma of the near rape and murder, and swings from hysterical distress to hysterical joy at their prospective liberation; Sardou's Floria is more business-like, instructing her Mario in his role. While Puccini's score is full of foreboding, hinting that Cavaradossi knows or at least suspects that he is about to die, there is no such suggestion in the play. The last scene of the play, which contains only twenty-six lines of dialogue, is there simply to allow Tosca to leap to her death. Perhaps most revealing of all, the last word of the opera is "God" ("Oh Scarpia, before God!," *Oh Scarpia, avanti a Dio!*), while the last word of the play is "scum" ("I'm going there [to join Mario], you scum!," *J'y vais, canailles!*).

I   *"Historico-topographico-panoramic Inexactitudes"*

Then, in making a sketch of the panorama for me, he wanted to show
the course of the Tiber passing between St. Peter's and the fortress!! I
told him that the river ran on the other side, under [the fortress], and
he, calm as a fish, said, "Oh, that's nothing!" Quite a fellow, all life
and fire, and full of historico-topographico-panoramic inexactitudes.[1]

$\mathscr{P}$uccini, seduced by Tosca and determined to make an operatic heroine of her, went to negotiate with her "father" Victorien Sardou with his eyes
open. The old Magician of the Paris stage (see fig. 1) cherished his reputation
as a writer of carefully researched historical dramas, but Puccini as an Italian knew perfectly well that Sardou's Rome—full of tyranny and heroism,
with ancient rivers leaping their banks for the convenience of set designers—
was largely a figment of the Frenchman's imagination. The composer didn't
care: his attraction to the subject had less to do with history than with a powerful mixture of economics and eroticism, a keen nose for the box office, and
a self-described "Neronic instinct" fired by the image of sexual guilt expiated
through physical and psychological torture. There was, his instincts must have
told him, something universal (if unsavory) in *La Tosca*.[2]

Victorien Sardou has now been reduced to "the oftenest referred to and
least read dramatist of modern times," but in his day he ruled the popular
stage.[3] He wrote more than seventy plays, most of them resounding successes,
and not one of them performed today. Born in Paris in 1831, he grew up in the
provinces, where his schoolmaster father worked. To please his father he began to study medicine at age twenty-one but soon abandoned science for his
one true love, the stage. Politically he considered himself a leftist. As a young
playwright he found inspiration in the stories told him by a red-haired old
Terrorist (in 1852, after the Terror had been sanitized by a distance of some
sixty years), and he espoused popular radical ideas in many of his plays. A
fervent if not particularly active republican, as a teenager under the short-
lived Second Republic (1848–52) he dated his diary according to the republican calendar (or at least he claims to have done so).[4] When Louis Napoleon

FIGURE I. Victorien Sardou, a photograph of the "Old Magician" taken in 1908. Published in *L'Illustration théâtrale*, no. 121, 19 June 1909 edition of *La Tosca*. Author's collection

Bonaparte did away with the Republic to create the Second Empire, Sardou (still a struggling student) adapted to the changing climate and turned his hand to frothy amusements and lightweight satires. His first play, *La Taverne des Étudiants* (The Students' Tavern), was produced at the Odéon theater in Paris in 1854, but it sank with scarcely a trace. The twenty-three-year-old would-be author, nothing daunted, set himself the task of learning his craft. He determined to follow in the footsteps of Eugène Scribe, the theatrical giant of his age, author of almost 400 plays who until his death in 1861 dominated, almost defined, French theater.

Scribe was the great master of what has come to be known as the "well-made play," a form of popular drama which depended for effect on ingenious and complex plotting and surprise endings. As an exercise, Sardou would read the first act of a Scribe play, and attempt to complete the story according to the clues laid out in the expository opening scenes.[5] The hard work paid off, and by the end of 1859 Sardou's original plays began to appear regularly in the theaters of Paris; they would remain there until after World War I.

In the 1860s Sardou dabbled in social criticism, poking fun at such easy targets as gullible peasants, the nouveau riche, and Americans and American-ized women in plays like *Les Femmes fortes* (Strong Women; 1860), *Les Vieux garçons* (The Old Boys; 1865), *La Famille Benoîton* (The Benoîton Family; 1865), and an 1873 vaudeville satire on American family life entitled *L'Oncle Sam.* By the early 1880s France's most popular playwright entered into a col-laboration with her most popular actress, Sarah Bernhardt (they became known as "The Two S's"). The golden-voiced Sarah (see fig. 2) was at her best in tragedy, and Sardou provided her with a series of historical melodramas: *Fédora* (1882), *Théodora* (1884), *La Tosca* (1887), *Cléopatra* (1890), *Gis-monda* (1894), and *La Sorcière* (1903).[6]

A self-proclaimed republican patriot and history buff, Sardou returned again and again to the period of the French Revolution and Napoleon (among others, this period provided him with material for hits like *La Tosca, Ther-midor, Madame Sans-Gêne,* and *Robespierre*) and larded his plays with ideological catch-phrases and appeals to chauvinistic nostalgia to which he knew his Parisian audience would respond. In 1887, the year in which *La Tosca* was first performed, the French badly needed the comfort of a little chauvinism. It was much more pleasant to look back to the glories of the tri-umphant Grande Nation of 1792–1814 than to contemplate the shoddy reali-ties of the current government. The Third Republic had been forced on France after the mortifying defeat of Napoleon III's Second Empire in the Franco-Prussian war, and the bloody horrors of the Paris Commune of 1871. Born in humiliation and civil strife, the Third Republic would be character-ized by meretricious political maneuvering and a succession of scandals. *La Tosca* had its premiere as two of the greatest scandals came to a head: Gen-eral Boulanger's threatened coup d'état, and l'affaire Wilson, in which the son-in-law of the President of the Republic was caught selling admission to the august Legion of Honor.[7] But social chaos is not necessarily a bad thing for the theater, and the master knew a surefire theme when he saw one. *La Tosca* had everything: a plum role for superstar Sarah Bernhardt as an amorous, temperamental performer (in effect, she played herself); plenty of sex and vi-olence; an exotic historical setting that offered the opportunity for gorgeous sets and costumes; and a vaguely left-wing plot glorifying both Napoleon and

FIGURE 2. Sarah Bernhardt, at about the time of the premiere of *La Tosca*. Foto Marburg/Art Resource, NY

the martyrs of liberty, and cashing in on the upcoming first centennial of the French Revolution.[8]

Despite muted voices of protest from the Right, this centennial was a triumphant celebration of republican issues. And a defining republican issue of the Third Republic was anti-clericalism, or laicism: that is, opposition to the power and influence of the Catholic Church in France. The most famous example of this struggle, the Dreyfus affair, came to the boil in January 1898 with Zola's famous pamphlet, *J'accuse*, but as early as 1868 Larousse's dictionary had defined "clerical" thus: "The clerical spirit is the negation of the conquests of modern science, the hatred of human dignity, the return to the bloody shadows of the Middle Ages, in a word, the opposite of the Revolution."[9]

The Third Republic was characterized by more or less constant warfare with the Catholic Church, a struggle understood by the Left as modernism rising above the darkness of superstition and tyranny, and by the Right as a diabolically inspired attempt to deliver France up to corruption and chaos. A chasm yawned between Left and Right, and virtually every aspect of French cultural life, from the Chamber of Deputies to the powerful newspaper press, reflected this division in one form or another. Catholics, encouraged by the Syllabus of Errors of 1864 and the declaration of papal infallibility of 1870, refused to cooperate with or even recognize the Republic. The Republic for its part openly attacked the Catholics with laws such as the 1882 law removing crucifixes from the schools, and the 1889 law subjecting seminarians to the draft ("priests, put on your backpacks!" the Left crowed), culminating in a series of legal measures between 1901 and 1905 establishing the separation of church and state.[10] Anti-clericalism was such a powerful force in French politics and society that Clemenceau refused to attend a 1918 victory Te Deum in Notre Dame cathedral.[11]

Ernest Renan, whose *Vie de Jésus* was an open attack on the divinity of Jesus and thus on the whole basis of Christianity, was at this time at the height of his popularity, and enjoyed great respect among the intellectual and anti-clerical party.[12] Anatole France's *Thaïs*, a thinly disguised commentary on the contemporary Paris of 1889, denounced what its author presented as Christian hypocrisy, sectarianism, and small-minded stupidity.

The intellectual tradition of republicanism and anti-clericalism was rooted in the work of Hugo, Michelet, Quinet, Spencer, and Taine, and was promulgated by such popular writers as Renan and Anatole France. Behind these ranks Sardou labored, intellectually negligible perhaps, but unquestionably influential. Sardou, like many of his fellow countrymen, dabbled in the warm margins of the boiling pool of revolution: he liked the nice bits but disapproved of the unpleasant incidents such as the Terror that had made the nice

bits possible. In 1891 this attitude would pitch the playwright into the center
of a furious controversy over his anti-Terrorist play, *Thermidor*. The plot concerns the misfortunes of a young girl who is denounced to the revolutionary
tribunal as a nun, and goes to the guillotine in the last hours of the Terror
after Robespierre's fall, rather than escape by claiming to be pregnant. The radical Left seized upon the play as an example of compromise with the Church,
and condemned it. The fuss was largely a tempest in a teapot and is now remembered if at all because it inspired Clemenceau's famous comment, "La
République est un bloc"—that is, the Republic (and the revolution that created it) cannot be subdivided: you cannot take Danton and not Robespierre,
liberty and not Terror.[13]

This sort of logic never bothered Sardou, of course. For him, anti-clericalism seems to have been primarily a button to push in order to get the reaction
he wanted from his audience. *La Tosca* is full of examples of this. One occurs
in the first act, where Floria chatters to her lover about the directions given
her by her confessor, directions which she is willfully but nervously refusing
to follow. After some playful interchanges with Mario about the book he has
loaned her—an autographed copy of Rousseau's *La Nouvelle Heloïse* that
she finds boring—she tells him that her confessor has directed her to induce
her lover to shave off his "revolutionary" mustache. But she hasn't mentioned it to him because she likes the mustache. And, she babbles on,

> I no longer dare go to confession and admit to him that your mustache is still
> there because I like to visit it. . . . But now my accounts are really in fine
> shape: I'm in a constant state of mortal sin, and if I were to die suddenly . . .
> [Hell!] . . . I wouldn't care if it were with you![14]

Sophisticated Parisian audiences could be relied upon to smile at this exchange, since denouncing confession as an instrument of clerical domination
had become a truism by the end of the century. *Priests, women, and the family*, Michelet's 1845 attack on clerical interference in family life, had been
reprinted at least eight times by 1875.[15]

If Floria's dithering over her immortal soul versus Mario's mustache was
intended to make audiences smile, Sardou had another and stronger card to
play with his Scarpia character. The villain's partnership with a shadowy papal government (necessarily shadowy, since in June of 1800 it did not exist)
was a personification of another bugbear of the French Left, the Throne–
Altar alliance. In France the Catholic Church was seen (often appropriately)
as an ally of a would-be resurgent Bourbon monarchy.

If the issues of anti-clericalism and republicanism made *La Tosca* an especially appropriate vehicle for France in the *belle époque*, the play con-

tained plenty of raw human emotion that did not depend on a specific intellectual context for its effect. Sarah Bernhardt, recognizing the crowd-pleaser
with which Sardou had presented her, took the show on tour soon after its
premiere. She took the play throughout Europe and the New World, but dis-
dained to translate it, on the surprisingly successful theory that her genius
made her meaning clear even to those who did not understand a word of what
she said.

Giacomo Puccini, a promising young composer whose second opera *(Edgar)* was about to open, saw one of Bernhardt's performances of *La Tosca* in
Milan at the Teatro dei Filodrammatici on 14 February 1889. Both he and *Edgar*'s librettist, Fernando Fontana, seem to have been struck by the play, and
by its operatic potential. They followed the show to Turin for another performance on 17 March.[16] It was this early experience with Tosca, when Puccini understood few of her words but all of her emotion, that started his on-
again off-again pursuit of the fictional diva. In May 1889 he wrote to Ricordi
urging his publisher and patron to secure the rights to Sardou's play, which,
he felt, "suits me exactly." Years later, when the Tosca project finally got un-
derway, Fontana would claim that he had been the first to propose the idea.[17]

The story of the genesis of Puccini's *Tosca* is long and byzantine in its complexity.[18] Shortly after Puccini urged his publisher to acquire the rights for
an opera based on *La Tosca*, Ricordi entered into negotiations with Sardou,
who finally allowed himself to be coaxed into signing a contract in 1891; early
in that same year Luigi Illica seems to have begun work on a libretto.[19] From
the beginning Ricordi wanted the opera for his new rising star, Puccini, but
at first Sardou (who no doubt felt that he could afford to demand the best)
seems to have been dubious about the relatively unknown young composer.
By November the playwright changed his mind, and a flurry of activity followed: on 26 November Sardou signed the contract; on 13 December, Puccini
signed; almost immediately Illica produced a scenario, which was sent to
Paris.[20] There followed a long hiatus. Sardou wanted more money. Sardou
didn't like Puccini's music. Puccini, offended, washed his hands of the project and turned his attention to *Manon Lescaut* and then to *La Bohème*. The
contract was canceled.[21] But the project refused to die. Early in 1894, a new
candidate for composer emerged: Baron Alberto Franchetti, a wealthy Turin-
ese aristocrat and another member of Ricordi's stable of promising young
composers.[22] Plans proceeded through the summer, and in the autumn Franchetti traveled to Paris to meet with Sardou, along with Illica, Ricordi, and
the great Giuseppe Verdi.[23] It was presumably on this occasion that Verdi was
deeply moved by Cavaradossi's farewell to life and art (later cut), and formed
the opinion that he himself would have liked to write the opera, "were I not

retired."[24] Verdi was not the only one to cast covetous eyes on *Tosca:* Puccini, perhaps inspired by forbidden fruit, was once again attracted to the lady.

There is a persistent myth that Ricordi and Puccini conspired to cheat Franchetti of the libretto; in fact, though there certainly was a rivalry between the two composers, Franchetti appears to have had trouble with the project from the start, and by May 1895 he had given it up. Not until the end of July of that year is there any mention of Puccini in connection with the libretto, and the actual contract for his resumption of control of the libretto does not appear to have been signed until August 1895.[25]

By the end of 1895, the final *Tosca* team was in place: Puccini; Luigi Illica, who had begun work on condensing the play three years earlier; and Giuseppe Giacosa, who would oversee the setting of the text in verse (see fig. 3). Not until November 1897 would Puccini finally get down to work on the score.[26] At that point, the real work began.[27]

The job of translating Sardou's old-fashioned, formulaic, and very French play into Puccini's intensely personal opera was complex and difficult, and involved no end of squabbling among the four men—Illica, Giacosa, Puccini, plus Giulio Ricordi—who had a hand in it. Part of the task lay in reducing a massive, cunningly constructed five-act play to a length suitable for an opera. An equally difficult problem was the "translation" of Sardou's French characters into individuals whose motivations and behavior would be appropriate for an Italian opera. Sardou's Floria Tosca is, of course, Sarah Bernhardt herself—sophisticated, vindictive, easy of virtue, long on charm, and given to tantrums. In the course of the libretto development she becomes kittenish and submissive to her lover, sincerely pious, and a victim quite outmatched by Scarpia. Sardou's Cavaradossi is charming, intellectual, politically articulate, cool, and very French. In the transition to operatic hero he loses all of his French characteristics and never succeeds in acquiring any really convincing Italian ones—perhaps because the librettists were determined to turn him into a nationalist Risorgimento hero and Puccini plainly didn't give a fig for Risorgimento heroes. Scarpia begins his translation to the opera with an air of understated elegance and decadent sophistication; his motives are complex, his lust frankly pathological, and he is not above outright trickery. He is cooler, slyer, and altogether nastier than in the finished opera.

Puccini, with all his anti-clericalism, gives his characters a much greater religious dimension than they have in Sardou's play. Floria Tosca is, with the possible exception of Suor Angelica, the Puccini character most clearly defined by religion (and by sex). Sardou's Chief of Police is a straightforward villain whose only use for religion is as a cover for crime; the operatic Scarpia is portrayed as a man who uses the power of the Church for his own ends,

FIGURE 3. The trio who produced *La Bohème* and *Tosca:* Puccini, Giacosa, and Illica in 1895. © Archivio Storico Casa Ricordi. Reproduced by permission

but his private religious feelings are not altogether clear. Is he a totally cynical and irreligious man? Or must we take at face value his exclamation, "Tosca, you make me forget God!"? When he sings, "God created different beauties, different wines; I want to sample as much as possible of the divine work," are we to read that as pure cynicism, or as a Rasputin-like attempt to provide a merciful God with as much as possible to forgive? In Sardou's play Cavaradossi has no religious dimension at all. In the opera, he is shown as a good man, but his goodness has nothing to do with religion: it is defined by loyalty in human love and friendship, by artistic passion, and by political liberalism. But even Cavaradossi almost acquired a religious dimension in the operatic text, though his two direct references to God were ultimately cut (see chap. 8).[28] He does retain a reference indicating that his view of his lover's religiosity is by no means totally negative, or even ironic. In Act III, praising the gentleness of her "sweet hands," he tells her that they were "destined for good and merciful works, to caress children, to gather roses, to pray, joined, for the unfortunate" (see chap. 9).[29]

Unlike the Sardou original, the various versions of the manuscript libretto are saturated with religious references, only some of which survived into the finished opera. The fact that many of these references present the institutional Church in a bad light is not the point: religion, good or bad, is recognized as important.

The sacristan functions as the active symbol of clerical obscurantism and represents the Altar side of the Throne and Altar alliance. In the final version of the opera he retains most of his ecclesiastical turns of phrase (such as *Liberami Domine!* and the like, or asking Cavaradossi if he is doing penance by not eating his lunch).[30] Other religious references have been dropped, notably in the scene that preceded Scarpia's entrance. In an earlier version the sacristan chuckles that the cannon shot announces "the resurrection"; later he will deny that he knows where the painter has gone, calling him "that heretic." The choir and clerics rejoice over the news of Marengo, shouting, "We'll celebrate the victory over the gang of heretics!" and "Viva Loyola!" This is one of two specific digs directed at St. Ignatius Loyola, the founder of the Society of Jesus, or Jesuits (suppressed in 1776 but reinstituted in 1815 and by 1890–1900 very much a thorn in the side of secular liberals in Italy as in France). The other reference is of course Spoletta's "Saint Ignatius, help me!" *(Sant'Ignazio, m'aiuta!)*, invoking Loyola as though he were the patron saint of police spies.

While in Sardou's play religion is simply a political issue, in the opera it has become much more complex. This is not only an aspect of the transition from

France to Italy, where relations between the State and the Church were more intricate (if not any warmer); it is also a reflection of an important aspect of Puccini's own life. Although in many ways Puccini's treatment of religion simply reflects the gender-related conventions of his day, it is nonetheless a revealing factor in his work.[31] In his mature period his women characters (with the possible exception of Manon, whose entire life is a flight from rules) always have a religious dimension, while his male characters (with the revealing exception of Scarpia, his only true villain) never do. Manon Lescaut avoids being sent to a convent and embarks on a life of sin for which she will pay dearly; Des Grieux, who in Prévost's novel tries to become a priest, does nothing of the sort in Puccini's adaptation. In *La Bohème*, Mimì keeps a prayer book and shyly confesses that she "doesn't always go to Mass"; even Musetta directs a heartfelt plea to the Madonna; Rodolfo and his friends' idea of religion is to dine out on Christmas eve. Madama Butterfly's conversion to Christianity marks a profound change in her life; Pinkerton hardly notices. Minnie, the Girl of the Golden West, teaches Bible classes while Ramerrez robs banks. Leaving to one side the *Trittico* operas and *La Rondine*, Turandot *is* a religion, albeit a starkly non-Christian one; but while at first glance Calaf seems to worship at her shrine, he is really a devotee of erotic, heterosexual love as the Life-Force, a Shavian sort of anti-religion that Puccini, and Cavaradossi, share.

John DiGaetani may overstate his case, but there is certainly some truth in his argument that *"Tosca* is . . . the clearest expression of Puccini's own religious and political views—that the Church is the enemy of humanity, that agnosticism is the only possible position with a God who does not respond to the needs of suffering humanity."[32] Puccini's troubles with the Church had deep roots, but one of them was certainly the blatant irregularity of the Puccini ménage. Elvira Gemignani (later Puccini), a married woman and the mother of two children, had abandoned her husband for the *bel* Giacomo. Despite the fact that cutting-edge modernists were beginning to make adultery fashionable among the intelligentsia, this was a time when such matters were taken seriously. Puccini could hardly have been surprised to find that he had brought down the wrath of the establishment upon his head. His cousin, Don Rodrigo Biagini (a priest), tartly advised the errant musician that "as for you, you should be catapulted from the roof of the Milan cathedral."[33] Another priest-friend, Dante del Fiorentino, got into trouble with the director of studies at the seminary for associating with "that loose-living Puccini, that sinner, that . . . !" The director saved his most damning condemnations for Puccini's new opera, *Tosca:* "'As if it were not bad enough that he himself was loose-living,' the director roared at me, 'there is the fact that in *Tosca* he has put the most sacred Te Deum side by side with his profane songs.'"[34]

Though Puccini had the reputation among his Tuscan neighbors of being an unbeliever—Del Fiorentino reports being told by an altar boy that "we never go there [to the Villa Puccini] . . . He's an unbeliever"—two priests, Del Fiorentino and Pietro Panichelli, wrote affectionate books of memoirs about him.[35] It may be worth noting that both of these friendships came about while Puccini was either working on *Tosca* or shortly thereafter: Panichelli, a Roman priest Puccini met in 1897, helped him with some of the clerical local color for his Roman opera, and Del Fiorentino, a fifteen-year-old seminarian at the time, first met Puccini when the great man broke his leg in an accident with the expensive motor car he had purchased to celebrate the success of *Tosca*.

Puccini's attitude toward religion, and toward the Roman Catholic Church, was predictably ambiguous. He was not an observant worshiper, and Panichelli suggests that his reputation as an unbeliever was well deserved. On the other hand, Puccini seems to have felt the impulse to invoke the blessings of the Church at the great turning points of life. After the death of Elvira's husband, the couple were married "quite suddenly," according to Del Fiorentino, in the cold dark of a late January night, with the church windows curtained in the hope that nobody would notice.[36] Before he died in a Brussels hospital, Puccini received the last rites from Bishop Micara, the Apostolic Nuncio at Paris.[37] It is not unreasonable to assume that the self-described "poor Christian" felt an occasional twinge of nostalgia for the Church, for what he revealingly referred to as "the faith of my mother." "Give me back, little priest, the faith that I had," Panichelli (the "pretino") reports Puccini as asking.[38] Del Fiorentino (Gonnellone, "Big Skirts"), who was always on the lookout for signs of spirituality on the part of his hero, quotes Puccini as saying "[I] never lacked respect for the faith of my mother" and "I never joined any anti-religious organizations."[39]

The same ambiguity can be found in *Tosca*, where religion can represent the gentle side of the heroine's character, and the church bells can suggest peace. In the libretto it is important to differentiate between references to institutional religion, which are almost uniformly negative, and direct or indirect references to personal faith, what Santi calls "everyday religion," which are much more likely to be positive.

This ambiguity is typical not only of Puccini as an intellectual, but of Italian Church–State relations in general, relations very close to their nadir in the last decade of the nineteenth century. Pope Leo XIII (1878–1903) was a gifted diplomat and willing to reach out to modern society (as he did with the encyclical *Rerum Novarum* in May 1891). He was conciliatory toward Bismarck, who was then conducting the Kulturkampf in an eventually fruitless attempt to crush the Catholic Church in the new German state. In France Leo pursued a policy of *ralliement* (coming closer) with the Republic, to the rage and frustration of the radical Left as well as the radical Right. But relations with the Italian state went less well, and in August 1898, just a year and a half before the premiere of *Tosca*, Leo had issued an encyclical instructing the faithful that it was the duty of loyal Catholics to abstain from political life in Italy as long as the Pope remained in his "intolerable situation." Leo and his successors withdrew from Rome and remained "prisoners in the Vatican" for another thirty years, until Mussolini and Pius XI signed a Concordat (the Lateran Treaty) in 1929.

In retrospect, it seems clear that the very fact of Italian unification had made these problems inevitable. The dream of unification—that is, that the peninsula known as Italy should become a single political nation—can be traced back to before the eighteenth century, but despite occasional patriotic outbursts and martyrdoms, it was not until the middle of the nineteenth century that the idea became anything more than a quixotic dream.[40] The problem was similar to that faced by aspiring German nationalists: although there was clearly a cultural group that shared strong linguistic and historical ties, each of the political entities among which that group was spread had its own traditions and institutions, and long-entrenched political organizations. Unification would require the destruction of a dozen or so states, some as small as the Republic of San Marino (which never did join the new Italy), some as large as the Kingdom of the Two Sicilies. Others had long been part of other states—such as Venice and the Veneto, which had to be wrested away from the Austrians, and Corsica, which still belongs to France. But the knottiest of Italy's problems was one that was uniquely Italian: the secular power of the pope. At the start of the nineteenth century there was a band of territory across Italy from Ancona in the north to Gaeta in the south that owed secular allegiance to the Papa-Re, or pope-king. After a brief flirtation with the idea of Neo-Guelphism—that is, that Italy should become a loose federation of states under the largely symbolic headship of the pope—the unavoidable fact had to be faced: an Italian state could only be created by open conflict with the papacy.

After a prelude in the revolutions of 1848–49 the Italian wars of unification began in earnest in 1859. Piece by piece, the Italian states were accreted to the Kingdom of Piedmont, by war, and by "Yes" or "No" plebiscite votes: Parma, Modena, Romagna, and Tuscany in March of 1860; Naples and Sicily in October of that year; in November, the Marches and Umbria. In July of

1866, Venice and its territories were ceded to Italy by Austria. It was not until 1870 that Italian troops took Rome which, after a plebiscite, was added to the Kingdom of Italy and soon became its capital.

Unfortunately, the Italian state that had begun so hopefully had by 1876 settled for cynicism, corruption, and government by *trasformismo*—political alliances that cut across party lines with little definable end beyond power. Puccini's tendency to ignore politics and concentrate on the personal was typical of a generation of Italians who came to maturity in this period. The industrial north found itself in an uncomfortable marriage with the agricultural center of the peninsula, and both were horrified to look across the pillow at the feudal *mezzogiorno* of the south. Italy's ventures into colonialism in Ethiopia met with humiliating defeat at Adua in 1896 when an Italian army was crushed by the Ethiopians under Menelik. Class relations within Italy were hardly better, and in the spring of 1898 Milan erupted into open war between workers and the army in the week of the Fatti di Maggio, 3 to 8 May. At the premiere of *Tosca* less than two years later the conductor Leopoldo Mugnone, fearing an assassin's bomb, fled the podium soon after the curtain went up on Act I. Although the bomb threat proved a hoax, Mugnone was not merely an alarmist: seven months later King Umberto would be killed by an anarchist.

Even without class conflict and political chaos, the new capital of Italy was having problems. When *Tosca* opened at the Teatro dell'Opera in Rome in January of 1900, the city was still shuddering under the impact of its transformation from a small, charming, slightly shabby papal capital, to the first city of the new nation of Italy. A modern capital required a modern bureaucracy, and soon the old city was filled to bursting with civil servants, their families, their hangers-on, and the labor force necessary to feed, shelter, and amuse them. The population shot up from under 200,000 in 1870 to about 460,000 by the end of the century. The first frenzy of building after 1870 was slowed only by a real estate crash in 1887, and it soon picked up speed again. When the curtain rose on the first performance of *Tosca*, the Victor Emanuel monument was a little over half finished; having been started in 1885, it was not completed until 1911. This sugar-coated monstrosity dedicated to Victor Emanuel II (the king of Sardinia who became king of Italy in 1861) looms over the city from what had been the end of the Corso, and leaves no one in the slightest doubt about who won the ancient struggle between pope and emperor.[41]

Between 1870 and 1914 the new Italian state, plagued by corruption, cynicism, and post-Risorgimento disillusion, joined the rest of Europe in its inexorable slide toward the Great War. The fin-de-siècle despair that produced

Wilde and Beardsley in England, Satie and Verlaine in France, and Klimt in Vienna, took the form of *verismo* in Italy, with its stress on police-blotter realism and the violence and bestiality of the common man.

Puccini, like many Italians, seems to have been alienated from political as well as from religious life. In this he reflected the changing psychic landscape of the west, chronicled by his contemporary Sigmund Freud (1856–1939). The young Viennese physician's *Traumdeutung* (The Interpretation of Dreams) was published in 1900 — coincidentally the year of *Tosca*'s premiere — and his psycho-sexual theories would soon filter down into a general culture that was ripe for them. Puccini himself has long been a favorite subject of Freudian analysis, drawing on the rich material of his father's early death, his dominant mother, his Don Juanism, and his tendency to equate sex with death.[42] Although it is easy to overstate the usefulness of post-mortem psychoanalysis, it is nonetheless true that the composer himself was keenly aware of the sometimes perverse nature of his artistic inspiration. He referred to his "Neronic instinct" and admitted (or boasted?) that he could not compose without his "puppet executioners." *Tosca* gave him plenty of scope for these feelings with the eroticism of torture, rape, murder, and suicide.

Jules Lemaître, in his review of the premiere of Sardou's play in *Débats*, spoke of "scenes of the butcher shop and the abattoir; indeed, there is nothing more tragic than torn and cut flesh, than bloody death. . . . Behold him [Sardou] taken over by the need for brutal sensations which lead him bit by bit to the Roman or Byzantine circus, to the mortal combat of gladiators. M. Sardou is thirsty for blood. He is the Caligula of the drama."[43]

Sardou's Caligula met Puccini's Nero, appropriately enough, in Rome, where pseudo-history and history can blend, as the following example of life imitating art imitating life suggests.

A politically committed young man, born in Paris to a Italian family, works in one of the great baroque churches in the heart of Rome. It is wartime, and the city is occupied by his enemies. He is handsome and well educated, he has everything to live for; but he defies the tyranny of the state and reaches out to save a comrade. Captured and tortured, he refuses to give any information; despite the frantic efforts of those who love him to save his life, he is executed by a military firing squad. The parallels with the life and death of the hero of *Tosca* are chilling, but this man's name was Maurizio Giglio, not Mario Cavaradossi; he worked in the church of Sant'Agnese in Agone, not Sant'Andrea della Valle (three minutes' walk away). He did not die heroically alone, on the platform of the Castel Sant'Angelo, on 18 June 1800 but in the confusing anonymity of a crowd, with more than 400 other Romans in the Ardeatine caves on 24 March 1944.[44] Unlike death on the operatic stage, this was cold, wasteful, and repulsive. There was no orchestral accompaniment, no cool and picturesque dawn with the sound of church bells and shepherd songs. Letters to loved ones went undelivered; some were found years later in what had been the pockets of jackets or trousers, illegible from contact with blood and decaying flesh.

And yet in the face of this real pain, and real heroism, we are joltingly reminded of the connections between theater and human life. The text on Giglio's memorial in the church of Sant'Agnese might have been taken from the libretto of Puccini's opera: "he fell, slaughtered . . . , defying with his death all forms of tyranny." [45] The people who raised the monument, and perhaps the young man himself, seem to have understood the dreadful events of that spring through the allegory of the musical theater—Puccini's operas were still very much a part of European popular culture in the first half of the twentieth century. Art in general, and opera in particular, has a way of bringing into sharp focus the intersection between the personal and the universal. On a sublime level, Michelangelo's *Pietà* contains every mother who ever mourned an adult son. On quite another level, Tosca can contain every woman who resisted rape, and every man who defied pain in the defense of justice.

Puccini's instincts were right. Despite the "historico-topographico-panoramic"—and religico?—"inexactitudes," there is something universal in *Tosca*.

2 Sede Vacante: Rome without a Pope

$\mathcal{R}$ome at the end of the eighteenth century was a small, placid little city with a declining population, an air of gentle decay, and a reputation as the most delightful tourist venue in Europe.[1] About 150,000 people lived there in an area built in classical times for almost one million, so a sparse population occupied roughly a fifth of the space within the shelter of the ancient walls. The Tiber flowed between sloping banks, usually sluggish but periodically flooding to devastate the low-lying marshy areas that lay between the seven hills. For foreigners the beauty of Rome was enhanced by its romantic emptiness, uncluttered by anything so vulgar as living people. There they could dream in the cool silence of its gardens and revel in its magnificent buildings that stood alone in the warm, liquid light. Poetic young men flocked from France, England, the German states, and even further afield, to admire the long vistas of ivy-covered ruins decorated, as in the engravings of Piranesi and the cityscapes of Vanvitelli, with the occasional human figure: a shepherd, some laundresses, or a little party of amateurs led by an antiquarian guide.

Eighteenth-century Rome was a city of faith, the center of a world religion. The bells of its more than 400 churches competed with those of almost 250 monasteries, seventy-three convents, and twenty-three seminaries. Tourists remarked that the city was filled with priests, but this was often as much a matter of fashion as of vows. The real clerics were outnumbered by men who dressed in clerical black in order to fit in, to gain respect, or simply to save money.[2] At the end of the seventeenth century one in every fifteen or sixteen Romans was in holy orders; by 1800 this had fallen to about three and a half percent of the population, or one in thirty or so.[3]

In addition to being a center of religion, Rome was one of the first great modern tourist cities. Often there were almost as many visitors as residents (an estimate based on the extra bread baked in 1700 suggests that there were 100,000 visitors in that Holy Year).[4] The pious came for the Holy Year's blessings, for the relics, and to make the ritual visit to the Seven Churches; the worldly came for the classical ruins, for the splendors of Renaissance art, for the music—in sum, for the polish of civilization that could only be acquired in the great cities of Italy and above all in Rome, the chief city of the world, the *caput mundi*. They came, too, for the fun: carnival, with its masquerades, horse races, and cross-dressing; the fireworks displays at the Castel Sant'Angelo; the dazzling illuminations of St Peter's dome. Rome was a city of theaters where the parts of women were taken by boys and by castrati, to the titillation of visitors. It was a city of fresh, running water, filled with fountains and crowned by the flooding of the entire Piazza Navona on summer weekends, to the delight of small boys who scrambled for coins in the temporary lake, and the ladies and gentlemen whose carriages splashed through it while they reclined eating ices. As in all Mediterranean cities, home was only for sleeping; life was a drama played out in the wider world of cafés and squares, or in the churches and great public buildings. Except in the great houses, food was prepared and eaten in the open.

Tourists like the Président de Brosses loved the city. Charles de Brosses, president of the parlement of Toulouse, traveled widely in Italy in the middle of the eighteenth century, and collections of his letters were published by his family after his death. "This Rome," he wrote, "is beautiful, so beautiful that everything else seems shabby by comparison." Tobias Smollett enthused over the view from the Janiculum hill at sunset, "that stupendous panorama of domes, towers, and golden cupolas, churches, palaces, green trees and sparkling waters."[5]

Not everyone was so completely charmed. William Hazlitt's sensibilities were repelled by "narrow, vulgar-looking streets where the smell of garlick prevails over the odour of antiquity," and in 1800 the English army officer Robert Wilson sniffed that "[i]n seven hours I saw all there was to see . . ." Even visitors more appreciative than Wilson noted with regret that the city was unusually dirty even by eighteenth-century standards. Hester Piozzi was appalled to note

> that the general appearance of a city which contains such treasures should
> be mean and disgusting, while one literally walks upon granite and tramples
> red porphery under ones feet, is one of the greatest wonders to me in a town
> of which the wonders seem innumerable; that it should be nasty beyond all
> telling, all endurance, with such perennial streams of the purest water lib-
> erally dispersed and triumphantly scattered all over it.[6]

But if fastidious tourists objected to having their classical fantasies mixed with the garlic and dirt of human habitation, they had kinder words for the Romans themselves. The lower classes were reported to be intelligent and amiable, with only two major faults: a disinclination to labor (this was the welfare capital of the world, as it had been in classical times), and an inclination to murder one another in hot-blooded duels. But the killing rarely extended to foreigners, and robbery was unusual. Visitors were fleeced more gently, by the enormous population of beggars and by an equally enormous group who did small tasks in the hope of tips from the bemused tourists.

The fact that Rome was undeniably full of poor people was related to the city's religious identity. For Romans poverty was not shameful because it was seen as a Christian virtue, and the availability of cheap or free food, shelter, medical care, and education, plus the temperate climate, made the city of the popes an attractive place in which to be poor. Rome's political structure did nothing to reduce the numbers of the needy. The city was the capital of the Papal States, a collection of thirteen political entities that stretched across the peninsula, roughly from the borders of the Kingdom of the Two Sicilies in the south, to Bologna and Ferrara in the north. In typical early modern fashion these states had been accreted higgledy-piggledy over the centuries, and each had its own traditions and style of government. The city of Rome, though it retained its older forms, was effectively ruled by men appointed by the popes, elderly clerics for the most part who held the reins of power lightly. Political theorists, especially French ones, sneered at Rome's old-fashioned government and railed against its tradition-laden inefficiency, dismissing as irrelevant the fact that this was the most socially stable and politically secure state in Europe.

By the end of the eighteenth century the people of Rome had been ruled by the popes for almost a millennium and a half, and most of them liked it that way. Ever since the empire had abandoned them in the fourth century, tucking up its robes, clutching its jewels and its books, and fleeing east behind the swords of its shaken army, the fortunes of the Romans had risen or fallen with the skill and power of the pope. Some of these men had been disasters, others had been heroes. Folklore related how Leo I turned back the Huns; how Gregory the Great protected the city from the Lombards; and how Leo III placed the imperial crown on Charlemagne's head, declaring the empire subject to the authority of the Church. Even the worst of popes brought with them the benefits of a great court, with plenty of attendant profit for the city's economy and morale. Long before the Middle Ages Romans had developed a proprietary attitude toward the pope and the universal Church and they guarded their privileges jealously, and often violently.

On those rare occasions when there was no pope in Rome the city suffered, as in the dark and dreadful years of the "Babylonian Captivity" (1309 to 1377) when, at least in the Roman view, the French kidnaped the papacy to Avignon and, as if in punishment, the plague traveled the Silk Road to devastate Europe. Since that time the Church had been led by scholars and warriors, sensualists and holy men, politicians and power-brokers, through the worldly splendors of the Renaissance, the horrors of siege and pillage, and the exuberant vitality of the Baroque. But not until the end of the eighteenth century, under the dark cloud of revolution in France, did history seem set to repeat itself with another French-inspired exile of the Holy Father.

Almost from the start the Revolution in France had been frankly hostile to Christianity in general, and to the Roman Church in particular. There were a number of reasons for this. The Enlightenment, which provided some of the intellectual underpinning for the Revolution, had seen Christianity as irrational and obsolete, and preached instead a gospel of rational secular benevolence. The Church was firmly identified as an ally of the old order, especially at the upper ranks of the hierarchy where the ecclesiastical and secular aristocracies were so intertwined as to be almost indistinguishable. Before heads rolled or armies marched, the National Assembly meeting in Versailles in 1791 had fired a decisive shot across the bows of the Church in France in the form of a Civil Constitution of the Clergy. Among other things, this set of laws provided that bishops and parish priests were to be elected by their congregations, and clerics, as state employees, were to be subject to an oath of allegiance. The Assembly deputies meant the Civil Constitution to be part of an overall reform program, but the oath of allegiance created a bitter and permanent split between clerics loyal to Rome and those whose primary loyalty was to France and the Revolution.[7]

Thirty to forty thousand French priests who refused to take the oath were deported in 1792, and many of them fled to Rome. There they joined tens of thousands of other refugees who clustered for safety around the papal throne. Many arrived with little more than the clothes on their backs, and lived on charity such as the daily distribution of bread that the elderly French Cardinal de Bernis organized for these wretched expatriates.[8] Even in the Roman state, welfare capital of the world though it may have been, the traditional alms and institutions for pilgrims were stretched beyond the breaking point by the unprecedented numbers of the needy. The problem was made worse by a crisis in papal finances created when the Church in France, for centuries Rome's major support, stopped sending its customary contribution to the pope.

At first money seemed to be the most important issue at stake as the revolutionaries busied themselves with appropriating Church property, an irresistible source of ready cash to a new nation born under a mountain of debt. Soon, however, the Revolution took on the characteristics of a religion itself, with martyrs, temples, and feast days observed with sacred rites and sermons. By 1793 the new religion had provided itself with a whole new calendar, purged at one blow not only of Christianity but of centuries of cultural tradition as well. It was all wonderfully rational and in the truest sense, radical.[9] As Revolution moved into Terror, life became more and more difficult for adherents to the old ways. Priests and nuns were lynched or guillotined along with anyone else suspected of being less than enthusiastic in support of the Revolution, and Robespierre introduced his Cult of the Supreme Being as the final answer to Christianity. This cult lasted about as long as Robespierre himself (he was guillotined in 1794) and the Church in France emerged from the ashes and began to put its house in order again. Within two years, however, the invasion of Italy led by the ambitious young General Bonaparte once again put the Revolution on a collision course with Rome.

The city that braced itself for another round of conflict was the proud birthplace of Western civilization; it was also a backwater state with a hopelessly outdated style of government, living on welfare and the forbearance of the powerful. Its defenses had long been more ideological and diplomatic than physical—there were no warlike eighteenth-century popes. Pius VI [Braschi] was the last of a series of amiable, relatively able men whose unusually long tenures and undemanding piety had made Romans comfortable with their old-fashioned state.[10] This pope was certainly no match for a wiry young descendant of the Lombards named Bonaparte.

Not only did Pius VI lose the uneven military struggle with Bonaparte, the popes lost the long-term propaganda war as well. One result of that loss has been the fact that, despite some excellent recent scholarship, eighteenth-century Rome retains the image of a romance novel where Casanova and Cagliostro pursue pretty little nuns, and painted cardinals pursue (and catch) pretty little castrati, while the Holy Office broods menacingly, if ineptly, over all. This conventional view long dominated the historiography of the era.[11] It continues to do so in non-specialist works in English, despite the work of Italian historians like V. E. Giuntella and Franco Venturi and their successors, and (in English) of Hanns Gross and R. Burr Litchfield. The image of a frivolous Rome persists at least in part because it is so utterly charming and derives from so many delightful contemporary sources: diaries, memoirs, and tour guides. It is woven from anecdotes and little scandals, many of them invented by imaginative adventurers like Casanova and repeated by northerners who came to Rome looking for the lush permissiveness and sweet decay of the south.

There is a darker side to this image, one put about more or less deliberately. The Enlightenment, or at least its secularizing, francophile spokesmen, saw Rome as the stronghold of the musty tradition and faith that had to be cleared away before reason could establish her beneficent rule. Revolutionaries correctly recognized Rome as the seat of a rival religion and were determined to discredit as well as destroy her. In the nineteenth century, architects of a united Italy knew that their nation-state could not be created so long as the Church, centered on Rome, continued to make rival claims on the loyalties of Italians. Italian nationalists had powerful and articulate allies in the English intelligentsia, who happily combined admiration for nationalism wherever they found it (except perhaps in Ireland) with a loathing for and suspicion of anything smacking of Roman Catholicism. It is hardly surprising that one of the results of all this was an enduring myth of papal Rome as frivolous, facile, inefficient, dirty, poor, and sustained by priest-craft and torture chambers.

Behind the myth lies a complex old regime city where formerly successful social and economic mechanisms were growing less and less adequate in the face of rapid change. Rome's main reasons for being were religious ceremony and social welfare, hardly appropriate aims in a modern, proto-capitalist world economy. By the eighteenth century tourism, always important under the name of pilgrimage, became the major (though not the only) industry, a situation that only increased the city's reputation for frivolity. Much of the contemporary anecdotal criticism of Rome and Romans sounds like a reflection of the eternal attitude of the tourist toward any site that both lures and fleeces him. Rome's other major source of income, the religious establishment, was proving less than reliable as the eighteenth century came to a close. As the capital of the universal Church Rome relied on collections from the Catholic world for the major part of her income, with the largest single group of contributions coming from the Church in France. These contributions were already decreasing during the eighteenth century under the twin attacks of secularism and jurisdictionalism (Church–State conflicts over authority).

Any analysis of the Roman social structure in the eighteenth century must begin with the fact that this was a city where the Church was the defining social, political, cultural, and economic institution. One result of this was that each social category was doubled, with clerical and lay representatives.

At the top of the pyramid was a dual nobility of old Roman families like the Colonna, alongside newer papal families such as the Braschi, always created by election and often not Roman in origin. The new papal families entered the ranks of the Roman nobility, where they and their descendants remained. Government was exclusively in the hands of churchmen.[12] Lay members of the great families of Rome were not involved with the court or government, except through ordained relatives. For this reason it was vitally important that every great family have a cleric, and preferably a cardinal, in every generation—a political imperative that sometimes led to highly dubious religious vocations.

Rome's middle class, like that of many old regime states, was small, though by no means negligible. It comprised the usual lawyers, physicians, and businessmen but it also had a strong artisan component, as one would expect in a city that lived by spectacle and ritual. At the top of this artisan middle class were the architects and master painters, at the bottom the carpenters and decorators. The clerical middle class included the parish priests, teachers, secretaries, and literati, down through the students and men in minor orders who scraped along on patronage and part-time jobs.

The poor were perhaps Rome's most characteristic social group.[13] Like the other social orders, this large group included both lay and clerical representatives. Most visible were the "begging brothers" more or less loosely associated with religious houses, and the freelance holy men and women who lived on handouts. The city's underclass also included an inordinately large number of casual domestic servants who attached themselves to prominent families in exchange for food and patronage.

Despite the disproportionate numbers of the poor, the city was rarely disturbed by social tensions or political violence; rather, it had the calm, unhurried air of a provincial capital.[14] By the end of the eighteenth century this pleasant civilization was living on borrowed time, but there was very little anyone could have done to avert the disasters that would soon put an end to it. Certainly it would have been quite impossible for the Papal States to defend themselves in any military sense. There was a papal army but these men were primarily concerned with marching in parades, keeping order at theaters, taking custody of criminals, and providing jobs for the powerful and the humble in the great chain of patronage that was the government of Rome. In reality the defense of Rome relied on the good will of Catholic powers like Austria, France, Spain, and the other Italian states. But the active support of these states grew steadily more problematic as the century rolled to a close. By the last decade of the 1700s Pius VI was well aware of the pitiful state of his army, and of the shaky condition of his diplomatic defenses. None of the Catholic states wanted to risk the precarious balance of peace by defending the pope; and Austria and Naples were perfectly willing to snap up chunks of territory from a weakened and tremulous papacy. To save his state the elderly pope danced on a tightrope, making concessions and paying millions in tribute. The young Bonaparte galvanized the French army of Italy into an irresistible invading force in 1796; in February 1797 Pius gave up huge tracts of papal territory in the Treaty of Tolentino, and thereby bought a few months' respite. But in the last days of 1797 his difficult and undignified performance ended when a clash between local radicals and angry working-class Romans backed by papal troops led to the (probably accidental) death of the young French General Duphot.[15]

The trouble began when a minuscule but enthusiastic band of pro-French, pro-revolutionary Romans, encouraged by French agents, made an ill-advised attempt at a coup. Instead of collecting popular support they stirred up a hornet's nest of anti-French protest among the touchy men of the Trastevere district and fled, pursued by a mob and by papal cavalry, to the Corsini Palace. There they hoped to take refuge with the French diplomatic mission and the ambassador, Napoleon's mild elder brother Joseph. Joseph and his staff came out from dinner to try to calm the situation, but in the confusion shots rang out and General Duphot fell mortally wounded. This was especially embarrassing as Duphot was not only a representative of the government of the French Republic (at this time, the Directory), he was also engaged to be married in two days to Joseph's sister-in-law and Napoleon's former fiancée, Desirée Clary.[16] The young lady collapsed, and Ambassador Bonaparte demanded his passports and left the city with his family and his entourage. Led by General Berthier, the avenging armies of the Republic marched inexorably on Rome from the north of Italy. In February of 1798 the city's defenses did not so much fall as dissolve. On the eleventh of that month (the 22nd of Pluviôse or the Rainy Month, Year VI of the Republican calendar) Berthier entered Rome as conqueror, but if he was expecting a liberator's reception, he was disappointed. In a letter to the Directory the general spoke of "provoking the crisis necessary to [the Republic's] birth," and "the stupor" without "a trace of patriotic feeling" that greeted his arrival.[17] Popular enthusiasm was not necessary, however. Berthier knew the drill and proceeded with the democratization of Rome according to regulations. Liberty Trees were erected and political prisoners (including the future consul Liborio Angelucci) were freed to dance around them; on 16 February the Roman Republic was declared (see fig. 4). On the following day the pope, eighty years old and ill, was told that he had three days to leave his capital. Richard Duppa, an English student of painting then pursuing his studies in Rome, says the commissioners began removing the furniture from the papal apartments as soon as they arrived, and had the place pretty well stripped before the pope was removed.[18] According to Francesco Fortunati, a priest who kept a careful chronicle of events during Pius VI's reign, on the 20th the pope was unceremoniously bundled into a carriage with two physicians, two attendants, and a handful of clerics, including his confessor, and sent on his travels (see fig. 5).[19]

FIGURE 4. The Declaration of the Republic in February 1798. The Liberty Tree erected for the occasion dwarfs the equestrian statue of Marcus Aurelius, perhaps an unconscious comment on the relative importance of the Roman Republic vis-à-vis the French. C. Vernet, engraved by J. Duplessis-Bertaux. Museo Napoleonico

The tyranny of the popes was declared to be over, replaced by a new state designed to welcome the French and reintroduce antique liberties to the city of the Caesars. The government of this new state was to consist of seven consuls (the classical constitution had provided for only two), among them Liborio Angelucci, one of the models on which Sardou based his character Cesare Angelotti. Another was probably Nicola Antonio Angeletti; see chapter 5. Angelucci, a surgeon and sometime obstetrician, was typical of the republicans in Rome, most of whom were middle-class professionals or the younger sons of nobles, along with some intellectual and idealistic churchmen. Born in Rome in 1746, Angelucci had an excellent reputation as a medical man and as a scholar, and was active in intellectual circles in the city.[20] In addition to his medical work, he edited (1791) the first Roman edition of Dante's *Divine Comedy*. He was in political hot water more or less constantly after 1792, first with the papal government and then with his colleagues in the Roman Republic. When the French agitator Hugon de Basseville (also a physician) arrived in Rome in 1792 Angelucci, one of the first Roman converts to the

FIGURE 5. Departure of Pius VI from Rome. The elderly pontiff was summarily deported from his capital when the French arrived in 1798. Museo Napoleonico

republican cause, immediately befriended him. Basseville was set upon and killed by a Roman mob in January 1793, an event that served as one of the first nails in the coffin of papal Rome. The following year a plot against the papal government was discovered, and Angelucci was implicated along with several nobles and some artists. The purported aim of the conspiracy was "establishing new laws to better assure the lives and property of subjects and to bring back prosperity in goods and monies."[21] Angelucci was certainly interested in "prosperity in goods and monies": he was implicated in the plot mainly because he was unable to explain the large amount of money found in his house. During his long and inconclusive trial Angelucci was held at the Castel Sant'Angelo until he either fell ill or attempted suicide (an intriguing and no doubt coincidental echo of the plot of *Tosca*) and was allowed to return home under house arrest. He was in even more serious trouble in August 1797 when he was accused of plotting to murder the pope. Only the intervention of the French, who had recently signed a treaty with the papal government at Tolentino, saved his life. He went into exile and, unlike Sardou's Angelotti, he went north, where he met up with General Bonaparte.[22] He followed Bonaparte from Milan to Rastatt, and then to Paris, lobbying for an invasion of the Roman states and the establishment of a republic. When

Berthier marched on Rome, Angelucci was close on his heels and was immediately included in the government, first as prefect, then as a consul.

Unfortunately, once he came to power he proved to be interested only in advancing himself and his family, and in keeping the French happy. He was soon extremely unpopular with the people as well as with his colleagues, who feared that he meant to take over and push them out (they seem to have had good reason for this, and were anxious to have the tribunate and the senate pass laws to prevent any consul from taking power on his own). He was attacked in the republican press and in the political clubs as a thief and a false patriot whose arbitrary and unconstitutional acts endangered the Republic.[23] In September the traditional Roman spokesmen for popular anger, the "talking statues" Pasquino and Marforio, indulged in a long satire on the consuls in general, and Angelucci in particular: "Be careful [Angelucci] doesn't hear you, because when he's in a rage he's a real beast and seems as if he's possessed by a demon, throwing out sword, pistol, syringes, and lancets!"[24] By summer Angelucci was so unpopular that his very presence caused riots, and his luxurious carriage was attacked in the street. The republican press accused him of enriching himself by buying up confiscated properties at absurdly low prices—he bought the palace of the Order of Malta on the via Condotti in his wife's name for a mere 5,200 scudi—and he was forced to resign.[25]

He made little attempt to defend himself from corruption charges and instead took the money and ran, taking refuge in the senate, as the constitution allowed. When the Neapolitans occupied Rome briefly in 1798 Angelucci followed the government in exile to Perugia. The following year, when the Republic fell again (this time for good), he stayed almost until the end. But unlike his fictional counterpart he left with the French, going to Marseille and then on to Paris. After Bonaparte's victory at Marengo he came back to Italy, but he was not allowed to return to Rome despite his offer to serve as a spy for the new pope's Secretary of State, Cardinal Consalvi! Only in 1809, when Napoleon occupied the city in order to give his son the title King of Rome, did Angelucci return to his home, but he would never again be a civic official.[26]

The Republic set up in February 1798 was the usual French-style affair, with antique Roman trimmings. There was a lower house that could debate but not legislate and an upper house that could legislate but not debate. The delegates, attired in toga-like uniforms with large plumed hats, were elected on the basis of limited suffrage from among the property-owning males. The government was headed by a group executive, the consuls, in theory chosen from and by the representative bodies but in effect selected by the French military and political envoys. Roman republicans had little to say about the actual running of the state: this was made clear from the start, when the republicans wanted to leave the pope in Rome (probably for economic rather than religious reasons) but were overruled by the French.[27]

One of the first acts of the new regime was to hold a splendid memorial service for the slain General Duphot.[28] Rome, more than any other Baroque state, had made skillful use of public spectacle as a tool of government; the revolutionaries, embarked on the difficult work of creating a new social and political order, were among their most adept pupils. The great Jacques-Louis David, "pageant-master to the Republic," had after all learned his craft in Rome.[29] Revolutionaries in Paris had leaned heavily on public spectacle and it is no surprise that their Roman colleagues, in the very home of classical antiquity and Baroque spectacle, should have gone into a frenzy of pageant-making. They were able to call on the services of a class of professional decorators and festival-makers, the *festaioli*, who shifted easily enough from decorating church interiors for feast days and building monuments to dead cardinals and princes, to celebrating republican triumphs and lamenting democratic martyrs. The great celebratory edifices (called *macchine*, machines) that regularly transformed the interiors of churches and public squares could be erected in as little as a few hours, with 150-foot tall displays representing mountains, palaces, fantasy kingdoms, or ships, decorated with fireworks and fountains dispensing free wine. Funeral *macchine* were more sober, though just as large and just as elaborate. The materials were much the same in any case: frames constructed from massive timbers, covered by canvas panels painted in trompe-l'oeil style, and given an architectural look by the use of stucco and carta pesta (a sort of papier-mâché), often painted to look like polychrome marble.[30] The addition of velvet draperies with gold and silver trim, torches and fireworks, trees and stages for actors and musicians completed the look.

Francesco Fortunati, a Roman diarist who disliked the new government, was nonetheless impressed by the show prepared to honor the ashes of the gallant General Duphot, as well he might have been.[31] All day on 23 February the guns of the Castel Sant'Angelo fired at five-minute intervals while a great funeral *macchina* was erected in St. Peter's square. In keeping with the sober neoclassicism of the occasion it was designed along strict and simple lines, making use of the popular Egyptian motifs that traditionally complemented the classical. Flanked with tall cypresses (uprooted and brought in for the occasion) the monument consisted of a pyramid on a raised dais, with four flights of steps leading up to the platform on which incense burned in braziers. The monument was surrounded by an enormous orchestra (Fortunati says it employed all the musicians of Rome, string and wind players alike); as soon as it was daylight on the 24th the orchestra was joined by a crowd of singers, intoning hymns in honor of the slain general and of Ambassador Bonaparte, specially composed for the occasion by Maestro Masi. The singers were led by the choir of the papal chapel, who were out of jobs now that their patron had been deported, and were presumably grateful for the work. The obsequies ended with soldiers parading through the city, their hats draped with cypress, escorting four sergeants who bore an urn containing the mortal remains of the unfortunate Duphot.

If the spectacle was intended to encourage the soldiers or to warm the hearts of Romans toward their new government, it does not seem to have worked. The junior officers of the French army, furious because they had not been paid, held a noisy public meeting at the Pantheon immediately after the funeral. The next day a fierce revolt broke out in the Trastevere district, whose inhabitants were traditionally the most independent, and least pliable, of Romans. The immediate cause of the revolt was outrage at the fact that the Jews (whose Roman community was at least as old as that of the Trasteverini) had been declared free and equal citizens.

The army took heavy casualties (about 200 soldiers were killed) but the revolt was suppressed and the reprisals were swift: twenty or so rebels were shot in the Piazza del Popolo.[32] Executions alternated with spectacles throughout the revolutionary period, as they do in the play and the opera, where Tosca within a few hours goes from performing at a gala concert in the Farnese palace to witnessing her lover's execution by firing squad. Such events were far more common under the Republic, when very few weeks passed without an execution, than they were under the reactionary rule of the Allies (when the events of *Tosca* are set). Republican executions were usually carried out in military style: the French did not at this time introduce their ultra-modern killing machine, the guillotine, but they did standardize the proceedings. Now, with equality before the law enshrined in the republican constitution, everyone, regardless of rank or crime, faced a firing squad. Those executed under the Republic were a mixed bag. They included quasi-political offenders such as the rebels from the Trastevere district and guerrillas (or bandits) from the hill towns; common thieves, whose activities naturally increased with the confusion of occupation and war; and deserters and soldiers convicted of breaches of military discipline. In November 1798 two minor clerics—a deacon and subdeacon—were brought to Rome and shot for taking down the Liberty Tree in their village and replacing it with a cross. Perhaps the most peculiar execution was carried out on 7 June 1799 when a soldier was shot for theft. Like Cavaradossi in the play and opera, he refused the attentions of the priest;

FIGURE 6. A Roman assignat. Imitating the fiscal policy of the French Republic, the Romans issued paper money, which quickly became worthless. Author's collection

unlike the hero of *Tosca*, he explained that he did not need them as he planned to be reincarnated immediately, in Paris. "And thus," comments Fortunati, "he entered upon the other life."[33]

While the French pursued their own interests and problems, the Roman Republic floundered and eventually sank, cordially loathed by most of its citizens. Even without the ideological conflicts that divided a profoundly traditional people from their innovation-loving new rulers, sheer economic troubles would have driven them apart. The people had been used to living on the bountiful charity of the pope; with him gone, the economic base of the city disappeared. Despite price controls the cost of food soared, and attempts to regulate the value of currency only made matters worse and contributed to the raging inflation (see fig. 6). The population of the city fell from 166,417 in 1796 to 153,004 in 1800, and continued to fall throughout the Napoleonic period to 117,882 in 1812, a total decline of almost 30 percent in sixteen years. (By contrast, the population of Naples rose by three percent in the same period.)[34]

Among the more serious troubles facing the Roman Republic was the fact that her liberators syphoned off vast amounts of goods and cash from the already bankrupt state. A small part of this loot went to support the French army, which was in dreadful shape, ragged, barefoot, and unpaid; more went to support local graft and corruption; but most was sent to Paris to disappear into the murky and bottomless depths of the French national debt. Rome was to be sucked dry and an expert, a commissioner named Haller, was sent to oversee the operation. Haller systematically looted the Vatican and the city's churches. Paintings, sculptures, draperies, books, manuscripts, furniture—whatever could be removed was packed up to be added to the stream of mule-drawn wagons that seemed to extend from Rome directly across the Alps in an unbroken line to the French capital. There the looted works of art would be converted to cash, or set aside to add to the glory of the newly created museum of the Louvre.

Perhaps in an attempt to distract Roman attention, patriotic festivals and entertainments began with Duphot's funeral and continued doggedly on to within a week of the fall of the city. Fortunati, hostile but fascinated, kept a careful diary of the Republic.[35] Between 17 February 1798 when the French marched into the city and 29 September 1799 when the Allies replaced them, he describes half a dozen major spectacles and dozens of *feste di ballo* and theatrical parties laid on to celebrate republican events.

The major republican festivals were the Festival of Regeneration, on 15 February (this fell during Lent in 1799); the Festival of Federation, on 20 March; Bastille Day, celebrated for two days on 14 and 15 July; and the anniversary of the French Republic on 22 or 23 September (this was also the first day of the republican calendar, which coincided with the fall equinox).[36] All of these festivals had common elements: military parades; *macchine* with fireworks and figures to represent classical characters or allegorical virtues or vices (labeled in case one missed the point); and grateful citizens, usually including a few pretty girls.

It was in the opera houses and the prose theaters that the new Republic had the highest hopes for influencing public opinion. A columnist in the *Monitore romano* admonished patriots to remember that "[a] single theatrical production is more effective than an infinite number of laws and declamations."[37] It was widely believed that the great deeds of "the brave French" were in large part inspired by their "Republican Music," and within the limits imposed by time, lack of money, and an indifferent or hostile population the republicans of Rome set about trying to follow the French example.[38] Public virtue, "the basis of all republics," was to be increased by a reformed—or as they put it, regenerated—theater. The first step was obvious: reformers banned the castrati from the operatic stage. Already out of fashion in the modern theater, these male sopranos and altos had thrived in Rome in part because of a papal ban on women performers on the public stage. The republicans took great pleasure in abolishing a custom they saw as the epitome of old regime degeneracy and a prime example of the pernicious nature of tradition. Romans, who by and large liked the castrati, were nonetheless intrigued by the idea of women performers; when the Republic fell the castrati returned, but the women stayed. (See chap. 4.)

Despite the occasional topical novelty piece like *Il matrimonio democratico* (The Democratic Marriage) and the requisite light comedies by Paisiello (such as *Il fanatico in berlina*; The Fanatic in the Pillory, originally *La locanda*), theatrical offerings under the Republic tended to be sternly virtuous and unremittingly uplifting.[39] For the Festival of Regeneration the Argentina—Tosca's theater—offered the patriotic drama *La congiura dei Pazzi* (The Pazzi Conspiracy). General Duphot's funeral employed thousands of musicians, and Liberty Trees were erected around the city, with bands and free wine. Metastasio's *Attilio Regolo* was given a Republican reading, and according to the *Monitore* was well received.[40] Voltaire's *Morte di Cesare* (Death of Caesar) was a hit, at least in part because the actors, a group of French amateurs, brought the statue of Pompey from the Campidoglio, so that the actor-Caesar could expire at the very feet where the original Caesar was said to have died.

The ediles, officials in charge of the theaters, regularly distributed free tickets to ensure that theater was available to all, even the poorest. Old-fashioned, non-republican theatrical pieces were sanitized by the addition of "patriotic airs" played and sung at intervals. Dire reprisals were threatened against those "aristocrats and enemies of democracy" who sneered at "the energetic spirit which republican music excites in the soul."[41]

Unfortunately, even the production of uplifting dramas was beset with difficulty. Theater managers like citizen ex-Duke Sforza Cesarini had to walk a tightrope between Romans fed up with solemn moralizing and touchy republicans on the lookout for crypto-aristocratic menace: in June 1799 Alfieri's historical tragedy *La congiura dei Pazzi* (The Pazzi Conspiracy) was whistled off the Alibert stage, while patriotic patrons of the Argentina were shocked by *La tragedia di Debora*, a drama based on the Old Testament story. The patriots sent a delegation to the ediles demanding that the show be taken off, on the grounds that it offered a bad example to the public women of the city, who might be encouraged to murder their customers in imitation of the heroine on stage.[42] In the last days of the Republic Voltaire's *Semiramide* caused an uproar among the patriots when one of the characters sat on a throne, an act that was seen as an outrage to democratic decency.

The republicans did not have a corner on moral outrage. Many Romans objected to irreverent portrayals of religious figures, as in *L'ingresso dei francesi a Faenza* (The Entrance of the French into Faenza), where several actresses dressed as nuns and an actor dressed as a prelate wearing a pectoral cross assisted at a "democratic marriage" under a Liberty Tree. Even more obnoxious was a show where devils were shown pinning a tricolor cockade onto God the Father.[43]

In addition to introducing new festivals and promoting democratic theater, the leaders of the Republic made half-hearted attempts to "nationalize" traditional Roman holidays and landmarks. The June feast of Saints Peter and Paul, for instance, was permitted but the bronze statue of Peter in the basilica, traditionally dressed in papal robes for the holiday, had his vestments limited to a modest episcopal mitre. The bronze angel who guards the city from the top of the Castel Sant'Angelo suffered an even greater indignity when in January of 1799 he was dressed up in a tricolor and red bonnet and renamed "The Genius of Liberty." The new revolutionary calendar with its ten-day weeks, or decades, was introduced and this had some unfortunate side-effects. In July and August the Piazza Navona was flooded and free ices were distributed as usual, but this summertime treat occurred every ten days rather than every seven days as before. More serious, the new calendar meant that there were to be no more Sundays. There was little serious attempt to interfere with Christian worship as there had been in France, although there was some talk of reducing or eliminating the Easter Week ceremonies.

The spectacles may have kept up the morale of committed Jacobins, but there were few of these. The rest of the Romans, who had never felt anything warmer than indifference toward the new state, became steadily more alienated. The French had never been secure in Rome, and as early as April 1798 the army was seriously considering withdrawal. Not only were they surrounded by a hostile countryside and under constant attack from bandits or irregulars if they ventured outside the city, but they were also caught between the Austrians to the north and the Neapolitans to the south, either or (more likely) both of whom were likely to attack sooner or later. Geopolitical developments in 1798 and 1799 made the survival of the sickly Roman Republic highly problematic. It was not more than three months old when its greatest defender, General Bonaparte, sailed from Toulon for Egypt. After some initial successes the expedition ran afoul of Admiral Nelson and on the first of August 1798 most of the French fleet was sunk in Aboukir Bay. Bonaparte and his hapless army were virtually marooned in Egypt.

Flushed with this triumph, Nelson returned to Italy and encouraged the
Bourbon King Ferdinand of Naples to march on Rome. On 22 November Ferdinand and his retinue moved into Rome; ten days later the king, preceded by
his queen and accompanied by his gentlemen-in-waiting, fled the city in undignified panic.[44] Angelucci and company, who had retreated to Perugia at the
approach of the Neapolitans, were carried back to their city by French arms.

In January of 1799 French forces pursued Ferdinand south and on 23 January the chaos in Naples coalesced into what would be the most romantic, and
ill-starred, of the Italian republics. Even less durable than her Roman sister,
the Parthenopean Republic at Naples survived only through artificial respi-
ration, between 23 January and 19 June 1799, and perished in a bloodbath that
ensured its immortality. This event is treated in more depth in chapter 5,
since the fall of the Parthenopean Republic provided the origin of much of
the political imagery in Sardou's *La Tosca*.

In Rome, through the spring of 1799, while supporters pretended that
their Republic was alive, the French position in Italy worsened. The string of
republics were at best urban islands in a sea of hostile peasantry; wherever it
became possible, Italians rose up to expel, or at the very least murder, their
liberators.

The Austrians and their allies, defeated the year before, recovered in 1799
and their victories in the north continued through the spring and into the summer. Archduke Charles drove the French back across the Rhine; Kray defeated
them at Magnano, and two weeks later Mélas (in whom Scarpia places such
hopes in Act II of the opera) and Suvorov, the Russian commander, did the
same at Cassano. Milan fell and the Cisalpine Republic was extinguished;
Suvorov entered Turin and Melas besieged the French General Moreau and
his troops in Genoa. As early as spring of 1799 Rome was surrounded by the
Allies, who paused and considered upon the best way to seize the nettle that
was Rome.

In the city the consuls, who had never been popular, were the subjects of
increasingly open and bitter satires and attacks. In mid-June, for instance,
the following story circulated after it was found nailed to the door of an unnamed consul:

> A consul died and presented himself at the gates of Paradise to be let in.
> St. Peter, however, told him that the consuls had stolen the keys to heaven
> along with everything else and, furious, threw him out. So he walked on and
> presented himself at the doors of Purgatory, seeking admission there. But
> one of the attendant souls told him sadly that since his fellow consuls had
> stopped all the pious petitions for the dead, Purgatory had had to be shut
> down. Finally he went to the door of Hell, where he found a huge number

of souls trying to get in. Presenting himself to the demon doorkeeper, the consul asked for admission; the demon took him by the arm and gave him a great shove, saying, "Go to the end of the line, and when it's your turn come right on in!"[45]

The French ambassador's door at the Bertolio palace did not escape the attentions of the satirists. On the morning of 25 June a picture was hung there showing a squealing pig surrounded by four lions representing the four dominant Allied powers (Naples, Austria, England, and Russia) who are saying, "You certainly won't run away from here again!"

The ancient spokesmen of the Roman *popolo*, Pasquino and his companion Marforio, had been commenting sardonically on the Republic from the earliest days. On the first of July the consuls, while packing to move into the Vatican palace (presumably to be closer to refuge in the Castel Sant'Angelo), issued an edict forbidding non-Roman priests to wear clerical garb. According to Fortunati, on the morning of 4 July Pasquino was discovered in full clerical regalia, with this vaudeville routine attached to the statue's base:

> MARFORIO: Tell me, Pasquino, what's up this morning that you put on the black *farajoletto* [clerical dress]? Is it some feast day?
> PASQUINO: I'll say! They've forbidden priests to wear it, so I put it on myself to bring the Holy Oil [to anoint the dying] to the Roman Republic.

On 5 July an unidentified man played what Fortunati described as a "good joke" on a group of patriots who gathered at a popular café on the Piazza Sciara. In what sounds like a parody of Cavaradossi's Act II outburst, the joker galloped up as if he had come from outside the city, shouting "Vittoria, vittoria!" and waving a sealed packet, which he said contained "good news" that he was on his way to impart to the consuls. The patriots seized the packet and ran back inside the café, only to find that it contained maps showing details of the victories of the Austrians over the French.

Everyone, including its adherents, knew that the Republic was doomed, but its death agony was long and undignified. The summer dragged on, with satires and jokes, with defiant parties and parades held by the republicans, with arrests and executions which increased in frequency as the inevitable surrender came nearer. By 16 August the French had retreated to the fortress and blocked the Bridge of the Angel to impede any attack; a few days later a Florentine merchant and his son were shot for carrying arms; they were followed by a curate from the church of St John of the Florentines in Rome, charged with preaching revolt against the French from the pulpit. The executions continued through August and September, and so did the "patriotic celebrations." As late as 23 September 1799 the anniversary of the French Republic was celebrated with horse races ("completely ridiculous!" sneered Fortunati), a military parade at St. Peter's square to honor twelve wounded soldiers who were crowned by "twelve patriot girls," and a gala dinner at the French ambassador's where speeches were made about defending Rome to the last drop of patriot blood. Two hours after sunset a fireworks machine was ignited ("surprising," admits Fortunati, "for the variety of its colors") and the evening ended with a ball at the Apollo theater.[46]

Less than a week later the Roman republicans were finally forced to recognize the realities of their situation. French losses on the Continent made Italy not worth the trouble of holding; deals were cut among the major powers, and the French agreed to an orderly retreat before the Allies, abandoning Rome and the Roman republicans as they had abandoned the other nonviable little republics—the Cisalpine, the Parthenopean—in the face of superior firepower.

While the Roman Republic had struggled in vain to become anything more than a pathetic front for the French military government, the pope had been trundled about Italy, a danger and an embarrassment to every state in Europe. While the Directors who now ruled France knew that they did not want the pope in Rome they had no very clear idea of what they did want to do with him. The Catholic powers shuffled their feet and avoided eye contact. Only Russia, with its quixotic tsar Alexander, considered attempting a rescue.[47] This curious state of affairs was partly, but not entirely, due to fear of revolutionary France. If the truth be told, the European powers were not displeased to have the papacy removed from their own political calculations: after centuries of struggle between pope and emperor, the final victory of the secular state seemed within reach. Still, not even those states most eager for a dissolution of the papacy were willing to go so far as to kill the old man. A white martyr, dying slowly, was bad enough; a red martyr meeting violent death was unthinkable. So the statesmen of Europe waited for nature to take its course, and dreamed of the day when there would be no pope in Rome or perhaps anywhere else.

But the more the Braschi pope suffered (and the more unwelcome the French made themselves) the more his spiritual and temporal subjects forgot his sometimes burdensome nepotism and vainglory, and the more they loved him. He was undeniably a sick old man bearing up under his trials with dignity and fortitude; worse, with a wry sense of humor.[48] He found temporary refuge in the lands of the archduke of Tuscany while the French Directory threatened to ship him to Spain or to Brazil.[49] In the spring of 1799 the French occupied Tuscany and dethroned the archduke as part of their continuing policy of willy-nilly democratization. Spurred on by rumors that one power or another was planning to snatch their embarrassing hostage, the French almost literally dragged the old man through northern Italy and across the Alps. On Bastille Day of 1799 he reached Valence, on his way from Grenoble to Dijon. He had been ill, half-paralyzed, and in pain since he left Rome; now he was obviously dying. On 29 August, one year, five months, and nine days after his calvary had begun, he died.

Rome, without a pope for almost a year and a half, now officially entered the period known as *sede vacante*, the time when the chair of Peter is vacant, a time of licensed chaos, for settling old scores and airing old grudges. It would be almost another year before a new pope, Pius VII, would come to Rome; he would arrive on 3 July 1800, two weeks after the events of *Tosca*. With the French gone, Naples, Austria, England, and Russia all pursued their own schemes for the fate of Rome. In stark contrast to Sardou's and Puccini's vision of a city crushed under papal tyranny, the opera and the play are in fact set in a lawless place where no hand clearly holds the reins.

3 The Painter's Rome

I have unfinished business here in Rome. I arrived at the moment when the French troops were leaving by one gate, while the Neapolitan army came in by another.

Cavaradossi to Angelotti, *La Tosca*, I, iii

The Cavaliere Mario Cavaradossi, coming as a stranger to his father's city, would have arrived on the last day of September 1799, the first of the three principals to reach Rome. Floria Tosca would certainly not have been there consorting with the hated Jacobins, much less singing in their godless theaters while the Roman Republic was in power. And Scarpia would not arrive until June 1800.

From the start, the historical Neapolitan occupation of Rome was very different from the images presented in the play or the opera. On 29 September the French General Garnier announced the terms of a treaty which had been negotiated with the Allies: adherents of the Republic, known as patriots, were to be allowed to remain in the city unmolested or leave with the French army, if they so chose; in either case the security of their property was to be guaranteed.[1] The next morning before dawn a column of French troops and a group of Romans, men and women who had supported the Republic, took the road toward Civitavecchia where, by treaty arrangement, they would be ignominiously evacuated by English warships seconded from the fleet of the victorious Admiral Nelson. Ironically, they were following the road by which, under papal government, convoys of petty criminals had shambled toward Civitavecchia and the prison galleys that never put to sea.[2]

As the French and their friends left, the Neapolitan troops marched silently in from the south along the Appian Way, entering the city through the San Giovanni gate "with no beating of the drum."[3] The Allies had been marking time in the suburbs, hoping to avoid any clash over the occupation. Each of the combatants seemed anxious to avoid the other; the suppression of the Parthenopean Republic in Naples during the previous summer had left a bad taste in everyone's mouth and none of the parties wanted a repetition of the embarrassing bloodshed. This was most particularly true for the republicans, whose blood it was that was under discussion.

The Neapolitans took possession of the city from the San Giovanni gate, and immediately sent a force to surround the ghetto to prevent the Romans attacking the Jews and sacking their homes. Then, still silent, the troops marched up the Corso to the Piazza Venezia. As they passed the site of the French Academy the bystanders spotted a young man they knew to be a patriot, the son of a politically active surgeon named Chinozzi. Confusion broke out as first the crowd, and then some of the soldiers, tried to arrest him. He ran; shots were fired. Finally he was run to ground near the Piazza Venezia, and what could have become a very ugly incident picked up momentum as another patriot (this time a churchman) was recognized and seized by the crowd. In Naples incidents like these had turned into lynchings of the most gruesome sort.[4] In Rome, however, this did not happen. The Austrian commander Marshal de Bourcard quickly ordered Chinozzi and the patriot cleric released, and made a public announcement of the terms of the treaty, whereby adherents of the republican regime were not to be molested. Disturbing the peace by breaking the treaty was to be punished with the death penalty (often threatened but never, so far as the records tell, carried out for political offenses of this sort).

All of this triumphant reaction would hardly have been a heartening sight for the hero of the play, a Parisian republican with family business on his mind. Even an artist eager to draw from the wellspring of European civilization could have been forgiven for turning around without unpacking his bags: the winners of the Prix de Rome between 1796 and 1801 wisely decided to wait for peace, and stayed in Paris. Presumably the fictional Cavaradossi, with a Roman name to counteract his French manner, is more confident, or more reckless.

There was much to tempt a young painter to recklessness. Recent scholarship has given the lie to the old idea that Rome was simply a museum where talented foreigners could browse among masterpieces from earlier centuries, and apply they observed there within the schools of Paris or Venice. The work of art historian Anthony M. Clark began to change that image by the 1970s. Clark's research revealed the fact that Rome was recognized at the time as a vital and influential center of painting, rivaled only by Paris.[5]

At the end of the eighteenth century perhaps the single most important non-Italian group working in Rome were the young French painters associated with Jacques-Louis David, the dominant neoclassicist and revolutionary painter par excellence. But the French by no means had the field to them-

selves. German and English painters abounded, many of them attached to
the "court" of Angelica Kauffmann (1741–1807), one of the most famous artists in Europe. The largest and most important (as well as the least studied)
group of artists was made up of Italians, the most famous of them probably
Pompeo Batoni (1708–87). These skilled professionals did the great bulk of
the commissioned work in the city, and continued a long and distinguished
tradition.

Rome was the center where every painter had to go to polish his (or in several cases, her) craft.[6] Here one found the great collections of Greek and Roman sculpture, and the monumental architecture all the more imposing for
its air of melancholy decay, breathing that "sense of the transience of all
things human" that was and would continue to be so dear to the Romantics.[7]
The patronage of the popes, the religious institutions, and the great families
had filled the city with so much great art that uncounted wonders remained
despite dedicated efforts at looting. "Rome," wrote Coyer in 1764, "will always
have the advantage of being the School of the World, because of the originals
it possesses."[8] Two enormous and much-copied canvases by Pannini, painted
in 1758 and 1759 for the French ambassador, offer graphic evidence of this
view of Rome. Titled *Gallery with Views of Ancient Rome* and *Gallery with
Views of Modern Rome*, these tour-de-force works show the interiors of two
imaginary galleries (fig. 7). One features paintings of the classical ruins of
Rome along with Greco-Roman statuary, sarcophagi, and architectural detail. The second is similar, but the paintings and statuary are Renaissance
and Baroque. Both show the riches of Rome laid out for the enlightenment of
scholars, patrons, and young artists.

It was in Rome that the German Johann Winckelmann defined the classical, and here the Frenchman Jacques-Louis David raised the neoclassical
style to the dominant political and artistic statement of the age. The city was
normally full of artists and intellectuals who had come to learn from the work
of their great predecessors.[9] Most either took no notice of the modern crises
and struggles of the Italians, or noted them with detached amusement. The
Romans in turn looked on these visitors with tolerance warmed by the expectation of profit. There were normally so many of them that one of the most
popular carnival characters was the Foreign Artist, a persona achieved by
putting on a long frock coat and hurrying up and down the Corso with huge
sketch pads and enormous pencils.[10]

By the 1790s painting, like everything else in Rome, had been politicized,
and working in the style of David could be indiscreet, but artists who kept
out of politics and avoided outrageous or openly anti-religious work were not
molested. For an artist like Cavaradossi to stay in Rome against the counsels

FIGURE 7. *Gallery with Views of Modern Rome*, 1759. Giovanni Paolo Pannini. Musée du Louvre. Erich Lessing/Art Resource, NY

of good sense would hardly have been an unprecedented thing to do. The famous Venetian sculptor, Antonio Canova, was working in Rome during the upheavals of 1799–1800. In November of 1799 he was happily at work on a larger than life portrait of Ferdinand of Naples. In a few years he would be equally happy, and busy, sculpting portraits of the large Bonaparte clan, an oeuvre crowned by his famous reclining nude of Napoleon's sister, Paolina (or Pauline) Bonaparte Borghese. The English artist and essayist Richard Duppa, whose account of the death of General Duphot we have already noted, arrived in Rome in 1798 when the papal government fell and stayed on under the Republic to continue with his drawing and research, and to note the political upheavals about him with the cool interest one would expect of a Shropshire man. His situation parallels that of Sardou's fictional hero. The Republicans would have considered Duppa an enemy alien, since France and England were at war; Cavaradossi, as a French national, would have been in much the same situation vis-à-vis the Allies. In view of the fact that the Republicans were more likely than the Allies to execute their enemies, Duppa was taking even more of a risk than Cavaradossi.[11] The young Englishman's interests, which stressed the works of Michelangelo and Raphael, were fairly typical of the standard tour guides and the memoirs of intellectuals and artists at the end of the eighteenth century. Among the first sights they all recommended were St. Peter's basilica, and the papal galleries at the Vatican and at the Quirinale, where the pope normally lived. By the end of 1799 the French had looted these with great energy and skill, but even the French commissioners had not found a way to remove everything.

Tourists and painters alike continued to make their pilgrimages to see Michelangelo's frescos in the Sistine Chapel, though some moderns found the powerful figures uncouth.[12] Raphael, admired for his spirituality and refined vison, was considered by many to be "the best of the modern painters" and artists were advised to study his *School of Athens* and the Vatican tapestries, and his famous *Transfiguration*, then found in the church of San Pietro in Montorio. A visit to the classical statuary in the Vatican and in private galleries was obligatory. Churches, then as now, were prominent on the artist's itinerary, for their architecture (considered useful for the history painter), and for the sculptures they contained, from the works of Michelangelo to those of Canova. Above all the attention of the visitor was directed to the wealth of paintings and frescos housed in the churches of Rome. Although some now consider it a trifle vulgar, the Baroque church of Sant'Andrea della Valle, with its frescoes by Domenichino, was then among the most admired, after St. Peter's and St. Paul's outside the Walls. Goethe visited the city in the golden days just before the French Revolution, between 1786 and 1788, and was delighted with the Pantheon, St. Peter's, the pyramid of Cestius, the Tomb of Cecilia Metella; the aqueducts and baths, and the Colosseum (preferably seen at night, by torchlight). The catacombs exercised a magnetic attraction, with the added shiver of danger from the bad air of the *campagna* outside the walls, and the peril of being lost in their labyrinthine passages.

Admiration was not unqualified. Some felt that Michelangelo's frescoes were too coarse to be truly artistic. Elisabeth Vigée-Lebrun (see fig. 8) could not bring herself to recommend Santa Maria della Vittoria and the "notorious" Bernini sculpture of St. Theresa in ecstasy "whose scandalous expression defies description," but few guidebook authors shared her scruples.

Works in the collections of the great Roman noble families were almost as available to well-bred tourists as they would have been in public museums. The Doria, the Giustiniani, the Barbarini, the Colonna, and the Borghese considered it part of the natural order that perfect strangers should tramp through their homes admiring their Pietro da Cortonas, their Raphaels, their Poussins, their Giuseppe Ghezzis, and their Guido Renis. Goethe commented on this Italian concept of "living nobly" as soon as he crossed the Alps, noting

FIGURE 8. Self-portrait by Elisabeth Vigée-Lebrun, whose fame as a painter rivaled
that of her compatriot Jacques-Louis David. Uffizi, Florence. Alinari/Art Resource

that in Verona the rich, if they wished to be considered gentlemen, had to tolerate the fact that their homes were considered public property; to do otherwise would be to live less than nobly.[13]

The amateur might lose himself in touring but the student or the professional artist sooner or later had to face the hard labor of preparing his own works. First came the critical choice of a subject. This was particularly important because art was seen as a means of shaping society, and history painting was considered the most exalted form of art because it drew on the past to convey messages of personal morality and civic virtue and was thus beneficial to society. The topic an artist chose was likely to be a scene from the Roman or Greek past. Republicans like Cavaradossi and David's students in general favored representations of Brutus, or Marius, or the Gracchi, all of whom were seen as stern and virtuous republicans opposed to aristocratic corruption and luxury. Other favorites were the death of Socrates (seen as a martyr to truth), and the blind Belisarius (heroic savior of Byzantium treated shamefully by his emperor Justinian).

Once a subject had been selected a specific episode had to be chosen, and then the artist had to determine the viewpoint through which he would interpret that episode. David's landmark work, *The Oath of the Horatii* (see fig. 9), was based on a well-known story, but the artist chose an unusual moment for his focus: instead of showing the father defending his surviving son before the Senate, David took the moment when the sons swore their oath to fight to the death against the Curtii. This is the definitive neoclassical painting, the statement of stern republican virtue against which all political painting of the day is measured.[14]

Painting, like theater, was a narrative art closely tied to the cultural values of the day. The painter, like the performer, used his or her skills to tell a story with the aim of stirring the audience to virtuous action, or at least to virtuous sentiments. Telling the story involved a great deal of hard work: the endless sketching of scenery, ruins, buildings, and landscapes; the selection of appropriate models, and posing them to the best effect; choices about light sources, color, tone, and balance. In addition the painter had to select and prepare his materials, an arduous task demanding a knowledge of chemistry and a strong right arm.

Sardou's Cavaradossi tells Angelotti that he is working in the church in order to disguise his radical politics.[15] He cannot, however, resist the temptation to incorporate a portrait into his mural (the portrait of Angelotti's sister the marchesa Attavanti). In fact, while the churches remained major employers of artists, by 1800 portraiture was the bread-and-butter work of the craft. When Vigée-Lebrun came to Rome in 1790 her main occupation was

FIGURE 9. David's *Oath of the Horatii*, the painting that revolutionized art and intro-duced neo-classicism. Musée du Louvre. Giraudon/Art Resource

painting portraits, and her memoirs include a useful essay for the instruction of painters engaged in this lucrative work.

The highest status, however, was accorded to the history painter. David, who did many portraits, made his major reputation with history paintings. This too could pay very well, if the artist had a head for business: in 1799 David put his *Intervention of the Sabine Women* on public exhibit for a fee of 1 fr. 80 per visitor, and made enough to buy a country estate with the pro-ceeds.[16] A Rome visit was of course essential for the preparation of a history painter. In his guide to the city "J. Salmon, antiquary, late of Rome" advises the student to pay particular attention to architecture, and recommends that he study medieval architecture, which may be used as background—a trick, he says, which Nicolas Poussin used to great effect.[17]

Individual artists and intellectuals were attracted to Rome for their own reasons, but art was a much more serious business in the eighteenth century than could be accounted for by the individual motives of painters. The arts were a major tool of statecraft, a means by which public opinion was shaped, and national prestige demanded that any important state maintain an artistic presence in Rome. The French Academy in Rome was established in February 1666, one of Colbert's schemes for advancing French cultural dominance.[18] The Royal Academy of Painting and Sculpture in Paris sent its best students to Rome in order to polish and perfect their skills. These painters, sculptors, and architects were maintained during their four-year tenure at royal expense until the Revolution. After 1793 the French Republic maintained the Academy, well aware of the propaganda value of such a stable of public-relations specialists.

During most of the eighteenth century the French Academy in Rome was located at the Mancini palace, an elegant building on the Corso. Its first director was the sculptor Bernini, but by the eighteenth century the Academy was an exclusively French outpost. The Président de Brosses, passing through the city in the middle of the century, found the institution under-utilized. He reports a handful of artists huddled together in a vast building that the crown could ill afford to keep up, and recommended that the Academy be combined with the Embassy in order to save money. But even in the leanest days the artists and architects managed to justify their existence, keeping the name and prestige of France before the eyes of the diplomatic corps. The students threw themselves into the Roman tradition of spectacle; not only were their talents called upon for the great fireworks machines designed for French royal occasions (including the most famous of all, the 1729 extravaganza at the Piazza Navona for the birth of the Dauphin),[19] they also distinguished themselves in their designs for carnival floats and diplomatic displays.

By the time of the Revolution the dominant figure in the French Academy in Rome was Jacques-Louis David (see fig. 10), who was not merely the most famous and successful painter of his day, but a revolutionary painter in every sense of the word.[20] Unlike most eighteenth-century painters who were from the artisan or craftsman class, David came from an upwardly mobile bourgeois family and felt at ease in the company of rich intellectuals like his fictional student, Mario Cavaradossi; indeed, he had every intention of becoming a rich intellectual himself. In this David was a typical French revolutionary bourgeois, frustrated by what he saw as the traditional aristocracy's monopoly on power, and eager to overthrow that class and replace it with his own. As a revolutionary artist he despised the old-fashioned sort of painter, who fit into the "feudal" social structure and saw painting as a trade or craft rather than a sacred calling. In a famous tirade to his students he dismissed the Academy as a "wig-maker's shop" where students learned "conventional movements . . . tricks . . . and mannerisms," useful only for those who "make a trade out of painting."[21] The job of painter, like that of musician, was in

FIGURE 10. Self-portrait by Jacques-Louis David, whose students dominated the Prix de Rome and the French Academy at the end of the eighteenth century. Uffizi, Florence. Giraudon/Art Resource

the process of change. Before the eighteenth century the status of the creative
artist normally fell somewhere between that of the courtier and that of a superior sort of servant; by the nineteenth century the arts had become liberal
professions that relied on public interest and approval for success. In a word,
the arts were being revolutionized. Art, for David—and presumably for his
putative student, Cavaradossi—was not merely a craft, a métier. It was either a noble enterprise or a highly lucrative profession. Or, preferably, both.

When the Revolution began in 1789 David was already a mature (one
might even say middle-aged) professional, successful and admired. At the
same time, as an ambitious bourgeois he loathed the Royal Academy of
Painting and Sculpture which he saw (perhaps rightly) as blocking his advancement to the professional triumphs of which he felt himself worthy. Long
before 1789 he was the hero of the artistic and political radicals, young men
who took up David's austere technique as a part of the typical radical critique
of pre-revolutionary France. This critique involved "unmasking" the deceptive style of those attached to the old regime. The radicals felt that truth and
virtue (in art as in politics) had to be plain and straightforward, rather than
concealed under the deceptive cover of "style."

David the radical painter was actively involved in the scandals and con-
troversies of the 1780s. He blatantly shattered the rules of painting, to the delight of philosophical and political radicals who saw this (correctly) as "an
appeal to a naturally seditious mass, an appropriation of high culture on behalf of once safely excluded outsiders." [22]

David had great influence on the French Academy in Rome, but he was in
that city on only two occasions. Between 1775 and 1780 he spent five years as
a "pensioner" of the French Academy. After three bitterly disappointing fail-
ures, he had finally secured the Rome Prize at the advanced age of twenty-
seven, and traveled to Rome with his teacher, Vien, the new director of the
Academy. David arrived in Italy swearing that he would not be seduced by
classicism; he left the most committed of neoclassicists. On his return to Paris
he was appointed first painter to the king—the same Louis XVI for whose
execution the painter would vote nine years later. The king personally commissioned *The Oath of the Horatii* and David returned to Rome between 1785
to 1787 to complete this work, which would make him the most famous painter
in Paris and the founder of an influential new school of art.

As the French state dissolved after 1789 David became ever more closely
associated with radical politics. In the first salon show after the Revolution,
in 1791, he presented a new sort of history painting in his study for *The Tennis Court Oath*, which represented a real event featuring still-living actors

rather than an idealized episode from the remote past.[23] This great narrative work had been commissioned by the Jacobin Club, whose members understood the propaganda value of having that moment of high political drama immortalized by one of their own. The thin line between David's politics and his painting blurred as the Revolution lurched willy-nilly toward the Terror. This was the period when, according to Sardou, the young Mario Cavaradossi was living in Paris after the death of his parents, in the studio of his teacher, David. These were exciting days, but it is hard to imagine that much was being taught in the great man's atelier after David the master painter and propagandist was elected to the National Convention. There, in January of 1793, he voted in favor of the execution of the ci-devant king, formerly Louis XVI and now an anxious, overweight family man known as Louis Capet. When Cavaradossi in the first act of Sardou's play refers to his teacher as a *conventionnel* or member of the Convention, he is referring to David's participation in this infamous execution which had taken place seven years earlier. For those who feared and loathed the Revolution—that is, most of the population of Rome—the celebrated David was a killer of his king. A decade later Pius VII, sitting for his portrait, would charm the brilliant regicide by commenting with gentle irony that he trembled to think what a man who had beheaded his king would do to "a poor papier-mâché pope."[24] Few Romans would have been as amiable.

But if the people and rulers of Rome were horrified by the ever more radical drift of the Revolution (and they were), the young men at the French Academy in Rome were delighted. By August 1790 the director, Ménageot, was pleading for permission to resign his post on the grounds that ideas of liberty and equality had made his young charges unmanageable. (Permission was denied.)[25] When the revolutionary agent Hugon de Basseville arrived in Rome in 1793 he set up his headquarters in the French Academy at the Mancini palace. There he sold off the images of former kings, along with tapestries and glassware; he encouraged the radicalism of the pensioners and caused riots by (among other things) dressing the Academy doorman in a revolutionary outfit complete with a tricolor cockade. The residents of the Academy were young, and they were artists in a culture where the artist's work was a serious political activity. Encouraged by their new government they swaggered about the city taking every opportunity to flaunt their politics with their demeanor, and most especially with their clothing. Sardou's Cavaradossi is meant to be a typical representative of these young men, though his description of the political implications of his own appearance is more appropriate to 1793 than to 1800:

... beyond the fact that my name has a singed smell to it because my father made a scandal in his time, the mere fact that I am a student of the *conventionnel* David, my way of life ... my clothes, and even the expression on my face—all of this calls me to the attention of the police. Here as in Naples, you know, the man is badly thought of who neglects the powdered wig, culottes, buckled shoes, and instead dresses and cuts his hair in the French style. My Titus haircut is outrageously liberal, my beard is freethinking, my boots are revolutionary! [26]

Sardou's hero is an exponent of radical chic where unkempt hair was intended as a statement that its wearer was too masculine, virtuous, and busy with more important matters to be bothered with it.[27] Sardou's idea of giving his hero facial hair in the style of the 1880s was anachronistic but there is some argument to be made for a mustache. (Early Cavaradossis regularly appeared with more or less luxuriant mustaches. The creator of the role, Emilio de Marchi, was relatively restrained; see fig. 11.) Mustaches were a military affectation, part of the cavalry officer's mystique along with long unwashed hair worn in braids to keep it out of its wearer's face. A similar fad was the unshaven look, where the beard was allowed to sprout to a heavy five-o'clock shadow, conveying the same message of sexually dynamic, nonconformist intensity favored today by rock stars and television personalities. Boots rather than low shoes were part of the same image. And of course the very term sansculotte ("without knee breeches") was such a powerful political image that it became a synonym for radical republican. As so often happens, the defiance of fashion became fashionable, and by 1800 these "revolutionary" styles had penetrated the general population. The conservative garb of powdered wig and knee breeches was hopelessly out of date everywhere but at formal court functions, and few young people, no matter what their politics, would have been caught wearing them anywhere else.[28]

In Rome in the early 1790s, however, such dress was indeed inflammatory. In the autumn of 1792 the French monarchy was declared abolished, and the Director advised that the Academy be closed, since staff and pensioners there were receiving neither pay nor stipends. Bad days for the administration were not, however, necessarily bad days for the students who were a long way from home, far from the inconveniences of Revolution, and basking in its long-distance delights.

It is hardly surprising to find that the revolutionary government was well-disposed toward art in general and the Academy in Rome in particular, especially when we consider the high-profile role that Jacques-Louis David was playing in the Convention.[29] David's interest in the affairs of the Academy

FIGURE 11. Emilio de Marchi, who created the role of Cavaradossi at the 14 January 1900 premiere in Rome, sported a jaunty mustache, as did most early Cavaradossis. Dr. Girvice Archer. Copy print made in 1999 by Michaela Allan Murphy

was not only based on his keen appreciation of art as propaganda, but also on the fact that Rome was full of his own students.

In the eighteenth century, the Rome Prize was granted by the Academy after a grueling series of competitions.[30] The scrambling for the award was fiercely competitive—some, like David's student Girodet, cheated. Winning was highly political: one can judge the ebb and flow of David's success with the Paris art establishment, and then in the worlds of revolutionary and imperial politics, by the numbers of his students who got the Prize. They maintained a constant presence in Rome, winning nineteen times from 1784 (when his favorite pupil and close friend, Drouais, won) up to 1814, when the fall of Napoleon put an end to David's dominance as the emperor's official painter. His pupils won prizes in 1787, 1789, 1791, and again in 1797, 1798, 1800, 1801, 1803, 1804, and 1805. Since a first prize was good for at least four years' residency, there was only one period for two or three years in the middle of the 1790s that there was no David student eligible to reside at the Academy in Rome. The gap in David-trained winners in the 1790s is probably related to the fact that the master himself was immersed in radical politics until the fall of Robespierre in 1794 and thereafter was in prison or keeping a low profile until 1796. By 1797, a year after Napoleon's first invasion of Italy, David's students were back in stride, with victories in all but two years between 1797 and 1804—by coincidence, one of those years was 1799, presumably the year when Mario Cavaradossi would have won.

David's most famous and successful pupil, Jean-Auguste-Dominique Ingres, won the prize in 1800 and in 1801, but his Roman trip was long delayed. French visitors, and especially French visitors suspected of radical sympathies (as David's students automatically were), became increasingly, and dangerously, unpopular in the city; in addition, the new French Republic did not have the money to support painters, embattled as it was on all sides. It was not until 1806 that the backlog of winners was cleared and Ingres got his chance.

The Baron François Gérard, another David pupil, offers some intriguing parallels with Cavaradossi, and one wonders if Sardou might have been aware of them. He certainly could have been: in the celebrations leading up to the first centennial of the Revolution, David and his students were commemorated along with other revolutionaries in a flurry of publications and popular interest. Gérard was a decade ahead of his fictional counterpart, winning the prize (at the age of nineteen) just as the Revolution broke out in 1789. In many ways the lives of the real and the fictional painters are mirror images. Both are members of the lower ranks of the nobility. Cavaradossi is born in Paris to an Italian father, and dies in Rome; Gérard was born in Rome to a French father (in the household of the French representative, Cardinal de Bernis), and died in Paris.

Gérard's correspondence with another David-trained Rome Prize winner, Anne-Louis Girodet, shows just how rapidly the shock waves from the 1789 revolution hit Rome, to the discomfort of the French students there, whatever their private political convictions. Girodet, like Gérard, was politically conservative, no supporter of his teacher's Jacobin party. This did not, however, prevent his coming to grief with the Roman populace and police. "Life," he wrote to Gérard in 1790, "is becoming very difficult for us here." The city was full of spies, and the French had to be careful to avoid being accused of fomenting revolution. "It is impossible to get a passport for Naples, and those French who came to Rome from that city are now being forced to leave."[31] In June on the eve of the feast of the patrons of Rome, Saints Peter and Paul, the painter went with a group of students to watch the traditional fireworks display at the Castel Sant'Angelo. Two years later Elisabeth Vigée-Lebrun would enjoy the illumination of the Castel Sant'Angelo with "thousands of firecrackers and flaming balloons thrown up into the sky." In 1790 there was, as usual, a huge crowd, all pushing to get a better view of the Catherine wheels and Roman candles that lit up the summer night. The young Frenchman (Girodet was twenty-three at the time), finding himself pushed up against one of the guards, got into an argument and then into a fistfight with the soldier. He was promptly arrested and frog-marched across the bridge to the fortress under guard by eight soldiers, four in front and four behind, armed with "bare sabres in one hand and guns in the other." There was a delay while an officer who spoke French was located—the painter, like so many Fellows at national academies in Rome then as now, had made no attempt to learn Italian.

His companions had meanwhile hurried off to inform Ménageot, the director of the Academy, who blustered and demanded his dependant's immediate release, which was granted. Rome, Girodet wrote to his friend in Paris a week later, was still buzzing with the news that a Frenchman had been arrested and taken to the Castel Sant'Angelo, without mentioning the fact that he had been released after a few hours.

Two years later two Academy pensioners from Lyon, the sculptor Joseph Chinard and a young student of architecture, Ildefonso Ratner, found themselves in considerably more serious trouble.[32] Although these young men were not students of David, David became involved in their case in his capacity as member of the Convention. The two had reputations as radicals and partisans of the Revolution, which, although it had not yet peaked, was already viewed with horror by most Europeans. Both Chinard and Ratner had been members of the revolutionary National Guard in their native town of Lyon. The Roman police, the infamous *sbirri*, were convinced that the French artists were spreading radical subversion, and on the night of 22–23 September they broke into their rooms while the two young men were away and lay in wait for their return. According to a letter that David read aloud in the Convention, the students returned home to find their rooms full of sbirri, who "garrotted them and dragged them off to prison"—first, to the Carceri Nuovi (New Prisons), and later to the Castel Sant'Angelo. The story of the garrotting is not at all unlikely: in the previous century Don Torarini, a priest arrested on suspicion of possessing illegal weapons, had the following experience: "one of the sbirri . . . hit him hard in the stomach . . . ; meanwhile, another grabbed him by the hair and a third delivered a punch right to his face; thus gasping and with bloody visage, they dragged him away." [33]

The French students might have considered themselves lucky to get away with a bit of garrotting. (A further discussion of the sbirri follows in chapter 5.) A few days later the police returned to the rooms and this time they carried away several models that Chinard had been working on—the most damning had the alarming if not particularly original title of *Jove striking with thunderbolts Aristocracy and Religion*. The civic and religious authorities in Rome naturally took this as an open attack on the foundations of their state. Additional evidence, if such were needed, was provided by a hat belonging to Chinard, which boasted a (French) national cockade—though according to David, the sculptor "only wore the hat when he was at home." By 1792 the tricolor cockade was recognized throughout Europe as a symbol of international revolution, not unlike the red flag of the mid-twentieth century. Rumors flew around Rome and Paris: Chinard, they whispered, had disappeared, and Ratner was said to be dead. The French were touchy in late 1792, having just declared war on Europe and being on the point of executing their king. The month when all this fuss began was also the month of the September massacres, when thousands of detainees were taken from the overcrowded prisons of Paris and literally butchered in the streets. The two arrests in Rome, plus a third in which a man from Avignon was also locked up in Sant'Angelo, threatened to become a major international incident. In Paris David stirred up a storm of patriotic frenzy, denouncing the "tyrannical Roman priests" and calling on his colleagues to defend the motherland and save the artists from "the Inquisitorial flames" (an interesting idea in the month after the guillotine had been first set up in the Place de la Révolution to deal with heretics who questioned the revolutionary faith). Madame Roland, who would soon be guillotined herself, added fuel to the fire with her denunciation of the "Prince-Archbishop of Rome." Protests and threats of reprisal were sent to

Cardinal Zelada, the papal Secretary of State. Zelada, apparently anxious to placate the French, replied that the three had been arrested for disturbing the peace; they had not been confined to the Inquisition prison, but rather were sent to the State prison apartments at the Castel Sant'Angelo, a facility "reserved for notable detainees who have to put up with none of the annoyances suffered by ordinary prisoners." And in any case, he pointed out, the students had already been released. They left the fortress on 13 November wrapped in a warm blanket of righteous indignation, and neglecting to pay the bill for the food they had consumed while confined. This denouement was, of course, of little interest to the Paris revolutionaries.[34]

Sardou, as a history buff writing during the first centennial of the Great Revolution, was well aware of incidents like this one, and seems to have accepted the David version of events as gospel. The image of the "artist as revolutionary martyr" and the corresponding idea of the iniquities of the clerical government were part of the climate of opinion in France in 1792 and would continue to be common currency. This complex of ideas formed much of the basis for the character of Mario Cavaradossi, radical artist and hero. Almost all of this characterization disappeared when Puccini, who had little sympathy with and less interest in revolutionary politics, translated the play into the opera.

Cavaradossi may have been turned into a "signor tenore" over the protests of Giacosa,[35] but his original character as created by Sardou was very different. As hero of the play he embodies the Gallic irony and charm, the well-bred cultural superiority and the progressive right-mindedness that Sardou admired and expected his audience of Third Republic Parisian bourgeois to admire as well. It is by no means an accident that Sardou made his hero a student of Jacques-Louis David, and a grand-nephew of the radical Swiss-born philosophe Helvétius. Cavaradossi is made up of equal parts of David's revolutionary activism, the Romantic concept of the artist as hero, and the Gallic self-image of sophisticated superiority appropriate for an heir to the intellectual tradition of the philosophes.

Sardou has given him a very specific bloodline: his father Nicolas Cavaradossi, a member of a noble Roman family, left the city and went to Paris, where he was introduced into the salons by Abbé Galiani. There Nicolas met and married a Mlle Castron, grand-niece of Helvétius. Sardou has thus removed his hero, via his father, from the reforming Roman tradition of Benedict XIV and placed him squarely into the secular Parisian Enlightenment. By allowing Nicolas Cavaradossi to marry into the family of Helvétius, Sardou has created a man from the haute bourgeoisie on one side (Helvétius, in addition to being a philosophe, was also a large-scale tax farmer, or *fermier général,* and a very rich man) and from the most venerable Roman nobility on the other.

In the person of Helvétius Cavaradossi has been given as an ancestor one of the very few eighteenth-century thinkers who frankly admitted to being an atheist, a philosophical position that was much more respectable at the end of the nineteenth century than it had been a century earlier. Helvétius's most influential work, *De l'Esprit,* created a storm of condemnation when it was published in 1758. Peter Gay (who approves) calls the book "a scandalous hedonist treatise." In it, Helvétius rephrased the ancient Greek philosophy of epicureanism, arguing that human beings are motivated exclusively by the desire to maximize pleasure and minimize pain. This potent mixture of motives, Helvétius argues, explains all human actions. Expanded to a social theory, this became Utilitarianism.[36] Cesare Beccaria, Milanese author of the influential work *On Crimes and Punishments,* admired Helvétius and acknowledged his influence. This Italian connection may have given Sardou the idea of adding the Swiss radical to his hero's family tree.

Perhaps to balance the cool atheism of Helvétius, Sardou has also given Cavaradossi a family connection with the prophet of sensitivity, Jean-Jacques Rousseau, introduced in the play as a friend of the painter's father.[37] In Act I we learn that Rousseau gave Cavaradossi père a copy of his popular novel *La Nouvelle Héloïse* (The New Héloïse), which Cavaradossi fils tries to convince his mistress to read. The book is an eighteenth-century version of the medieval romance between Abelard and the "old" Héloïse, and preaches a warm and fuzzy moral message in the style that prefigures the Romantics. The "new" Héloïse, like the "old," has a guilty passion for a scholar that she sublimates into a noble platonic affection. In the novel duty forces her to marry an elderly landowner, but her heart belongs to a poor but honest young tutor with the knightly name of Saint-Preux. If Abelard, the towering, quarrelsome medieval theologian, has been reduced to a Swiss tutor, Héloïse has fared no better: a conventionally dutiful and unlettered young woman, she conveniently dies after saving one of her children from drowning. Floria has no patience with this long-winded, pseudo-pious nonsense, dismissing it with, "They talk all the time, and never make love."[38]

Cavaradossi evokes the mainstream encyclopedists as well as his hedonistic grand-uncle Helvétius and the irrationalist Rousseau.[39] His father Nicolas, a "bit of a heretic in his own time," is said to have been an admirer of Voltaire and "closely associated" with Diderot and Alembert—three names that Sardou seems to have pulled straight out of a list of the most recognizable names from the Enlightenment. Voltaire (François-Marie Arouet, 1694–1778) was, of course, the great bugbear of conservatives for his tireless work as the gadfly, and for the mischievious delight he took in deviling the Catholic Church (as in his well-known motto, *Ecrasez l'infame*, "Crush the infamous thing"). Denis Diderot (1713–84), who together with Jean le Rond d'Alembert (1717–83) edited the *Encyclopédie*, was a protean thinker who among other topics turned his hand to art criticism and wrote a series of monumental commentaries on the salon exhibits of the 1760s in Grimm's *Correspondance littéraire*.

Sardou lards his work with so many historical nuggets that it is a great temptation to look for individuals who can be labeled the "real" Tosca, Scarpia, or Cavaradossi. This is, of course, pointless since what we are dealing with here are not eighteenth-century realities but rather a series of rather shallow projections backward from a century later. But because of the way in which the playwright made use of history, it is possible to look for templates, for people who contained elements that Sardou could cannibalize to concoct his thin but attractive creations. Cavaradossi, made up of revolutionary artist, romantic individualist, Enlightenment intellectual, and Gallic charmer, contains recognizable bits and pieces of French artists and intellectuals. He also contains aspects of the Italian nobility. Sardou is coy about giving a title to the Cavaradossi family, though he has the painter's servant tell the nosy sacristan, "My master is Roman, and from an old patrician family."[40] There is no such Roman family, but there is an Italian family onto whose genealogical tree one could graft the character rather nicely.

The name of this family is so similar to that of the operatic hero as to be virtually the same, with one of the five syllables transposed. The Caravadossi, like Giuseppe Garibaldi, are from Nizza, a maritime Italian-speaking city that was absorbed by France in the nineteenth century. Their coat of arms is blue, with two gold-crowned lions rampant, facing one another and holding between them a fleur-de-lys. Below them is a flaming heart *al naturale*, reflecting the family motto of *candor illaesus*. The family held two titles, baron of Toetto della Scarena and count of Aspromonte. It adds a piquant note to the opera's Act II interrogation scene to think that Mario's arrogant tone comes from the fact that, as a brother or nephew of the baron Scarena, he is not overly impressed with the baron Scarpia.

Nizza became Nice when it was given to Napoleon III on 24 March 1860 in payment for the French emperor's intervention on the Italian side in the first phase of the wars of national unification, or the Risorgimento. Like the hero of the opera, like the uneasy collaboration between Sardou and Puccini, the Caravadossi of Nizza/Nice stand as an example of the tangled relationship between France and Italy. If we follow those threads they will lead us back to a young Louis Napoleon Bonaparte testing his imperial ambitions in the

Italian secret societies of the 1830s, and to the French occupation of Rome (1848 to 1870) that outraged anti-clerical liberals in both states (Sardou certainly among them).[41]

The Caravadossi of Nizza are a family that, like so many Italian noble families, rose during the Renaissance by climbing the civic ladder—probably after having made money in some enterprise connected with shipping. In the same year that an ambitious son of neighboring Genoa discovered what would turn out to be a new world, Giovanni Caravadossi achieved the less earth-shaking triumph of becoming mayor of Nizza. After 1492 the family had little impact on history, but they kept their social and economic status: in 1728 they produced an ecclesiastical noble in Pietro Girolamo Caravadossi, Bishop of Casale. It was only in the latter part of the eighteenth century that they acquired secular nobility when in 1770 a grand-nephew of the Bishop, Baldassare Caravadossi (a name to conjure with!) acquired a fief and the title of Baron of Toetto della Scarena. Thereafter the family had some minor success in the grand old noble game of title collecting. Baldassare married Maria Giuseppa Grimaldi, the daughter of another baron and connected with the counts of Aspromonte on her mother's side; in the fullness of time (February 1833) Baldassare and Maria's son Giulio added the title of count of Aspromonte to the family coffers. A cadet line of the Caravadossi descended from Giulio's younger brother, Felice, a man who held no titles but who would no doubt have been given the courtesy title of Cavaliere. Felice involved himself in the Italian wars of independence of the mid-nineteenth century, but unlike his fictional analogue he seems to have been a sensible man who survived to father four sons.[42]

There is, of course, no evidence to suggest that Sardou borrowed this name for the hero of his play, though he certainly could have heard it. If he had, it would have appealed to him. Although it is too long to run trippingly off an Anglo-Saxon tongue, to a Latin it is redolent of aristocracy. It also has echoes of a noble Italian name that was certainly in Sardou's mind as he worked on *La Tosca:* another multi-syllabic name beginning with a "C," the name of the Neapolitan commodore Francesco Caracciolo, a revolutionary sympathizer who was hanged from the yardarm of his own flagship at the order of Admiral Nelson in 1799. (See chap. 5.)

The name "Cavaradossi" would also have pleased the French playwright for its evocation of the painter Caravaggio. At the turn of the twentieth century Caravaggio (Michelangelo Merisi da Caravaggio, 1573–1610) was seen as a defiant rebel genius flinging his democratic subject matter and radical painting technique into the face of papal Rome. The great Mannerist certainly had a genius for trouble. He fled Rome after killing a man in a barroom brawl, burned himself out, and died young; a very different sort of character from Sardou's cool aristocrat repairing the frescoes at Sant'Andrea. And Caravaggio, for all his violence, seems to have been a conventionally pious son of the Church.

In addition to an appropriate family name, the playwright also gave his hero what, from Paris, appeared to be the appropriate appurtenances for a Roman patrician: a palazzo on the Piazza di Spagna, a country estate near the Appian Way, and a history of *romanità* that extends back to the sixteenth century and the Medici popes.

The Piazza di Spagna has long been one of the most famous sites in Rome. For at least two centuries any tourist or would-be tourist could be counted upon to recognize this as an exotic place where artists and their models gathered, along the Spanish Steps, the square's most dramatic feature (built between 1723 and 1726). A guide to the city published in 1800 tells the visitor that this area "is inhabited principally by foreigners, for whose accommodation it contains many good lodging-houses, while antiquaries and guides, or ciceroni, flock around it."[43] The area grew up around the Spanish embassy at a time when that country was still among the most powerful states in the world, and the diplomatic immunity attached to Spain's ambassador extended to the whole district. This had the effect of giving foreign visitors a base that was Roman yet removed from the more restrictive regulations of the papal city.

The area was particularly popular among French tourists. Charles de Brosses, counselor and later president of the parlement of Burgundy, visited Rome in 1738–40 and stayed in a house on the Piazza di Spagna that he rented from a Signora Peti. It was located in front of Bernini's *barcaccia* fountain and at the foot of the famous stairs, which he describes as "the largest and grandest staircase in Europe, interrupted by eight terraces." The painter Elisabeth Vigée-Lebrun came to Rome in 1789, an early refugee from the barely begun chaos of revolution. She lodged first at the French Academy but found the room too small and the street too noisy, with a shrine to the Madonna frequented by bagpipers (this was December and the time of the annual invasion of piferi players from the hills). She moved to the nearby Piazza di Spagna, where she took rooms in the home of a French landscape painter named Denis, and found this area even worse. It was busy and noisy, with the coming and going of coaches through the day and night, and "a motley crowd [that gathered] there after I had gone to bed, singing choral pieces charmingly improvised by young men and women. . . . this perpetual concert, which would have delighted me had it taken place during the day, irritated me beyond belief at night."[44] The distinguished portraitist had a terrible time trying to find a quiet place to live. After she left the Piazza di Spagna she took an apartment which seemed quiet, but where laundresses on the ground floor worked the pump all night; she then moved to a private mansion empty except for her, full of filth and rats who ate her paints; finally she moved to accommodations where she was kept awake by "countless worms chewing through the joists." "I remain convinced," she complains, "that the most difficult thing to find in Rome is a place to live."

Cavaradossi is extraordinarily lucky. Not only has he inherited a family home ("on the Piazza di Spagna, in an old house that still carries the pretentious name of the Cavaradossi palace," he tells Angelotti), he also has access to a suburban retreat. Since Sardou could never resist detail he gives a long and complex history behind this site, too. It was built by an ancestor (Luigi Cavaradossi) on the ruins of an ancient villa. It was Luigi who first discovered the well in which Angelotti conceals himself, and the same Luigi who first used it, escaping from the archers employed by a Medici pope (whether Leo X, 1513–21 or Clement VII, 1523–34 is not specified).[45]

The villa or *podere* (small farm holding) is located in the suburbs in what Sardou has Cavaradossi call "my vineyard, as they say here." In the eighteenth century, while Rome was a small city surrounded by open countryside, the nobility as well as many of the charitable and ecclesiastical institutions held estates that were suburban but still within the old city walls. The Cavaradossi "vineyard" is located in a particularly evocative section, along the road leading to the Appian Way and quite near several of the most romantic Roman ruins: the baths of Caracalla, the tomb of the Scipios, and the tomb of Cecilia Metella.[46] In 1800 Salmon described this as a district "a great part occupied with villas, gardens, and vineyards, full of the surprising ruins of temples, baths, palaces, aqueducts, and many other conspicuous buildings that have withstood the devastations of enemies and time" with many "country estates, with gardens of oranges, citrons and grenadines, filled with statues and fountains."[47]

The area was traditionally deserted in summer because of the Romans' almost superstitious terror of the "bad air" of the *campagna*, the swampy area around the city. This exodus created just that air of melancholy and decay that tourists loved: "all of this countryside is the most piquant theater for the amateur," abounding with evocative and suggestive ruins. And, of course, this would have made it all the more useful as a hiding place.[48]

Sardou's placing of the "Cavaradossi palace" and the villa is one of the more revealing touches in his style, cut from the same cloth as the Venetian girl musicians and the Bourbon repression in Naples (see chaps. 4 and 5). These are all instantly recognizable references that the average Parisian theater-goer could plug into his own sketchy awareness of Rome and say, "Ah ha, of course!" A bourgeois who had never been further east than the Bois de Vincennes would immediately visualize the colorful array of flowers and the models who, as *tout le monde* knew, draped themselves along the Spanish Steps (more a nineteenth-century than an eighteenth-century custom). The Piazza di Spagna is in fact not a particularly appropriate location for the town home of an old Roman family, but that sort of detail quite rightly did not interest the popular dramatist or his audience.

What did interest Sardou was the image of a city living in terror under an oppressive regime. There is barely enough truth in that image to lend a slight semblance of historical accuracy. As early as 15 October 1799, two weeks after the arrival of the Allies, foreigners were ordered to leave Rome; many of those who ignored the order soon found themselves in the Castel Sant'Angelo, waiting to be marched under guard to the frontier.[49] (Cavaradossi, with his Roman family and Roman estate, would not have been liable to obey this order.) Beyond this, at least in the early weeks of Allied rule, there was surprisingly little official prosecution of political undesirables, though there was certainly a great deal of triumphalism—Te Deums and celebratory Masses and parades ordered by the governor. Liberals and French sympathizers also had to put up with a certain amount of mockery. On 11 November a satire circulated around the city, "in praise of the Patriots, Jacobins, and Hebrews."[50]

Street boys took up the harrassment of local Jacobins with predictable enthusiasm. The patriots got a new nickname, and instead of sansculotte ("without knee breeches") were called *senza culo*, "butt-less." Galimberti tells a story about a crowd of little boys who got a bit too close to two of their victims, so that one of the children found himself picked up by his belt and held out at arm's length by an indignant patriot who thus put at least a temporary end to the annoyance.[51]

Despite Allied victories, the war continued through 1799 and into 1800, and all the problems of provisioning a major population center continued as well. Food shortages were exacerbated by the Romans' traditional expectation that their material wants would be provided by their spiritual overlords. When affordable bread, meat, and wine failed to appear, the result was public outrage. A man like Cavaradossi would certainly not have gone hungry, but no one could have escaped the unrest in the city, or the crime wave fueled by shortages and by the presence of large numbers of unpaid, undisciplined foreign troops. A politically liberal small manufacturer named Saverio Pediconi, who lived in the neighborhood where Sardou located his hero, took the precaution of arming his workmen.[52] Looting, drunkenness, and general disruption were the normal consequences of the occupation by thousands of

Allied troops. Soldiers were regularly flogged or shot in the public squares for infractions of military discipline.[53]

The Romans were fascinated by the more law-abiding of their exotic visitors. They were particularly intrigued by the unusual spectacle of 1,500 Russian troops, part of a delegation of 15,000 sent by Tsar Alexander, who arrived on a rainy evening in early November with their big guns and their peculiar musical instruments.[54] When the strangers arrived the Romans fell in behind them to march to their barracks on the Piazza San Giovanni Laterano, until everyone, Russian and Roman, was marching along and singing. The Russian commander was said to have been so touched by the welcome that he wept.

Relations between the northerners and the Romans were not, of course, confined to singing and tearful bear hugs. On the 13th, about a dozen Muscovite soldiers wandered into a druggist's shop while the proprietor was busy dressing a soldier's wound (medical care, like food and billeting, tended to be on a do-it-yourself basis). The Russians crowded in to watch, and then left with a stolen carafe of opium, which they tried to sell to a barber. The barber, having no use for the opium (and perhaps taking a malicious pleasure in the obvious ignorance of the thieves), offered to buy the empty carafe. Reluctant to let anything potable go to waste, the soldiers sat down and drank the contents. "Four died right away," the diarist Galimberti notes, "and the other seven went to sleep and won't wake up again."[55] Their commander, having lost eleven men, demanded that the barber and the druggist both be arrested.

But despite the entertainment provided by the misadventures of foreign troops Rome was not happy, and even the theater and the extended carnival season did not improve matters much.[56] The free and easy dress and manners of the Republic came under fire, and edicts were issued directing clerics to put their black habits back on, and ordering that women should "cover themselves decently," especially in church. However, the diarist notes that the authorities soon gave up that particular attempt as hopeless.

Carnival proper began after the octave of Christmas, in a city that was wet, cold, hungry, and thoroughly discouraged. The nobility did their best to pretend that life had returned to normal with the end of the Republic, taking up subscriptions for masked balls and the traditional horse races. But nothing seems to have worked out as planned. The horse-racing got off to a bad start in 1799–1800, and Duke Cesarini (a French sympathizer who also owned the Argentina theater, and whose horses consistently won) had to sweeten the crowd's temper with free wine and the distribution of coins. The public carnival balls at the Alibert theater were badly attended, and it was so cold that they broke up before midnight. Diego Naselli, the military governor of the

city, at first refused to allow masking or even costumes. In the face of popular disgust at this incivility he relented on the question of costumes, but remained adamant on the masking. And what was carnival without masking?

Traditional carnival costumes took certain predictable forms. One of the
most common was the eternally popular *travestimento*, where men (especially
coachmen) dressed as women while their female friends dressed as men and
hitched rides as the coaches paraded up and down the Corso. Pulcinella, the
Neapolitan commedia dell'arte character, was another favorite. Scholars and
antiquarians saw him as the heir to the ancient Roman clowns, and at carnival he made the fullest possible use of the freedom of the clown, verging close
to obscenity (which might be allowable) and to political satire (which could
be dangerous). Revelers dressed as foreign artists hurried up and down the
Corso. Others put on old-fashioned clothes and created characters known as
"Quakers." These were fussy old men with red cheeks who pursued loose
"women" who were in fact men wearing low-cut blouses.[57]

Carnival costuming and masking was less a matter of simple display than
of creating and acting out little dramatic scenarios, veering close enough to
satire to be understood, yet not so close as to attract the attention of the sharp-
eyed police agents. In 1800 it was perfectly acceptable to satirize the consuls
and other pseudo-classical representatives of the late and unlamented Republic. Pompous men wrapped in the elaborate costumes of republican officials
strode about "confiscating" horses and women, issuing absurd decrees, and
holding impromptu courts at which the "prisoners" had to buy their freedom
with outrageous bribes. It was a great deal less acceptable to comment on the
difficulties of the current state. A man dressed as a physician went about announcing in solemn tones that "for the present epidemic I prescribe washing
one's feet, and a strict diet." His reference to the filthy streets and the food
shortages failed to amuse the sbirri and he was arrested.[58]

Getting arrested was easy in a city which for almost two years had known
little but chaos, and the interest of the great majority of Romans narrowed
down to one subject: the price and availability of bread. Feeding Rome had
been a problem since before the days of the Empire, but citizens of papal Rome
had long been used to a guaranteed bread supply. As in every early modern
city prices were controlled by a paternalistic government keenly aware that a
well-fed city is easier to govern than a hungry one. As governor, Diego Naselli
continued the policy (no public official of the time would have dreamed of
doing otherwise) but the prices crept inexorably up. With supply lines broken
by the war less and less grain made the voyage to Civitavecchia; and what
reached that port often rotted on the wharves. At times there was simply no
bread to be had for any price, or the bread that was offered was made from

hay, from fava beans, or from barley.[59] Angry crowds surrounded bakers'
shops, riots broke out almost daily, and there was fear of a general uprising.

By January the situation was intolerable. Bakers armed themselves against
the mobs; the mobs armed themselves against the bakers, and against the soldiers who had been set to guard them. With three armed groups confronting
one another, violence inevitably escalated. Slogans of "Bread or Death" were
scrawled on walls during the night. People, often innocent bystanders, were
injured or killed when troops fired on rioters. A boy was trampled; a baker
and a Neapolitan soldier shot one another. A furious crowd of three hundred
angry women gathered at the Farnese palace where Diego Naselli, as representative of the monarchs of Naples, had taken up residence. Naselli, "much
agitated," promised to improve conditions within three days, and distributed
coins to calm his unwelcome visitors. In the meantime he called for additional troops to disperse them.[60]

With carnival came chaos, and the government turned to the body of men
who had always acted as intermediaries between the state and the people: the
priests of the city's parishes. A commission was formed to study the problem,
and they came up with a scheme whereby bread would be distributed according to a system of tickets to be issued by the parish priests. At the same
time, the troops would be moved away from the bakeries and replaced by un-
armed volunteers, to be called Amici, or Friends.

On 18 January 1800 the volunteers met at the palace of Prince Doria, who
had reluctantly resumed the direction of the Foodstuffs Commission. According to Galimberti the meeting quickly turned farcical. The head of the Amici,
a Neapolitan named Vitolomeo, greeted his men with the following speech:

> Gentlemen, I am your chief. You are not Civic Guards, nor Urban Guards,
> but rather Friends, men of good reputation. You will have no guns to stop
> the people. Instead, you will carry staffs as symbols of your authority . . .

Many laughed. Others demanded—and got—guns.[61]

As darkness fell in the city that same January night there was a less laugh-
able demonstration of the violent interface between the people and the state.
In the late afternoon (5 P.M. French time, the twenty-third hour in Roman
time) a young man left the Quirinale palace and began his long walk through
the city. At his right and at his left walked two robed and masked members
of the Confraternity of St John the Beheaded. Around them mounted troops
kept the curious at a distance. It was carnival time, and in its way this procession was a part of carnival as such processions had always been. Their route
led them through the Piazza di Spagna; a young painter recently arrived
from Paris could hardly have avoided the show.

They must have walked slowly through the crowds. By the time they made their way up the Via del Babuino to the Piazza del Popolo it was already three-quarters of an hour after sunset (twenty-four and a quarter hours, Roman time) and the square was lit by the flare of torches. More troops surrounded the scaffold that had been built there, and Maestro Titta, the young hangman of Rome, waited there with his assistants.[62]

The condemned man and his hooded companions went into a makeshift chapel where they knelt and prayed. They were coming to the end of an intense period that had begun when the sentence of death was handed down by the Council of War only four hours earlier.

The prisoner's name was Gregorio Silvestri. He was a twenty-three-year-old notary who lived in lodgings on the Piazza di Spagna, and he had been arrested and condemned for plotting against the new government. Some said that he had been caught distributing French propaganda; others said that he was guilty of "satire, and plotting," and of placing himself at the head of a mob of 6,000 rabid Jacobins who planned to meet outside the Porta del Popolo and butcher the Neapolitans.[63] The records of his case are no longer in the state archives with the other Jacobin trials; what we know about him comes from diarists and from the chronicles of the confraternity. They tell us that, when he heard the sentence, he protested his innocence; whether he meant that he denied the act of treason, or that the act was justified, we don't know. In any case, there was no time for lamentation. The handcuffs were tight, bruising his wrists. He asked that they be loosened and this was done. The brothers urged him to confess and be absolved of his sins, and the condemned, a political radical but (unlike the fictional Cavaradossi) unwilling to face eternity unshriven, had done so. Then came the need to put his earthly affairs in order, to complete the small bits of unfinished business—the novel about Telemachus borrowed from the girl who did the embroidery work; be sure she gets it back (if there was any other message for her the brothers did not record it); the silk stockings left to be repaired at the shop near the church of Sant'Andrea della Valle: have them collected, the estate is small and their value will help make it larger; and don't forget the six scudi and the watch left behind in prison, and the new coat and muslin handkerchief, and the shoes and stockings, and the books. There are small debts to be paid, and a borrowed lamp to be returned to the priest who lives near the Church of the Coachmen. When everything is sold, the money is to be divided into two parts. Half of it is to be spent for Masses to be said for the repose of his soul. The other half is to be given to his father, "but in a way that won't distress him."

The priest from the nearby church of Saints Vincenzo and Anastasio came with the host for communion. After more prayers the party left the chapel.

The precise and careful ritual of death was almost over. With "great courage" Silvestri mounted the steps to the scaffold; one of the confraternity brothers, Abate Gozzi, stayed at his side while the sentence was carried out. The body of the executed man was taken down and laid on the waiting bier, and by torchlight, again surrounded by the cavalry, the brothers walked to their church of St John the Beheaded, bringing with them what remained of Gregorio Silvestri to be buried "with the greatest honors of the Church, to the glory of God and of our patron."

Four blocks away at the Alibert theater the nobility and officers were gathering to attend a gala entertainment. Across town the curtain rose on a musical comedy at the Valle theater, where a reluctant prima donna was starring in a new intermezzo by Maestro Caruso. The audience gleefully looked forward to fireworks, and they were not disappointed: there was a quarrel which quickly became a shouting match between the soprano on stage and the composer in the pit; the audience joined in enthusiastically, and the performance ended in a riot.

The carnival season of 1800 had begun.

4 The Singer's Rome

*Four years later [after the pope released her from the convent where
she was a ward] she made her triumphant debut in Nina and then,
at La Scala, at San Carlo, at La Fenice . . . wherever you turn, there's
no one else but her. As for our liaison, we met when she came here
on short notice to sing at the Argentina. . . .*

Cavaradossi to Angelotti, *La Tosca*, I, iii

Floria Tosca, love child from Verona and darling of the Italian stage
from Milan to Naples, would have been the answer to an impresario's prayer,
arriving "on short notice" to rescue a theater season that had been an unqualified disaster from the start.[1] Show after show and singer after singer were
hissed and whistled off the stage in 1800; the only moderate success, Paer's
Gl'intrighi amorosi (Amorous Intrigues) at the Valle theater, occurred at
the end of the season in mid-May.[2] The most unseemly exchanges between
composer/director and performer became three-way battles with audiences
throwing themselves enthusiastically into the fray. Laws forbidding "demon-
strations of favor or disfavor" in the theaters, reinforced with dire threats of
fines, prison, or corporal punishment, had no perceptible effect.

Public theater in Rome had always had a precarious existence. Virtually
all old regime states recognized the power of the theater and acted to control
it, but papal Rome even more than most regarded secular theatricality with
a suspicious eye. Depending on the philosophy of the reigning pope, public
theater was either banned altogether or permitted only during brief seasons
under rigid censorship. Despite the fact that some seventeenth- and eighteenth-century popes were theatrical and musical dilettantes, public theater
was never more than tolerated in their capital city. Even private performances
in noble houses were looked upon with suspicion and not infrequently banned.
Any disaster—an earthquake, a bad harvest, a war, the death of a prominent
person—meant that theaters would be closed for an indefinite period.

After 1738 the office of the governor of Rome developed an organic body
of laws dealing with theater. These laws were primarily intended to insure
the physical security of the theaters, to control box-leasing arrangements,

and to oversee the comportment of the public and of theater people. The
court took a special interest in musical theater, because the three theaters in
Rome where musical shows were regularly performed—the Argentina, the
Alibert, and the Capranica—were constantly plagued by money troubles. Financial problems in the theaters translated into social problems which the
state was most anxious to avoid. The governor therefore regulated these theaters with an eye to keeping them solvent. He banned lavish, expensive productions, he regulated competition to ensure that there was enough custom
to go around, and he made impresarios pay large security deposits, which
could be used to pay off performers and craftsmen left high and dry by the
failure of a season or of a theater.[3]

Through most of the eighteenth century theaters in Rome were permitted
to operate only during the carnival season, which could begin as early as the
day after Christmas and ran until the beginning of Lent on Ash Wednesday
(four to six weeks later). The opening date could, and did, vary depending
on local events and on the date of Ash Wednesday; a particularly short carnival season could justify an early opening.[4] Each year, an Edict on the Theaters would be published giving the authorized opening date, along with the
licit time for performances to begin, and the maximum price of tickets for
each theater. Even within the limited season there were no performances on
Fridays, feast days, or the eve of feast days.

In 1780 Pius VI authorized an extended season of spring and autumn performances. The unforeseen result was that impresarios found themselves
scrambling for their share of a small audience: Romans were not used to going to the theater outside of carnival time. The following year the pope decreed that only one theater at a time could be open during the new seasons.[5]
Pius VI was unusually friendly to theater. When the 1798 season had to be
canceled because of the precarious political and military situation, the pope
directed the Apostolic Camera to reimburse impresarios some 4,000 scudi.[6]

Whether the reigning pope was well-disposed toward theater or not, performances and venues were strictly circumscribed. The defining aspect of
Roman theater at the end of the eighteenth century was its absolute ban on
female performers in public, or commercial, theaters, but there were many
other regulations that had to be respected. Theater buildings could not be
distinguished by any special façades or markings that would identify them as
places of entertainment. Any disturbance at or around theaters was regarded
as especially serious and punished accordingly. Performances and texts were
heavily censored and the slightest hint of criticism of government or religion
could close a show. Performers were regarded with suspicion, and misbehav-
ior, whether broken contracts or inappropriate liaisons, often led to jail or an

escort out of town. None of these restrictions was uniquely Roman. All had been normal practice throughout Europe in the early modern period: for instance, La Fenice, built in 1793, was the first Venetian theater to have an identifiable façade (though La Scala in Milan had been built with a notable façade in 1778, and the opera in Vienna had a façade of sorts by the 1750s). But if the popes were hardly alone in being suspicious of the effect of theatricality on public order and morality, their role as both secular and sacred rulers put them in a unique position to control it. The consequence was that in Rome these rather old-fashioned restrictions continued in force until the old regime there came crashing down around everyone's ears in 1798. Even then they hung on stubbornly in Rome: reinstated with the restoration of 1815, many of these rigid theatrical regulations endured through most of the nineteenth century.

Despite the atmosphere of official hostility, by the last decade of the eighteenth century there were six or seven public theaters in Rome which regularly specialized in musical and prose dramas and attracted audiences from all ranks of society. A lively undergrowth of less elevated, and less permanent, venues catered to the lower end of the audience spectrum, and featured puppet shows, acrobatic exhibitions, short comic musical pieces, and animal acts. Recent archival research has uncovered at least eighty-eight separate venues where theatrical productions took place.[7]

Most theaters offered both prose and musical shows, but musical productions were by far the most popular and profitable. Very few of the operas that packed the houses are ever performed now—no Mozart opera, for instance, was ever produced in an eighteenth-century Roman theater. The composers came from the courts of Italy and most often from Naples—Domenico Cimarosa, Giovanni Paisiello, and Niccolò Piccinni, and a host of others whose names are forgotten by everyone but students of the history of music: Rinaldo di Capua, Giuseppe Maria Curcio, Giuseppe Nicolini, the Guglielmis, father and son. Theater bills featured the name of the opera and the lead singer or singers, then the rest of the cast, then similar information about the secondary show, usually one or more ballets. One has to search for the name of the composer, rather in the way that one has to search to find the name of the writer as the credits roll for a film or television show.

The parallel with television is a useful one.[8] Although some shows were successful and popular enough to be repeated or taken on the road, the majority were designed to be disposable, written for the occasion and then discarded. Like today's popular entertainment, they could be either serious or comic. Serious operas *(opere serie)* had been significantly modified by the end of the eighteenth century, but they maintained their popularity into the nineteenth century and continued to fulfill their stated aim of improving public morality.[9] Their plots were usually based on Greek or Roman classics or on biblical stories, and their themes invariably dealt with nobility of birth and of character. The most famous of these had texts written by Pietro Metastasio, used and reused by composers as the occasions demanded. Like the comic operas, serious operas always ended on an uplifting note of optimism and harmony.

By the middle of the eighteenth century the light or comic operas (opere buffe) had completed their evolution from amusing between-act entertainments, or intermezzi, to full-scale works in their own right (though a class of short works called intermezzi continued to be popular). In a real sense these comic operas were "situation comedies," light, charming formula pieces where the humor arose from the conventional situation, enjoyable because the audience knew exactly what was coming next. Typical of these were the "fanatic" shows: the fanatic for music, for astronomy, for antiquity, for medicine. All of these plots centered around clever young lovers who hoodwink pretentious amateurs, usually older men with absurd designs on the ingénue.

Most productions, serious or comic, featured ballets, or balli, between the acts or as secondary items on the bill. These balli, which could run to several acts, had elaborate costumes and plots that were often derived from literary sources. Like the operas, they could be serious, semi-serious, or comic (grotesque). And as in the operas, their casts in Rome were exclusively male, though the male dancers underwent no surgery to qualify them for their female roles.[10]

The parallel with modern popular entertainment breaks down in one important respect: no one in the eighteenth century, no matter what his or her political persuasion, defended the idea that public entertainment was morally neutral or a matter of individual choice. The Christian view had long been that theater was a leftover from paganism, to be tolerated only in order to avoid worse vices. This attitude persisted well into the eighteenth century despite a movement in favor of theater as a useful tool (the position taken, for example, by the Jesuits).[11] By the end of the century, secular theorists and ecclesiastical censors alike saw the theater as a key element in public order and decency, and looked to entertainment as a means of teaching cultural, political, and religious values. To this end the state issued minute regulations, and enforced them by highly intrusive policing. This did not end with the collapse of the old regime: in Rome under the Republic and the Kingdom of Italy, papal censors were replaced by civil functionaries whose strictures were, if anything, even more intrusive and more rigorously enforced. With the restoration of 1815, the clerical censors returned, more nervous than ever, and kept close watch until the arrival of the unified Italian state in 1870 brought yet another change of ideology, and another generation of theatrical watchdogs.

Despite the fact that before 1800 it was illegal to build a Roman theater with a façade that identified it as such, Baroque Rome was filled with theaters and theatricality, in the colleges and in noble and citizen households, and in the papal court. However, theaters (in the sense of buildings specifically constructed to offer indoor performances to respectable paying audiences) were largely an eighteenth-century innovation for Rome. Four of the seven major theaters were built after 1715, and the remaining three opened between 1670 and 1691. The major houses were the Argentina, the Alibert or Dame, the Valle, the Tordinona (later renamed the Apollo), the Capranica, the Pallacorda, and the Pace; among the lesser theaters were the Granari, the Ornani, and the Corea amphitheater.[12]

The Tordinona, which opened under the patronage of Christina of Sweden, was the oldest of the Roman theaters and briefly achieved the remarkable distinction of featuring female singers, between 1670 and 1674; they would not return for another 124 years: in April of 1798, women took the soprano and alto parts in a musical comedy titled *Chi si contenta, gode* (He who pleases himself, enjoys himself), with music by Giuseppe Mosca. This show featured not one but three ladies, Susanna Banchieri, Anna Priori, and Concetta Matrilli.[13] In 1800 the Allied commander of the Castel Sant'Angelo demanded that the Tordinona (by this time renamed the Apollo) provide him with free tickets, on the alarming grounds that the theater was "under the guns of the Castel." The demand was indignantly refused.[14] Since the theater was open in 1800, producing shows by Cimarosa and other popular composers, it would have been a likely place for Sardou to employ his heroine but, like the Alibert (below), it was apparently not glamorous enough.

Another of the oldest of the commercial theaters was the Capranica, built in 1679. By 1692 members of the ambassadorial corps to the Holy See were fighting duels with one another for access to its best boxes: visibility was vital to national prestige. Like several other theaters, the Capranica was closed during 1800.

The Pace, a little wooden theater with a U-shaped hall and narrow boxes, opened in 1691 to offer musical dramas. The Pallacorda opened in 1715, a small popular theater built on the site of a tennis court from which it took its name. Between stage performances it offered variety shows and gymnastic displays. We have no record of shows produced there in 1800.

The Alibert, like the Pallacorda, began as a sports center (in this case, a handball court). It was named for Count Jacques d'Alibert, Christina of Sweden's secretary, who had first planned it. It opened as the largest theater in

Rome, with seven tiers of thirty-two boxes each, and as de Brosses notes drily, "it passes for the handsomest." [15] The popular name of the Alibert, Teatro delle Dame (Ladies' Theater), came from the fact that for a long time this was the theater patronized by the nobility. After the arrival of the French in 1798 female sopranos appeared at the Alibert, starting with the temperamental diva Teresa Bertinotti. In 1800 the Alibert, with its star Cecilia Bolognesi, was the finest of the theaters that remained open, and assumed the status of official theater.[16] It was very close to the Piazza di Spagna and the putative palazzo Cavaradossi and therefore would have been much more convenient for the lovers than the Argentina. But Sardou would have none but the most prestigious venue for his heroine, and by the end of the century the Alibert was losing the competition for premier theater to the newer Argentina.

The Valle, a close neighbor of the church of Sant'Andrea, opened in 1727. It was built in the new horseshoe shape with five tiers of boxes and the interesting innovation of benches with distinct seats in the pit, to avoid scuffling for places among the holders of the cheaper tickets. It tended to offer farces and light romantic comedies rather than "serious opera." Along with the Apollo and the Alibert, the Valle was open in 1800. By Sardou's time it was strictly a prose theater, and Sarah Bernhardt, for whom the role of Tosca was written, made her Rome debut there in *La Dame aux camélias* (Camille, or The Lady of the Camellias) in January of 1898.

Floria Tosca's theater, the Argentina, first opened for the carnival season of 1732 starring the popular castrato Giacinto Fontana, known as Farfallino ("Little Butterfly"). Built as a rival to the Alibert, it was slightly larger and shaped in the new horseshoe floor plan. It was famous enough to be featured in the 1773 edition of Diderot's *Encyclopédie* in an illustration that shows the large hall and the simple façade, which, according to custom and law in Rome, gave no hint that it concealed the entrance to a luxurious theater (see fig. 12).[17]

The Argentina is only about a block from Sant'Andrea della Valle if one uses the back entrance of the theater and goes in the side door of the church. But Sardou, who was vague on the details of Roman topography, no doubt chose it for his heroine because it was the most famous theater in the city in his day and one of the great opera houses of Europe. In 1816 Rossini directed the premiere of his *Barbiere di Siviglia* (The Barber of Seville) there; in 1838 Giuseppina Strepponi (not yet Signora Verdi) starred there in Donizetti's *Lucia di Lammermoor,* and Verdi wrote two of his early operas, *I due Foscari* and *La battaglia di Legnano* (The Battle of Legnano), for the Argentina. Angelica Catalani—surely one of Sardou's templates for his Tosca character (see below)—was booked at the Argentina to repeat her Milan debut role in

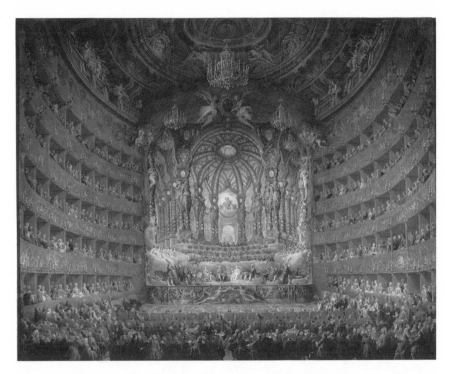

FIGURE 12. Interior of the Argentina theater as it appeared in a painting by Giovanni Paolo Pannini. The production was a spectacle put on to celebrate marriage of the dauphin in France. Musée du Louvre. Art Resource

Mayr's *La Lodoïska* for the start of the 1797–98 carnival, but all Roman theaters were closed because of the war. In 1800, though it was officially closed, the impresarios of the Argentina advertised a production of Paisiello's *Barbiere di Siviglia*, which may or may not have gone on.

In addition to these major theaters there were dozens of small theaters and venues, some of which (like the Corea amphitheater) held outdoor shows along with bullfights and balloon ascensions. Others, like the Granari or the Ornani, were rented rooms where puppet shows and animal acts were offered for an admission fee of a few pennies a head. Still others were more or less private facilities, like the outdoor Greek-style theater of the Arcadian academy.[18]

The French and their partisans took control of the city in 1798 and theater, like everything else, was revolutionized. Sala notes in his diary that the chief consul Bonelli ordered the theaters open, with women singers, because "the priests and monks don't give the orders here any longer."[19] Women, banned from the Roman stage by Sixtus V (1585–90), returned; they would not leave again. Strange though it may seem to the modern reader, their return was not an unqualified success.

Until the last two years of the eighteenth century musical theater in Rome had been dominated by singers known variously as musici, virtuosi, evirati ("unmanned ones"), or, more graphically, castrati.[20] These were singers who were surgically emasculated before puberty so that their voices remained flexible and treble but, as they matured, developed the strength and volume of male voices. They seem to have first appeared in Ferrara and Rome in the middle of the sixteenth century, perhaps arriving from Spain. The last castrato we know about was Alessandro Moreschi (1858–1922), who sang in the Sistine choir from 1883 until 1913; his voice was recorded on primitive equipment in 1902 and 1904.[21] Although castrati are generally thought of now as theater singers, most of them made their careers in church choirs with only occasional forays into the opera. Women were not allowed to sing in church, and so the creation of permanent male sopranos and contraltos solved one of the great problems of working with the choirboys, whose voices changed just as the singers became really proficient at their work. Although theologians disagreed about whether or not the operation was licit, few *maestri di cappella* asked probing questions about how a capable singer came to lose his masculinity. A surprising number of boys were said to have been attacked by pigs, which was as good a story as any.

Between 1650 and 1750 the powerful, flexible voices of the castrati dominated the Italian opera. And in the states of the pope, with their ban on female sopranos, the young castrati regularly appeared as prima donnas, taking the roles that had been written for, and in other cities were performed by, women. Why women were excluded from the public stage is a question that has been much argued and little understood. Earlier generations were content to attribute the custom to hostility to females or a taste for pederasty; neither hypothesis now seems adequate. Certainly some of the reasons were religious. Saint Paul was merely expressing a moderate version of the generally accepted opinion when he advised that women should be silent in the assembly.[22] Another factor was probably the desire to preserve order. Traditionally all performers have been regarded as disruptive influences; women who performed were considered courtesans or worse by definition, and therefore even more dangerous than their male counterparts. Perhaps at the root was the conviction that the female principle was too powerful to be presented directly, that it could best be portrayed symbolically, with masks, dolls, or other sorts of "artificial women." The concept is by no means confined to Rome, or even to Europe. One has only to look to the female impersonators of the Chinese opera, the Japanese kabuki, or the south Indian kathakali. The castrato voice was often described as "angelic"—an adjective that referred to its quality of transcending gender.[23] The castrati seem to have been perceived as less tied to nature and therefore more capable of personifying the abstract values of love and sacrifice that were central to the traditional culture.[24]

By the middle of the eighteenth century many intellectuals had arrived at exactly the opposite opinion. One of the greatest of the eighteenth-century Italian reformers, Lodovico Antonio Muratori, saw the castrati as exaggerating and amplifying, not ameliorating, the female principle, and therefore encouraging the "feminine" vices of irrationality and lust. Muratori deplored the "modern musical theater" as "leading to immoderate effeminacy" because

> the effects of our modern dramas, and particularly of hearing our great musici, is to inspire a certain softness and sweetness which secretly serves to make the people more lowly and dedicated to base loves, drinking in the languidness of the voices, tasting the vilest emotions, seasoned by unhealthy melody.[25]

Polemicists like Voltaire used attacks on the castrati as part of their attack on tradition in general and traditional religion in particular. According to the canon of the Enlightenment, these singers were freaks and perhaps sodomites, and represented the ultimate decadence of a decadent and corrupt society. Because most castrati ended up singing in church choirs they made a useful stick with which to beat traditional religion, that most unenlightened of social institutions.

But though late eighteenth-century intellectuals relegated the idea of the male soprano to the status of an embarrassing hangover from the unenlightened past, the singers themselves continued to be popular. As is often the case, the progressive elite preferred innovation but the conservative populace clung to the old-fashioned musici. In Rome they were so popular that, when female sopranos were introduced, the response was often public outrage. David Silvagni, by no means a partisan of tradition, speaks of the "revulsion" that Romans felt at the sight of women on stage. When the liberal Cardinal Consalvi permitted women to continue on the stage with the papal restoration of 1800, "the public took it badly, and always protested in favor of their beloved musici, recalling Farinelli, Caffarello, Catena, and their most powerful and recent favorite, Velluti."[26]

Outside of the Papal States the castrati had never displaced female sopranos. Serious operas usually called for both male and female sopranos and altos, and castrati were rarely cast in comic operas at all except in Rome.

Nevertheless, the castrati continued to be a presence in opera into the first decades of the nineteenth century. Girolamo Crescentini (1762–1846; fig. 13), a sweet-voiced contralto who specialized in the pathos of Romantic roles, was one of Napoleon's favorite singers, and a friend and sponsor to Angelica Catalani (see below). Luigi Marchesi (1754–1829; fig. 14), brilliant, handsome, and temperamental, had a devoted following, especially among women. Stendhal was intrigued by these female fans, who identified themselves by wearing medallions of their idol. After the turmoil of Republic and restoration the famous Velluti starred in the 1816 season in Rome and continued to sing until 1830, virtually the last of the important operatic castrati.[27]

Despite the continued popularity of the male sopranos and their virtual monopoly on the Roman stage, outside of Rome the second half of the eighteenth century was one of the great ages of the diva. These bewitching, infuriating, transcendent performers processed in triumph from opera house to opera house, accompanied by adoring retinues and shimmering with the aura of glamour, power, and glory. Audiences rioted, men fought duels, girls yearned to emulate them, and impresarios, cursing them, dug deep into their pockets to pay their ruinous fees. This is the sort of diva on which Sardou based the character of Tosca. In typical Sardovian style, the first act of the play includes a long monologue in which one of the characters (Cavaradossi) tells another (Angelotti)—and the audience—all about her:

> This exquisite creature was discovered in the fields, in a state of nature, looking after goats. The Benedictine nuns of Verona, who took her in for charity's sake, barely taught her to read and pray; but she is one of those people who learn quickly what they need to know. Her first music teacher was the organist of the convent. She profited so well from his lessons that by the time she was sixteen she already had some small notoriety: it was the thing to do to go hear her on feast days. Cimarosa, brought there by a friend, took it into his head to contend with God for her and to make her an opera singer; but the nuns did not want to give her up to the devil. There was quite a battle: Cimarosa conspired, the convent intrigued. All Rome took sides, for or against, so much so that the late pope had to intervene. He had the young girl brought to him, heard her sing, and, charmed, patted her cheek and said: "Go in freedom, my child. You will touch all hearts, as you have touched mine, you will make sweet tears fall . . . and that too is a way of praying to God." (Cavaradossi to Angelotti, *La Tosca* I, iii)

Before the age of recording, the voice and charm of a singer was as ephemeral as the sparkle of a firefly; once they passed out of living memory little remained, and their names are largely forgotten now except by scholars and

FIGURE 13. Girolamo Crescentini, one of the great castrati of the late eighteenth and early nineteenth centuries, made his 1778–79 debut in Rome at the Valle theater as Livia in Cimarosa's *L'Italiana in Londra*. Dr. Girvice Archer

Ludwig Marchesi.

FIGURE 14. Luigi Marchesi, shown here in an early nineteenth-century German engraving, sang female parts at the Alibert in Rome in 1773, and appeared at the Argentina in 1783 in Cherubini's *Quinto Fabio*. Dr. Girvice Archer

aficionados of operatic lore. There are, however, exceptions, and in Sardou's
day a major one was Giuseppina (or Josephine) Grassini, remembered less for
her singing than for her status as Napoleon Bonaparte's mistress.[28] La Grassini was born on 18 April 1773 in Varese, a country resort at the foot of the
Alps frequented by the Milanese nobility. She was the daughter of Antonio
Grassini, who worked for the local convent, Our Lady of the Holy Mountain,
and Isabella Luini, who seems to have claimed the interesting distinction of
being descended from Leonardo da Vinci. The future diva's full name was
Maria Camilla Giuseppina Grassini and her first teacher (like Tosca's) was a
local church musician, one Domenico Zucchinetti, organist in the church of
Santa Vittoria. Zucchinetti recognized her talent and proposed that the child
(she was barely sixteen) be sent to Milan to study for the opera; her mother,
a violinist, feared for her daughter's virtue, but was eventually won over. As
is so often the case, mother was right. Soon after the little singer arrived in
Milan, Prince-General Alberigo of Belgioioso "made her a woman," as one of
her biographers delicately puts it.[29] She had chosen her deflowerer well. Alberigo Barbiano of Belgioioso and Este was military advisor to the Austrian emperor, viceroy of Lombardy, and widower of Anna Ricciarda of Este, illegiti-
mate daughter of the last Este duke of Modena. His musical family (it boasted
two amateur singers and a dilettante composer) made room for the pretty
provincial, taught her polite manners and musical polish, and saw to it that
she made her debut (still at age sixteen) as second female lead at the ducal
theater in Parma in operas by Guglielmi (*La pastorella nobile*; The noble
shepherdess) and Cimarosa (*La ballerina amante*; The loving ballerina).
Small roles in comic operas were not really suited to her contralto voice, and
she made little impression until 1793 when she appeared in Zingarelli's *Artaserse* (Artaxerxes), with the famous castrato Marchesi and the tenor Lazzarini. Her friendship with the young castrato Crescentini improved her musical taste, and she was an established star by 1797 when the French, led by
General Bonaparte, marched into Milan.[30] The general, who had left his new
wife Josephine behind in France, was especially struck by the charms of the
twenty-six-year-old diva.

Grassini's status as Bonaparte's mistress made her famous in France, and
that fame experienced a considerable revival during the centennial celebrations toward the end of the nineteenth century; Sardou could not have avoided
thinking of her when he created his Italian opera singer, La Tosca. Her biog-
rapher André Gavoty describes her "supple neck and expressive face," her
soft skin, opulent black hair, brown eyes, and "the imperious arch of her
well-formed eyebrows," her upturned nose and fleshy lower lip. A French admirer who saw her in Naples in 1797 admired her magnificent contralto voice,

her figure, and her noble and elegant height. "Never," he sighed, "has such a ravishing creature appeared on the stage."[31]

Angelica Catalani, another ravishing Italian diva, began her career at the end of the eighteenth century (see fig. 15). Like Grassini (and Tosca) she was convent-educated; as in the case of Grassini, a romanticized biography of Catalani would have been easily available to Sardou when he was patching together his own raven-haired heroine from bits and pieces of her colleagues. Unlike Giuseppina Grassini, who never sang in Rome, Angelica Catalani was a star at Tosca's own theater, the Argentina, during the carnival season of 1798–99 when, at the age of nineteen, she appeared in *Ifigenia in Aulide* by Giuseppe Mosca. Her reviews were at first highly favorable:

> Citizeness Catalani [the republican newspaper reported] unites to the sweetness of her voice, which has no natural defects, an infinite and peerless attention to agility, a vigorous vibrato.[32]

The show continued for a month, closing on 7 March (16 Ventoso in the republican calendar), by which time the *Monitore* reviewer was less enchanted with her style. A later review accused her of indulging in "too powerful vibrati that degenerate into howls," encouraged by a circle of "ignorant louts in the pit" who, the reviewer warns the singer, "either don't know the difference, or who are making fun of you."

Catalani was young and beautiful with a brilliant and flexible voice, but as the *Monitore* critic seems already to have noticed, she did not have much education or natural taste. She had made her debut in Milan at the age of seventeen with the famous and elegant castrato Crescentini. Crescentini, who sang with and advised Giuseppina Grassini, seems to have offered to do the same for Angelica, to less satisfactory effect. Fétis, who heard her sing and knew her friends, states that although Crescentini tried to teach her some singing technique, "she didn't seem to understand." Fifteen years later she gave up the direction of the Théâtre-Italien in Paris in order to go on tour with a handful of bravura showpieces guaranteed to bring her audiences to their feet. She is reported to have been a fine comic actress and she could also do well in tragedy, but she had little interest in drama or character, and apparently became bored with operatic performances when they required her to do more than stand still and make glorious noises.

The biography of Catalani most likely to be available to Sardou, and the one he would have found most appealing, appeared in a romantic and only tangentially accurate work on the lives of female singers published by Marie and Léon Escudier in 1856.[33] According to the Escudiers, Angelica was born

ANGELICA CATALANI

Painted by I.Neigh　　　　　*Engraved by G.J.Fossi*

Published by the Proprietor

FIGURE 15. The lovely Angelica Catalani, one of the probable templates for Sardou's character of La Tosca. Dr. Girvice Archer

in Venice in 1785 (in fact, she was born at Sinigaglia, near Rome, in 1780), entered a convent (in fact, her father was an employee of the nuns), and learned
to sing at the knee of the convent organist. In a typical "discovery" story, like
Lana Turner sitting at the drugstore soda fountain, she was said to have been
discovered by the director of La Fenice theater in Venice, desperate to replace
his prima donna who had inconveniently died just as the carnival season
loomed. So, like Floria in the Sardou play, she was first heard singing in
church, then wrested away from the convent and plunged into a triumphant
operatic career. There is even a story of an ecclesiastical protector, Cardinal
Onorati, who struggled to keep Angelica from the world, but failed, as Floria Tosca's protectors failed to keep her away from the stage.

At the age of seventeen, Catalani made her debut at La Fenice in *La Lodoïska* by Johann Simone Mayr. Mayr's opera was a version of a popular story
on which Cherubini had based his French Revolutionary propaganda opera
of the same name. Several versions of the opera appeared in Italy during the
Revolutionary period. In a set of coincidences which may or may not have
been known to Sardou, the Cherubini opera includes a series of similarities
between its heroine and Tosca. Most striking is the fact that the leading character's name, "Lodoïska," when pronounced in French, is barely distinguish-
able from the name—La Tosca—that Sardou, after much agonizing, chose
for his heroine.[34] Cherubini's opera, set in Poland, was written in Paris just
before the Terror. It is a striking example of revolutionary propaganda in the
theater. La Lodoïska is the fiery lover of a liberal noble, who defends herself
from the lustful designs of the evil reactionary noble.[35] Although it is difficult
to imagine the pious and conservative Floria Tosca appearing in a work designed to glorify the most radical of the French revolutionaries, La Catalani
seems to have experienced no such qualms, despite the fact that a contemporary, Giacomo Gottifredo Ferrari, praised her modesty and religiosity, and
her custom of having Mass celebrated in her home on feast days. In 1801 she
married a French officer who took over the management of her career; from
all accounts she was a "good wife and a good mother." Pious and loyal she
may have been, but she also seems to have been stunningly vain, and rather
stupid.

The *Monitore* which was initially so enthusiastic about Citizeness Catalani was equally delighted with another diva, Citizeness Teresa Bertinotti
(later Bertinotti-Radicati), who sang in Rome in 1798. The journal reported
that:

> she sang with grace of carriage, with agility, and with admirable expression
> which went to the heart, especially with two scales of descending semitones

in the last rondo, carried out with surprising rapidity, sweetness, and majesty.[36]

By the time Teresa Bertinotti sang in the theaters of the Roman Republic the twenty-two-year-old diva had, like Floria Tosca, appeared at La Fenice and La Scala. In Rome Bertinotti appeared at the Alibert with the tenor De Lorenzi, her sometime lover and sometime enemy, in a series of light operas: *La disfatta dei macedoni* (The defeat of the Macedonians, with music by Giuseppe Maria Curcio), *La selvaggia nel Messico* (The savage girl in Mexico, with music by Giuseppe Nicolini), and Francesco Federici's sentimental *Virginia*, a dramma serio in which she shared the stage with another female soprano, Anna Bertozzi, and two castrati, Vitale Damiani and Giuseppe Batazzi. Prima donnas were new to Rome, but in Bertinotti the city apparently started off with a stereotypically fierce one. Two parties quickly formed, those supporting the soprano and those who took the side of her tenor ex-lover; and in the best Roman tradition, the supporters of one rioted whenever the other sang. Since they were appearing together, the result was that evenings at the Alibert became "an inferno of shouts, whistles, and applause," to the general delight of the public and the horror of the authorities. Bertinotti absolutely refused to sing the duet with her despised former lover. The audiences went mad. There were fistfights, objects soft, hard, and rotten were hurled, and challenges to duels were issued and accepted. At one point, Bertinotti walked to the footlights and made a rude gesture at the audience (the *corne*, which can be compared to flipping the finger at them); the quarrel became a police matter, and the soprano was charged with disturbing the peace. The state intervened and closed the theater until the diva relented and sang the duet; thereafter life at the Alibert once again became tranquil and the opera was performed uninterrupted. Unfortunately, reviews suggest that it was not worth the wait.[37]

The career of Floria Tosca contains elements similar to, and probably borrowed from, all of the above singers. From the temperamental Teresa Bertinotti she borrows some of her fire, and her appearance in Rome in 1800. Like Grassini and Catalani she is dazzlingly beautiful, a simple girl from the country, convent-educated, and trained by the church organist. The career of Maria (or Marietta) Marcolini, a pretty young Florentine contralto, also contains tantalizing hints of La Tosca. Although born in Florence, she seems to have begun her career in Venice, where she appeared in 1800 (age twenty) at the Teatro San Benedetto. Like Tosca she sang in Naples and at La Scala in Milan, and in 1806 she was a star at the Argentina theater in Rome. At least one contemporary source describes her as Veronese (from Verona) (see fig. 16). She became a star young, and pursued an international career at an age when today's

A . MARIA . MARCOLINI . VERONESE

PER . SOAVISSIMO . CANTO

PER . GENTILISSIMI . MODI

FIGURE 16. Maria, or Mariana, Marcolini who, like Tosca, sang in Rome. Dr. Girvice Archer

singers are just entering the conservatory. To these characteristics, Floria adds another romantic element: she is a foundling.

The remarkable Italian institutions dedicated to the care of the children of the poor were famous throughout Europe, and Sardou, who wanted his heroine to be an elemental Child of Nature, could hardly resist placing her in their care. Rome was the first city in Europe to make universal primary education available to both boys and girls, in free schools run by religious orders.[38] Girls were generally taught reading, catechism, and women's work, but special attention was given to teaching orphan girls the skills they would need to support themselves.[39] In Rome, this almost always took the form of some sort of textile work; in the cities ruled by Venice (such as Verona), as in Naples, charitable institutions developed during the seventeenth and eighteenth centuries which specialized in professional musical training.

If Sardou wanted his heroine to be an opera singer, he had two patterns from which to choose: first, the famous singers who seemed to have sprung full-blown in their teens from the convents and church choirs of Italy (like Grassini and Catalani). The second was the romantic image of the Venetian conservatories. None of the divas who sang in Rome under the Republic or the restored papacy was a product of these conservatories; Sardou, however, could not resist giving his heroine at least the aura of these famous institutions.

Floria Tosca, the foundling goat-girl raised and taught by the nuns of Verona, recalls the images of the orphan girl musicians of Venice who inspired Jean-Jacques Rousseau, the eighteenth-century's prophet of sensitivity, to transports of delight: "I cannot conceive," he writes in his *Confessions*, "of anything so voluptuous and so moving as this music."[40]

More than a century later Philippe Monnier, looking back through the rose-tinted lenses of reports such as Rousseau's, describes the girls as "orphans and love-children" whose patrons rejoiced "to see the first-fruits of talent and the graces of body unfold at the same time."[41] For the nineteenth-century taste, the girls' immaturity and the supposed spirituality of their upbringing only added to their erotic potential.

The reality was less romantic but rather more interesting. Where Rousseau and (later) Monnier saw delectable blossoms ripe for the plucking, the people and rulers of Venice saw tangible proof of the wisdom of the state. The schools began in the sixteenth century as efforts to deal with the problem of poverty. By the eighteenth century the conservatories had become centers for training women musicians, and the chief alternatives to theatrical entertainment in Venice. Their audiences, listening as the young women sang out of sight behind screens, enjoyed the idea of the lovely children, dressed in white with bunches of pomegranate flowers behind their ears, singing and playing under the direction of the most famous maestros in Italy, men like Vivaldi, Porpora, Hasse, Galuppi, and Cimarosa. In the mythology of Venice as the ideal society, these *figlie di coro* (choir girls) represented a public-relations triumph as Venice transformed the children of her poor into angelic beings. The image is charming but profoundly (and deliberately) misleading. These young women were professionals, rigorously trained by the best musicians in Italy—which is to say, the best in the world.[42] Clearly Sardou preferred the vision of a Child of Nature singing like a canary; the reality was in most cases quite different.

Sardou, having got his heroine into a convent cum orphanage, had to extricate her. In order to do this he generalized from the Catholicism of Italy as a whole to the idea that the pope would be the logical choice to resolve a conflict between the patrons of a convent in the Veneto and influential parties favoring the theater. This idea was made even more attractive by the fact that the pope in question was Pius VI, with his nineteenth-century reputation as a gentle martyr. Unfortunately, the idea of Pius VI or any other pope involving himself in the sort of controversy described by Sardou is absurd. Training women to participate actively in the liturgy was thoroughly un-Roman and against papal policy of the time. Defying Rome in this fashion was a typically Venetian thing to do, but no institution in the Veneto would have allowed a pope to assume control of patronage appropriate to the Venetian state. The only way Floria could have ended up in the papal court would have been if she were kidnapped. But kidnapping a young woman from a convent, with or without her willing cooperation, was a capital crime anywhere in Italy, and not even Domenico Cimarosa could have got away with it.

Sardou credits the start of Floria's career to the two most famous composers of eighteenth-century Italian opera; or more precisely, to the two eighteenth-century Italian composers whose French connections ensured that they were still household names in Paris long after they were dead. Napoleon had an extravagant admiration for Domenico Cimarosa (1749–1801), and he made Giovanni Paisiello (1740–1816) his court composer. Both worked primarily in Naples, but could demand top prices anywhere in Europe, or farther afield: from 1782 to 1788 Paisiello was court musician to Catherine the Great; when he could bear Russia no longer, his place was taken by his compatriot and sometime rival, Cimarosa. Both composers were products of the famous musical conservatories of Naples: Cimarosa was a charity student at the conservatory of Santa Maria di Loreto; the more prosperous Paisiello family sent their son to the conservatory of Sant'Onofrio.

Both composers got into serious trouble in 1798–99, when the Parthenopean Republic went down in ruins. Paisiello found himself charged with having been "director of National Music" under the rebel regime, but managed to convince the court that he had done nothing to earn that title. Cimarosa wrote music for a patriotic hymn ("to accompany the burning of the images of tyrants") and then, with the fall of the Republic, rapidly ground out anthems and cantatas in praise of the reaction. He was nevertheless arrested in December of 1799 and held for four months. On his release he went to Venice, where he died ten months later. The medical report identified the cause of death as a stomach tumor, but rumors persisted that he had been poisoned on orders from the Queen of Naples.[43]

Paisiello, on the other hand, survived his brush with revolution and by 1802 had hitched his wagon to the rising star of Napoleon Bonaparte, whose court musician he would be from 1802 to 1804. Before this, however, he spent an anxious year or two, as Sardou shows him, trying to get back into royal favor with the monarchs of the Two Sicilies. It is not known precisely where he was in June of 1800, but his music was performed or scheduled to be performed in Rome at the Argentina theater that spring. It is perfectly plausible to imagine him there, hiding behind the diaphanous skirts of his fictional protégée, Floria Tosca.

We know only one of Floria's roles for certain: the title role in Paisiello's *Nina, o la pazza per amore* (Nina, or the girl gone mad for love). And we know, or suspect, that the same composer's *Barber of Seville* was produced at the Argentina in 1800 while that house was supposedly closed. Tosca might also have sung Carolina in Cimarosa's hit opera, *Il matrimonio segreto* (The secret marriage), based on an English play, *The Clandestine Marriage*, by Coleman and Garrick.

Nina is a sentimental part, much more lachrymose and without the self-mockery of the characters in *Il matrimonio segreto*. *Nina*, like Cimarosa's opera, is a domestic drama involving paternal tyranny, daughterly duty, and young lovers reunited in the end. The plot is simple and, while not remotely believable, deals with naturalistic characters and relationships. Nina spends most of the opera in a state of gentle madness, wandering about the stage simply dressed and confused, with flowers in her hair.[44] This sweet, melodic tearjerker is skillfully composed but makes few demands on the voice. The singing is meant to be as simple and "natural" as the characters; Nina, even in her mad scene, almost never sings either above or below the staff and none of the other characters is called upon for more than an octave's extension.[45]

Paisiello's *Barber of Seville*, which was advertised for the Argentina in 1800, was one of the most successful operas of the late eighteenth century, and one of the few to enter any sort of standard repertory. Composed in Russia in 1782, the opera was based on Beaumarchais's *The Barber of Seville* (the first of his "Figaro" trilogy), which had premiered in Paris only seven years earlier. Paisiello's opera was long considered the definitive operatic adaptation of Beaumarchais. When the young Rossini dared to compose his own version in 1816 he took over much of Paisiello's libretto, and was strongly criticized for his presumption in trying to rival the older master's witty genius.

If Floria sang Carolina, Nina, or Paisiello's Rosina she would need to be capable of realistic acting in situations that seem, at least to the characters, to be serious. The last quarter of the eighteenth century had seen a great burst of enthusiasm for more convincing operatic acting. Truly naturalistic acting would not become popular until the technology of theater changed, making the soft-spoken close-up possible, but opera singers, like stage actors, were already trying to create convincing and moving characters and dramatic situations. In a treatise published in 1774, Giambattista Mancini advised that "acting is the final and most important duty of the opera singer, the motions of the face and body working to portray the evolving passions of the drama." [46]

The fall of the Roman republic in 1799 presented the city's impresarios with challenges that went far beyond problems of stagecraft. There was no question of allowing the season to continue as planned. But there was little time to make the preparations necessary for a completely new season. Only three of the Roman theaters were open on a regular basis that year: the Valle, around the corner from Sant'Andrea; the Alibert, the Argentina's rival as first theater in Rome; and the Apollo, formerly known as the Tordinona, across the Tiber from the Castel Sant'Angelo. There were also puppet shows at the Pallacorda, and no doubt many of the small popular theaters offered shows and music on an occasional basis.

The Alibert assumed the status of official theater, and Governor Naselli and the royal representatives took up residence in two boxes joined together to make one imposing box. They held a great carnival ball at the theater on 19 January for 1,200 guests led by Naselli, Acton, and the representatives of the Bourbon monarchs and the Austrian Empire. The boxes were draped in white silk trimmed with gold fringe, and the stage transformed into a brightly colored pavilion for dancing with a great (and expensive) display of candles and torches.

The Apollo opened its carnival season with Cimarosa's *L'italiana in Londra* (The Italian girl in London), a "lukewarm success." The second item on the bill, a ballet called *Gli sogni di Telemaco* (The dreams of Telemachus), was booed off the stage. A month later *L'italiana* was recalled to replace a forgettable little item called *Il matrimonio in cantina* (The wedding in the cellar) which, like most shows that season, had met with hisses and catcalls and closed on the same night it opened.[47]

The prima donna at the Valle, La Bussoni, was a young woman of definite opinions who did not hesitate to bring the show down around her own ears. As a result the Valle was having an even worse season than the Apollo. On 18 January a new show by Maestro Caruso opened with the active hostility of the prima donna, who as a partisan of the rival composer Guglielmi was intent on doing everything she could to ruin the Caruso piece. Caruso, directing the opera from the pit, listened with mounting frustration and rage as she whispered her way through her part. Finally, unable to bear more, he screamed, "Cavi la voce!" (Let the voice out!) She pretended not to hear; he screamed again; she remained obstinate; the audience joined in with shouts of derision, and the prima donna stormed off the stage.[48] A month later, however, an opera by Guglielmi did no better, falling on its face even with the soprano's cooperation.

The spring season, which Floria Tosca was presumably brought in to rescue, fared little better than the carnival one. On 27 April the Valle opened with a farce by Paisiello, *Lo spazzacamino* (The chimney-sweep). Despite its popular composer it too was whistled off the stage by the few people who bothered to attend. The May show, Paer's *Gl'intrighi amorosi* (Amorous intrigues), seems to have been the only show to succeed during that season.[49]

For spring, the Alibert put on a new opera, *Roma liberata* (Rome liberated), with music by the Neapolitan composer Giuseppe Curcio and words by a Roman poet, Francesco Ballani. Despite the return of the old regime, female singers remained on the Roman stage: the part of Faustina was taken by Cecilia Bolognesi. The dedication makes it clear that the libretto, nominally about the liberation of Rome by Constantine from the tyrant Maxentius, was meant as a transparent allegory of the deliverance of the city from the godless republicans. Constantine, the first Christian emperor, was to be understood as representing "our beloved, our common father, the generous, the great, the pious . . . ," that is, the newly elected pope, Pius VII, whose arrival was eagerly awaited.

The classicism of *Roma liberata* was continued in the next opera, Guglielmi's *La morte di Cleopatra* (The death of Cleopatra) with Cleopatra, like Faustina, played by Cecilia Bolognesi. This was not a new opera, as it had been performed in Naples in 1796 at the San Carlo, but it was put on "as a compliment to Don Diego Naselli." The effusive dedication praises "our liberator," Ferdinand IV of Naples, but popular enthusiasm for the liberator was no greater than popular enthusiasm for the opera, which failed. Romans did, however, like the otherwise untitled "Chinese dance" that accompanied it.

It was a season badly in need of rescue, but in cold reality, none came. Perhaps if Paisiello's *Barber of Seville* had gone on at the Argentina as planned, perhaps if a singer of the caliber of La Catalani had been available, the season might have been saved. Surely Floria Tosca, the celebrated interpreter of Paisiello and Cimarosa, could have turned the tide. In some dimension where fact and fiction overlap, she slips out of the stage door of the Argentina, away from rehearsing her role as Rosina, away from the worried composer desperate to recover his reputation, and breathing a little rapidly with anticipatory excitement, hurries through the sun-drenched streets of Rome toward the locked doors of Sant'Andrea della Valle. The world is hers to command. She can sing in London and in Saint Petersburg, and within a few years she will be invited to sing at the court of the new emperor of the French, the victor of Marengo; perhaps she will have to deal with the predatory instinct that beautiful performers sometimes inspired in him. She can marry her Parisian-Roman painter if she chooses, and have as many children as she wishes, without interfering in the least with her work. She can retire in 1825 or 1830, having sung the early works of Rossini and Donizetti, and perhaps live to see a new wave of revolution in Italy in 1848 and the start of the movement to national unification. But we know, of course, that none of that will happen. Instead, the painter and the singer will find themselves at the mercy of the law, and it will all end badly at dawn on 18 June 1800.

5 The Policeman's Rome

*An investigation, witnesses, a summation by the defense? We hardly
have time to amuse ourselves with such trifles. His Catholic Majesty
has simplified the procedure . . .*

Baron Scarpia to Tosca, *La Tosca*, IV, iii

$\mathscr{S}$ardou and Puccini present us with a Rome where the word of the
Regent of Police supersedes all law. As usual the reality was quite different: in
fact the law was ubiquitous and inescapable. As in all old regime states, there
was a dense underbrush of legal foliage in Rome, complete with suckers and
thorns, growing out of the rich loam of traditional society. Institutional courts
rose like moss-crusted trees; and if we follow the analogy much further we
will find the lawyers scuttling about under the matted vegetation.

His "Catholic Majesty"[1] Ferdinand certainly may have wished for a strong
herbicide with which to remove the underbrush and "simplify the procedure"
but not even in Naples in 1799, with the active participation of Admiral Nelson and no outside interference, did he manage to do away with courts. The
best, or worst, he could do was to set up a layer of kangaroo courts of his own
to hand down the desired sentences—a fact for which both Paisiello and Cimarosa had reason to be profoundly grateful, since both were acquitted by
such courts despite their more or less active cooperation with the Parthenopean Republic.

In Rome even more than in Naples justice suffered less from high-handed
tyranny than from a flamboyant proliferation of legal systems. There were
multiple courts, each reflecting one of the many layers of civil and Church law.
Church courts not only dealt with separate offenses from civil law, but also
dealt with the same offenses in separate jurisdictions. The most famous of
these Church jurisdictions was the court of the Holy Office or Inquisition,
which was still active in Rome, though by 1800 it had been abolished in most
Italian states. The Inquisition was, of course, a bugbear for liberals of the
revolutionary age, and many were convinced (and remain so) that Rome was
honeycombed with subterranean dungeons where heretics groaned in the
pitiless hands of their inquisitors. This had probably never been true and it

certainly was not the case by 1800, when the court of the Holy Office sat under the direct supervision of the pope, heard only cases of sorcery and direct attacks on religion, and rarely passed any sentences at all. The Inquisition in Venice had been reduced to a staff of one by the middle of the eighteenth century, and its abolition was less the overthrow of a powerful enemy of reason than an after-the-fact bit of housekeeping, sweeping the remnant of a previously useful institution into the dustbin of history.[2]

The Inquisition was only one, rather minor, example of the many legal institutions of papal Rome. The court system of the city was a hopeless tangle of overlapping and often conflicting laws and jurisdictions. Each institution, each authority in Rome had its own court, from the hundreds of religious orders which each maintained a presence here, to the governor, the chamberlain, the cardinal vicar, and heads of other departments of state.[3] All and each of these had his own court and judicial personnel, and his own legal prerogatives, all jealously guarded. The largest and best-managed of the courts were those of the governor, which heard cases involving serious crime (they were the only courts that, in normal times, could hand down the death penalty). They were kept very busy—in 1780, they heard 3,565 cases.[4]

Minor cases involving such matters as petty theft were heard by the court of the senator of Rome (there was only one "senator" in the eighteenth century). There was no appeal from the decisions of this small-claims court but the senator heard the cases with the help of assessors who advised him.[5]

The cardinal chamberlain and monsignor treasurer general oversaw another layer of courts, those which dealt with currency violations and unauthorized exports. This included control over the sale of objects unearthed by antiquarians and sold to foreigners as well as guaranteeing the authenticity of bonds and financial instruments. The court of the cardinal vicar dealt with issues of morals and family matters, and with the Jews in the ghetto. There was no shortage of appeals courts. The highest of these was the Rota, but there were many others; some historians estimate that there were as many as seventy-two such courts, including the Camera Apostolica, the congregations of the Immunità and Buon Governo, the signatory court, and the assessor of the Inquisition.[6]

There was nothing exclusively Roman about this sort of institutional tangle: it was the normal way in which Western law functioned before the codifications of the late eighteenth century. But in Rome, by definition, tradition was more than usually tenacious. The most reforming of popes (and there were many through the centuries) found it easier to add a layer and prune back its rivals than to attempt the outright abolition of any courts or laws. The result was a tangle of law administered through innumerable tribunals, all of which had competing claims to jurisdiction. Contradictory rulings were not only possible but likely; appeals courts were as confusing as the primary courts, and cases dragged out for decades; and the whole business was run by a group of elderly, vaguely benevolent amateurs distracted by endless rounds of feast days.

If the courts were a nightmare of inefficiency, the prison system was the most enlightened in Europe. The state prison was the Castel Sant'Angelo, which we will examine in some detail in chapter 8. In normal times it held few prisoners, and these were usually kept in cells on the upper levels of the fortress, not in the ancient dungeons so admired by tourists.

Ordinary prisoners were normally held either in small prisons around the city, or at the New Prisons on the Via Giulia (the Carceri Nuove). The New Prisons were built across the Tiber from the Castello between 1652 and 1655. There, for the first time in the history of European penology, ordinary prisoners were held in individual cells. They were separated by age and by sex, and (another innovation) persons awaiting trial were kept separate from those already sentenced.[7] As everywhere in Europe, prisoners were expected to pay for their food and lodging. This meant that the rich could live almost as comfortably in prison as they did at home. The poor were, as always, at a disadvantage, but in Rome there were several confraternities which competed with one another to pay food, lodging, and legal costs for those who could not afford them.

The relative mildness of Roman prisons was probably due to the nature of the state. From the religious point of view, the aim of punishment was repentance and the reclamation of the strayed one. Sentenced criminals were often held in convents and monasteries, under circumstances no harsher than those experienced by the voluntary residents of these institutions. Worse, the pope and his government considered themselves bound to Christian forgiveness. Consequently, to the outrage of the penal theorists like Beccaria, they scattered amnesties and clemency about with a free hand.[8]

Even without pardons, few convicts spent any length of time in prison.[9] Most minor infractions of the law were punished directly by public corporal punishment such as the *cavaletto* or the *tratti di corda* (or *strapado*), or simply by being placed on display near the instrument of these penalties, or paraded around town on donkey-back with a placard around their necks describing the nature of their offense before being sent off to serve their time on road gangs (see fig. 17).[10] More serious crimes could be punished by exile, or by the *galera*, a term that can be translated either prison, or galley. Two or three times a month lists of prisoners sentenced to the *galera* were published, and the little convoys were marched under guard to the coastal town

FIGURE 17. Nicola Antonio Angeletti, a nineteenth-century Italian revolutionary who was whipped through the streets of Naples, is another possible model for Angelotti. The humiliating nature of this punishment may have given Sardou his idea for sentencing his Angelotti to the galleys. Engraving, published in Vanucci's *I martiri della libertà italiana*. Author's collection

of Civitavecchia. In the Sardou play Angelotti has already served three years in this form of imprisonment. Although Sardou seems to have understood the Italian term *galera* ("galley") literally, and entertained visions of slave labor such as that depicted in novels like the recently published *Ben Hur,* this was a misapprehension.[11] There was no papal fleet to speak of for the *galeotti* to row, and their confinement seems to have been minimal. Prisoners worked at odd jobs and at street cleaning, for which they were paid rather better than the soldiers who guarded them, and lived in barracks which they could leave with little difficulty. Escape was notoriously easy, but few bothered; securing a pardon or remission of sentence was almost as easy.[12]

Despite the popular perception of later eras, the papal government (like most old regime states) had a serious disinclination to execute anyone, even murderers. In 1786 there were sixty-two murder trials in Rome, though there were certainly many more than sixty-two murders. Of these trials, one defendant was condemned to death—and he was reprieved. Ten were sentenced in absentia, and none of these was executed. If anything, the papal government was excessively lenient; some commentators believed that this was the reason why murder was so common in Rome.[13]

By far the most frequent sort of murder was knifing. This usually took place in the street, the result of a quarrel or vendetta, and was thought to be a personal matter between the quarreling parties; the winner was popularly considered to have been in the right, through some variety of *cavalleria urbana* or trial by battle.[14] Only rarely would the police attempt to intervene in such cases, and even more rarely did they get any cooperation from neighbors or potential witnesses. Statistics are hard to come by since arrests were relatively infrequent, but estimates of the number of murders vary from one a day to four a day. In a city with a population of under 150,000 this is a truly horrifying statistic but Romans seem to have taken it in stride. Even those cases that came to court in normal times were often dismissed; and in the extremely rare case when a death sentence was handed down (about one a year, and by no means all for murder) pardons were relatively easy to get. (In the Roman tradition, Tosca assumes that she has only to throw herself on the queen's mercy to obtain a pardon for her lover.)[15]

If the court system of eighteenth-century Rome was more lenient (albeit confused), and the prison system milder and more humane, than a modern observer might expect, the policing was spectacularly worse. The modern Western police are an invention of the nineteenth century, with some precedents in late eighteenth-century reform movements.[16] Generally speaking, there was very little interest in establishing such a force before this time. Policing, it was felt, was a nasty job that should most appropriately be done by men who were little if at all better than criminals themselves. In Italy, and most particularly in the Roman states, there was a vast, unbridgeable gap between the judiciary who made the laws and the sbirri (cops) who enforced them. The horror inspired by the blood-tainted professions clung even to butchers and surgeons; it made police, jailers, and executioners virtually untouchable. In addition, the very act of confining criminals was considered despicable, and as degrading to the police as to the detainee. The name itself, sbirro, was and remains an insult, comparable to the "pig" of the 1960s.

Steven Hughes has appropriately compared the Roman sbirri (fig. 18) to the more marginal sheriffs of the American West, distinguished from outlaws and civilians only by a badge and an array of weapons, and so badly paid that they lived on the edge of absolute poverty. The sbirri tended to supplement their income with various forms of extortion at the expense of criminals and citizens alike. They set up illegal roadblocks and demanded money from people coming into the city; echoing the plot of *Tosca*, they offered clemency in exchange for bribes and sexual favors from the female relatives of men accused of crime, and their harassment of prostitutes was infamous. They were not above burning down houses to capture suspects; they kicked and beat prisoners unless they were bribed to stop the maltreatment. If a suspect like Cavaradossi managed to arrive at the office of the chief of police without a black eye or a bloody nose, it could only be because a generous tip had changed hands.

Sbirri wore no uniforms and were employed by no central law-enforcement agency. Rather, they worked for the *bargello*, or captain, of a specific court, such as the court of the governor or, during the interregnum of 1800 when *Tosca* is set, for the Governing Committee, or Giunta di Stato. In terms of *Tosca*, Spoletta is functioning as *bargello* for the chief of police, employing at least "tre sbirri" (three cops). He shows the usual contempt for his men, referring to them as "i miei cagnotti," my [big, lousy] dogs. In 1790 there were 115 sbirri employed by the various Roman courts; it was a far from adequate force, and its inadequacy became more obvious as the social order broke down. Their numbers were supplemented by soldiers, both before and during the occupation of 1799–1800, but this was hardly a recipe for peace. The records are full of conflicts between the sbirri and the soldiers, and the confrontations often degenerated into shoot-outs.

The sbirri were universally loathed not only because of their low reputation, and their penchant for random violence, but also because they were the ones who, under the direction of the executioner, carried out most of the torture called for by the legal code. This aspect of their professional work was rare by 1800, but it was still widely resented. Torture as such was not formally

FIGURE 18. Roman sbirro, one of the infamous cops of papal Rome, in a typically pugnacious pose. Ron and Jackie Juge, after contemporary drawings

abolished in Rome until the reforms of 1831, though most procedures had been
done away with as early as 1735, when the governor of Rome banned the use
of torture to extract confessions in the case of heinous crimes.[17] When Pius VII
reinstituted papal government in Rome in 1800 he directed his staff to work
on law reform, including reform of the use of torture. Nevertheless, torture
remained on the books until 1831, when Gregory XVI's *Regolamento organico
e di procedura criminale*, Article 348, stated: "The use of any indirect means
whatever, of any false statements, tempting, seducing, or menacing interro-
gations in order to extract replies which the interrogated person would not
have naturally [or freely] given, is forbidden."[18]

Serious scholars have tended to avoid the topic, but recent research indicates that the use of judicial torture was normally subject to a complex and
stringent set of regulations related to the law of proof.[19] Despite the enormous
complexity of old regime law, certain factors tended to remain constant. One
of these was a great reluctance to impose the death penalty without absolute
and irrefutable proof of guilt—what was called "full proof." Circumstantial
evidence, no matter how strong, was not enough. For full proof the court had
to have one of two things: either unimpeachable and demonstrably disinterested eyewitnesses, or a full and free confession, verified by independent
sources.[20] The confession, "the queen of proofs," was absolutely essential until quite late in the evolution of European judicial thought. John Langbein argues convincingly in *Torture and the Law of Proof* that it was only after
other, "weaker," forms of proof came to be accepted in capital cases that
courts could dispense with torture. Ironically, the high value placed on human
life made what we consider to be inhuman procedures essential if justice were
to function at all. Because of course if a confession were necessary, then a
confession would have to be procured.

But even that was not nearly so simple as one might imagine. In the absence of full proof, a magistrate or police official needed at least what was
called "half proof" before he could legally prepare a warrant ordering a suspect to be questioned under torture. And half proof was quite specifically
defined: either one acceptable eyewitness, or the sort of circumstantial evidence that would put the matter beyond reasonable doubt.

If the accused person persisted in denying his (or less commonly, her) guilt
under torture the court was forced to acquit. Only when circumstantial proof
was overwhelming could any sentence be passed, and that "extraordinary
sentence" had to be less than that which would have been passed if the accused had confessed (for example, prison rather than execution, or exile rather
than prison).

If the accused confessed under torture, however, this did not in itself provide "full proof." The confession had to be verified, either by corroborating evidence, or by a repetition once all effects of the torture had passed. If the accused refused to confirm the confession, of course, the torture was repeated—but this could not be done more than one, or in exceptional cases, two times. A person with strong nerves and a relative insensitivity to pain could escape conviction by the simple expedient of confessing as soon as the torture began—at which point it would have to be stopped—and then refusing to verify the confession later. No matter how frustrated the torturer or the investigator might become, they could only proceed at the risk of a lawsuit. This is why a major objection to torture was the complaint that it was inefficient, favoring courageous criminals over more easily frightened innocents.[21]

There were two forms of torture in use in Rome during the second half of the eighteenth century. One was the *corda*, which calls up such nostalgic yearnings in Spoletta ["O bei tratti di corda," he mutters, "Oh for a few good jerks of the rope"].[22] The machine for administering the *corda* stood near the Farnese palace in the Campo dei Fiori, at the entrance to an alley that still carries its name (the Via della Corda). The machine consisted of a scaffold with a crossbar and a series of ropes and pulleys. The sentence was carried out in the following way. After sentence was passed the condemned was escorted from the prison to the scaffold, as for a public capital execution. His arms were tied behind his back with the rope connected to a pulley, and he was hauled up to a height of between seven and ten meters. He was then dropped, gently or roughly depending on the severity of the punishment, as many times as called for in the sentence (three was the usual number). The *corda* could be considered a form of the classic rack, but it was more commonly used as part of the sentence than as a method of extracting information. Three *tratti di corda* or jerks of the rope was the standard penalty for violations of public order in the first half of the century, a category which included ticket-scalpers. Many of the victims were carriage drivers, a tough and independent segment of the population whose upper body strength seems to have sometimes mitigated the severity of the torture. An eighteenth-century grand tourist, Lalande, tells about watching a driver undergo his three *tratti* and, after his release, swagger to the front of the scaffold and offer to do it again if someone would tip him a scudo.

After 1798 these traditional forms of law and law enforcement were interrupted by war, invasion, and revolution. Each successive government in Rome scrambled to solve the usual problems, plus a host of new ones: disruption of the court system; the presence of undisciplined and often unpaid troops; shortages and rumors; and banditry, always a plague in the countryside, which now moved into the city.

The 1798–99 Republic was never secure enough to establish a functioning judicial or penal system, though its supporters (many of whom, in Rome as elsewhere, were lawyers) saw law reform as one of their major policy goals. Decrees aplenty were issued, and a criminal tribunal of the Department of the Tiber was set up to replace the old-fashioned tangle of laws and courts. The ideas of Cesare Beccaria, whose 1764 treatise *On Crimes and Punishments* had become the bible for law reformers, were to be introduced into Rome. One of the few tangible results was the fact that the scaffold for the *tratti di corda* was removed from its traditional site on the Campo dei Fiori. Beccaria's arguments against capital punishment, however, fell on deaf ears, and the firing squads were far busier under the Republic than the *boia* (or executioner) had been under the popes.

With the fall of the Republic in 1799, Roman law entered an even more confused phase. The cardinals whose job it was to run the papal system would not arrive back in the city until late June of 1800. In the meantime the Neapolitans were careful to preserve what they hoped would be a fiction, that is, that they were there merely to administer the capital until her legitimate sovereign, the pope, could assume his throne. Until that piously desired, but hopefully long-delayed, day came, the agents of the king of Naples would ensure tranquillity and work to free the state from "the plague of democracy." Diego Naselli, who arrived from Palermo on 10 October 1799, set up a new court to deal with subversives. This Giunta di Stato, or Governing Committee, was headed by Cavaliere Don Giacomo Giustiniani; Monsignor Giovanni Barberi, a distinguished jurist, served as *avvocato fiscale*, or public prosecutor, and three judges were appointed: Alessandro Tassoni, Giovanbattista Paradisi, and Francesco Maria Rufini.[23]

The Committee was somewhat hampered by the terms of the treaty by which they took control of Rome, which offered amnesty for supporters of the Republic. However, the amnesty applied only to acts carried out before the arrival of the Allies: stubborn adherence to the Republic, or opposition to the new state, could and did result in arrest for subversion.[24] Non-Romans without specific permission to remain in the state were ordered to leave, and passports were made available to them. Religious functions suspended under the Republic were reestablished, churches were reopened, and the Jews were ordered to return to the ghetto and to wear distinguishing marks when outside it (rules like these help account for Jewish sympathy for the Republic and the presence of many Jews in plots against the new state). Freedom of the press was limited by an edict of 21 October, since this freedom was considered to be "the most seductive and surest way to corrupt men's hearts and alienate them from their true rulers."[25]

Defense and cross-examinations were allowed before the special courts, which were to be conducted on the same basis as the traditional Roman courts. An ex-Jesuit, Agostino Valle, was appointed to head the defense team. Valle was an experienced and respected lawyer, and had formerly worked as assistant to Monsignor Altieri of the Rota Romana, the highest of the Roman appeals courts. By all accounts he and his team did a conscientious job, speaking out against the Committee or the provisional government whenever the attempts of these bodies to evade the treaty became too blatant.[26] Their acquittal rate was respectable; and in at least one case, that of Saverio Pediconi, Valle saved his convicted client's life by legal maneuvers and delaying tactics. The archives of the Governing Committee are far from complete, but they are substantial, consisting of twenty-four files subdivided into 263 fascicles, each of which contains procedural papers for one or more trials. The Committee handed down 559 sentences, as follows: two death sentences (one of these was later commuted); eleven sentences of imprisonment; 103 sentences of exile from the Roman state; 150 of internal exile, within the state but away from the immediate area of the city. In the other 293 cases prisoners were cautioned and released. It is difficult if not impossible to say how many were arrested: even those men and women brought before the Committee could have been arrested on orders from other tribunals or directly by the military. In some cases even the Committee could not figure out why a particular prisoner was in custody, and ordered his release.[27]

This is not surprising given the circumstances. People were often arrested after a petition to Naselli or the Committee from "a friend of the good cause"— Scarpia's *suddito fedele* or "faithful subject" (in Act II) comes to mind. Since the tendency was to arrest first and investigate afterwards, this arrest by petition could be, and no doubt often was, used for personal vendettas.

Twelve men were executed in the first six months of 1800, ten for banditry or desertion and two for political reasons. Only one of these men, Ottavio Cappelli, was sentenced by the Governing Committee. Cappelli, a revolutionary mystic and libertine and a friend of Cagliostro, had been in trouble in Rome long before the revolution. During the Republic he was notorious for hosting "angelic dances" where the participants reportedly cavorted nude. However it seems probable that Cappelli was executed not because he was a mystic and libertine but rather because he held a commission from the Russians and was suspected of being a spy for that Allied but by no means always friendly power.

Valle had his work cut out for him defending Cappelli. Because the accused man was from Siena his defense attorney argued that he was not a subject of the pope and so could not be accused of lèse-majesté (high treason) against him, but this argument was not accepted (and so presumably would not have helped Cavaradossi to explain away his Act II "Vittoria!" outburst either). He had a record: in 1795 he had been arrested by the Holy Office and sentenced to seven years in prison, but had then been pardoned by Pius VI, and exiled. He was arrested on charges arising after the treaty: ignoring the order for foreigners to leave Rome, breaking the terms of his exile by return-ing to the city, and having compromising papers and illegal weapons (*armi proibiti del primo grado*)—all charges that carried a potential death penalty. In the end, Valle lost the case and Cappelli was hanged in the Piazza Sant'An-gelo on 29 January 1800.

The other death sentence, handed down but not carried out, was against Saverio Pediconi, whose sentence was commuted (thanks to Valle's defense) to life imprisonment on 10 June 1800, one week before an Angelotti–Cavaradossi case would have arisen. There were others executed in Rome that year, such as Gregorio Silvestri (who was condemned by a military council, not by the civil authorities), and six men convicted of operating a particularly vicious robbery and murder gang, but only Cappelli, Pediconi, and Silvestri were condemned for overtly political offenses.

Most political cases were less dramatic, such as that of Count Alessandro Scotti, the lawyer Carlo Fea, his cousin Agostino Guerrini, and a German re-ferred to as "Giacomo Grund," all arrested in November 1799. Accused of treason, Fea was able to prove his innocence. Scotti was in more trouble since he had been arrested with incriminating letters; also a secret accusation was placed against him by the architect Giuseppe Valadier, and confirmed by Stanislao Tatti, to the effect that Scotti spread rumors that 16,000 French troops were approaching Rome to expel the Neapolitans. The other two ac-cused said they had nothing to do with politics. A letter from General Bour-card indicates that Fea was released, and that Guerrini was dismissed with a sentence of exile, as was Grund. The letter says nothing of Scotti, and he was still in the Castel Sant'Angelo in March of 1800.[28]

Throughout the spring of 1800 Naselli continued to assure his king that Rome was tranquil, while murders, thefts, and the ransacking of churches were the order of the day. Rumors and accusations reached the royal ear in Palermo. One letter charged that "the Jacobins daily break the laws with plots, alarming and seditious talk . . . and they are not punished but rejoice in their iniquity." The same writer lamented the laxity with which the laws were en-forced and the general apathy in political affairs.[29] The diarist Sala, among others, noted that "the French managed to make themselves obeyed, but it seems as if no one takes any notice of these Neapolitans!" One Andrea Guidi was arrested for complaining that the state was soft on Jacobins, rarely arresting them and letting them go even when arrested.[30] Palermo demanded an explanation from Naselli, who lamented that, while he knew that there were patriots in Rome, he was prevented by the treaty from dealing with them unless they committed new subversions.

Certainly the Roman republicans were less than terrified. Some, fearing the sort of wholesale repression that had occurred in Naples, had left Rome at the end of 1799 and traveled to Civitavecchia with the intention of leaving with the French. In that city they continued to dress "Jacobin style" (sporting the tricolor cockade) and called themselves the Republic in exile. Many did not leave the state but hung about waiting to see what would happen, and when they discovered that the repression was neither particularly severe nor particularly efficient, they decided to go back to keep an eye on their property, even at the risk of arrest.[31]

From Governor Naselli's point of view matters grew steadily worse as winter passed into spring of 1800. Insurrections and banditry in the countryside were added to the usual problems of shortages, Jacobin insolence, and general crime. Certainly there were enough problems in and around Rome in the late spring and early summer of 1800 to justify sending for a specialist, and according to Sardou that man was Baron Scarpia. In the play, Scarpia arrives in Rome only a few days before the action begins, coming from Naples where he has made his reputation as a "pitiless enforcer of the law." Here in Naples, and specifically in the bloody suppression of the Parthenopean Republic in 1799, we find the roots of the Scarpia character, along with a clear demonstration of the axiom that "bad history can tell us as much as good history." It is therefore important that we turn away from Rome and examine a city, and a series of events, that do not appear at all in the opera, though they are discussed ad nauseam in the play.

La Tosca resonates with echoes of the events in Naples in 1799. This is hardly surprising, given the way in which nineteenth-century popular history took the suppression of the Parthenopean Republic to its collective heart. The event was one of the best-known episodes from the Napoleonic period, and even now Emma, Lady Hamilton and her affair with Horatio, Lord Nelson is the stuff of myths as well as of novels.[32]

The cast of characters provided by history are indeed larger than life. In the role of The Complacent Husband is Sir William Hamilton, an elderly career diplomat who represented Great Britain at the court of Naples. Emma Lyon, as The Faithless Wife cum Devoted Mistress, was a young woman with a checkered past. She was also a woman with ambition, sensitivity, and talent, so much so that in 1791 Sir William married her. Introduced to the court, she utterly charmed the king and, above all, the queen, to whom she became a confidante and friend.[33] The third figure in the triangle, The Lover, was Admiral Horatio Nelson, Hero of the Nile and the diminutive savior of England. Between 1796 and 1799 Nelson sailed in and out of the strategically vital port of Naples, often returning missing body parts—an eye here, an arm there. Eventually he and the ambassador's wife became lovers, with the knowledge and at least the tacit consent of the ambassador.

This love triangle was played out against the background of the war, and of the Neapolitan court with its uncouth but energetic king, Ferdinand, and its controversial queen, Maria Carolina, daughter of Habsburg Empress Maria Theresa and sister of the unfortunate Marie Antoinette. Ferdinand was famous for his familiarity with and affection for the *lazzaroni*, the underclass of Naples, to the extent that he was said to catch fish and hawk them in the market, and eat macaroni with his hands in the royal box at the San Carlo. Although he was conscientious about siring a family (as the queen's seventeen pregnancies amply attest), he took little interest in the management of his state, leaving much of the business of policy to his council and, after the birth of an heir, to his wife.[34]

History has not treated Maria Carolina kindly, a fate she shares with other powerful women such as Catherine of Russia. Even now it is difficult to be objective about her. Enemies have described her as a mannish harridan; as stupid, vindictive, and hysterical; as the disastrous power behind the throne of her lumpish husband. Her defenders point to her strength of character and her skill in the game of power politics.[35]

Emma Hamilton and her influence at the court of Naples feature prominently in the Sardou play, though she never appears on stage. As Angelotti explains at length to Cavaradossi in Act I, the escaped prisoner's political troubles are rooted in his youthful affair with Emma Lyon, before she graduated to the status of kept woman and then wife. In fact, Lady Hamilton functions as a sort of offstage female Scarpia in the play, exacting political vengeance for a sexual rebuff.

When Napoleon invaded Italy in 1796 the English fleet both protected Naples and made it a target. The Kingdom of the Two Sicilies might have escaped occupation had its rulers behaved with some modicum of diplomatic sense. They did not. In 1798 King Ferdinand allowed himself to be tempted into a disastrous filibustering attack on Rome. The French not only expelled him and his troops, they pursued them and, while the court and their supporters fled to Palermo, Championnet's army occupied Naples. There they set up a puppet state, christening it with the Greek-style name of the Parthenopean Republic.[36] Like all of the revolutionary statelets, the Parthenopean Republic was supported only by a relatively small group made up of some members of the upper middle class and the liberal nobility and clergy. Grudging toleration was the best it could inspire in the people of the city, and the *lazzaroni* to a man loathed it as an alien imposition and yearned to be rid of it.

This attachment to the monarchy on the part of the *lazzaroni* has been the subject of much scorn by liberal historians who see lower-class hatred of the Republic as evidence of ignorance, superstition, and general wrong-mindedness. But while their rejection of the Republic may have been based to some degree on affection for their king, their politics had a great deal more to do with a hatred for modernizing liberals and their French protectors who were seen (quite accurately) as aliens who brought war, taxes, and destruction of the traditional prerogatives of the people. Republicans, devoted to a powerful central government, were the natural enemies of the sort of particularism beloved by the lower classes of Naples. Worse, the new rulers had the infuriating habit of denigrating old customs and beliefs, along with an insistence on holding the moral high ground that added insult to injury.

The Parthenopean Republic did not outlive the French occupation, and never effectively controlled much more territory than the city of Naples. Five months after the new state was established the course of the war drew the French north, and the French commander Macdonald marched his troops out of the city and left the Republic and its idealistic supporters to sink or swim. Irregular armies loyal to the king closed in from the land, and the English fleet commanded the harbor; the republicans scrambled to make terms of surrender.

The surrender terms provided that supporters of the Republic were to be allowed to withdraw from the city along with those French troops who had been left behind. This was a standard enough provision, and one that was routinely honored in eighteenth-century warfare. The king and queen of Naples, however, backed and encouraged by their trio of English friends, categorically refused to honor any such terms. The republicans were unceremoniously hauled off the ships they had already boarded. From the shelter of Nelson's flagship the Bourbon monarchs called for vengeance, and the police and court systems of Naples delivered it. Thousands were arrested and hundreds were executed in the public squares, while an uncounted number were unceremoniously butchered by the *lazzaroni*.

These killings became an important part of the Left vs. Right debates during the following two centuries. The martyrs of the Parthenopean Republic entered mythology: men like the aristocratic republican soldier Ettore Caraffa, who defiantly refused a blindfold and lay face-up on the headsman's block; women like Eleonora Fonseca Pimentel (see fig. 19) whose last words were quoted from Virgil, "Perhaps one day we shall rejoice to remember even

ELEONORA FONSECA PIMENTEL.

FIGURE 19. Eleonora Fonseca Pimentel, one of the idealistic middle-class liberals executed in Naples after the disastrous Parthenopean Republic. Author's collection

this."[37] But no story was more famous, or more heartrending, than that of Luisa Sanfelice Molina, whose story mirrors that of *La Tosca*. La Sanfelice was especially popular during the nineteenth century, when she was portrayed as a frail and foolish beauty, more sinned against than sinning, doomed for love. The story had everything the Victorians liked: romance, illicit sex punished, and (like Tosca) a politically naive woman entrapped in masculine snares through her own weakness, coming to a perfectly revolting end. In Luisa's case, the nervous executioner bungled the job and had to hack her head off with a knife; in Floria's, her plunge from the battlements would have smashed her body on the paving stones in the courtyard below.

La Sanfelice's troubles came about because she betrayed a conspiracy in which one of her lovers, a royalist, was involved, for fear that another lover, a republican, would be harmed if the plot succeeded. The royalist lover and his brother were executed. When the Republic fell the powerful family of the dead men worked hard to ensure that Louisa was condemned and executed for her treason.[38]

The whole disgraceful and grisly episode of the suppression of the Parthenopean Republic was made even more shocking by the fact that the victims, like Cavaradossi, were idealistic members of the upper and middle classes, neat, well-educated, modern, and for the most part young and good-looking. It is not at all surprising that parts of the Parthenopean affair emerged in the guise of a Sardou melodrama, and soon after, a Puccini opera. It is only surprising that the whole story of Tosca was not set in Naples. Certainly some of the more lurid details would make more sense there, such as the threat of torture, and the extraordinary powers of a relatively minor official like Scarpia. What is missing from a Neapolitan setting, however, is revealing: the overwhelming presence of the Roman Church. Nevertheless, a great deal of the story shows this inclination toward a Neapolitan setting. Tosca herself is given Neapolitan connections, having sung at the San Carlo, and making her debut in a Neapolitan opera, Paisiello's *Nina*. Like Emma, she is a favorite of Queen Maria Carolina.[39]

Angelotti, not very reasonably, is made a Neapolitan as well as a Roman, so that he can be among the partisans of the Parthenopean Republic, but above all so that he can run afoul of Lady Hamilton. Angelotti shows other traces of his Neapolitan origins, such as the curious parallels between him and the executed Neapolitan admiral Caracciolo, both discovered hiding in wells.

Scarpia's origins lie even farther to the south, and buried deeper in historico-mythology. The first mention of the chief of police in Sardou's play refers to him, not by name, but as "a Sicilian with the reputation as a pitiless enforcer of the law." This vague *sicilianità*, "Sicilianness," is central to the character. Sicily's reputation in the 1880s was even worse than the Mafia has made it now. War, depression, and the destruction of the vineyards had caused this once-wealthy island to hemorrhage people, who left their homes to seek work.[40] Consumers of French popular literature tended to see Sicily as a savage, pitiless land ruled by an arrogant feudal nobility, with an oppressed underclass that defended itself only by banditry and mutual brutality.

Sardou's villain embodies both that nobility, and that underclass. The aristocrat in Scarpia owes a great deal to Don Diego Naselli, commanding general and governor in occupied Rome in 1799–1800 (although Sardou, perhaps fearing lawsuits, was very careful to separate Scarpia from Naselli).[41] Naselli, a thoroughly blue-blooded descendant of a Lombard family that had moved to Sicily in the thirteenth century in the service of Frederick II, was viceroy of Sicily in 1820.[42]

The other side of Scarpia's lineage is to be found in the Neapolitan countryside where, as in the Roman *campagna*, insurgent bands harried republicans and French occupation forces alike with results very similar to those recorded by Goya a decade later in Spain. Most of the fighting was done by irregulars, with predictable results in terms of tales of roasted captives, cannibalism, and blood-drinking bandit chiefs. It is impossible, and perhaps not even useful, to disentangle the real from the symbolic atrocities.

The terms "Sicilian" and "bandit" were almost synonymous in the nineteenth-century tradition, and Sardou makes certain that his villain, unlike Naselli, has a strong whiff of the bandit about him. In one of his long Act I speeches, Angelotti describes the atrocities of these so-called bandit leaders:

> When the royal army returned [to Naples] I succeeded in escaping to Rome,
> while at Naples the patriots, my friends, were drawn and quartered, blinded,
> mutilated, burned alive by the Neapolitan rabble, who devoured their
> charred flesh, and in the countryside, tracked down by Holy Faith-ers in the
> pay of a Fra Diavolo or a Mammone, that monster who pierced the throats
> of his prisoners in order to drink their blood . . . (Angelotti to Cavaradossi,
> *La Tosca*, I, iii)

Sardou almost certainly found his villain's name among these irregular commanders who supported the king in Naples, though Angelotti never actually accuses Scarpia of being one of them. Gherardo Curci, nicknamed "Sciarpa", was one of several Bourbon irregulars who were ennobled for their efforts on behalf of the monarchy. Some of these were classic bandits while others appear to have been popular leaders at the village or provincial town level, typical of the leaders of peasant revolts in the early modern era.[43]

Curci, or Sciarpa—the nickname (meaning scarf or sash) seems to refer to an item of paramilitary clothing—features prominently in contemporary accounts of the fall of the Parthenopean Republic. Republican historian Vincenzo Cuoco considered him to be "one of the greatest and most lethal of the counter-revolutionaries." He was created a baron by Ferdinand IV in May of 1800, in recognition of his services to the kingdom, but his enemies portrayed him as a crude figure, wearing "a piece of pigskin badly attached with a string" for shoes, and exuding peasant cunning and religious hypocrisy. Nicola, a royalist who remained in Naples during the time of the Republic, mentions him in military bulletins, where Sciarpa appears with Michele Pezza, and both of them are described as competent commanders.

Michele Pezza, whose nom de guerre was Fra Diavolo or Brother Devil, was the most famous and probably the most characteristic of these bandit-hero-monsters. The nickname, clearly intended to be intimidating, includes the suggestion of religious perversion that Sardou and, to a greater extent, Puccini built into the Scarpia character.

Pezza was typical of leaders of the rural proletariat, born into a moderately prosperous family, relatively well educated, and capable of functioning in the wider world. He fought the French and the local Jacobins in the countryside around Naples; after the fall of the Republic he moved on to harass the enemy in the Roman *campagna*. There was certainly hostility between Pezza and the more conventional representatives of the Allies in Rome, and he was arrested by Bourcard and Naselli and held at the Castel Sant'Angelo on charges of looting. He either escaped or was freed by order of the king.[44]

Vincenzo Speziale shares a set of initials with Sardou's Baron Vitellio Scarpia.[45] A Sicilian like our baron, Speziale was a member of the Governing Committee (Giunta di Stato) set up in Naples to deal with the aftereffects of the Parthenopean Republic, much as the body of the same name was instituted in Rome. The composer Domenico Cimarosa was brought before Speziale, and acquitted. Like Fra Diavolo and the others, Speziale drew the fire of the anti-Bourbon historians of the early nineteenth century. Not only did he feature in their chronicles, he also made his way into fiction (as a villain in Cesare Riccardi's *The Restoration of 1799, or the Martyrs of Naples*) and song (in an irreverent "Calabrese Te Deum").[46]

Gaetano Mammone was another of the pro-Bourbon partisans, the one whose name attracted the nastiest of the war atrocity stories in a guerrilla campaign where there was no shortage of atrocities. He had the reputation, as Angelotti notes, of "piercing the throats of prisoners and drinking their blood." It is worth noting that the term *buveur de sang*, or drinker of blood, is a common French epithet, comparable to the adjective "blood-thirsty" in English.

Rome in the spring of 1800 may well have been a city in need of the services of a troubleshooter; it certainly did not need, and would not have tolerated, a "drinker of blood." Domestic violence and family tangles, then as now, made up much of the work of the police. The case of the baroness Gavotti is fairly typical, though the high rank of the participants made it noteworthy. In April of 1800, after a complicated bit of police work, the baroness was arrested for trying to poison her husband. This investigation was carried out by the real, as opposed to the fictional, head of the police in Rome: Giovanni Pietro, Cavaliere Guglielmi. She was taken to the Castel Sant'Angelo, but poisoning husbands (at least, by baronesses) seems to have been looked upon with a certain tolerance. After her trial she was sent to do her repenting in the relative comfort of an Ursuline convent.

Another case that unfolded at almost the same time as the events of *Tosca* shows the intimate interest that the state took in questions of marriage and social class. Don Peppe Buoncompagni, the second-born son of the Prince of Piombino, was arrested in April 1800 for contracting an illegal clandestine marriage. In an age of individualism such as ours it is difficult to imagine how seriously the old regime took questions of marriage, especially marriages of the nobility. In this case not only were the young man and his wife (the daughter of one of his servants) arrested, so were the witnesses to the wedding. During the trial it was argued that the woman had been Buoncompagni's mistress for some time, and they had two children. If he were determined to marry her, he could have easily done so under the Republic, when such a match would have been legal, but instead he had waited until the restoration and defied the law. This showed bad judgment. The couple were sentenced to five years each (he at the Castel Sant'Angelo, she in a convent), and the witnesses, who were presumably older and should have known better, were sentenced to ten years in prison. When the *duchino* ("dukelet") and his companions heard the harsh sentences they appealed to General Naselli. Naselli referred the case to the Council of War, which ruled that all the defendants should be released on condition that they go home and "say no more about the matter."[47]

The edicts posted on the walls of Rome that spring show that Cavaliere Guglielmi, the chief of the Roman Police, was busy with the prosaic nuts and bolts of police work.[48] From his offices in the Madama palace (now the seat of the Italian Senate) Guglielmi issued proclamations ordering the usual registration of foreigners in Rome. Guards at the city gates were to take careful note of the names and addresses of non-Romans coming into the city, and innkeepers—in 1800 as today—were ordered to provide police with lists of their guests and their travel documents. Detailed directions were posted explaining the procedure for applying for passports. The sbirri were, as usual, a problem; Guglielmi's papers include a booklet of instructions on how to keep the peace between them and the troops who acted as auxiliary police. Thirteen men were sent to the Castel Sant'Angelo in June 1800 on a variety of charges and sentences. Three forgers, apparently arrested as a group, were sentenced to detention "at the pleasure of the state" while a fourth man was sentenced to three years in prison for dealing in counterfeit money. Four were imprisoned for theft of one sort or another, with sentences of either one to five years, or "at the pleasure of the state." A recaptured escapee got three years. A murderer drew five years while a polygamist got the longest sentence of all: seven years.

In light of the fate that Sardou decreed for Floria Tosca, the most ironic edict issued by the head of the Roman police in June 1800 was a reissue of one of those civic regulations that appeared each year as the summer began. In a rather fussy tone the police chief lectured Romans on the need for giving good example and condemned the "impudence" of anyone, but most especially of women, who "bathe or swim in the Tiber"! [49]

As summer began it was finally clear that the pope, in the person of the newly elected Pius VII (Chiaramonti), would arrive to take possession of his capital city despite the best efforts of the Neapolitans. The question had been in some doubt, and it was only in June that Naselli finally received instructions from Palermo to turn the city over to the papal government. It was agreed that the commission of cardinal-legates would assume authority on 22 June (four days after the supposed death of Floria Tosca), and the pope himself would enter the city in triumph on 3 July. It might be reasonable to imagine that a "troubleshooter" like Scarpia could be sent from Palermo, where the court of Naples had moved in 1799 and from whence King Ferdinand stubbornly refused to budge. In the last few weeks of Allied rule there were surely a number of little problems that needed to be cleared up in Rome— matters that could be embarrassing once the pope had returned, such as, perhaps, the judicial murder of a former lover of Lady Hamilton's?

One of the few things we can say for certain about justice in Rome when the fictional Scarpia would have been in charge is that it was in transition and confusion. This was, after all, at least the fifth major upheaval in the administration of the city in a little over two years, and within days there would be yet another disruption with the imminent return of the pope. Citizens of Rome had gone from papal rule, to French rule, to a paper Republic that fell to Naples for a week or so, then returned only to collapse under an invasion force made up of Neapolitans, Austrians, English, Russians, and Turks. If chaos is fertile ground for injustice, a Scarpia would have had ample opportunity for skulduggery and high-handed defiance of the law. Despite the

treaty, and despite the public defender, it is not beyond the realm of possi-
bility that a matter involving an escape from prison could have been shunted
off as a simple routine police matter and left entirely in the hands of the chief
of police. Rome was on the point of being handed back to the pope; and a
resurgent France in the person of First Consul Bonaparte was on the point
of transforming Europe. Given this scenario, it is possible to imagine that
Scarpia, on hearing the news from Marengo, is astute enough to realize that
under cover of this stunning reversal he can get away with subverting the law
he has sworn to uphold.

$\mathcal{M}$idday, 17 June 1800

The curtain rises suddenly on the action of the opera. Three menacing chords seem to pursue a ragged man, Cesare Angelotti [see fig. 20], as he staggers into the deserted church of Sant'Andrea della Valle.

The opera grabs the listener by the throat in the first instant with three violent chords played triple forte by the entire orchestra: B-flat major, A-flat major, and E major (see ex. 6.1).[1]

Ex. 6.1. Scarpia/Tyranny (I, 1–3)

After a pause, the curtain rises as another motif is punched out, "extremely lively, with violence." This one, syncopated and suggesting breathless staggering, will be associated with Cesare Angelotti, the political prisoner whose escape sets the tragedy in motion (see ex. 6.2).

Ex. 6.2. Angelotti (I, 4–6)

Vivacissimo con violenza

ff (si alza il sipario)
(the curtain rises)

Even for those who know little or nothing about the plot of the opera, the effect of the three initial chords is profoundly unsettling. Bernard Keefe, following the usual practice of assigning the chords to the character Scarpia, comments that the music tells us more in six seconds about the personality of a sadistic psychopath than would six minutes of exposition.[2] With further study the chords become even stranger and more troublesome. Puccini indicated no key signature for them, and Burton has observed that "there is no diatonic collection that contains all three of these chords."[3] The Scarpia/Tyranny motif as heard at the beginning of the opera is a sequence of major chords on B♭, A♭, E, suggesting an incomplete whole-tone scale. Its implications will gradually be confirmed as the motif is ever more closely linked with the action of the opera.[4] To add to the effect, the interval outlined by the bass notes, B♭–E♮, is a diminished fifth—the infamous *diabolus in musica* of the Middle Ages that had become common musical currency by Puccini's time but still retained its restless, potentially chaotic suggestions.

Traditionally these three chords have been identified exclusively with Scarpia, but this attribution may be only part of the story. Puccini referred to them simply as the *motivo di prima intenzione*. Recent scholarship has suggested that they may play a vital role in the organization of the entire opera. The chords might more appropriately be identified both with Scarpia's evil, and the ambience that makes that evil possible: the Throne–Altar alliance. For this reason, I will refer to this as the Scarpia/Tyranny motif. From their first, dramatic appearance these chords tie the villain so closely to the Church, both as a location and an institution, that we might even reverse the attribution, and associate them with the oppressive power of the institutional Church as demonstrated in the person of Baron Scarpia. We first hear them immediately before the curtain rises—to reveal not a political or a military power base (the scenes of Act II and Act III respectively), but a church. And not just any church but a very specific one: Sant'Andrea della Valle, one of the great churches of the city (its dome is the largest after Saint Peter's), and like all great Roman

Figure 20. Hohenstein costume drawing for Angelotti, from the original production of *Tosca*, which for many years was the only production allowed under license from Ricordi. © Archivio Storico Casa Ricordi. Reproduced by permission

churches the seat of a Cardinal-Prince—an office that by its very nature combined religious and temporal power. The chords, and the musical structure that is built upon their bass notes, resonate through the entire opera. If they represent Scarpia, then he hovers over the entire drama, omniscient, sadistic, and inescapable.[5] Girardi has identified twenty-seven different occasions on which the chords or fragments of the chords are heard, not all of which seem directly related to the character of Scarpia.[6] They thunder in the very first sounds made by the orchestra. They spring out like a quickened heartbeat just before Cavaradossi snarls his denunciation of Scarpia as a "bigot, a satyr" (I, 769). They appear in a distorted version at Scarpia's death (II, 1028–29 and 1060–61). In the portrait of dawn that begins the last act, they are whispered, like a malevolent exhalation hovering over the sleeping city (III, 36). They even insinuate themselves into the shepherd's song (III, 59).

> *Angelotti, gasping out his relief, scrabbles to find the key to one of the chapels. He finds it, opens the grill, and hides himself. In Sardou's play, the escape took place on the previous evening, at sunset. In the opera, it is midday on 17 June 1800, and the church lies silent and empty in the noon heat.*

In the first weeks of June 1800 it was hot in Rome, but not unseasonably so. Francesco Luigi Gilii, forty-five-year-old priest and director of the Vatican observatory, habitually stuck an old letter into his pocket before climbing to the top of a tower in the Vatican palace where his instruments were measuring the condition of the atmosphere. Twice each day, between 6 and 7 in the morning and between 2 and 3 in the afternoon (modern or "French" time), he made the climb and, a dutiful son of both the Church and the Enlightenment, he observed and recorded this tiny sample of the laws of Nature and of Nature's God.[7]

Fr. Gilii's records tell us that temperatures ranged between 27 and 28 degrees Celsius, or in the middle 80s Fahrenheit. The days were calm and bright with the prevailing winds out of the southwest, but there was rain toward the middle of the month—typical Roman summer rain, a few heavy drops toward evening, or a brief downpour with lightning and thunder. The moon was waning, and on the night of Tuesday to Wednesday, 17 to 18 June—when the action of the opera and the play climaxes in the death of every major character—it was 24 percent illuminated (the following midnight it would be only 16 percent illuminated). The moon will be full *(luna piena)* only in Floria's imagination.[8]

The plot of *Tosca* begins with an escape from the Castel Sant'Angelo and ends with an execution and suicide there. Sardou's Angelotti tells us precisely what happens at the fortress on the day of his escape. At sunset on 16 June (the day had been bright and clear, and the night would be calm) a jailer glances nervously to the right and left, then slips into a cell with an armload of rough workmen's clothing. Inside he hastily unchains a prisoner, then slips out again leaving the door closed but unlocked. The jailer's name is Trebelli, and his precautions will be useless. Within eighteen hours his complicity in the escape will be discovered and his confession under torture will send the police hurrying to Sant'Andrea della Valle.

Despite its reputation, the Castel Sant'Angelo was far from impregnable. The swashbuckling goldsmith Benvenuto Cellini had escaped in the sixteenth century, breaking his leg in a jump from the lower wall. In 1800 the bandit captain Fra Diavolo walked out (probably with help from the highest quarters). During the French occupation of 1798–99 it had leaked like a sieve as soldiers imprisoned for desertion rubbed shoulders with rich men locked up until they disgorged the "contributions" demanded of them, and with the workmen who would, in Sardou's play, provide cover for Angelotti. These workmen had a massive job on their hands, repairing the damage that had been caused in June of 1795 when a powder magazine blew up. The shock of the blast broke windows all over Rome and rocked the Borgo district, causing a crack that is still visible in Michelangelo's Sistine ceiling fresco.[9] The fortress itself was almost gutted, and five years after the explosion attempts to repair the damage continued.

Although the fortress-prison had a (carefully cultivated) grim reputation, it operated in much the same way as did prisons all over the Western world at the time: there were levels of accommodation depending on the purse and status of the prisoner. Even if a newly arrived Scarpia were intent on making life difficult for him, the fictional Angelotti (like the historical Angelucci) was a rich man; we must assume that he had the luxury of his own cell, even if he was chained to the furniture.

The evening Angelus, Angelotti's signal for escape, sounds at half an hour after sunset, the first hour in Roman time.[10] The workers, rough men from the Trastevere district dressed in homespun woollen breeches and stockings and wide-sleeved shirts, leave the fortress in small groups under the not-so-watchful eye of the Neapolitan garrison, to whom one Roman no doubt looks a great deal like another.[11]

If Angelotti has nerves of steel he can simply walk directly across the Bridge of the Angel through the Piazza Sant'Angelo (see map), where executions are normally carried out. Only six weeks earlier, six men were hanged there for robbery and the murder of a priest. Because the crime included sacrilege their heads and arms were cut off and posted at the Angelica gate and the St. Sebastian gate, and their corpses burned.[12]

Once through the square Angelotti would not have to worry about avoiding street lights. Romans considered street lighting an imposition that threatened their civil liberties, and managed to resist it until well into the nineteenth century (see fig. 21). A few years earlier, the French traveler Charles de Brosses had written:

FIGURE 21. Rome did not approve of street lighting, but in times of crisis the night watch would patrol the streets, stopping people like this indignant citizen drawn by Giuseppe Barberi during the Roman Republic of 1798–99. Museo di Roma

We had to limit ourselves to one modest little candle fixed to one of the shafts [of our coach]. All around us, the Roman coaches were moving mysteriously in the night, groaning like souls in purgatory. Often a voice would call out in the profound silence, "Volti la lanterna!" ["turn the lantern away"] In other words, don't disturb whatever I'm up to. And everyone obeyed at once.[13]

Because of this custom Angelotti can move with some security, particularly since sunset is too early for the patrols to be out. Past the square he would enter a maze of narrow streets (demolished a century later to make way for the Corso Vittorio Emanuele) and find his way to the back door of the Theatine church of Sant'Andrea della Valle. Sant'Andrea is one of the most imposing of the Baroque churches, built between 1591 and 1665 on land that Costanza Piccolomini of Aragon, Duchess of Amalfi, gave to the Theatines in 1590. Their Roman church was built on the site of Pompey's theater, where Caesar died; in imperial Rome the area was a valley containing an artificial lake and canal where Nero held some of his most infamous orgies.

Sant'Andrea contains chapels dedicated to the great families associated with the church: the Barberini, the Strozzi, the Rucellai, the Ginetti-Lancellotti. In all, eight private chapels open off the nave. Unfortunately, none of them fits the description of the "Attavanti" (or Angelotti) chapel, since all are open to view on two or three sides. There is, however, one with a secret, or at least difficult to notice, refuge. The first chapel on the left from the main entrance, the Barberini chapel, conceals in the street wall a shallow little chamber separated from the chapel proper by an ironwork grill (see fig. 22).[14] This is the shrine to Saint Sebastian, marking the spot where Lucina, a pious Christian woman, found the entrance to the city's sewers that led her to the body of the martyr Sebastian, later buried outside the city walls in the catacomb that bears his name. Perhaps more useful as a refuge is the crypt of the Barberini family, accessible by way of a heavy grill set into the floor in front of the chapel altar. The Marquis de Sade admired this chapel. It is no doubt a coincidence that the only image of the Magdalene in the church is in this Barberini chapel. It is a statue rather than a painting, but she is a typical Magdalene, beautiful, penitent, and half-naked, with her breasts covered only by her hair and by a strategically placed cross.

As Angelotti disappears into the chapel a sacristan arrives, grumbling under his breath. This unhappy cleric has been assigned to assist the painter, who is working on a mural in the church, and he thoroughly disapproves of the man, his dirty brushes, his liberal politics, and his inappropriate models.

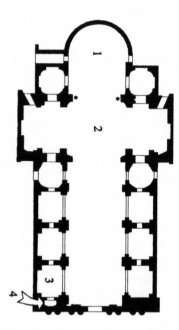

FIGURE 22. Floor plan of the church of Sant'Andrea della Valle, showing (1) the apse, (2) the nave, (3) the Barberini chapel, and (4) the shallow recess in that chapel that could serve as a hiding place. Ron and Jackie Juge.

Sardou's Sacristan, who bears the learned name of Eusebius, or Eusèbe, is almost exclusively a comic character. A superstitious, hair-splitting fool (the theological puzzle of whether or not the damned sleep in hell overwhelms his small mind), he spends the long first scene of the play trading gossip (i.e., exposition) with Cavaradossi's young servant; he gloats over the supposed royalist victory over Napoleon; he complains about the inadequacy of the painter's tips. In Puccini's hands the character becomes darker. He retains his "comic relief" identity, with a twitchy little motif, played "jokingly" (see ex. 6.3).

Ex. 6.3. Sacristan (I, 101–3)

A buffoon, he talks to people who aren't there, grumbles under his breath, stutters in terror when confronted. He represents ignorance and superstition, falling to his knees at the sound of the Angelus bell and coining absurd, vaguely ecclesiastical oaths like *Sante ampolle!* ("Holy oil jars!"). His darkest function is that of the willing (if inept) tool of oppression: he mutters about "Voltairean dogs" and "enemies of the Holy Government," and falls all over himself to implicate Cavaradossi when questioned by Scarpia.

By the time the opera's libretto reached its final draft the character had lost his name and become merely "Il Sagrestano," the Sacristan. In earlier drafts Puccini called him "Lo scaccino," the cleaner or janitor, and considering the menial tasks he is assigned in the opera, this is a much more appropriate title.[15] Certainly by Puccini's day, the job of sacristan had pretty much degenerated to that of a janitor. The word "cleaner," however, lacks the strong clerical overtones of the word "sacristan," and whether or not this was a conscious factor for Puccini and his librettists, it is as "the Sacristan" that we know him. Around this time the real sacristan of Sant'Andrea was a priest named Giacomo Sabatucci; his assistant, also ordained, was Giovanni Lafreddi.[16]

As our Sacristan shoos out the last of the worshipers he walks through the church to make sure that no criminal, no Jacobin intent on sacrilege, has remained behind. Six weeks before the action of the opera, in the real Rome, thieves broke into the nearby French church of Saint Louis and took a pyx, much of the altar silver, and the embroidery-encrusted altar cloths.

The ancient right of sanctuary, abolished under the Republic, was reintroduced in practice if not in law with the arrival of the Allies. When the police pursued a suspected Jacobin into Sant'Andrea on 23 February of 1800, the case had to be referred to Governor Naselli before he could be arrested.[17] In mid-June there may well be a collection of petty malefactors hanging about the church taking advantage of the refuge, and if there are they will have to be herded back into the living quarters adjacent to the church for the night. After locking the street doors the Sacristan would look up and down the short transept, climb the steps to the main altar, perhaps even move the altar cloths aside. He might or might not climb the long steps up to the pulpit halfway down the nave, but he would certainly rattle the grillwork barriers leading to the chapels to be sure they are locked. Candles were a major expense in running any church, and the Sacristan would not want them wasted; he snuffs them out as he checks each area, and finally takes the last of them away with him, through the high, vaulted, echoing space of the sacristy, and then back to the living quarters. The church, lit by starlight and the pale glow of the waning moon, settles into silence broken only by the sound of small, careful

movements and perhaps the low, grinding snip of scissors as a man cautiously, guided only by his fingers, cuts away at eight months' growth of hair
and beard.

Puccini's librettists, in order to give Angelotti a dramatic entrance and
tighten the action, have moved his escape from the perfectly reasonable time
of nightfall on 16 June, to the wildly improbable time of just before midday
on the 17th. This first plot change from the play to the opera foreshadows a
whole series of changes whose effect will be to heighten the drama, and de-
crease the realism of the plot.

As the action of the opera begins, the Sacristan has been up since matins.
He lives in the monastery behind the church, and his ordinary duties include
taking care of vestments, acting as altar server if no one else is available, su-
pervising the choir and the students, and collecting and accounting for the
small offerings for candles and the poor box. We know a fair amount about
these petty day-to-day finances of Sant'Andrea. The French commissioners
in 1798 inventoried the church with a view to confiscating its silver and paintings; in 1800 and 1801 the canons of the church filed for compensation for
losses during the French occupation; and the ordinary account books of the
church and monastery detail income and expenses for food, charity, vestments, candles, artists, and other calls on the community purse.[18] In June of
1800 the chapter of Sant'Andrea della Valle took in 169 scudi, 52 paoli, and
half a quattrino. Forty of these scudi came from interest on investments, and
about 32 from paying guests. Expenses exceeded income by about 12 scudi.
Almost half of the money went for food, about a third for candles, and the re-
mainder for clothing, medicines, and incidentals. Only nine scudi was paid
out on salaries in June, though in July and August the church paid artists
(probably decorators) as much as 30 scudi a month. The Cavaliere Cavaradossi, being a gentleman, is of course not on salary.[19]

*The Sacristan's greatest interest is the painter's untouched lunch
basket and especially the bottle of wine therein. Most stage directors (taking a note from Sardou, who gave the wine great
play) show him actually reaching for this when the midday
Angelus bell stops him.*

The Angelus is a very old Roman Catholic devotion that since the sixteenth century has been recited three times a day, early in the morning, at
midday, and at sunset (or since clock reforms in the nineteenth century, at
6 A.M., noon, and 6 P.M.). The prayer consists of three brief Latin couplets relating the angel Gabriel's annunciation to Mary of the news that she has been

chosen to bear the Christ, Mary's acceptance, and the subsequent incarnation of God as Jesus. Each couplet is normally separated by an Ave Maria (Hail Mary), but Puccini has not included these longer prayers.

In the opera the Angelus marks the first use of one of Puccini's favorite instruments of local color, church bells. Mahler, who despised Puccini's work in general and *Tosca* in particular, especially loathed these bells. Bells are used liberally throughout the first act ("a continual clangor," Mahler writes), and will play an even more critical role in the last act, signaling the dawn in the prelude, and finally ringing the fatal "fourth hour" of Cavaradossi's execution ("again mighty tintinnabulations").[20]

The soft tone of the bells (I, 186–87) brings the Sacristan to his knees, where he intones the prayer (the score directs that he begin "Andante religioso.") As he proceeds the dynamics gradually fade to triple piano, the tempo slows down before starting up again with a jerk—the sound of a man whose mind is wandering, whose "prayer" is merely the meaningless repetition of Latin syllables.

This scene does not exist in the play. While Puccini and his librettists shared Sardou's anti-clericalism, they understood the role of religion in Roman life much better than the Frenchman did, and made quite different, and more effective, use of liturgy and religiosity. At the very start of the opera we are presented with Angelotti at the feet of the Madonna (he is the first but by no means the last character to relate to her). Cavaradossi's entrance is defined by the Angelus. Seeing the Sacristan on his knees, he asks "What are you doing?" The fact that he does not recognize this most familiar of Catholic devotions would have sent a powerful message to Italian audiences in Puccini's day.

> *The painter enters and uncovers his work-in-progress, which includes a portrait of Mary Magdalene. The Sacristan recognizes the portrait's model as a frequent worshiper and is shocked by this most recent example of Cavaradossi's impiety, but the painter is delighted with himself and with his work. The mystery of art has allowed him to combine his lover, Floria Tosca, with this unknown blonde to create a single desirable woman. ["Recondita armonia"] The Sacristan sees only lust, and does not hesitate to say so.*

Before we look at the first aria, "Recondita armonia," it is worth pausing to examine the underlying structure of the opera in a series of parallels between Act I and Act III that caused Mosco Carner to call *Tosca* "one of the best-constructed operas in the repertory."[21] The first and last acts are a triumph of symmetry in which the last functions as a distorted reflection of the first. Each act begins, after the scene is set, with a tenor aria. (It is intriguing to note that despite the dramatic dominance of the baritone and the soprano characters, the tenor has what many consider the best arias.) "Recondita armonia," in Act I, shimmers with sunlit yearning; "E lucevan le stelle," in Act III, is deeply poignant music of the night. The frames of mind portrayed are dramatically different, but each is an expression of a value system and each has as its motivating force the painter's love for Tosca.

In both the first and third acts the tenor aria is followed by an extended love scene. Each of these scenes contains an arioso for the soprano which is less a set piece than a part of the action; neither is of the melodic caliber that would tempt singers to use it as a separate concert extract. Both are addressed directly to Cavaradossi. In the first, "Non la sospiri," Tosca looks forward to what she hopes will be a night of love-making; in the second, "Il tuo sangue e il mio amore," she recounts in a jumbled, half-crazed fashion the horror of that night as it actually transpired. Neither love scene is a duet proper, since the principals rarely sing together.

These scenes are very different but include common dramatic themes. In each the lovers are absorbed by their romantic hopes and dreams—hopes and dreams which in both cases are illusory. Tosca, the innocent, deluded victim, is bothered, even distracted, in both by whispers of uneasiness—in Act I by her jealousy, in Act III by her preoccupation about making the execution seem convincing—but in both cases she misses the real danger. Attavanti, and the firing squad, are indeed deadly, but not in the ways that she imagines. Cavaradossi in both cases knows more than he admits. In Act I he is constantly aware of the hidden Angelotti; in Act III the question of what he knows or does not know is unresolvable, but he is arguably aware of the danger of the coming execution and at least suspects that he may not survive it. The lovers reverse roles between the two scenes. In Act I Tosca wants to talk about love while Cavaradossi wants to get back to the political reality (Angelotti); in Act III she returns again and again to the political reality (the execution), while he wants to talk only about love.

Finally, both acts (in fact, all three acts) conclude with a coup de théâtre involving the Church and the chief of police. In the Act I finale Scarpia lays his plans against the backdrop of religious ceremony; in Act III, with St. Peter's dome dominating the brightening skyline, those plans are completed, though not in the way that Scarpia had foreseen.

According to Sardou, who was meticulous in his stage directions, Cavaradossi is working on a painting (*toile*, literally, "canvas") titled "The Resurrection of Lazarus," a scene which could include in its cast of characters Martha and Mary of Bethany, the sisters of the resurrected man.[22] The operatic stage directions refer to Cavaradossi's work simply as a *quadro*, or picture, showing "a Mary Magdalene with large blue eyes and a great fall of golden hair." In both the play and the opera Mario refers to her as "the Magdalene." It was (and is) common to identify Mary of Bethany with Mary Magdalene, and both of these with the unnamed penitent who anointed Jesus' feet and dried them with her hair.[23] The Magdalene was a popular saint in the early modern period (see fig. 23). She was the patron of reformed prostitutes and thus represented an important form of charitable activity, in aid and shelter for these women; she also gave painters the opportunity for works that ranged from the pin-up to soft porn. Floria's instinctive reaction to the woman in the painting could reflect the burden of meaning that such a subject traditionally carried, plus a more personal awareness of what was likely to be in the back (or forefront) of this particular painter's mind.

If Mario is telling Floria the truth, he sketched a pretty stranger the day before and this morning transferred the face to the mural. Now he is ready to start work on the drapery of her robes. With this in mind, and neglecting to say anything to the Sacristan, he has wandered away toward the ghetto (a short walk from Sant'Andrea) in search of a length of fabric with which to experiment.[24] The Jewish section of Rome is one of the oldest in the world, dating at least to Imperial times and boasting such famous residents as Saints Peter and Paul. It was enclosed behind a wall during the rigors of the Reformation in the middle of the sixteenth century, and remained isolated until 1870; the walls were finally demolished in 1887. During the eighteenth century the main gate of the ghetto was normally open but it could be closed and locked in times of crisis, either to keep the Jews in, or to keep hostile Christians out.

When Mario returns to the church in time for his Act I entrance, the Sacristan's talk of the "unknown woman" draws his attention back to the face of the Magdalene. He calls for the palette and works rapidly for a few moments with the newly cleaned brushes. Then he takes a miniature of Floria from his vest pocket (see fig. 24).

"Recondita armonia" begins with two flutes moving in fourths and fifths, suggesting light, rapid brush strokes. The Attavanti motif (see ex. 6.4) blends

Ex. 6.4. Attavanti (I, 266–69)

Cavaradossi

e te bel-ta - de i - gno - - ta,_____

FIGURE 23. Mary Magdalene was a favorite subject for painters long before Cavaradossi incorporated her into his mural. This one is by Tintoretto, and includes the usual large, expressive eyes, and bright hair that serves as the only covering for her naked body. Musei Capitolini, Rome. Alinari/Art Resource

FIGURE 24. A miniature of the sort that Cavaradossi might carry. This dark-eyed beauty is Christine Boyer, painted by Jean-Baptiste Isabey. Museo Napoleonico, Rome

with a musical symbol for Tosca (ex. 6.5), providing the "recondite harmony" implied by the text.[25] The aria is a celebration of erotic love, like its Act III parallel "spiritualized" to point toward a deeper meaning—in this case, the mysterious capacity of Art (the initial capital is essential) to blend specific individual beauties into a transcendent ideal. This exaltation of feminine beauty is paralleled by the sanctimonious disapproval of the mean-spirited and suspicious Sacristan, who keeps up a running commentary. Faith and Art are two rival systems for finding meaning in life, and we are left in no doubt about which one Puccini approves.

Ex. 6.5. Tosca (I, 411–14)

(Tosca entra con una specie di violenza, guardando intorno sospettosa)
(Tosca enters impetuously, looking suspiciously about her)

Andantino sostenuto
dolcissimo e con tutta l'espressione

The aria ends on a high B♭, with a ringing declaration of the painter's un-diluted devotion to his mistress, the dark-haired, dark-eyed singer. But, as Roger Parker has pointed out, the music that follows is a motif associated with the Marchesa Attavanti and with love.[26] Should we conclude that Cavara-dossi does indeed fancy the blonde? Certainly there are hints of amatory am-biguity in the earlier versions of the libretto. At one point the Sacristan's mut-tering included the following:

> *e sono più di una! Or l'altra verrà,*
> *quella di tutti i dì, quella de' fiori*

[And there are more than one! Now the other will come,
the everyday one, the one with the flowers][27]

There is considerable confusion about whether or not the painter knows the identity of his model. In the play, where Cavaradossi and Angelotti are strangers to one another, there is no ambiguity about the painter's relation-ship with his involuntary model. He knows perfectly well who she is, though he does claim to have seen her only once, "by accident." In the opera libretto, where the two men have been made old friends, Angelotti's sister becomes an annoying loose end. Mario refers to her, even when talking to himself, as an "unknown beauty" *(beltade ignota)*. Even the Sacristan, a professional busy-body employed in the church where her family chapel is located, calls her "that stranger" *(quell'ignota)*. And yet when Tosca recognizes the woman in the portrait as the Marchesa Attavanti, Mario (who has not yet had his conversation with Angelotti) laughs and congratulates her on getting it right *(Brava!)*. At one point in the opera's evolution the librettists resorted to stage directions to suggest that Mario recognizes her at the same time that he recognizes Angelotti (see below). In any case it is interesting to note that Mario is lying when he tells Floria that he saw her only "yesterday, but it was pure chance" *(la vidi ieri, ma fu puro caso)*: we know from the Sacristan that she has been coming to the church for several days *(ai dì passati)*.

This Act I aria shows us what kind of man Cavaradossi is; this is the point from which he changes. He has the overwhelming egoism of a young man for whom everything is going well, and his music here is a mixture of confidence, unself-conscious paganism, and sensuality (in the precise definition of focus on and understanding through the senses). He is certainly very much in love with Tosca, or at least with the Tosca he perceives. But at this point in the opera he is so little aware of the real woman who needs him to love only her, that it does not occur to him that she might object to being "confounded" with this very different woman. He can blend the two and call it Art—which it is, but it is also wanting to have his cake and eat it too. There is, in fact, a little infidelity here; a very little one, but nonetheless real, and Floria will sense it unerringly.

The Sacristan takes this opportunity for a thorough if sotto voce denunciation of the "Voltairean dogs," enemies of the Holy State, as represented by the sensualist painter and his all-too-obvious relish for "these skirts who set themselves up as rivals to the Madonna, and give off a whiff of Hell." While he mutters, he prepares the colors, grinding the solid pigments to the finest possible powder (tube paints were not in common use until almost the middle of the nineteenth century.)

The Sacristan completes his task and his tirade, ostentatiously making the sign of the cross with something of the air of a man repelling vampires. "Your Excellency, I'm going." The painter merely waves him away with, "Do what you like." He tries again: "The basket is untouched, are you doing penance?" That barb too fails to provoke a response. But his injunction to lock the door succeeds in exasperating the painter: "Go away!" And the Sacristan, pleased with his work of irritating the infidel, chuckles, "I'm going!"

The Sacristan has no sooner left than Angelotti emerges from his hiding place, recognizes the painter, and is in turn recog-

nized as a Consul of the late Roman Republic. Cavaradossi of-
fers to help with the escape but they are interrupted by Tosca's
voice calling for Mario. Angelotti staggers with exhaustion and
hunger; Mario presses the basket filled with food and a bottle
of wine on him, and hustles him back into his refuge.

Sardou makes it clear that Angelotti does not know Cavaradossi and decides to throw himself on his mercy only after overhearing the Sacristan and
the painter's apprentice discuss Cavaradossi's pro-French sympathies. The
fact that the men are strangers of course facilitates their long and tedious exchange of biographies in which we learn everything but the name of Lady
Hamilton's dog. Puccini's librettists, in an attempt to compress the action
and motivation, and also perhaps to personalize it, made them old friends.
Angelotti greets Cavaradossi joyfully, though it takes the painter a little
longer to recognize Angelotti.

One of the drafts for the libretto, with minute attention to motivation,
outlines Cavaradossi's train of thought when he sees the intruder. Angelotti
says, sadly, "Prison changed me so much, then!" (see fig. 25). Mario, puzzled,
repeats, "Prison!" Then he understands: a glance at the woman in the painting, then back at the man in front of him, and he recognizes both of them at
once.[28]

Mario runs to lock the door of the church, then wholeheartedly and without hesitation asks what he can do to help. The two are plunged into a male
world of whispered plots in darkened rooms; Floria Tosca's voice cuts
through this like sunlight—and as welcome as sunlight to a pair of moles.

Theater people work late hours (in the play Mario offers to come and
wake Floria up at midday *[midi]* the next day). It is not at all clear what
Tosca is doing at the church in the middle of the day. She may be coming
from a rehearsal, or she may intend to go to one later: in an early version of
the libretto she says that Paisiello is waiting for her to rehearse.[29] If she has
come with the idea of sharing her lover's lunch and then going to work later
in the afternoon, she is understandably annoyed when he chases her away!

If she is coming not from the theater but from her home, she could be
coming from the Palazzo Venezia. As a famous artist and a native of an important city in the Veneto, Floria Tosca might well be given apartments in the
diplomatic headquarters of the Venetian state in Rome. Venice became an
Austrian possession in 1797 and the embassy also became the property of the
Empire (it would remain the Austrian embassy until just before World War II).
But this change of ownership, while critical to the creation of an Italian state
in the nineteenth century, would have had little effect on Floria Tosca: she

FIGURE 25. Cavaradossi and Angelotti, as shown in one of the many series of post-cards made to illustrate the action of the opera. Dr. Girvice Archer

FIGURE 26. Claudia Muzio, one of the great early Toscas, in a scene from the first act. Dr. Girvice Archer

would simply have gone from being a loyal subject of the Most Serene Republic to being an equally loyal subject of the Holy Roman Emperor Francis II.

Both the Palazzo Venezia and the Argentina theater are relatively close to Sant'Andrea (see map). Whether Tosca has been rehearsing or has come from her apartments, she has been hurrying and then standing on the church steps in the sun; it is mid-June and she is probably perspiring so that her dress clings. In both the play and the opera she enters with a great bundle of flowers that she has brought for the Madonna (see fig. 26). This is a typically Roman gesture and one that continues to be common to this day, when the outdoor markets are filled with brilliant and relatively inexpensive flowers, both locally grown and imported. Today the largest of these markets in the center of the city is in the Campo dei Fiori, the fruit and vegetable market that caters to tourists, housewives, small shopkeepers, and opera singers hurrying to midday assignations. Floria, who likes the stimulation of conflict, would love the jostle and the bargaining and the shouting of the Campo. Surely she never paid the asking price for anything. Late that night, numb from the horror of what she has seen and frantic for her lover's safety, she will still have the presence of mind to demand, "How much?" And not even the chief of police will get the price he expects for the commodity he has for sale.

Floria could have picked up her flowers in the Campo, or she could have selected them from any of the vendors along the streets: in mid-June everything would be in season, great armloads of zinnias and roses for a few pennies.

Floria's suspicions have been aroused by the locked door and she questions her lover sharply. Placated by his response, she arranges her flowers at the statue of the Madonna and then sets about planning a rendezvous for that night.

Tosca and Cavaradossi cannot have known one another for long; this helps explain both the passion of their relationship, and the fact that they do not trust one another (it does not occur to him to tell her the truth about Angelotti, and she immediately suspects the worst of him at Scarpia's insinuations). As soon as Mario opens the door she bursts in, annoyed and suspicious. This is hardly irrational when we remember that she probably does overhear "whispers and furtive movements," just as she says; Sardou's hero answers ingenuously, "I was whistling, you heard me whistle"; the operatic Mario insists that he was talking only to her. But unless Cavaradossi is an experienced and talented liar, Tosca can no doubt tell that he is hiding something.

Tosca enters to the sound of rippling triplets over a sustained melodic line, played "very sweetly" and "with all possible expression" in the strings (see above, ex. 6.5). But the stage directions in the score seem to contradict this amorous exultation, telling us that she comes in "with a sort of violence"; in an early version of the libretto she was described as searching like a hunter for her prey.[30] Does this musical motif, as Keefe, Schuller, and Burton have suggested, represent the heroine's piety, the gentler side of her nature?[31] The same music recurs in Act II when she refers to her "sincere faith." It is music for entering the church, for decking the Madonna with flowers, for sincere faith; but it is also music that can accompany "violent" and "suspicious" actions inspired by jealous rage. The motif may be seen not only as a comment on the gentleness of her character, but also a reference to the unregulated passion of her love for Cavaradossi, which dooms them both.

Mario distracts her by trying to kiss her, and she immediately remembers the Madonna (does his embrace threaten to crush the flowers?) and pulls away. In an early draft of the libretto Mario, the indulgent lover and unbeliever, laughs and nods at a column which stands between himself and the statue of the Virgin, and says, "She can't see us here." In reviews of the Sardou play as it was performed at the end of the nineteenth century, the scene between the lovers in this act is described as a comic scene, involving a great deal of teasing, lounging, and love-making on the scaffolding.[32] Puccini has raised the erotic and emotional temperature of the scene so that in most productions of the opera little comedy remains.

Floria has a more personal relationship with the Madonna than any of the other characters has, but each character in the opera in turn at least acknowledges her. Angelotti, the first person on the stage, turns to her for the key to safety. The Sacristan grumbles to her when no one else will listen to him, and kneels to recite the Angelus at her feet. Even Cavaradossi acknowledges her authority, ironically giving up his rights to kiss his mistress. Scarpia, although he does not mention the Madonna directly, takes holy water from the stoup by her statue and offers it to Floria, in a finely balanced piece of hypocrisy and lust.

> *Mario, preoccupied with the escaped prisoner, is at first uninterested in her plans and then, after her enthusiastic description of love-making under the stars* ["**Non la sospiri la nostra casetta**"], *responds with appropriate ardor. Floria recognizes the unfinished Mary Magdalene as a portrait of the Marchesa Attavanti, but Mario succeeds in calming her jealous suspicion and after more passionate reassurances from him she leaves.*

Floria pays her respects to the Madonna (the motif of her entrance again underscores her piety), and then turns to other pleasures. "Now stop that," she directs, "and listen"; and she begins to issue instructions for the evening.

Mario raises his head to look at her, but it's a blank look, like that of a stranger: "Tonight?" (The motif of Angelotti's escape tells us where his mind is.) She doesn't notice at first, her mind is too full of the promise of the night, the two of them alone, him making love to her. When she realizes that he is not responding she is hurt: "You say it badly." She begins in a playful tone: "Don't you yearn for our little house . . . ?" A glance assures her that she has caught his imagination and the song quickly becomes happy and frankly sensuous, describing warm scented nights in a private, starlit place, the place and the stars that he will remember while he is waiting to die, breaking off when he thinks of her naked body because he can't bear to remember any more.

A little teasing and a lot of kissing, and things seem to be back to normal. Then he does it again: "Now leave me to work." A suggestion of the Scarpia/ Tyranny motif (I, 516) tell us what is really pressing him, but for Tosca the effect is that of a slap across the face, and when she sees the painting she turns all of her frustrated anger on that. Even when Cavaradossi eases her away she continues to stare at the eyes, knowing that there is something terribly wrong with them but not knowing just what it is. The painting is not nearly so important to Sardou, who merely uses it as a device to catch Scarpia's attention and to give Floria a chance to pout.[33]

The interrupted love scene resumes. In a broadly lyrical phrase that will come to be identified with Cavaradossi's love (ex. 6.6) he dismisses her fears

Ex. 6.6. Cavaradossi's Love (I, 641–44)

about the blue eyes of the portrait, assuring her that no eyes in the world could compare with hers. He is expertly and enthusiastically charming, and a submissive Floria dissolves into his arms. An 1898 set of working papers includes the following duet sketched out in Illica's hand:[34]

Tosca	Cav: *(holding her close)*
Yes, it is agony	How I love you
that torments me	all on fire
and deceives me!	with an offense
I think, I cry out,	you've imagined!
I fly . . . and then	(. . . in the air?)
at only one	You come in, you cry out,
word from you	then . . . you smile

I laugh at myself	and your harm
and in a kiss	you change to kisses
I believe and . . .	your anger and . . .
	(kisses her on the mouth so that her
	words are mingled with a sigh)
and I am silent!	and you are silent!

Only traces of this submissive Tosca, bending to the will of her dominant lover, survive in the text. At the climax of the duet as it now stands she pleads with him to go on—as in the last act he will ask her to go on talking—and he responds with a motif simply identified as "Love," a motif that will recur in the last act as she hurries toward him (I, 641 and III, 214) (see ex. 6.7).

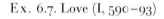

Ex. 6.7. Love (I, 590–93)

Andante passionale
Cavaradossi
con grande espressione

Mia vi - ta, a-man-te in - quie - ta, di - rò sem - pre:"Flo - ria, t'a - mo!"

The stage directions in the working papers for the libretto describe Mario as leaning back against the scaffolding at this point, pulling her to him, and starting to undo her hair. The dialogue in the draft makes this scene altogether more physical than the relatively chaste version that survives. Floria says that she belongs to him ("sono la tua cosa"); Mario strokes her hair "voluptuously" and speaks about "freeing the ocean waves of your hair," and "plunging into your eyes and dying there": all frankly erotic late nineteenth-century code-words. (Here Puccini has noted, "Più caldo che . . ." Warmer than . . .")[35] With a little gasp and a guilty look at the Madonna, Floria pulls away. "My God," she says, "what a sin!" There is no reason to assume that she is refer-ring simply to her mussed hair. (There is no parallel to this scene in the play—Puccini and his librettists took both sex and religion much more seri-ously than did Sardou.) This time when Mario tells her to go, she obeys, paus-ing only to tell him that he can work until nightfall, but no woman of what-ever description is to keep him company, and ending with a repetition of her demand/request that the color of the Magdalene's eyes be changed to black ("Ma falle gli occhi neri!")

This love scene seems to have caused no end of trouble to the librettists. In his 1995 edition of the vocal score Roger Parker notes numerous changes in the text as late as the 1900 printed edition of the full score.[36] Among the more interesting changes from the point of view of characterization is one which occurs at I, 637. As it is performed today, Tosca's words are "Say it again, the word that consoles, say it again" *(dilla ancora la parola che consola, dilla ancora)*; in the first printed edition of the vocal score, the words were "I am vanquished, I abandon my life to you" *(Vinta sono, la mia vita t'abbandono)*. Again (I, 610), where Floria now says, "[how well you know] . . . the art of making yourself loved" *(l'arte di farti amare)*, in the autograph score the phrase was "the art of entering me, in [my] heart" *(l'arte d'entrarmi in core)*, a phrase that moves past the suggestive and comes very close to being physically graphic.[37] "Più caldo," indeed.

> *As soon as Tosca is gone the two men discuss Angelotti's escape and he prepares to leave, bringing with him the disguise his sister provided but inadvertently leaving behind a fan marked with the Attavanti crest.*[38] *A cannon shot announces that his escape has been discovered and they hurry out together.*

When Mario returns from locking the door behind his mistress he is once again filled with conspiratorial enthusiasm. Tosca, he tells Angelotti, is a good girl but a believer who keeps nothing hidden from her confessor. So he has told her nothing. This is so obvious a course of action that Angelotti makes no comment at all. Instead the fugitive, who has meanwhile eaten all of the food and drunk the wine (we know this because the Sacristan will later find the basket empty), loosens up enough to discuss his precious sister. Sardou tells us that as part of the plan she has left Rome and waits in the nearby hill town of Frascati. If all goes according to schedule Angelotti will join her there and together they will consider what to do next. Perhaps he will remain at Frascati behind high walls in a suburban villa. Or he may leave the state, traveling toward Naples and family properties there; or go north toward Tuscany, where the Attavanti have lands; or try to reach the French in the north; or perhaps go to the coast at Civitavecchia and then, defying the dangers of the English fleet, cross to the French-held island of Corsica. In any case his beautiful sister will stay away from Rome so long as there is the slightest danger from the vile Scarpia.

Mario denounces Scarpia as a bigot, a satyr who uses the confessor and the executioner for his own lascivious ends, while the orchestra, echoing the text, sounds the Scarpia/Tyranny chords that again tie the chief of police to the institutional Church. Mutual accusations of moral turpitude were common eighteenth-century political currency. In the play Scarpia reverses the accusation in his conversation with Floria, telling her that she should beware of believing in a man who himself believes in nothing: "atheist in religion," he warns her, "atheist in love."[39]

Inspired by his own denunciation of the evil chief of police, Mario works himself up to a pledge to save his friend even at the cost of his own life. This has an authentic neoclassical ring to it, and in the opera the vocal line rises to a high B♭ in a very Italianate display of intensity. This is another instance of Puccini's librettists inserting a scene that is not found in the play. Sardou's cool hero makes a joke of helping Angelotti, lightly claiming, "I have an adventurous streak, things like this amuse me," and discounting the danger to his own life by saying that it is no more than anyone would do, comparable to jumping into a river to save someone from drowning.[40]

On a more practical level, Mario recognizes the urgency of getting the escaped prisoner away from a public place like the church. Now that the streets are deserted during the heat of the day, he advises Angelotti to slip out of the chapel into a nearby orchard whose walls are in disrepair, then by way of a cane-break cross several fields to "a villa of mine." Sardou describes the villa in great detail, and the third act of the play is set there. Puccini and his librettists have cut out almost all of this talk, on the grounds that the two men are already acquainted. ("I know it," Angelotti replies when the villa is mentioned.) The working papers, however, suggest that the librettists were not comfortable with this shorthand, as they made curiously extensive efforts to describe the refuge and, even more oddly, to describe the key to the villa. In the draft libretto Mario spends several lines telling Angelotti how to get down the well, and insists on making it clear that there is water at the bottom so that any searcher who drops a stone into it will be fooled into thinking that it is a well and nothing more.[41] Further, he tells him that the hole in the well shaft is in fact an opening into an undiscovered catacomb. (Since the villa is within the ancient city walls this is highly unlikely: the catacombs are burial chambers, and burials were allowed only outside the walls.)

The key to the villa, we are told, is small and finely engraved and kept on an elegant gold chain. This suggests that the villa is very important to both of the lovers, so important that Cavaradossi has had an expensive key made which he keeps on a special chain. His giving it to Angelotti then becomes a significant symbolic act, almost an act of betrayal.

No sooner has Angelotti been given the key than we hear a cannon shot, which Cavaradossi immediately interprets as the signal to close the city gates. As we will see later, Scarpia is annoyed by this slip-up. Whether or not a single cannon shot from the fortress was the appropriate signal, it was certainly possible to close the gates in 1800, though it would have required a major effort: Rome had twenty gates, "preserved and in good repair," set into fifteen and a half miles of walls.[42] And while walls were no longer as reliable a defense as they had once been, they maintained the integrity of the city and the gates were used as customs posts as well as for military checkpoints.

In both the play and the opera the sound of the cannon is meant to convey to characters and audience alike the image of teams of efficient secret police springing into action. This faith in early modern policing is probably misplaced. Brutal efficiency of the kind demonstrated by Scarpia was an invention of the Napoleonic period, and while this sort of precision may have existed in nineteenth-century Vienna or Paris, this was never true of Rome. There were certainly hordes of police spies and informers, but we need only remember the miserable state of the sbirri to doubt their infallibility. Cavaliere Guglielmi as the (real) chief of Roman police did his best, and solved some impressive cases, but clockwork inexorability was not the style of the day.

The cannon shot is followed in the opera, logically enough, by the music that accompanied Angelotti's first entrance. But immediately on its heels, as the two conspirators hurry out, comes not the Scarpia/Tyranny chords but rather a flurry of the Sacristan's music, rising to fortissimo *(più crescendo ancora ed incalzando)*. The Sacristan himself tumbles in, breathless, having just barely missed the two men (I, 859). Charles Osborne sees this as incongruous.[43] But given the anti-clerical assumptions of Puccini's Italy there is nothing at all incongruous in the image of a fleeing, terrified victim of the Church-State harried by a silly, malicious buffoon, like a stag set upon by dogs.

The Sacristan returns with news from Marengo. Disappointed at not finding the painter there (he had counted on annoying him with the bulletin), he assembles the excited choir singers and shares the news with them, telling them to prepare for the Te Deum that has been ordered.

This Te Deum is negligible in the play, where Act I ends with Scarpia merely directing his men to join the prayers giving thanks for victory. He does not speculate on the possibilities offered by Tosca's involvement until much later in the play. Puccini, however, ends this act with a spectacular scene built around the liturgical set piece. The librettists begin to build that closing scene here, at the Sacristan's entrance, with specific directions about the crowd of people summoned by the Sacristan's clapped hands. These are "clerics and altar boys, confraternity members, students, and singers of the chapel choir." The working papers add "preti scagnozzi" (down-at-the-heels hacks of priests), which Girardi sees as evidence of Illica's fervent anti-clericalism.[44] The disparaging reference to priests was deleted, as was the specific song this motley crew was supposed to be singing: a French revolutionary ditty called

the *Carmagnole* (which in fact Romans did sing to make fun of local Jacobins). The choir would certainly have been delighted at the news of an extra
service with extra pay. Musicians' pay in the balance books of Sant'Andrea,
as elsewhere, was generally a scudo per month, but for exceptional occasions
(such as the Te Deum) they could earn another scudo, doubling their income
with a single service (as the chorus exclaims, "doppio soldo!"; fig. 27).[45] This
rate of pay seems to have been fairly standard. For example, in the first years
of the eighteenth century the Roman church of San Luigi dei Francesi kept a
small professional choir and paid them roughly one to one and a half scudi
for a special-occasion Mass such as the feast day of their titular saint.

It is difficult to compare old regime salaries with modern ones, since they
were complex affairs made up of cash, kind, tips, and perquisites apportioned
on an elaborate and often unwritten scale. Musicians' pay was especially peculiar, and partial pay was common, so "double pay" would have been very
welcome. The band of the Castel Sant'Angelo, a group consisting of trumpet-
ers, pipers, and drummers, worked on a pay scale that ranged from nothing
through quarter pay and half pay, up to a full pay, depending on seniority
and the importance of the festival for which the musicians were playing. In
1797 the seven musicians on full pay were paid 6.50 scudi a month, plus a
gratuity of 42 scudi which they divided among themselves on each of four
special feasts (the anniversary of the pope's coronation, Easter, the feast
of Saints Peter and Paul, and Christmas) for an average monthly pay of
8.50 scudi.[46] When the new pope arrived in July of 1800 the superannuated
musicians at the fortress were pensioned off at "half the normal honorarium."

*Scarpia arrives with several agents, on the trail of the escaped
prisoner. The terrified choir flee and the Sacristan leads the police to the Attavanti chapel. They search and find the lunch basket and a fan. Scarpia recognizes the portrait of the Marchesa
Attavanti and, seeing Tosca, forms a plan to trick her into leading him to her lover.*

Puccini and his librettists entertained a number of ideas about the words
to accompany Scarpia's entrance, some of them surprising, given those three
shattering chords that accompany him. In one early version Scarpia comments, "Very good, dancing in church. A nice sort of respect!"[47] Although
there is no similar scene in the Sardou play it is the sort of entrance the French
Scarpia might make, slyly appearing out of nowhere with a deceptively soft,
ironic comment with murderous undertones. Puccini's villainous baron
brooks no opposition or delay. "A bacchanal in church! Very respectful!" He
dismisses the choir, stops the cowering Sacristan in his tracks, and sets the

FIGURE 27. "Doppio soldo! Te Deum! Gloria!" The choir singers celebrate the prospect of "double pay" as the Sacristan tries in vain to control them. Metlikovitz watercolor. © Archivio Storico Casa Ricordi. Reproduced by permission

sbirri to watching the church, "arousing no suspicion"—our first clue that he is trying to make this a low-profile operation.

In the timescale of the opera, Angelotti's escape must have been discovered almost immediately. Thereafter, the course of (offstage) events is much the same in both the play and the opera. News would then be sent by courier from the Castel Sant'Angelo to the Farnese palace, a horseman galloping out of the sally gate, across the Bridge of the Angel and along the Via Giulia to a back entrance to the Farnese. Minutes after leaving the fortress the messenger would be running up the great staircase to the baron's apartments. Within a quarter of an hour of the discovery, the regent of police would know of it; within minutes he would have informed the governor (also resident in the Farnese palace), and his immediate orders would precede him to the fortress: no one is to leave, especially none of the guards. The baron himself would arrive on the heels of his orders to begin his investigation. At the fortress we know that Scarpia conducts a rapid, and brutal, investigation of the escape—rapid and brutal enough to give him the information he needs in time to come within minutes of catching his man. Once the jailer Trebelli breaks and gives away the plan, Scarpia, attended only by a small group of sbirri, hurries to Sant'Andrea, perhaps on horseback with the carriage following. He has chosen the sbirri rather than a detachment of Neapolitan infantry in order to keep the affair quiet. It is only two weeks before the arrival of the new pope, the city is nervous over news from the front, there have been bread riots, and hostility to Neapolitan rule is growing more open: this is no time to stir up more trouble by the noisy arrest of a well-known, if not well-loved, prisoner.[48] The sbirri, who did not wear uniforms, spread out through the church while their commander finds and enters the Attavanti chapel, noting that it has been opened by a different key than the one on the Sacristan's belt. They soon have the only prey they will find: an empty lunch basket, and a fan. It takes Scarpia fewer than a dozen bars of music to recognize the Attavanti crest on the fan, and then zero in on the portrait of the woman herself, in the attire of Mary Magdalene. In yet more hyper-speed sleuthing, he finds that the portrait has been painted by a man whose name he knows: a subversive, and the unworthy possessor of the most desirable woman in Rome. No sooner has he established this instant dossier than he catches sight of Tosca. All of this takes under three minutes of stage time.

> *Floria has returned to tell Mario that she must sing at court and cannot meet him as they had arranged. Scarpia uses the fan to convince her that her lover is with the Marchesa Attavanti. She hurries out, and the police follow.*

Scarpia's entrance opens the second part of Act I of the opera. Sardou's first act ends very shortly after the baron arrives, finds the fan, sees the portrait, and kneels for the Te Deum. Puccini's three-act opera has been painstakingly adapted from a five-act play, and some of the seams in the dramatic structure are still visible. The first of these major seams is here, two-thirds of the way through Act I (I, 1057), when Tosca returns to the church. Essential plot details from Sardou's Act II (set at the royal reception) are grafted on to the extended Act I of the opera, along with some but by no means all of the playwright's local color. Here the pastel tones of Sardou's drawing room have been transformed into the purple, scarlet, and gold of the High Mass.

Tosca's return to the church created major problems for the librettists. Their first attempt at bringing her back had Floria and Mario agreeing that she would hurry through her rehearsal and then return to share his meal. This was unsatisfactory, and the draft papers for the libretto contain two extremely peculiar scenes showing Floria's return, both involving conversations between Floria and the Sacristan, overheard by Scarpia. In the first, she tries to bribe the Sacristan to report on Mario's activities. She offers him money and, indicating the painting, asks: "The woman who comes here to pose for the Magdalene . . . the model . . . at what time does she usually come?" To her annoyance the Sacristan confirms Cavaradossi's story that the woman came to the church only to pray.[49]

This thoroughly unsympathetic behavior on the heroine's part was, fortunately, rejected. A second attempt to convey the same information was no more successful, as Floria interrogates an infuriatingly uncooperative Sacristan. This version resurrects the lunch motive.

SCAR: *(steps aside, and listens)*
TOSCA: *(having looked around in vain, turns to the Sacristan)*
       Where is he?
SACR: Who?
TOSCA: Mario.
SACR: *(annoyed)* Unknown.
TOSCA: What!
SACR: There's no such name in the calendar [of saints].
TOSCA: The painter.
SACR: I see.
TOSCA: I'm asking you, where is he?
SACR: I could ask you the same thing.
TOSCA: He was here . . .
SACR: When?
TOSCA: Before, with me
SACR: He was here, and now he's not here.

TOSCA: He was waiting here for me, for lunch.
SACR: For lunch! Brava!
       [retrieving the basket Scarpia has discarded]
       Here are the leftovers.
TOSCA: Who ate it?
SACR: Bah! I surely didn't!
TOSCA: He lied to me, he was lying all the time.
       I was nearly mad, and in the insanity
       of love, I came to him all joyful.
SCARP: *(listening and observing Tosca)*
       Tosca! The painter is her [illegible]. Is she an accomplice per-
       haps? No, she is too pious. Rather, I'll make her my accomplice.
       She's a jealous one . . . If I only had a weapon . . . Ah, that fan![50]

Both of these variations of the conversation, overheard by Scarpia, are of course meant to give him the material from which to concoct his story about the fan.[51] As the opera stands today, Scarpia decides to use the fan before Floria opens her mouth. She returns, finds her lover gone, and immediately leaps to the conclusion that she has been betrayed.

At this point (I, 1085) the church bells begin; they will continue off and on to the end of the act. Stepping forward from the shadow of the scaffolding, the chief of police dips his fingers into the holy water and offers it to the singer; he then launches into a heavy-handed flirtation (she answers distractedly) that oils its way to insinuation, then to outright gossip: this fan, he tells her, was left behind on the scaffold by the painter's startled lovebird. And Tosca, on no more convincing evidence than the sight of the Attavanti crest, believes him. One might well ask, why?

In Sardou the first, and most convincing, argument that Scarpia has on his side is the painter's political ideology. If Mario is certain (correctly as it turns out) that Scarpia is a lascivious hypocrite, the chief of police is able to make an equally convincing argument that the liberal painter is a sexual predator. Tosca obviously fears that Scarpia may be right about her lover's character. All of her doubts, created by Cavaradossi's patent lying, the whispers and the shuffling feet, and the seductive portrait, suddenly crystallize into the conviction that she has been betrayed.

The opera's Floria is heartbroken before she is angry; Sardou's heroine (who "discovers" the betrayal in the middle of the queen's soirée) flies into a simple, murderous rage. Moving this scene from one act to another, and from one vision of Floria's character to another, led Puccini and his librettists to experiment with some peculiar ideas. In an early version Floria angrily brushes aside her tears. "Was Cavaradossi here when you arrived?" she demands of Scarpia. On being told that he was not, she laughs bitterly and launches into a furious monologue which, the directions tell us, gets gradually louder and louder, and ends with her expressed determination to "tear her out of his arms" and the astonishing invitation to Scarpia to come along with her:

SCAR: *(to himself)* I've achieved the effect!

TOSCA: *(giving a start and angrily brushing away her tears)*
Cowardly tears!

SCAR: What's wrong?

TOSCA: Nothing. When you arrived,
did you find Cavaradossi still here?

SCAR: No.

TOSCA: *(laughs bitterly)* He would be working,
the wretch said. And meanwhile,
with me there beside him, he was dreaming
of her vile caresses. The wretch!

SCAR: Prudence!

TOSCA: *(becoming agitated and raising her voice ever louder)*
And that shameless hussy
was here in her filthy pleasure,
and at my cries she quickly
ran away. I understood those soft whispers.
Thief!
(threatening, indicates the Magdalene of the painting)

SCAR: Beware!

TOSCA: I know the path
to their hiding place.
I'll fall on them unexpected,
and I will know how to tear her out of his arms.
Are you coming?

SCAR: No, I remain.

TOSCA: *(turning to the painting, almost shouting)*
You won't have him tonight. I swear it.

SCAR: *(shocked)* In church?

TOSCA: *(bursting out into a long sob, indicating the altar with a voice full of weeping)* God, forgive me . . . He sees that I'm weeping.
(runs out)

This invitation to Scarpia is something that not even Sardou's Tosca was tough enough, or foolish enough, to suggest. Fortunately, this exchange was vetoed with an underscored "No," probably in Puccini's hand (see fig. 28). Tosca, weeping, leaves the church alone.

As the Te Deum begins, Scarpia plans the capture of the rebels and his conquest of Tosca.

The Te Deum (so called for its first words, "Te Deum laudamus," We praise you, Lord) is a long prayer of thanksgiving. Like many important liturgical

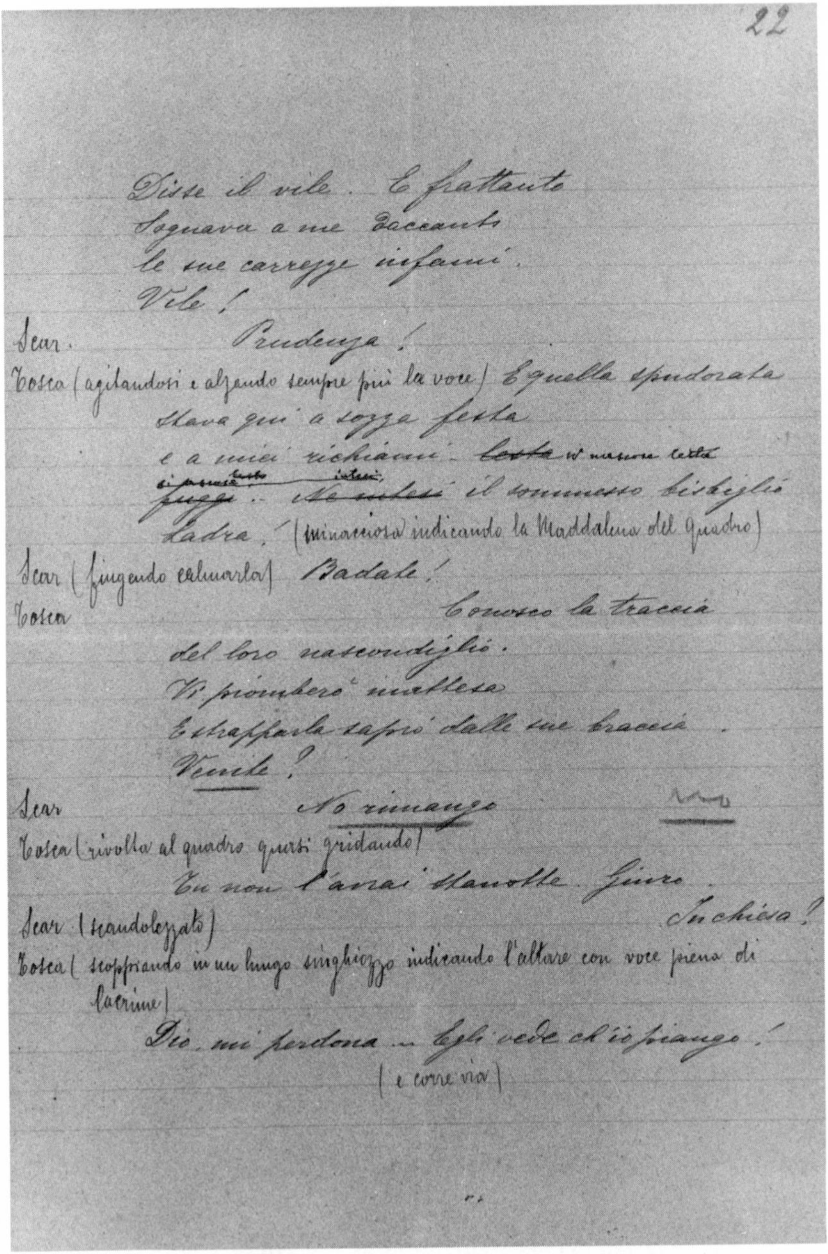
22

Disse il vile. E frattanto
Sognava a me daccanto
le sue carezze infami.
Vile!

Scar. Prudenza!

Tosca (agitandosi e alzando sempre più la voce) E quella spudorata
stava qui a sozza festa
e a miei richiami ~~tosta~~ si nascose lesta
~~si nascose~~ ~~fuggì~~ .. ~~Ne intesi~~ il sommesso bisbiglio
Ladra! (minacciosa indicando la Maddalena del quadro)

Scar (fingendo calmarla) Badate!

Tosca Conosco la traccia
del loro nascondiglio.
Vi piomberò inattesa
E strapparla saprò dalle sue braccia.
Venite?

Scar Io rimango

Tosca (rivolta al quadro quasi gridando)
Tu non l'avrai stanotte. Giuro.

Scar (scandolezzato) In chiesa!

Tosca (scoppiando in un lungo singhiozzo indicando l'altare con voce piena di lacrime)
Dio mi perdona... Egli vede ch'io piango!
(e corre via)

Figure 28. An early sketch for the Act I libretto, showing ideas for a scene between Tosca and Scarpia that were later rejected. © Archivio Storico Casa Ricordi. Reproduced by permission

chants it has inspired numerous settings, with music often specially composed for specific occasions.[52] Paisiello composed at least one: his Te Deum was played for Napoleon's coronation in 1804. Puccini's grandfather Domenico, a student of Paisiello's, wrote two for his hometown of Lucca, one of which was composed to celebrate the Austrian victory over the French at Genoa and was actually performed ten days before the events of the opera. Another Te Deum to celebrate this event was heard in Rome on 15 June. In a supreme irony for those who know *Tosca*, General First Consul Bonaparte attended a Te Deum in Milan on 18 June, four days after his Marengo victory and the day after the fictional operatic ceremony.[53]

The choristers of Sant'Andrea della Valle would have had no difficulty singing a Te Deum on short notice, since the prayer was routinely offered for any sort of good news such as a military victory or a papal celebration. The traditional plainsong version would have been part of the choir's ordinary repertory and the singers would have been happy to prepare a newly composed work, for extra pay. But while the choir could have easily produced a Te Deum to order, any celebration in the real world involved a great deal more preparation than that allowed for at the end of Act I of the opera. Only in the fantasy world of opera does it take under an hour to assemble a state occasion complete with a cardinal, fully robed attendant clerics and choir, official representatives of the government, soldiers, and the Swiss Guards (who would not in any case have been there unless the pope happened to be in attendance—and, of course, we know that there was no pope in Rome on 17 June 1800). At a Te Deum offered on 4 November 1799 in thanksgiving for the fall of the Roman Republic, the square of St. Peter's was lined with 4,000 troops, with a procession of carriages accompanied by drums and marching bands. The basilica was draped and illuminated despite the fact that most of the heavy scarlet silk and gold braid draperies, and the lamps and torch-holders, had been stolen or sold under the Republic, and few churches could scrape together a full set without borrowing. In the basilica the great bronze statue of St. Peter was dressed in pontifical robes with the triple crown on his head and the ring of the fisherman on his finger. The Mass was sung a cappella by the united choirs of St. Mary Major, St. John Lateran, and St. Peter's. Unfortunately, the Te Deum on this occasion, composed by the popular opera composer Guglielmi and critiqued like any other theatrical production, "did not please." Volleys of artillery were fired by the troops in the square at key points during the ceremony (Puccini has substituted the booming of the cannon).[54]

This juxtaposition of religious ritual against Scarpia's monologue is the Throne and Altar alliance made visible and as such was an irresistible target for Puccini and his librettists. However, creating the actual form of the

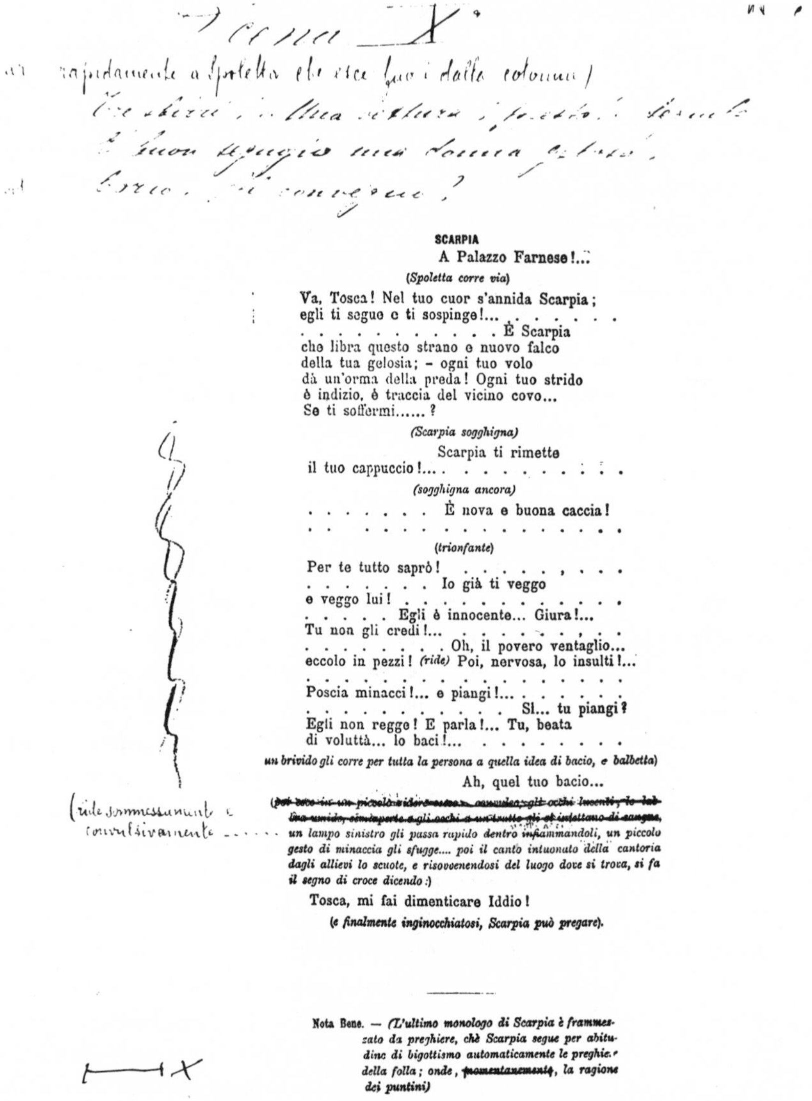

(rapidamente a Spoletta che esce fuori dalla colonna)

SCARPIA
A Palazzo Farnese!...

(Spoletta corre via)

Va, Tosca! Nel tuo cuor s'annida Scarpia;
egli ti segue e ti sospinge!... . . . .
. . . . È Scarpia
che libra questo strano e nuovo falco
della tua gelosia; – ogni tuo volo
dà un'orma della preda! Ogni tuo strido
è indizio, è traccia del vicino covo...
Se ti soffermi...... ?

(Scarpia sogghigna)
Scarpia ti rimette
il tuo cappuccio!... . . . .

(sogghigna ancora)
. . . . È nova e buona caccia!
. . . .

(trionfante)
Per te tutto saprò! . . . .
. . . . Io già ti veggo
e veggo lui! . . . .
. . . . . Egli è innocente... Giura!...
Tu non gli credi!...
. . . . Oh, il povero ventaglio...
eccolo in pezzi! *(ride)* Poi, nervosa, lo insulti!...

Poscia minacci!... e piangi!... . . . . . .
. . . . Sì... tu piangi!
Egli non regge! E parla!... Tu, beata
di voluttà... lo baci!...

un brivido gli corre per tutta la persona a quella idea di bacio, e balbetta)
Ah, quel tuo bacio...

(ride sommessamente e convulsivamente . . . . . . *Poi due un piccolo idiota... annuda gli occhi innocenti, le labbra umide, imperla e gli occhi... e tutto gli si infiamma di sangue, un lampo sinistro gli passa rapido dentro infiammandoli, un piccolo gesto di minaccia gli sfugge.... poi il canto intuonato della cantoria dagli allievi lo scuote, e risovvenendosi del luogo dove si trova, si fa il segno di croce dicendo:)*
Tosca, mi fai dimenticare Iddio!

(e finalmente inginocchiatosi, Scarpia può pregare).

———————

Nota Bene. — *(L'ultimo monologo di Scarpia è frammeszato da preghiere, chè Scarpia segue per abitudine di bigottismo automaticamente le preghier della folla; onde, ~~momentaneamente~~, la ragione dei puntini)*

FIGURE 29. An early idea for Scarpia's monologue that closes Act I. © Archivio Storico Casa Ricordi. Reproduced by permission

monologue was troublesome; Giacosa was never satisfied with it, and in the end washed his hands of the whole affair. The working papers for the libretto contain two versions of the monologue, only the first and last lines of which bear any relation at all to the "Va, Tosca" as we know it today. It consists of two parts: an expansion on the "falcon" image of the hunter, and a series of fragmented stream-of-conscious interjections in which Scarpia gloats and chuckles to himself (see fig. 29). A note in the stage directions indicates the meaning of the spaced dots: "Scarpia's last monologue is mixed with prayers, because from his habit of bigotry, Scarpia follows the prayers of the congregation automatically, hence all those suspension dots at this point."

SCARPIA: To the Farnese palace! *(Spoletta runs out)*
Go, Tosca! Scarpia makes his nest in your heart;
He follows you, and urges you on! . . . . . .
. . . . It is Scarpia
who frees this strange new falcon
of your jealousy;—every flight of yours
gives a track toward the prey! Every cry of yours
is a clue, a path to the nearby lair . . .
If you allow me . . . ?
                    (Scarpia leers)
Scarpia will replace
your hood! . . . .
                    (Scarpia leers again)
. . . . It's a new hunt, and a good one!
                    (triumphant)
Through you I will know everything! . . . .
. . . . I already see you
And I see him! . . . .
. . . . He is innocent . . . he swears!
You don't believe him! . . . .
. . . . Oh, the poor fan . . .
Behold it in pieces! *(laughs)*
Then, distraught, you insult him! . . .
. . . .
Then threats! . . . and tears! . . . .
. . . . Yes . . . you weep?
He cannot bear it! He speaks! . . . You, blessed
by desire . . . you kiss him! . . . .

Scarpia goes into paroxysms of voyeuristic lust at the idea of their reconciliation, their kisses (see fig. 30). The stage directions go far beyond mere instructions for movements, and take on instead the characteristics of a novel:

FIGURE 30. One of a series of watercolors that Metlikovitz prepared for Ricordi as part of the publicity for the first production of *Tosca*. This shows an Act I kiss between Tosca and Cavaradossi. © Archivio Storico Casa Ricordi. Reproduced by permission

A shudder passes through his whole body at this idea of a kiss, and he mur-
murs, "Ah, that kiss of yours . . ." then a dry convulsive laugh escapes him,
his eyes shining, his lips moist and partly open, and his eyes suddenly become bloodshot as a sinister flash passes rapidly through them, inflaming
them; a small gesture of menace escapes him . . . then the murmured song
of the choir students rouses him and, recalling the place where he finds himself, he makes the sign of the cross, saying: "Tosca, you make me forget God!"
And, kneeling at last, Scarpia is able to pray.

If we are right about the importance of anti-clericalism in *Tosca*, this is
the place in which we will find its fullest statement. Certainly the scene is
among the most effective spectacles not only in this opera, or even in opera
as a genre, but arguably one of the greatest in theater. Whence does the scene
derive its power? It lies at least in part in the contrasting of two immense and
apparently opposite passions: religious fervor and sexual frenzy. Even more
effective is the slow, inexorable "crescendo," in drama as well as in volume,
which builds from one man, dressed in black and all but alone on the stage,
speaking quietly to his self-effacing subordinate, to the whole panoply of secular and religious power in all its splendor of color and motion, with a sound
that crashes down on the listener like an avalanche. In this scene, as in the
tenor's last-act aria, "E lucevan le stelle," the music rises to a climax that
seems to replicate the physical act of love.

We must first remember that Puccini, a church musician bred in the bone,
knew all of the tricks of ritual drama: the hint of chant; the ecclesiastical atmosphere created by the modal scale; the rhythmic pulse of massed unison
voices; the intertwining of organ and bells. He uses all of these, and more, in
this Act I Finale.

The spectacle as it finally emerged from the struggle of libretto-making is
well worth a detailed examination. The scene begins when Tosca leaves the
church on her fatal mission, accompanied by the poignant sweep of music associated with Mario, and Love.

The music of love dies away to a pianissimo and the mood shifts as suddenly as if a mask were torn away. Scarpia's "real self" emerges, and his first
and most urgent preoccupation (the music tells us) is not erotic, but political: Angelotti's music is punched out in the lower strings, marked "very loud,
energetic, as powerfully as possible."

The motif slows to a sudden pianissimo as Spoletta, the bloodhound, steps
out from behind a pillar where he has been lurking. Before his chief gives his
orders, however, there are three slow measures of nothing but the deep sound
of bells. The bells have been with us off and on since before Scarpia's entrance, but now they change character. Marked "broadly religious" *(largo*

religioso) and "very sustained" *(sostenuto molto)*, they seem to swing rhyth-
mically, replicating the strongly accented swing of the heavy gold censers.

On the last half of the last beat of the fourth bar Scarpia begins to issue
his clipped instructions: "Three sbirri . . . a carriage . . . quick . . . follow her
wherever she goes." In dramatic terms the drawn-out pause before these instructions are delivered is bothersome: Tosca has hurried out, the spy has
been summoned with an imperious gesture, the church is filling. But Scarpia
waits for three long bars to set his men on their all-important mission. Must
the machinery of the State wait on the ponderous pace of the Church?

Scarpia has not finished his curt instructions when a sinuous pattern of
triplets begins a new motif (I, 1231), this one suggesting that Scarpia has
shifted his attention from business, to lust. His voice, with the bells and the
serpent-like movement of the orchestra below it, is joined by a melody line
played by the organ (I, 1237–38) as the procession, and Scarpia's aria proper,
begin simultaneously: "Va, Tosca!," "Go, Tosca" he sings as the cardinal and
his retinue advance toward the high altar.

After four bars the rhythmic firing of the cannon begins, and will continue
off and on until the end of the act. This is the same cannon we heard earlier,
firing the warning shot to close the city gates when Angelotti's escape is discovered.[55] Now the gunfire thunders out the news of the military triumph by
the State that is being solemnized by the rites of the Church.

Soon (I, 1263) another layer—the muttered prayers of the congregation—
is added to the bells, the cannon shots, and the organ. Puccini was obsessed
with this "muttering" effect, even though he knew perfectly well that no such
prayers are said before the start of the Te Deum. He didn't care: In August of
1898 he sent hectoring letters to his clerical friends, demanding "a few verses"
for the people to "mutter" before the beginning of the Te Deum. "I've decided
on the muttering, and by God I won't give up the effect."[56] Eventually he
settled on a mixture of words, a few from the Psalms, a few from Genesis, a
few from the Doxology: "Adjutorum [*sic*] nostrum in nomine Domini / Qui
fecit coelum et terram / Sit nomen Domini benedictum / Et hoc nunc et usque
in saeculum" (Our help is in the name of the Lord / Who made heaven and
earth / May the name of the Lord be blessed / Now and forever; I, 1263–68).
As impatient as Sardou shrugging off the actual course of the Tiber, Puccini
insisted that his dramatic reality must supersede any reality of the workaday
world. He knew the effect he wanted. The increasingly frank lust of Baron
Scarpia—lust for violent death, but above all his consuming lust for this
proud woman—is to be overlaid by layer upon layer of religious ceremony.
The character's language becomes more and more graphic—from "Scarpia

has made his nest in your heart," to the determination to see the fire in her
eyes become languid, post-coital fashion, with the spasms of love she will experience in his arms ("illanguidir con spasimo d'amor": the stage directions
say that these words should be sung "con passione erotica"). The regular pulse
of the cannon shots throbs in accompaniment.

The intertwining of Church and State is made musically graphic by the intertwined musical material. Scarpia reaches a climax with an ascending line
of six notes rising to a high F on the words "the other in my arms" *(l'altra
fra le mie braccia)*, while the first note of the Te Deum proper elides with his
word, "arms." Then the baron recalls where he is, and his high F exclamation
leads to the final phrase of the hymn (at I, 1289) when the voices of the congregation and the celebrants thunder out the anthem in unison, to excited
jingling triplets of bells (see fig. 31). Scarpia, emerging from his trance, cries
out, "Tosca, you make me forget God!" (an interesting example of diverting
the blame onto the victim), and "with religious fervor" sings "con tutta
forza," the Latin words "Te, aeternum Deum, omnis terra veneratur" (You,
Eternal Father, all the Earth adores!) Although the act, and the aria, end
here, the Te Deum is just beginning: "Te Deum laudamus: te Dominum con-
fitemur. Te aeternum Patrem omnis terra veneratur . . ." There is a rapid,
powerful recapitulation of the Scarpia/Tyranny motif, and the curtain falls
suddenly.

Despite Puccini's cavalier attitude toward the liturgical details, an enormous amount of effort went into making sure that the Te Deum looked authentic. While Puccini and the librettists struggled with the words and music, Giulio Ricordi was collecting information with a view to duplicating a
papal procession at the end of the eighteenth century. In August 1899 Ricordi
received a letter from Guglielmo Canori reporting that he had managed to
discover eighteen color prints showing the costumes of the papal court in
1825—a quarter of a century after the events of the opera, but Canori as-
sured Ricordi that "the papal court had not changed much between Pius VI
and Pius IX."[57] Canori also offered a description of the order of the procession, noting that, since Sant'Andrea della Valle is under the patronage of the
municipality, the procession should also include representatives of the city
government. The eighteen prints that Canori purchased for Ricordi eventually became the basis for Hohenstein's costume drawings—including friars
of various orders, deacons and subdeacons, choir and altar boys with lighted
candles and thuribles, mace bearers, and members of the municipality (see
figs. 32–34). This search for authenticity in the procession is typical of the
approach to history in general during this project: the producers of the opera

FIGURE 31. Scarpia kneels as the procession approaches the main altar for the Te Deum at the finale of Act I. Watercolor by Metlikovitz. © Archivio Storico Casa Ricordi. Reproduced by permission

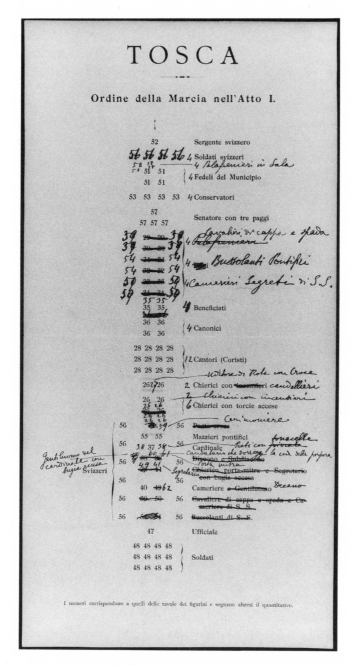

FIGURE 32. The procession order for the Te Deum scene was planned in meticulous detail, based on prints provided by Canori. The numbers are keyed to Hohenstein's costume drawings. © Archivio Storico Casa Ricordi. Reproduced by permission

FIGURE 33. Hohenstein costume drawing of a choir singer from the Te Deum scene of Act I. © Archivio Storico Casa Ricordi. Coristi, Act I, no. 28. Reproduced by permission

went to extravagant lengths to recreate the panoply of papal ceremony, while everyone concerned cheerfully ignored the fact that there was no intact papal court in Rome at the time.

In terms of theatrical effect, of course, none of this historical carping matters a bit. When done well (and it is difficult really to mess it up) the finale of Act I of Tosca is one of the most pulse-quickening, sweaty-palmed scenes in the entire theatrical repertoire. Effective though they are, the torture, the attempted rape, the murder, the execution, and the suicide must take a backseat to the sheer power of this finale.

FIGURE 34. Hohenstein costume drawing for a monk in the Act I finale, apparently a member of the Dominicans, the order that staffed the Holy Office. © Archivio Storico Casa Ricordi. Frati, no. 30. Reproduced by permission

What is it all about? Is it merely another of Puccini's workmanlike but relatively simpleminded appeals to the gallery, full of sound and fury and signifying not much beyond melodrama? Scarpia's musings, political as well as erotic, are woven directly into the liturgical ceremony. Is this because, as Carner and others have suggested, Puccini, unlike Wagner or Verdi, was incapable of portraying two separate frames of mind—one religious, the other obsessed with worldly power—simultaneously? Girardi rejects this thesis, arguing that it is essential that the police chief *not* be differentiated from the atmosphere that surrounds him, that his reflections are fed by the pious context in which he finds himself. I would suggest that not only are the baron's fantasies fed by the splendor and ceremony of the altar, they are directly bound to the institution which these ceremonies represent. We are left with the image of tyranny and erotic obsession blended with and amplified by the power of the Church.

7 *Entr'acte*

*A*fternoon and early evening, 17 June

The events that would doom Tosca and her lover during the night of 17 to 18 June had begun a week earlier, as two armies moved toward conflict at Marengo, in northern Italy.

Six days before the news from Marengo arrived in Rome, on Thursday 12 June, heavy drops of rain fell off and on during the day, Roman rain that mercifully if temporarily sweeps the streets clean.[1] At night there was a thunderstorm.

In the north, the geo-political struggles over the fate of Italy were coming to a crisis. Russia had withdrawn from the European front and would soon abandon the anti-French Coalition, but Bonaparte's absence—after his return from Egypt he spent some months consolidating his power in France—had offered an opportunity for the Austrian general Melas. In May, Melas's troops had taken Nice (then Nizza, an Italian city) and on 4 June the Austrian siege of Genoa had finally succeeded. Now Melas turned north, toward Milan, and toward Bonaparte, who in mid-May had accomplished the impossible by bringing his army across the Alps, like Hannibal.

On Friday in Rome the day was cloudy. On Saturday, 14 June, although no one in the First City of the World suspected that such a thing was happening, French and Allied troops closed in battle near Milan at a hamlet called Marengo. In Rome, the day dawned bright and clear but as time passed the clouds increased, a pathetic fallacy for the battle in the north. The day began well for the Allies—the French were outnumbered by Melas's troops and by mid-morning the Allies controlled the field. Bulletins announcing an Allied victory were sent out, and a courier departed for Naples and Palermo to bring the good news to the Bourbon court. It would take three days of hard riding to reach Rome, on the way south. By the late afternoon, however, Bonaparte was reinforced by fresh troops who arrived under the command of Marshal Dessaix; the Austrians, tired and caught off-guard, soon retreated in disarray. As he gathered the shattered remnants of his army around him, Melas sent a second courier on his way with news of the defeat.²

The following day, Sunday, was foggy and damp in Rome, and the rain hung on. Humid and hot, it was a disappointing sort of weekend for lovers eager to escape to the country. But as so often happens, Monday (16 June) dawned bright and fair with a few light clouds that burned away to leave yellow-gold sunshine followed by a calm night—"Notte serena," Monsignor Gilii noted. By nightfall on Monday the courier from the north must have reached Siena, halfway on his ride from Milan to Naples with false news of an Allied victory.

On Tuesday 17 June the weather was almost as pleasant as it had been on Monday. The morning was clear and bright (Floria shops for flowers in the Campo dei Fiori) as the first courier approached the city. In mid-afternoon, while Mario and Angelotti make their way across the city to the farm near the Saint Sebastian gate, a thin covering of cloud developed briefly, then dispersed. By nightfall, as the second courier passed Civitavecchia, the air was calm (Spoletta's "bloodhounds" ransack the villa searching for Angelotti) and the sky was blue-black velvet. By midnight the moon was barely a sliver. Just before dawn, as Cavaradossi waits for execution, the stars in the moonless sky glittered like diamonds in a jeweler's display case over the quiet streets of a city that disapproved of street-lighting.

Dawn on 18 June arrived at about the eighth hour, or 4:30 in the morning (this is near the longest day of the year). By 7 A.M. modern time (news of Scarpia's murder will be buzzing in the streets by now) the air was hot and heavy, with light clouds that would darken by mid-morning; soon it would rain, hard, with thunderclaps (in the world of fiction, does Rome mourn the deaths of its beloved diva and her lover?).

The opera omits any look at the police work that occupies Scarpia during the afternoon and early evening, though much of the play's second and third acts concentrate on this process.

As soon as the Te Deum was over Scarpia would order a gradually widening circle of arrests—a process that would have begun already with the information given by the driver who betrayed Trebelli, and speeded up by the jailer's confession. After the race to Sant'Andrea della Valle, Cavaradossi has moved dramatically to center stage in the lineup of suspects. His name is not unknown, he already has a dossier (Puccini's Scarpia exclaims, "un uom sospetto, un volterrian!" and Sardou's villain notes that he is "a liberal, like Monsieur his father"), so there are plenty of leads to follow even without the Sacristan's enthusiastic rush to testify.

The inquisitorial legal system, under which Scarpia operates, worked by asking every witness to tell everything he knew about the smallest detail of the event in question; the process was then repeated with anyone who was as much as mentioned in any of the testimony.[3] Trebelli's confession implicates a number of people, among them the wife of the Marchese Attavanti. In the play Scarpia is still toying with the idea of sending troops to Frascati to arrest her. He hesitates only because her husband is a favored courtier of unquestioned loyalty and the chief of police must tread carefully. Roman nobles who involved themselves in the Republic, unlike Neapolitan nobles, were generally left unmolested. Francesco Borghese, whose brother Camillo would marry Pauline Bonaparte in 1803, was a passionate and active supporter of the Republic, but the only inconvenience he suffered for this was a trip to Vienna to apologize personally to the emperor, plus a few weeks cooling his heels at one of the family's country estates.[4]

If circumstances or caution put the Marchesa Attavanti temporarily out of Scarpia's reach, she is not his only suspect. The Jacobins of Rome were a small minority, but there were several hundred of them, and they were not shy about expressing themselves. The treaty more or less protected them from prosecution for offenses committed before the fall of the Republic, but in May and June many of these men were arrested as news from the front became more problematical and rumors of Bonaparte's return circulated. Two ex-consuls released in March after the uprisings in the countryside were re-arrested in May; in mid-June the prisons would be full of men who knew Angelotti (Angelucci) and knew his friends. All of these are interrogated. We need not imagine Rome pullulating with torture chambers and torturers working overtime. Clerks and magistrates would be adequate for the job, and simple questions backed with nothing more threatening than the majesty of the law would apply enough pressure; if anyone remotely resembling the fictional Scarpia had been in charge, the man's unspoken menace would have loosened most tongues.

During the afternoon of 17 June the Sacristan is summoned, interrogated, and then released. Cavaradossi's assistants, including the boy Gennarino, are arrested. All of his servants and the staff of the palazzo Cavaradossi (such as Fabio, the coachman mentioned in Act I of the play) are questioned, as are all of the painter's friends and acquaintances, especially any known to have the wrong political philosophies.

The circle might or might not widen to include Floria Tosca's associates. Scarpia seems to regard her as a loyalist (as indeed she is), and if he is counting on the element of surprise he will not want to stir that hornet's nest before time. But if he does choose to look in her direction he might begin with the performers and staff of the Argentina theater. The unlucky Paisiello, so recently escaped from the attentions of the Neapolitans, will certainly catch his eye.

While Scarpia pursues his own interests, the two men for whom he is searching have gone to ground in a rustic house just inside the city walls.

Sardou has given Cavaradossi a country villa in the most romantic part of Rome, just inside the walls between the Saint Sebastian gate and the Latina gate, where the most famous of the Roman roads, the Appian Way, enters the city.[5] The fact that the house is within the walls means that the men can reach it even after the gates have been closed, though it would be a very long and difficult walk from the city center. They would have to skirt the Capitoline and Palatine hills, passing the grassy ruins of the Circus Maximus and the baths of Caracalla, then head out into open countryside of vineyards and estates and the beginnings of the legendary Appian Way. On foot or by carriage the trip would take over an hour. In the opera the two fugitives simply run out the back door, after Cavaradossi has told Angelotti not to bother with the disguise since "the path is deserted" *(il sentiero è deserto)*. The French Mario of the play is cooler, and more calculating: he sends Angelotti off to get into women's clothing and make his way out a side door of the chapel [there is no such door], while the painter sends for his carriage and leaves by the great doors opening onto the Piazza Valle.[6] The "woman" would then presumably clamber up into the painter's carriage and they would leave together. And that would indeed have taken some explaining to Floria the next day!

Sardou describes Cavaradossi's "suburban farm" (*podere suburbano*, as Scarpia calls it) in detail. The set for Act III of the play is a room dominated by an arcade, beyond which can be seen a loggia shaded with vines, and beyond that a moonlit Renaissance garden with a fountain and cypress trees, and a well (see fig. 35). Furnishings other than the usual tables and chairs include a large sarcophagus which can be used as a seat(!), and a temporary artist's studio with easel, paintings, and "the shaft of an ancient column." Sardou's loquacious hero tells his new friend all about the site and the house:

> We are here, my dear guest, as you could see in the moonlight, between the baths of Caracalla and the mausoleum of the Scipios. . . . There is nothing around us but ruins and tombs, all the debris of ancient Rome . . . a crumbling desert with a few oases of marshy cultivation. But this same sadness is not without charms. I love this solitude, filled with heroic memories, where I hear nothing but the bark of a watchdog, the rumble of distant carriage wheels, the nearby bells of St. Sixtus and St. John; and the muffled noises of

FIGURE 35. Set design for a production of Sardou's *La Tosca* showing Cavaradossi's villa, scene for Act III of the play. *L'Illustration théâtrale*. Author's collection

the living Rome which speak less to my mind than does the silence of the dead one.[7]

This is a portmanteau of images of Romantic Rome: the moonlight, the delights of melancholy, the silent "desert" on the outskirts of the city, and above all, the yearning for the superior delights of the ancient city and contempt for the modern one. The area Mario is describing here is near the Saint Sebastian gate (see map), in 1800 sparsely populated and filled with romantic ruins and dangerous catacombs where the unwary tourist could fall victim to the "bad air" *(malaria)* or, worse, lose his way and never be seen again. Mercier Dupaty, writing in 1788, waxed poetic over the flowers "growing in the shadow of death," an image that recalls Floria's sensuous "flower, you vast fields; tremble, sea breezes" *(fiorite, campi immensi, palpitate aure marine!)*. Dupaty, a French tourist, sitting on the grass under the blue vault of heaven, worked himself into a "delicious reverie" that he was anxious to share with the reader. As a sensitive and enlightened tourist Mario would no doubt have armed himself with this and other guidebooks.[8] His bookshelf would also include contemporary Italian books such as *Roman Nights*, written by the very enlightened Count Alessandro Verri, formerly of the *Caffè* journal of Milan and now, in 1800, living in Rome as a social and literary lion.[9] Verri's book was inspired by the discovery, in 1780, of the long-lost tomb of the Scipios, practically in what would have been Mario Cavaradossi's back yard. It was located while the Sassi brothers, owners of an estate just outside the Saint Sebastian gate, were enlarging their cellar. Breaking down an old wall, they found themselves inside one of the most exciting discoveries of a century that had included the finding of Herculaneum and Pompeii. The Scipios were among the greatest families of the Roman Republic, and every schoolboy in 1780, as in 1880, knew the story of Scipio Africanus, conqueror of Carthage, and of his daughter Cornelia, the mother of the Gracchi. Verri's book, built around these characters, is an elegiac collection of essays in which a series of ghosts describe classical Rome for the benefit of the eighteenth-century tourist. The ghostly accounts of the deaths of the Gracchus brothers are among the most moving passages of the book. Gaius and Tiberius Gracchus have been traditionally seen as champions of popular rights in Republican Rome, and both were murdered by mob violence in support of conservative Senatorial rule. They made appealing models for Italian republicans, who saw themselves as unappreciated saviors of a populace who loathed them.

The family of the Cornelii Scipioni built their tomb in the traditional Roman style with three galleries connected by a transverse gallery. The great stone sarcophagi containing the bodies of the family's dead were placed in narrow niches that opened off the galleries like little rooms. These are obviously the "broken sepulchers" *(franti sepolcreti)* of Floria's first-act arioso. If Mario and Floria were to explore these tombs by candlelight (and they could hardly have resisted) they would enter from the Appian Way by means of a low archway topped by greenery and leading to a column-lined vestibule.[10]

When Sardou has his hero speak of his villa being located in a "crumbling desert" he is referring to the popular idea that Rome was surrounded by deadly miasmas and quagmires. This image survived well into the nineteenth century, but by 1800 it was no longer entirely appropriate. Early in his long pontificate Pius VI had begun the work (completed by Mussolini) of draining the Pontine marshes.

The "melancholy" of the area was to some degree a romantic fiction, but the district was certainly dangerous in 1800. War and its attendant disruptions had precipitated a crime wave, and the empty suburbs provided a natural refuge for deserters from a variety of armies, as well as for the more traditional bandits who were getting closer and closer to the city as conditions worsened, rather like wolves encroaching on a medieval village.[11] Mario in the play is shocked by Floria's imprudence in venturing into the area alone, accompanied only by her armed coachman. He intends to send his tenant farmer's son along to escort her back to the city—but in the play, the police arrive at the villa before she can leave and the "torture scene" takes place there. In the opera she returns to sing at the Farnese palace. In both cases, she learns the secret of the hiding place shortly after arriving at the country house.

Angelotti's hiding place, as devised by Sardou, is cunningly tied in with real historical events. Like the Sassi brothers enlarging their cellar and falling upon the tomb of the Scipios, Cavaradossi is endowed with a Renaissance forebear named Luigi who cleared out an old well and tripped across a secret refuge, a relic of ancient Rome. Sardou of course tells us a great deal about it. The water for the well comes from the Marrana river. The entrance to the hiding place is twenty feet below ground level, vaulted, and so narrow that it has to be entered on one's hands and knees, but the chamber itself is large enough to stand up or lie down in. From the scraps of pottery and coins, Luigi Cavaradossi could tell that it had been used in classical times, a refuge for "an escaped slave, an enemy proscribed by Marius or by Sulla, a Christian promised to the beasts." Luigi kept the hiding place a secret, and used it himself to escape from the papal archers.[12]

The well gets short shrift in the operatic libretto—the only description comes from Mario in Act I, when he tells Angelotti that "[t]here's water at the bottom, but halfway down the shaft there is a small opening leading to a dark chamber." An early version of this speech identified the hiding place as an undiscovered catacomb to which there is no other entrance; Mario's father, a cautious man, kept it as a potentially life-saving refuge.[13]

The idea of hiding in wells sounds rather more effective than it usually proves to be. Sardou was probably thinking of the case of the Neapolitan admiral Caracciolo, who was captured hiding in a well on one of his country estates. Coincidentally there was another capital case in Rome in the spring of 1800 which involved a well. Saverio Pediconi, a prosperous scrap-metal dealer, used the well in his courtyard to hide a quantity of lead, from which he reportedly planned to make bullets. The police had no trouble finding this, though perhaps they were working on a tip.[14]

In the timeframe of the play, which is much more logical than that of the opera, Tosca spends the afternoon at rehearsal and then in the evening goes, all unsuspecting, to the Farnese palace. Only then does she become suspicious and hurry to the villa, followed by Scarpia.

Floria's midday meeting with her lover at Sant'Andrea is interrupted (in the play) by the arrival of her maid, who delivers a humble plea from Paisiello. Tosca, referring to the composer as "that crazy old man," reads it out loud so that Mario (and the audience) will know that the first, inaccurate,

news of the battle of Marengo has arrived. Paisiello has composed a cantata
for the night's festivities, and hopes that she will lend her "prestigious talent"
to a rapidly arranged rehearsal.[15] In the play, as in history, the royal celebrations have already been ordered for the occasion of the fall of Genoa to the
Allied General Melas, which took place on 4 June: the Marengo cantata is
merely a last-minute embellishment concocted on the spur of the moment.
Eusèbe (the Sacristan) reads from an imaginary newspaper:

> Maria Carolina . . . has hurried here from Livorno where she is en route to
> Vienna in order to give, this evening of 17 June, a great fête at the Farnese
> Palace in honor of this victory. There will be a concert followed by a ball,
> with the piazza Farnese illuminated as if by daylight, and music . . . at all
> the squares near the Palace.[16]

The official journal of Rome, the *Diario di Roma*, published the following
(real) notice on 18 June:

> . . . all the good people of this population are filled with joy and . . . showed
> their jubilation with illuminations. Especially the people of Genoa, who cel-
> ebrated the liberation of their native place by the Austrian armies; they dec-
> orated their church of San Giovanni with damasks, velvets, silver crepe, and
> gold fringe . . . on Sunday 15 June there was a solemn Mass accompanied by
> two choruses of select musicians, followed by exposition of the Sacrament
> and a Te Deum, sung by the same musicians.[17]

Gala parties at the Farnese like the one in which La Tosca is supposed to
sing were not uncommon. On 6 May 1800 Governor Naselli entertained the
Duc de Berry (son of the Comte d'Artois and nephew of the beheaded king
Louis XVI) with a mock battle followed by a banquet and a ball at the palace.[18] On other occasions windows throughout the city were draped with dam-
asks, and all the houses were illuminated (as for the arrival of the pope on 3
July); nobles processed through the streets in their carriages, accompanied
by bands and drums (4 November 1799); troops lined the squares near the
palace, bands played, cannon were fired, and free chocolate, ices, and wine
were distributed.

There is nothing out of the ordinary about music being composed for special occasions, sometimes on very short notice indeed; Paisiello's fictional feat
of composing Tosca's cantata between noon and nightfall is perfectly plausible. Pieces such as this were normally composed by the same men who wrote
the music for the season's theater pieces, and the real Paisiello was hard at
work that spring. It is not completely outside the bounds of real-world pos-
sibility that he could have passed the job of writing such a victory cantata on
to a student of his, Puccini's grandfather, Domenico (1772–1815). In Janu-

ary 1799 the young composer was in Naples studying with the great Paisiello when he was caught up in the political turmoil of the Parthenopean Republic and its suppression. In a letter to his father he speaks of "detestable anarchy" in which non-Neapolitans were in "mortal danger" of being accused of being Jacobins "and given a shotgun 'pill' in the chest."[19]

Before going to Naples, Domenico had composed two characteristically Lucchese works, "mini-operas" called *tasche*.[20] The two surviving *tasche* by Domenico Puccini include the sort of political references that could easily earn a young man a "shotgun 'pill'" in a city like post-Parthenopean Naples. His 1793 music drama was titled *Spartacus*, after the leader of a famous slave revolt against the power of Imperial Rome. In 1797 his theme was Castruccio, another patriotic story, in which the hero struggles against a tyrannical government in the name of Luccan liberty.

This glorification of revolutionary patriotism was not unusual in the *tasche*, which were written to accompany the annual three-day election of civic officials and whose purpose was to inspire patriotic pride. But it would be pleasant to think of Puccini's grandfather, like his teacher Paisiello, composing a cantata for a singer like Floria Tosca in praise of the triumphant forces of reaction, and all the while cherishing private political sympathies more in accord with those of a Mario Cavaradossi.

Having the music and the singers ready for an evening performance would not have been difficult; musicians were meticulously trained and sight-reading presented no problems, especially with the formulaic music that busy eighteenth-century composers were accustomed to produce rapidly, on demand. The problem with a full-scale celebration for the victory would lie not with the musicians, but with the men who had to make the preparations needed for decoration and illumination.

Rome, a city that specialized in public spectacle as a form of government, had a large class of professionals, called *festaioli*, who worked on these productions. Like theatrical set designers, or makers of carnival floats, they had an elaborate and traditional stock-in-trade. This consisted primarily of fireworks, and of silver crepe de chine or scarlet silk draperies, with gold fringes and embroidery; and candles and torches in gilt holders, for illumination (see fig. 36). The *festaioli* required time to scrape up enough drapery and lighting for a decent celebration. This was always a substantial project and in 1800 it was made immeasurably more difficult by the fact that under the Republic the great gold and scarlet draperies, the fringes, the lanterns, and the candlesticks had mostly been sold to the highest bidder (or, more likely, to businessmen who had bribed the commissioners).[21]

The great day of fireworks machines had been earlier in the century, but

FIGURE 36. A Roman decorator at work, draping columns for a festival. This is one of a collection of sketches made by Giuseppe Barberi, a Jacobin who was active in the Roman Republic of 1798. Museo di Roma

FIGURE 37. One of the great examples of Roman fireworks machines, in a Pannini painting of the celebrations ordered in Rome to celebrate the birth of the Dauphin in France. This *macchina* was set up in the Piazza Navona. Musée du Louvre. Erich Lessing/Art Resource, NY

the Roman tradition of "artificial fire" was still strong in 1800, as it is now (see fig. 37). Workers under the direction of an expert from the bombadier's guild used thousands of stars, fountains, spinning tops, and uncounted "chestnuts," or firecrackers, attaching them to "machines" that could tower more than 100 feet into the air. The show could last up to two hours, as the machine seemed to explode (in fact, they were not burned) from hundreds of containers hidden in the structure.[22]

As dusk falls on Tosca's Rome on 17 June, while the fireworks engineers put the finishing touches on their machines, the singers gather, sight-reading from a few hastily prepared bits of manuscript. After the rehearsal the diva will return to her apartments at the Palazzo Venezia for the complex and taxing ritual of putting on court dress. Baron Scarpia, having sent his men to the suburban villa, waits.

8 *Act Two*

*L*ate in the evening, 17 June 1800

In his apartments on an upper floor of the Farnese palace, Scarpia is waiting for two events that will signal the next phase of his investigation: Spoletta's return from his search, and Tosca's arrival at the royal gala.

Act II, like Act I, opens abruptly, and like Act I it begins with a motif associated with Scarpia. Before the curtain rises, descending octaves set the tone for this act, and seem to show Scarpia in a reflective mood (see ex. 8.1).[1] This motif ("Scarpia's Plan") acts as an interlocking set of "brackets" to enclose ever more complete developments of the chief of police's scheme as it unfolds: after the first statement (I, 1–3) a rapid succession of themes provides a map to Scarpia's train of thought. As with his musings in the church, Angelotti (cf. ex. 6.2) comes first, then Love (cf. ex. 6.7), and finally the love between Tosca and Cavaradossi (cf. ex. 6.6)—*il bel Mario*, "the handsome Mario," as he will contemptuously call him.[2] Scarpia's first words are in keeping with these thoughts: "Tosca is a good falcon! Surely by this time my trackers have seized their two prey! Tomorrow the dawn will see Angelotti and the handsome Mario hanging from the noose."[3] (At the mention of Mario the Scarpia/Tyranny theme is punched out "allegro energico.") Another repetition of Scarpia's Plan motif occurs at II, 18–20. The motif also marks the end of Scarpia's aria (called the Credo) at II, 98–99. This aria (discussed below) is an elaboration and justification for the plot he is shaping as the act progresses: Tosca will come to his apartments in response to his note; and for love of her Mario, she will allow herself to be used for Scarpia's pleasure. Finally, at II, 618–21, as the plot is completed—after Tosca has given away the secret of Angelotti's hiding place, after Mario has cursed her for her betrayal, and after the news from Marengo has had its devastating effect and Tosca is pleading for Mario's life—the sequence recurs: Angelotti's escape, then Love . . . and then (softly) the completion of the theme we have called Scarpia's Plan. Even

Scarpia's physical actions indicate completion. At the first statement of the motif he was seated at his dinner table; now he returns to that same table, once again turning his attention to his meal.

EX. 8.1. Scarpia's Plan (II, 1–3)

If the scene of the first act was a religious power base, this second-act stronghold is political: Baron Scarpia's apartments at the Farnese Palace, the seat of Bourbon authority in Rome. The Farnese is universally admired as the handsomest palace of the high Renaissance in Rome.[4] Built by a family with ties to the Borgias, to Michelangelo, and to the throne of Spain, it is a perfect symbol of papal magnificence and papal corruption, and a fitting setting for Puccini's dark vision of the power of the State allied with the power of the Church. It is said that Alessandro Farnese, who started work on the palace, owed his advancement to the stunning beauty of his sister Giulia, wife of Orsino Orsini and mistress of the Borgia pope Alexander VI. For the sake of the sister, gossip had it, Alexander made her brother a cardinal; and in 1534 Alessandro became pope himself as Paul III. The building of the Farnese was an exercise in Renaissance vainglory and excess. The family hired the greatest architects of Italy for the job of building their palace: Antonio da Sangallo began it, and when he died in 1546, the task was taken up by Michelangelo, who planned a bridge to connect the palace gardens with the Farnesina palace on the opposite bank of the Tiber. The next architect, Giacomo Della Porta, shelved the bridge plan after Michelangelo's death. But if the Farnese failed to accomplish their most grandiose schemes they nonetheless in the end managed to produce an architectural wonder, and guidebooks from the sixteenth century on invariably urged the cultivated traveler to see it.

An 1800 guidebook calls the Farnese "the most beautiful [palace] that exists in modern Rome," with its majestic staircase, its grandiose apartments, and its immense gallery covered in "poetic and allegorical" paintings by

Annibale Carracci.[5] Its formal entryway is high enough for a man on horse-back to ride through without dismounting or bending. Inside, the great stair-case leads to one of the most famous rooms in Europe, the Salon of Hercules, so called after the monumental figure of the demi-god, signed by Glycon of Athens, which was found in the baths of Caracalla in 1540.[6] The 1992 "real-time" *Tosca* broadcast live from Rome centered Scarpia's apartments on this splendid room. Long galleries lead from the salon to the Carracci gallery where lush and frankly pagan figures from Ovid's *Metamorphosis* cavort around the central Bacchus and Ariadne. Carracci, whose work in this room changed dec-orative painting in Rome, was badly paid for the job, took to drink, and died young.

When the male line of the Farnese died out in 1731 the family property was inherited by Elizabeth Farnese, the second wife of Philip V of Spain. Her son Charles became king of Naples as Charles VIII, and then King of Spain as Charles III, passing the throne of Naples to his son Ferdinand, husband of Maria Carolina, Scarpia's employer and Tosca's patron. Through this tangle of dynastic property arrangements the palace built by one of the great Re-naissance popes came into the hands of the rulers of Naples; Ferdinand took up residence there during his brief occupation of the city in 1798. When he was chased out after a week the Farnese, like the property of the pope, was ran-sacked and looted, and "all the furniture, goods, and belongings of the king of Naples were sold" for the benefit of the new state. When the tide turned yet again in 1799 the palace became the quarters of Ferdinand's representa-tive, Don Diego Naselli, the governor of Rome. Presumably by the time when the opera is set the state apartments were once again habitable and at least some of the stolen furniture had been replaced.[7]

While the quarters in the Farnese are perfectly suited to a monarch or a viceroy, they are not particularly appropriate as headquarters for the chief of police. Sardou, torn between Scarpia as bandit chief and Scarpia as deca-dent aristocrat, gave him rooms in the Castel Sant'Angelo. The playwright no doubt imagined him ensconced in the papal apartments, a core of luxury and splendor in the heart of the fortress. In fact, the Cavaliere Guglielmi, the real chief of police in 1800, lived and worked in quite a different palace, the Ma-dama, now headquarters of the Italian Senate. The presiding officer of the Governing Committee, or Giunta di Stato, who also exercised judicial au-thority in the city, lived and worked in the papal palace of the Quirinale.[8] Whether at the Farnese, the Castel Sant'Angelo, the Madama, or the Quiri-nale, officials like Scarpia certainly used their residences as office space, so there is nothing so very peculiar about the activities that go on in Scarpia's apartments in the second act of the opera.

While he waits for news of the search, Scarpia pauses for a meal, listening to the dance music from the royal apartments below him on the piano nobile.

In the usual Roman style, the Farnese palace is arranged in an open rectangle around a central courtyard, so that all of the rooms have windows opening either onto the loggia of the courtyard, or onto the street. At Scarpia's order the window is opened, and the sounds of dance music that Puccini (and Scarpia) describes as a gavotte drift up (II, 2). Like the Te Deum in Act I and the shepherd's song in Act III, the offstage music of Act II is "real" music, heard by the characters within their world. The gavotte, a popular dance of the eighteenth century, was already old-fashioned by 1800. In fact, what Puccini has written is more a "neoclassical gesture" than a gavotte: the authentic version of the dance had a very characteristic rhythmic pattern, which this one lacks.[9] The tune used here seems to have come from an exercise book of Michele Puccini (Giacomo's younger brother), which includes a gavotte in G major, with corrections by his teacher.[10] For the opera, Puccini has transposed it to D major. The tune is light, elegant, and charming, with none of the dark overtones of the drama. For twenty-five bars Vitellio Scarpia, the courtier, observes the surface charm of the world of the court.

Sardou, who as a playwright did not have the luxury of imposing a musical score on his characters, took full advantage of onstage music in Act II of *La Tosca*, set at the royal reception that we hear offstage at this point in the opera. His onstage ensemble gives a concert that includes (at various strategic points in the action) dance music—a gavotte, a minuet, and a saltarello—as well as formal concert music—what he describes as "the andante from Haydn's Symphony in D major" (Carner speculates that he may have meant the last of the London Symphonies, no. 104),[11] and the first tantalizing chords of a putative cantata by Paisiello (in B♭, as Tosca hisses to the unfortunate composer).[12]

Sardou's Scarpia is an intimate of the court, carefully maneuvering within the intricate hierarchy of power.[13] Puccini and his librettists, however, knew better (see fig. 38). Autonomous and all-powerful, the man before whom all Rome trembles reigns supreme in his apartments in the Farnese, aloof from his nominal sovereign and indulgently contemptuous of the court and its entertainments on the floor below him ("they're scraping away at gavottes," he comments while waiting for Paisiello's cantata to begin).[14] Puccini's villain laughs at Tosca's idea of appealing for royal clemency: by the time Maria Carolina could intervene, Scarpia would have already killed his prisoner, with no apparent fear of retribution. Even though he admits (or claims) that he "cannot grant a pardon publicly" *(non posso far gratia aperta)*,[15] we don't believe him and wonder why Tosca should.

FIGURE 38. Eugenio Giraldoni, who created the role of Scarpia. Dr. Girvice Archer

But though Scarpia is a wonderfully effective villain, he is not always a convincing one. The Te Deum at the end of Act I works because it plays out Scarpia's hypocrisy and lust against the splendor of the ritual of the Church. On the other hand, his Act II monologue *(Ha più forte sapore)* falters both musically and dramatically. If Scarpia is presented as an up-dated Iago (and both the drama and the score are full of indications that he is), then this is his Credo, his statement of faith, which parallels Iago's Credo in Verdi's *Otello*. As it turns out, at the core of Scarpia's persona is a savage perverse eroticism.[16]

Scarpia actually describes himself as following in Iago's footsteps: "Iago had a handkerchief, I a fan" *(Iago ebbe un fazzoletto, io un ventaglio)*. But Scarpia's evil seems shallow compared with Iago's. Shakespeare's villain precipitates a towering tragedy by destroying a virtuous woman and a good and noble man who trusts him. The weakness of which Scarpia makes use is a far less elevated passion: Othello's jealousy is an obsession; Floria's is either a ploy or a bad habit. Even more important, Iago is in control: virtually every plot twist before the final scenes of *Othello* has been engineered in cold blood by Iago. Scarpia, on the other hand, often seems to be improvising, merely taking advantage of opportunities that offer themselves. And while he is perfectly willing to wallow in sadism and corruption, he is more or less doing his job. Cavaradossi, though he has our personal and political sympathy, is unquestionably guilty of the serious crime of which he is accused: he and his friends fully intend to destroy the state in which they live. Scarpia is a hypocrite, a libertine, and a sadist; but he is no Iago and the attempt to make him sound like one is doomed to failure. When Puccini concentrates on Scarpia's hypocrisy, his sadism, and his lust, he is far more convincing.

In the score, throughout the opera Scarpia's music is in clear contrast to that of the lovers. Theirs is lyrical, his is declamatory, much in the style of the music Verdi gave to Iago in his *Otello*. One could even say that the musical conflict of the opera is between declamation and lyricism (again, as in *Otello*), in which the lovers' attempts to "sing" are constantly interrupted or frustrated by events controlled by Scarpia. However, the Act II monologue (his "Credo") contains broadly lyrical phrases, such as the one found at II, 69–70 (ex. 8.2). Carner finds this phrase too sentimental, reminiscent of Cavaradossi's Love motif (cf. ex. 6.6), the melody of "Qual occhio al mondo?" from the love duet. The phrases are in fact quite similar and seem out of character for Scarpia. But an examination of the text shows what may be really going on. When he lyrically (and ironically?) describes the sort of "normal" behavior that he despises, the sort of behavior he ascribes to Cavaradossi ("honied consent," "sighs and milky dawns," "guitar chords," and "horoscopes of flowers"), the aria is in A-flat (the same note as G$^\sharp$, on which one of

the Scarpia/Tyranny chords is based). But it modulates to Scarpia's characteristic note of E (II, 81–83) when he proclaims his own style of love-making:
"I desire. I pursue the desired thing, I satiate myself, and I throw it away."[17]
What Puccini seems to be doing here is "composing out" two of the notes
most clearly associated with Scarpia.

Ex. 8.2. Scarpia's Credo (II, 69–72)

We get the sense that the librettists insisted on this Act II Credo, and in
literary terms it works nicely. Scarpia's code is the mirror image of the themes
that define the love between Floria and Mario—he sneers at music ("guitar
chords") and nature ("horoscopes of flowers"). (Carner notes that here Puccini introduces descriptive touches: "harp arpeggios at the words 'guitar
chords,' the clarinet flourish at 'horoscopes of flowers,' and the bird calls at
'cooing like a turtle dove.'")[18] Cynical where the lovers are committed, he
compares women with wine, both pleasant, both consumable, and both easy
to replace once consumed.

Puccini's villain gains stature in comparison with the men who surround
him. The librettists not only slashed the numbers of minor characters from
twenty to six (with five more as non-speaking parts), they reduced the surviv-
ors to pygmies. At one point in the libretto's evolution, even the Sacristan dared
to question Scarpia (though he did it in an appropriately groveling manner):

SACR: *(aside)* It seems empty!
SCAR: What did you say?
SACR: Me? That basket in the hand
of your Excellency, puzzles me.
Where was it? Oh, may your Excellency excuse me
if I question him!
SCAR: Come!
His Excellency replies.
It was found in the middle of the chapel.
SACR: Empty?[19]

In the final version the Sacristan merely exclaims to himself, "Empty! Empty!" *(Vuoto, vuoto)*. Scarpia, who misses nothing, peremptorily demands an explanation, which the Sacristan provides, babbling with terror.

The characters of Sciarrone and Spoletta began life in Sardou's play as courtiers of some stature. Sciarrone (or Schiarrone, as his name is transliterated into French) joins the baron at the queen's gala as a fellow guest, and sits to discuss the case with him as a colleague; Spoletta is a respectable Neapolitan Captain of Carabinieri. By the time they arrive in the opera, Sciarrone has become a glorified footman and Spoletta, even more disgracefully, has been demoted to the chief of a gang of sbirri.

Spoletta, cringing, brings the unwelcome news that he has failed to find Angelotti. He has, however, arrested the painter. Before he begins the interrogation, Scarpia sends Sciarrone to fetch the necessary judiciary officials: the judge of the criminal court, and "Roberti," the executioner.

In both the play and the opera Roberti is a walk-on part with no dialogue, but he is a character with a considerable depth of background.[20] Between 1796 and 1864 the executioner (that is, the *boia*, or *carnefice*) of Rome was Giovanni Battista Bugatti, popularly known as Mastro Titta.[21] Bugatti was a short, stocky, vigorous man who was always clean-shaven and particular about his appearance. He was conventional and pious, and seemed untroubled by his dreadful profession. He dispatched 516 persons during his record-breaking tenure of sixty-eight years, helping them to "cross over the bridge," as the Roman idiom went.

At the time of the events portrayed in the opera, Bugatti was twenty-one years old; he served as Rome's executioner until 17 August 1864, when he retired at the age of eighty-five. He began his career with the old-fashioned methods of death—hanging, with embellishments such as dismembering and beheading; and a Roman specialty for "atrocious" crimes, stunning with a hammer and then cutting the throat.[22] During the military occupation of 1798–99 executions were carried out by firing squad, but when the French took over the city in 1808 they brought with them their new machine, the guillotine, and Mastro Titta welcomed it with the joy of a true professional. He called it "a new edifice for the cutting of heads," and he had plenty of opportunity to use it between 1810 and 1813, when there were fifty-six executions in four years (compared with the one or two a year that was normal under the popes).[23]

The executioner would normally oversee any application of judicial torture, though as we have seen the use of torture was tightly circumscribed by 1800. Hohenstein's costume drawing shows "Roberti" as a relatively well-dressed, respectable man—certainly more respectable than either the sbirri or Spoletta, who are distinctly seedy-looking characters (see figs. 39–41). The instrument Roberti uses is certainly unconventional, a circlet that can be tightened to produce pressure on the skull, cutting into flesh and bone. Sardou may well have got the idea for this peculiar device from one of the fantastic etchings in Piranesi's *Carceri* (prisons) series, entitled "Man on the Rack" (see fig. 42). The etching shows a bound, seated figure tied to the rack and capped with a metal implement of some sort. The device, whatever it is, seems to have been the creation of Piranesi's imagination.[24]

> *Cavaradossi is brought in under guard as the cantata begins in the royal apartments below. He denies any knowledge of the escaped prisoner.*

Scarpia has been thwarted in his original plan, which was to arrest Cavaradossi with Angelotti, and present Tosca with a lover already condemned. Now he quickly begins to form a new one. The stage directions tell us that he

> (walks about deep in thought; suddenly stops. Through the open window is heard the cantata being performed by the choristers in the Queen's apartments; so Tosca has returned [from the villa]—she is there—below him. . . . a thought occurs to him and he suddenly speaks to Spoletta . . .)[25]

He orders Cavaradossi brought in and sends Sciarrone for Roberti, and the Judge. As Cavaradossi enters a menacing theme begins, one that will recur throughout the interrogation (II, 184–89; see ex. 8.3). Played "very loud, strongly emphasized, and sustained" (*ff, marcatissimo* and *sostenuto*), it will thunder when the door to the torture room is opened (II, 324). When Cavaradossi is carried back, unconscious, the same theme will recur, this time played "with sorrow" (*doloroso*) and transposed up a minor third (II, 528).

Ex. 8.3. Interrogation (II, 184–89)

(Spoletta e tre birri introducono Mario Cavaradossi)
(Spoletta and three agents bring in Mario Cavaradossi)

FIGURE 39. Hohenstein costume design for Spoletta, Scarpia's henchman and chief of the sbirri. © Archivio Storico Casa Ricordi. Reproduced by permission

The interrogation scene that follows Cavaradossi's entrance is worth a close look, as Puccini once again plays the "real" music (the cantata) against the events of the drama, as he did with the Te Deum. As the interrogation proceeds the cantata moves from a simple line for three female voice parts to the full choir with soloist, sometimes standing out to mark a pause in the

FIGURE 40. One of the sbirri, a distinctly down-at-the-heels group as portrayed in the original costume designs for Act II. © Archivio Storico Casa Ricordi. Reproduced by permission

onstage exchanges, sometimes underscoring or contrasting with them. Finally, the choral work rises to climax, grating against Scarpia's nerves (and ours) like fingernails against glass.

The cantata begins twenty-four measures before Cavaradossi's entrance. The text is less than inspired; Eduardo Rescigno has commented that it is so poor it seems unlikely to have been the work of the librettists![26]

FIGURE 41. Hohenstein's costume drawing shows Roberti, the executioner, as a respectable professional in contrast to the scruffy sbirri. © Archivio Storico Casa Ricordi. Reproduced by permission

The human canticle[27] ascends and rises,
Through space, through the heavens,
By way of unknowable, empyreal suns,
Foretold by the Gospels,
It comes to you, O King of kings.
May this hymn fly to you,

To you may this hymn fly,
Supreme God of Victory.
God who was before the ages,
To the canticles of the angels,
This hymn of glory
May it now fly to you.
The human canticle ascends and rises,
Through space, through the heavens,
It comes to you, O King of kings.[28]

> CAV: *(haughtily, coming forward imperiously)*
>   Such violence!
> SCAR: *(with studied courtesy)*
>   Cavalier, please
>   be seated . . .
> CAV: I want to know . . .
> SCAR: *(pointing to a chair at the opposite side of the table)*
>   Sit down.
> CAV: *(refusing)*
>   I'm waiting.
> SCAR: So be it.

The chorus slows on the words "comes [to you] O King of kings"—a reference to the combined power of Church and State?—as Scarpia "looks fixedly" at Cavaradossi before beginning to question him. While he pauses, the male voices, led by the basses, begin the phrase that will culminate in Tosca's entrance as soloist.

> SCAR: You know that a prisoner . . .
>   *(breaks off as he hears Tosca in the cantata)*
> CAV: *(hearing Tosca's voice, he exclaims, deeply moved)*
>   Her voice!

Scarpia pauses for four measures, noting the effect that Tosca's voice has had on his prisoner (who realizes the implications of her presence as well as Scarpia did when he improvised this plan).

> SCAR: You know that a prisoner
>   escaped today from the Castel Sant'Angelo?
> CAV: I'm not aware of it.
> SCAR: And yet it is alleged that you
>   hid him in Sant'Andrea, provided him
>   with food and clothing . . .

Offstage, Tosca completes her entry line with an ending in a high C phrase—the first of three high Cs she sings in the opera, perhaps carefully selected for this spot in order to stress her role as a star performer.[29] Her high C underscores Cavaradossi's denial.

FIGURE 42. One of Piranesi's fantastic series, the *Carceri* (prisons), this one seems to show a man on a rack with a torture device similar to that suggested by Sardou in *La Tosca*. Sardou had a copy of this print in his private library. Musée du Louvre. Art Resource

> CAV: *(boldly)* Lies!
> SCAR: *(maintaining his calm)*
> . . . and guided him
> to a suburban farm of yours . . .
> CAV: I deny it. The proof?
> SCAR: *(unctuously)*
> A loyal subject . . .
> CAV: Get to the facts: who accuses me?
> *(with irony)*
> Your cops rummaged through the villa in vain!

The cantata has continued through this dialogue, with Tosca's voice high above the chorus. Here (II, 250–51) the expected C major resolution is disturbed by a return to the Interrogation motif, creating the effect of a sudden chill in the mood. Scarpia's response to Cavaradossi's demand for legal proof is cool, flat—the line is almost spoken.

> SCAR: Proof that he is well hidden.
> CAV: The suspicions of a spy!

There is a brief verbal scuffle as Cavaradossi sneers at Spoletta's search, the outraged spy responds with accusations, and Scarpia is goaded into a show of anger by the arrogance of Cavaradossi's reply:

> SPOL: *(offended, interrupts)*
> He laughed at our searching!
> CAV: And I'm still laughing, I'm still laughing!

The chorus takes up the melody of the cantata again—slow, regular, insistent—as Scarpia rises in anger.

> SCAR: *(rising, grimly)*
> This is a place for tears!
> *(threateningly)*
> Be careful!
> *(tensely)*
> That's enough now! Answer!

The divided chorus begins a crescendo that will end fortissimo as the voices build, once again emphasizing the words, "O King of kings!"—first bass and second tenor together; then first tenor, then contralto, then second soprano, first soprano, then Tosca's voice. As the lowest bass line joins the choir, Scarpia, furious, strides to the window and slams it shut, cutting the voices off in mid-phrase.

Scarpia orders Cavaradossi to speak, but the painter maintains his insolent refusal, even under a barely veiled threat of torture ("angoscia grande . . . ") In the orchestra there is an intriguing extension of the Scarpia/Tyranny motif (II, 296–97): following the two major chords on B♭, A♭/G♯ (see ex. 6.1), a third chord on F♯ is now added before the concluding E-major harmony, resulting for the first time in a true whole-tone sequence of four major chords (see ex. 8.4). This extension will occur again (II, 315–16) just after Scarpia has asked "for the last time" where Angelotti is hiding and Mario has repeated his denial.

Ex. 8.4. Scarpia/Tyranny expanded (II, 296–97)

When Tosca hurries in Mario manages to whisper to her to keep quiet, "or you'll kill me." He is taken away, and the game of cat and mouse begins in earnest.

After a doleful interlude as Cavaradossi is led away (see fig. 43), Scarpia again becomes the courtier. Gallant, formally polite, the baron reassures his guest, suggesting that they chat, "like good friends," and resumes the conversation, and the innuendos, he had begun at the church. This little scene of gentility and politesse only heightens the tension, superimposed as it is over the brutal violence that we know (although Tosca does not) is taking place offstage. The music is almost exactly reflected at the end of the torture scene, when Scarpia will once again put on the cloak of politeness.

Formal receptions such as the one Tosca has just left normally began at the first or second hour of the night, nine or ten o'clock in mid-June. And since (in both the play and the opera) the party has been going on for some time before the diva arrives, we can guess that by the time the cantata is finished and the diva makes her excuses and hurries up the stairs to the office-apartments of the chief of police it is at least 11 P.M. This rapid journey upstairs is another example of operatic telescoping, made necessary by pasting two Sardou acts together: Tosca has only 150 bars of music, or less than

FIGURE 43. "Mario Cavaradossi, qual testimonio il giudice v'aspetta." Cavaradossi is led away to torture, while Tosca remains alone with Scarpia. One of the publicity series prepared by Metlikovitz for Ricordi at the premiere of the opera. © Archivio Storico Casa Ricordi. Reproduced by permission

four minutes, from the time the cantata begins until she appears at the door of the baron's apartments, understandably out of breath. She has only a moment in her lover's arms before the grim machinery of the State grinds into action and he is taken away.

Had Tosca been a real historical person she would not have been surprised to see Cavaradossi under arrest. By spring of 1800 getting arrested was a very easy thing to accomplish. About six weeks before the fictional Cavaradossi case, a real episode occurred, which neither a Tosca nor a Cavaradossi could have avoided knowing all about, as it began in the Valle theater during a performance. On the evening of 28 April, two weeks after Easter and at the height of the spring theater season, Crispino Abbondi, a young Roman with liberal sympathies, joined some noble friends in their box. The conversation turned to military rumors and Abbondi commented that, according to what he heard, the French were steadily gaining ground in the north despite the Allied bulletins so confidently posted in the *Diario di Roma*. In fact, he told his friends, rumor had it that the French would be back in Rome before the first of June. It took governor Diego Naselli less than twenty-four hours to get word of this conversation. The young man was invited to an interview with the governor that recalls phrases and attitudes from the second act of the opera. Galimberti writes that "with pleasant manners" Naselli tried to get his involuntary guest to say just who the Jacobin was who had said these things. But Abbondi, in best operatic fashion, drew himself up and announced that Naselli "could kill him if he liked, but he would never tell him anything." And so he went to the Castel Sant'Angelo to join the 900 or so prisoners who were clogging up the penal system.[30]

Abbondi's was a relatively informal interrogation, apparently with no physical force used to encourage cooperation (see fig. 44). The case against Ottavio Cappelli was a great deal more serious; Cappelli was hanged at the end of it. But his lawyer could with no apparent sense of irony or daring state that "Extra-judicial confessions are not valid, and everyone knows it. It is up to the court to prove the truth of an extra-judicial confession."[31]

Equally serious was the case against Saverio Pediconi, a self-made man who would have been a neighbor (though not a social equal) of Cavaradossi. Pediconi was arrested on 20 November 1799 when a quantity of arms was found in his home, along with a great deal of lead discovered hidden in the well. Antonio Negri, the notary who was called in to witness the arrest, described the event: "I was called to the house of the accused at around the seventh hour of the night [around 2 A.M.]. When I got there I saw, by the light of several lamps and torches, the defendant Saverio Pediconi under arrest, locked in a room in his house."[32]

FIGURE 44. An eighteenth-century propaganda illustration purporting to show the *tratti di corda* being applied to a liberal (identifiable by his haircut) by the Inquisition. Author's collection

The Pediconi case contains hundreds of pages of evidence, arguments, questions and statements by witnesses, accusers, defenders, co-defendants, soldiers, notaries, and officials. At one point (on Sunday, 8 December 1799) a co-defendant stated "I thought about adding to my testimony in order to prove my innocence better, but I wanted to hold off until I could notify the public defender . . ." (that is, Agostino Valle). This is not the language of people being tortured, or threatened with torture.

The incriminating evidence in the Pediconi case leans heavily on three points: the immoral character of his life (a girl's brothers and father accused him of seducing her); rude and offensive comments about the emperor (Francis II of Austria) made in the hearing of some of his employees ("If you're waiting for that fucking pig of an emperor . . ."); and his ongoing association with known republicans. The first and third points, and perhaps the second as well, are also applicable in the Cavaradossi case: the fictional hero is a man involved in a blatantly sexual liaison, a man who barely attempts to hide his political opinions, and (if we can take his sarcastic treatment of Spoletta, or his Act I comments on Scarpia, as any indication) a man with little good to say about the rulers of Rome.

The most notable thing about the Governing Committee cases is that there is very little sign of a Terror. While getting arrested was fairly easy, most defendants were released for lack of proof, or found innocent, or sentenced to exile or short prison terms. Others were released after paying large "contributions"—so that Floria's contemptuous demand to know "How much?" *(Quanto?)* in Act II of the opera is a perfectly reasonable one under the circumstances.

If we superimpose the fictional drama of the second act of *Tosca* over the real Rome of 1800, the result is the following: Mario Cavaradossi has certainly broken any number of laws and is by his very nature a dubious character. But the political affair with which he has entangled himself should result in nothing worse than a police beating and a hefty bribe; at worst he would have to submit to the stress and expense of a long and annoying trial, and after that perhaps exile (no burden for a rich man planning to leave the city in any case). Instead, he faces torture and death. Clearly Scarpia is acting at the outside limits of the law. Above all, he is walking on very thin ice by having Cavaradossi tortured. The law required at least what was called "half proof" before an official, even a Scarpia, could legally prepare a warrant ordering a suspect to be questioned under torture. Half proof had to consist of one unimpeachable and demonstrably disinterested eyewitness to the offense, or else the sort of circumstantial evidence that would put the matter beyond reasonable doubt. In the case of the Crown v. Cavaradossi Scarpia has neither.

The law could, of course, be bent. If he were quite sure of getting the proof he needed and if the judge were agreeable (and this judge seems to be living, as they say, in Scarpia's pocket) then the chief of police could get away with saying that he had more proof than he actually had—thus the fictitious "loyal subject" *(suddito fedele)* that Scarpia suavely produces when Cavaradossi (who understands the law as well as anyone) demands to know the identity of the witnesses against him *(Chi m'accusa?)*. Confident that there

can be no such person, Mario assumes that the police will have to rely on Spoletta's testimony; and Spoletta has found nothing *(i vostri birri invan frugar
la villa)*. The painter simply misjudges how far out onto a limb Scarpia is
willing to climb.

In the time between sending for the judiciary officials and ordering them to
proceed using "the usual methods" *(le forme ordinarie)*, Scarpia would make
out a warrant (probably on a printed form) on his own authority, directing
that the suspect be questioned under torture. The judge, for his own protection, would never proceed without such a warrant in his hands.[33] In it Scarpia would refer to his files containing half proof such as the "loyal subject"
and the circumstantial evidence already recorded in Cavaradossi's growing
dossier: the portrait, the fan, the Sacristan's evidence about the lunch basket,
Spoletta's testimony, and the statements of other relevant witnesses.

For the prisoner, the presence of the judge and public executioner would
be reassuring rather than alarming: if Scarpia has decided to act within the
law, then the protection of the law could tip the balance in favor of the accused. For one thing, though the proceedings are certain to be horribly unpleasant they will not be fatal nor will permanent injury be likely. It was not
unknown for accused persons to bring charges of excessive brutality against
the official torturer and his assistants—and win their cases.[34] Even more important, Scarpia has apparently staked everything on a confession, and all
Mario has to do is see to it that he doesn't get one. The Cavaliere Cavaradossi
is certainly a well-educated young man, if a somewhat reckless one. When he
needles Spoletta into arresting him (no doubt to get the police away from the
villa) he can hardly expect that events will take the turn they soon do. Nevertheless, he would know something about Roman and probably Neapolitan
law. On that basis his behavior is neither foolishly heroic nor irrational: he is
simply a man of rather more than average courage who has found himself in
a dangerous but by no means hopeless situation and is making the best of it.

In the real Rome, the cards on the table between the two men as the second act begins would have been rather more evenly distributed than they appear to be in the opera. In this context Mario's words to Tosca—"Sprezzo il
dolor"—might be loosely translated, "The pain doesn't matter." And he's
right, it doesn't. What matters is that no one should talk. It is perfectly reasonable, from his point of view.

What he has not reckoned on, and what Scarpia has staked everything on,
is Floria Tosca's political naïveté (to say nothing of her understandable distress at hearing the man she loves screaming in pain). As a good royalist she
would have refused to believe the rumors about events in Naples the previous summer, but now, confronted with the undeniable reality, she would re-

member all of them and imagine the very worst: her lover, she would be certain, is being killed, and in a particularly horrible fashion. She is wrong. Mario knows it and tries to tell her so, and Scarpia knows it, though he is of course delighted to let her believe what she will. Thus Mario's fury when he finds out that she has given away his secret is not simply that of an idealist thwarted in his attempt to sacrifice himself; nor is it merely the outrage of a proto-nineteenth-century male whose mistress has done something he has expressly forbidden (though there is certainly an element of that). Rather it is the frustrated rage of someone who has gone through a great deal in a very dangerous game with the law and has almost won.

Spoletta, Sciarrone, and the sbirri take Cavaradossi into an offstage room.[35] **The judge, the clerk, and Roberti follow. Tosca and Scarpia remain alone on the stage.**

The torture scene required a great deal of work from the librettists. Sardou used it almost exclusively as a showcase for Sarah Bernhardt's histrionic talents. Scarpia was confined to irony and implacability, while Cavaradossi had only a few short lines in which to reassure Tosca and forbid her to speak. Puccini, with his self-described Neronic impulses, was certainly attracted by the prospect of setting the scene to music. Illica had long objected to the drama because it seemed to call for a long series of scenes involving only two characters. While he was still preparing a libretto for Franchetti, he seems to have viewed this scene as an opportunity to vary the musical menu with a quartet.[36] The results, as we see below, were both stilted and graphically sadistic.

TOSCA: *(always toward the entrance, twisting her hands in sorrow)*
Mario! . . . Speak to me, Mario!
Let me hear you! . . . Just one . . .
Just one word! . . .
(she stops at the voice of the Procurator and listens again)
They're killing him! . . .
(against Scarpia)
Ah, assassin!
(terrible)
A heartless mother gave you birth!
But beware, Scarpia, this lament of mine
is being marked by Christ in God's book!
On that day I will be there! With you, and implacable!
All the torments and the pain of hell
You will have, and your lament will be eternal!
PROCURA: Why so cruel with you?
SPOL: Speak!
PROCURA: He will not answer!
(to the assistants)

Tighten again!
(amid Mario's groans the Procurator's voice continues
to insist)
Where [is he]? Where? Where?
SPOL: *(muttering prayers and invoking the names of saints)*
Beautiful Lady of the Seven Sorrows..
My Lord Jesus! . . . All the martyrs . . .
(Cavaradossi gives a smothered groan)
CAV: *(between groans and cries of pain)*
You* can make me suffer
thousands and thousands of fierce pains,
thousands and thousands of miseries!
You* can kill me!
But the outrages
won't tear a cry from me!
Break me apart! Tear me to pieces!
Lacerate my temples and my brow!
I defy your* torture!
I defy your* death!
SCAR: *(silent, always calm, cold, and impassive, he remains standing*
near the table, not moving) [37]

The scene as it now exists is a tightly focused duel between Scarpia and Tosca, who is gradually and inexorably beaten down until she can only gasp out the secret of the hiding place.

As Tosca sobs, Spoletta mutters a verse from the Dies irae, the sequence in the Requiem Mass: "When that Judge takes his seat that which was hidden will be seen, in the end nothing will be remain unjudged."[38] Scarpia signals for the resumption of the torture. Tosca, unable to bear her lover's suffering, tells Scarpia where Angelotti can be found.

Just before Tosca reveals the secret, one more chord is is added to the sequence in the Scarpia/Tyranny motif (II, 498–500), further expanding the series of four first noted at II, 296–97. Now there are five major chords in the whole-tone progression: C–B♭–A♭–G♭–E. The whole-tone scale is almost completed here, except for the revealing omission of one chord, on D Major.

Dramatically, the gradual expansion of the whole-tone sequence is connected with the struggle between Scarpia and Cavaradossi over Angelotti, but more important, over the possession of Tosca. This is a struggle that Cavaradossi will at first lose because his lover cannot keep the secret he unwillingly entrusted to her, but will eventually win, taking her with him in death (a fact

---

*All of these second person references are in the singular, and in the familiar ("tu"), and are thus presumably addressed, insultingly, to Scarpia.

that might go some way toward explaining the controversial end of the opera; see pp. 254–56).

At this point in the action Tosca has collapsed and there is a lull while Spoletta intones a verse from the Dies Irae. Once again Puccini ties the institutional Church to the oppressive tyranny of the State. Spoletta, who earlier in the act appealed to Saint Ignatius for help, now mutters his Latin as if he were singing chant. After a fermata, we hear "a prolonged and high-pitched cry of pain" from the tortured Cavaradossi, and then, Allegro vivace, the almost completed whole-tone sequence—missing only the previously stated D major—followed by Tosca's gasping out of the secret: "In the well! . . . in the garden!" *(Nel pozzo! . . . nel giardino!)*.

> **Scarpia orders the now unconscious Cavaradossi released and brought back to the salon. As he regains consciousness he asks Tosca if she has talked. She lies but Scarpia ensures that the prisoner knows what has happened. Furious, he pushes her away, cursing.**

As the agents carry the unconscious Cavaradossi into the room (the dirge-like Interrogation motif [ex. 8.3] accompanies them, followed by Cavaradossi's love motif [ex. 6.7]). The stage directions tell us:

> Cavaradossi, in a faint, is carried in by the agents and laid on the sofa. Tosca runs to him, but is stricken with horror at the sight of his bleeding face and stops, covering her eyes with her hands. Ashamed of her weakness Tosca approaches Cavaradossi and covers him with kisses and tears.

She is gentle, sure, protective, holding him close and maybe rocking him slightly in her arms. Gradually he revives, recognizes her, and then asks "Did you talk?" *(Hai parlato?)*.[39] And she lies with absolute assurance, like a mother soothing a restless child by keeping away knowledge he is not ready to cope with.

This is the little tableau that Scarpia chooses to shatter. He is both a sadist and a voyeur; watching the lovers and using his imagination is half his pleasure. But now he wants to see the next scene. He turns to Spoletta and gives his orders—loudly, so that Cavaradossi will know that his resistance has been useless, he has been betrayed by the woman he loves, and both he and his friend are doomed: "In the well in the garden. Go, Spoletta!" *(Nel pozzo del giardino. Va, Spoletta!)*. Scarpia's triumph, pieced together during the interrogation and torture, is now total, and both of the lovers are helpless before him. Immediately, Allegro violento and fortissimo, comes the full expansion of the scale (II, 544–47; ex. 8.5).

Ex. 8.5. Full expansion of Scarpia/Tyranny (II, 544–47)

Vittoria!

It is at this musically satisfying point that the most unconvincing dramatic transition in the opera occurs. Puccini and his librettists, in order to get rid of Cavaradossi and clear the way for Scarpia's murder, drag in a version of the dramatic episode with which Sardou ended his second act, at the royal reception: the arrival of the stunning news that Bonaparte has after all won the battle of Marengo. This is one of those points where Sardou seems to come very close to actual historical events, though his use of the episode is pure fiction.

Queen Maria Carolina of Naples was not in Rome on 17 June 1800. She had arrived at Livorno three days earlier and bobbed about outside the harbor for two days on Nelson's flagship the *Foudroyant* waiting for the weather to clear, and debarked on 16 June.[40] The first news from Marengo arrived on the following day, while she was still in Livorno. Later the same evening the second bulletin arrived, with the astounding news that the French had in fact won the battle. Pietro Colletta, a contemporary who loathed the Bourbons and whose sense of drama easily overbalanced his sense of objective accuracy, gives the following account of the event:

> Awaiting the second report, [the Queen] left orders to be awakened when the news arrived, no matter the hour. Thus it happened that in the middle of that same night, the message arrived; she was awakened and, while opening the letter, said: "Let us read of the end of Bonaparte's presumptuous military exercise." But when, stupefied and incredulous, she read the news of Mélas's defeat, she had to reread it to confirm for herself the sad message. Then her voice failed her, and she collapsed on the woman who had awakened her. Revived, she saw the loathed letter once more and fell ill.[41]

Sardou transposes this event to the Farnese palace, and makes it even more dramatic by having the Queen read the letter aloud to her assembled guests at the royal reception. As she realizes what the words she is reading mean, she faints. Whatever the circumstances under which she received the news, it was certainly a terrible shock. On 28 June, almost two weeks later, she wrote to Palermo, "I very nearly died," and, "for several days I have been stupefied, my memory gone, my head quite empty." [42]

Even if Maria Carolina had been in Rome, Tosca would have had very little luck appealing to her for a pardon for Cavaradossi. Not only would the news from Marengo have erased any trace of sympathy the Queen might have had for rebels (and she never displayed much of that), she would not even have been conscious to hear the appeal.

The news from the north was at least as momentous as the play and the opera suggest. In a dazzling display, Bonaparte had returned from Egypt, consolidated his power in France, and then crossed the St. Bernard Pass over the Alps into Italy. Late in the afternoon of 14 June 1800, in a textbook example of the cliché, he snatched victory from the jaws of defeat. Overnight, Italy passed from being dominated by Austria and Naples to being under French control, and it would remain thus until the overthrow of Napoleon in 1814.

News of the battle reached Rome during the evening hours of 17 June, according to Galimberti. The recorded reaction of men like Cavaradossi was hardly more dignified or reasonable than that of the operatic tenor, and they didn't even have the excuse of being semiconscious. They sang and danced in the street, and built a large bonfire as close as they could get to the Castel Sant'Angelo, for the sole purpose of annoying the soldiers there (see chap. 9).[43]

Puccini brings in the bulletin from Marengo at the moment when Cavaradossi, who has just learned that Tosca has given away Angelotti's hiding place, pushes her away violently. Sciarrone bursts in with news of the battle and the room erupts.

An early draft of the libretto includes a scribbled version of a formal expository trio that Illica (again trying to escape the monotonous series of duets) designed to follow the announcement of Napoleon's victory at Marengo. It was no doubt rejected because its rather old-fashioned form was judged inappropriate for the dramatic context, as indeed it is. One might ask, however, if the version that was finally accepted—a hysterical outburst from Cavaradossi, with broken pleas and interjections from Tosca and sardonic mutterings from Scarpia—is much preferable. Despite its old-fashioned form and high-flown language, the earlier version contains some interesting characterizations. Mario includes Floria in his rejoicing, seeing both her and himself as victims of tyranny. Floria's response is more practical—"What does that matter to us?"—as she pleads with Scarpia not to listen to him, all the while trying to get her lover to leave, not yet realizing that her confession and his outburst have condemned him. Scarpia, for his part, laughs at Cavaradossi and, as in the final version of the libretto, informs him that he is "already dead."[44]

CAV: *([illegible] . . . avidly)*
Is it victory?
(to Floria, with great enthusiasm)
Victory,
that brings the butcher down
and makes the victim powerful!
We are avenged, Floria!
Let him tremble who forced the soft lips
of a trembling woman
to make the grave accusation
that kills her lover!
(with supreme enthusiasm)
I exult! I live! and I forget!
Atheist, I believe in God!*

TOSCA: What does that matter to us?
(goes to take Mario's cloak)
Put this on and let's leave . . .
(to Scarpia)
Don't listen to him!
(to Mario, her voice filled with fear and [illegible])
Be still!
First let us get beyond
this dark door.
Our victory—kisses,
our glory—love.
No! *(to Scarpia)*
Come! *(trying to pull Mario away)*
(menacing Scarpia) Ah, traitor,
this is vile! . . . Vile! . . . you made a spy of me
and now . . .
(interrupts and trying desperately to hold on to Mario, cries out desperately to Spoletta)
Don't take him away from me!

SCAR: *(sneering at Cavaradossi)*
Victory?
(runs to the window and [illegible] gestures toward the Castel Sant'Angelo)
Look there in the heavy air;
look at the Castel Sant'Angelo!
Your victory is a scaffold!
Dying man, exult in your brief joy!

---

*As late as the first printed libretto (1899) the "Vittoria" trio was preceded by Cavaradossi's words, "Ah, there is an avenging God!" *(Ah, c'è un Dio vendicator!)*.

You'd do better to pray in the hour of your death agony.
(to Spoletta)
Come now, end it! Get him away from me!
(and while Spoletta and the sbirri take hold of Cavaradossi, tells him, ironically)
Scarpia is still the strong one here,
and your name is Death!

Once Cavaradossi has been ejected, the frantic music dies away (II, 615–18) and the shattered woman can only groan ("come un gemito"), "Save him!" It is here (II, 619–21) that we see the final expansion of the motif we have called Scarpia's Plan (ex. 8.1). The stage directions are quite specific here: Scarpia goes toward the table, sees his interrupted meal, and is once again calm and smiling. The chief of police again assumes a mask of courtesy as he had done when Tosca first arrived in his rooms.

Scarpia's formal, almost ritual, courtesy fills a number of functions. It illustrates the hypocrisy that was, for Puccini and his librettists, such an important part of Scarpia's character. It places him squarely in the gallant, courtly world of the eighteenth century, perceived as insincere and corrupt from the vantage point of a century later. And it makes the "cat and mouse" game that he plays all the more chilling.

Tosca, well aware that Scarpia is a corrupt official, offers to pay for Cavaradossi's release. She is not, however, prepared for the price.

A change occurs in the relationships among the characters at this point, a change that is lost in English but is obvious in Italian. The historically defined class structure can still be seen in the grammar of most European languages. In the late nineteenth century Italian, unlike English, retained (and still retains) two quite different forms of the second person singular pronoun, and of the second person plural. In English, "you" does service in both the singular and the plural for polite intercourse as well as for addressing intimates and inferiors (once addressed as "thee"). In the Italian of Puccini's day, a superior, or a person in a formal situation or relationship, was addressed as *voi*, while an inferior or intimate was given the *tu*.[45] Scarpia drops the polite *voi* with Cavaradossi surprisingly late in the game: throughout the interrogation and torture, he addresses the Cavaliere, as is appropriate to his rank, in the polite form. (In the final version of the libretto Tosca slips once during the torture, when Scarpia laughs at her, and she exclaims, "You *(tu)* laugh . . . ?" *(tu ridi . . . ?)*; II, 450). It is only during the *Vittoria!* outburst that Scarpia's courtesy gives way, in phrases like "Get out! You're a dead man, the scaffold is waiting for you *[tu]*" (*il capestro t'aspetta;* II, 600–601). He continues to use the *voi* with Floria, again throughout the interrogation and torture, and as he offers her a glass of Spanish wine to restore her spirits he phrases the offer in the formal: "to give you *[voi]* courage" (*per rincorar*vi; II, 641). But when he rejects Tosca's offer of money he begins to address her in the second person familiar—as *tu* rather than *voi:* "a little while ago I saw you *[tu]* as I had never seen you before" (*poc'anzi* ti *mirai qual non* ti *vidi mai;* II, 689).

It is at this point, when he drops the formulas of polite society, that we see him clearly as what he is: a sexual sadist.[46] Puccini, who liked to walk the dark corridors of the human mind, moved this element of his villain's character to the foreground, though the librettists toned down Scarpia's most graphic language from the play, where he could say:

> That's how I want you! A woman who gives herself, a polite affair, I'm fed up with those. But your loathing, your humiliation and anger . . . to break your resistance and feel you twist in my arms . . . By God, that's the flavor of the thing, resignation would ruin it for me! [And later:] . . . that you should be mine, with rage and grief, that I should feel your outraged soul struggle . . . feel your revolted body tremble with passion despite yourself, in forced abandon to my loathsome caresses, to feel all of your flesh enslaved to my flesh! What revenge for your contempt, what vengeance for your insults, what a refinement of voluptuousness, that my pleasure should also be your torture![47]

This is clinically sadistic language, and historically Scarpia would have been a contemporary of the Marquis de Sade, who was born in 1740 in Paris and died in the madhouse of Charenton in 1814. De Sade liked to consider himself a latter-day *philosophe,* and although few liberal thinkers were willing to admit him as a colleague he was in fact representative of a major facet of Enlightenment thinking. Much of the literature that was banned in the pre-Revolutionary period as "philosophical" was frankly pornographic.[48] Certainly an energetic police official would have considered it his duty to confiscate any copies of de Sade's work that he found, and it is piquant to think of Scarpia furnishing his bedside reading table with works appropriated from the libraries of liberals.

The libertine, of course, has a much longer pedigree than the eighteenth century. Ovid's *Ars amatoria* offers a view very similar to that of Scarpia:

> "Oh, but I should hate to use brute force," you say. Why, that is exactly what girls like: they often prefer to enjoy themselves under duress. The victim of a sexual assault is generally delighted, for she takes your audacity as a compliment; whereas the girl who could have been raped but was not is bound to feel disappointed.[49]

Sardou's play includes the following exchange between Tosca and Scarpia, set at the royal reception. Scarpia, not quite sure whether or not Tosca is directly involved with Angelotti's escape, initiates a conversation laden with sado-masochistic eroticism, a conversation in which the convent-bred Floria Tosca more than holds her own and which suggests that she, like Scarpia and Ovid, was not entirely repulsed by the idea that women "prefer to enjoy themselves under duress":

> SCAR: *(leans over the sofa behind Floria, taking the hand that she has rested on the arm of the sofa and pressing it softly between his two hands, smiling)*
> Are you aware, Signora, that I could put handcuffs on this pretty wrist there and send you to the Castel Sant'Angelo?
>
> TOSCA: *(calmly, preoccupied with her sheet music, not taking her hand back)*
> Arrest me?
>
> SCAR: Absolutely.
>
> TOSCA: Why?
>
> SCAR: For displaying seditious colors.
>
> TOSCA: My dress?
>
> SCAR: This bracelet! Rubies, diamonds, and sapphires: clearly a perfect tricolor.
>
> TOSCA: *(quickly taking her arm back)*
> Ah! It's true! If the queen were to see it . . .
>
> SCAR: I'm only teasing. No one but I would notice. You are too well known for your devotion to the Church and the king . . . *(sitting next to her)* . . . unfortunately!
>
> TOSCA: Why unfortunately?
>
> SCAR: *(gallantly)* Oh, yes! I would take great pleasure in having you as a prisoner.
>
> TOSCA: *(gaily)* In a dungeon?
>
> SCAR: *(the same)* And under triple bolts, to keep you from escaping.
>
> TOSCA: And you'd torture me, too, maybe?
>
> SCAR: Until you loved me.
>
> TOSCA: *(picking up her music again)* If that's the only way you could manage it!
>
> SCAR: Well, women don't mind a little violence.
>
> TOSCA: It's true that there are some very ugly rumors about what goes on there, with women.[50]

The relationship between the policeman and the singer in this exchange is a classic example of libertine gender relations, in which the woman was by definition prey. Little or no shame attached to a man for taking the merchandise that was available. If Scarpia has some slight twinges of conscience (or is at least aware that he *should* have twinges of conscience) about selling his official influence ["Già, mi dicon venal"], he certainly has none about raping the mistress of a political subversive who is unable to protect her. The fact that she is both an orphan and a performer makes her even more vulnerable.[51]

If Puccini's Floria seems unaware of her status as merchandise, or the spoils of war, she has been misled by circumstances. Her convent upbringing, which would have stressed chastity and honor, and the papal order that set her on her career, no doubt encouraged her to think that, far from being defenseless, she enjoys the powerful protection of the Church. Unfortunately for her, in Rome on the night between 17 and 18 June 1800, in a city without a pope, this protection is not enough.

Floria, we know, has a flexible conscience. Sleeping with a man to whom she is not married is not in her view a particularly important sin. While this was not a canonically acceptable view, it certainly was (and remains) a common one.[52] Since the grave sin of adultery does not enter into the question, it might indeed seem a minor transgression in a nation where the sins of the flesh were never considered anywhere near as dangerous as the sins of the spirit or the intellect. Tosca does have problems with her confessor, but they center around Cavaradossi's "revolutionary" mustache, not his love-making.

Within a few hours these frivolities will disappear and be replaced by true moral dilemmas. Can she reveal a secret she has sworn to keep, when revealing it will cost one man his life? and keeping it has such dreadful consequences for another? Once that terrible decision is made, she is faced with an equally difficult one. Sex with a man she loves is one thing; submission to a patently evil man who terrifies her is quite a different one. Even rape would be morally ambiguous in her eyes; she would be required to do everything possible to avoid it, even at the risk of her life (she briefly, and not too convincingly, threatens suicide ["Ah, piuttosto giù mi avvento!"]).

Scarpia has made her submission infinitely more difficult in moral terms by making it a matter of choice.[53] Some interpreters of the role, as well as some opera lovers, see Scarpia's willingness to allow her to leave and his insistence that she freely choose to agree to his demands as evidence, not of sadism, but that the baron's fascination with the singer at least totters on the edge of the line between lust and love. There is, however, little evidence of self-sacrificing love on Scarpia's part in either Puccini or Sardou. In the play he taunts his helpless victim:

> If the bargain doesn't appeal to you, go ahead, the door is open. But I dare you to do it. You will cry out, insult me, invoke the Virgin and the saints! Waste time in useless words. After which, having nothing better to do, you will say "Yes."[54]

She must freely choose to break every rule that she respects—the law of the Church, the lessons of the convent that reared her, and her own moral code that demands fidelity to, as well as from, her chosen partner. In spite of the late nineteenth-century view that sexual morality was unimportant in Italy (an opinion that often had as much to do with wishful thinking as with objective observation), even in Venice, the "party capital" of Europe, the schools that trained orphan girls took chastity very seriously indeed.

Floria, horrified, seizes upon another traditional recourse: she will appeal to the Queen for mercy.

Tosca is free to go to the Queen because she is not under arrest. The arrest of a person like Floria Tosca would certainly have led to riots, and no one wanted popular uprisings on the eve of the new pope's arrival. Not only is she a much-loved theatrical star, she is also an acknowledged pet of Maria Carolina, who might ask very pointed questions about her arrest, and not like the answers.[55] Worst of all, as a native of Verona, the singer is a distinguished citizen of the Empire, which had recently absorbed the Republic of Venice and its dependent territories in the Veneto. Her position is comparable to that of the sculptor Antonio Canova, who lived for a time in the Venezia palace and enjoyed what almost amounted to diplomatic immunity.[56] For a Neapolitan police official to arrest and mistreat an Imperial citizen on evidence as flimsy as Scarpia's would be to risk the fury of the powerful Austrian state; and Austria was clearly calling the shots in the Roman situation: Naselli, operating on orders from Palermo, was trying his best to hold on to Rome, and it was pressure from Austria that finally pried his fingers loose. Scarpia would have to be either maddened by lust, or impulsively seizing the opportunity offered by the confusion after the news from Marengo, to even consider doing what he tries to do.

Floria, whose political naïveté is obvious to everyone, does not recognize the strength of her own position, but she does assume that she has some chance of influencing the Queen. Maria Carolina, even more than most monarchs, was given to passionate affection for her pets. Her most famous favorite was Emma Hamilton, who, like the fictional Floria Tosca, was beautiful, a talented performer, and not entirely respectable. In Sardou's play, the Queen has been kind to Floria, and might incline to indulgence. However, Scarpia has strong motives for executing Cavaradossi before a royal pardon can reach him. Scarpia has already overreached his authority with extrajudicial torture and soliciting a bribe; both would be easier to deny if the gentleman in question were dead.

Any final resistance on Tosca's part is crushed when she hears the sound of drums which, as Scarpia points out, accompany the last escort for the condemned.

The military drums, which appear here and at the very close of the act, are yet another example of Puccini's including "real" music from the world of the characters. This dramatic moment, in which Scarpia brutally extinguishes the last flicker of hope his victim might cherish, occurs only in the opera. Scarpia, his voice echoing the rhythmic pattern of the drum, coldly points out that "your [*tuo*] Mario, by your choice, has only a hour of life left." The drumbeat rises to a climax, and begins to fade (II, 775–77). The orchestra staggers back, as if exhausted, and dies away, and Tosca, alone and abandoned, softly begins the troublesome aria, *Vissi d'arte*.

The aria has been dismissed as a self-dramatizing whine, a cry of self-pity, and Puccini himself disliked it for stopping the action (which indeed it does, though this tends to be true to one degree or other of operatic arias in general). There is, however, a psychological insight here, one that illustrates the often observed fact that Puccini was in many ways a cinematic composer.[57] The aria provides a "freeze frame" in which time stops for one character and her life passes before her eyes.

If Floria Tosca is remembering her life, what is she seeing? The aria is introduced by chords that Girardi and Carner have described as vaguely ecclesiastical, "psalm-like melody,"[58] followed by music nearly identical with that of her Act I entrance (cf. ex. 6.5; I, 411) where she swept into the church of Sant'Andrea with flowers, to the warm embrace of her lover. Her words tell us that she has lived "for art and for love." But here, as in the first act, her description of romantic love seems inextricably combined with her religious observances—harming no one, giving alms, prayers, and flowers.[59]

After this first claim to virtue comes the plea, or the complaint: "Why? Why, Lord, do you reward me like this?" She then returns to the heart of her self-justification—her gifts of jewels and music to "make the stars and the heavens more beautiful." The only trace of love in the text of this aria is *caritas*, or almsgiving. While we can hardly expect a woman threatened with rape to discourse on the joys of physical love, as Mario will in Act III, it is nonetheless odd that she makes no reference, however chaste, to her love for the man who got her into this trouble in the first place. Only the orchestra hints at their love, and that only within the context of the church, where physical love and piety become entangled. Whether or not the aria is dramatically justifiable, it does offer a tantalizing statement of the fin-de-siècle conflation of love, art, and religion. Here art (in this case, music) is portrayed as indistinguishable from religion, and both blend with romantic love into a typically Puccinian mélange.

Vissi d'arte is yet another case, and one of the most revealing, of a scene and a characterization that have no parallel in the Sardou play. The French Floria is desperate, raging, heartbroken, or vulnerable, but she is never introspective and she is never sincerely religious, not even in a self-pitying sort of fashion. Any mention of God or the saints on her part is merely a way of teasing Cavaradossi or cursing Scarpia. The closest parallel to *Vissi d'arte* in the play has her spitting invective at her tormentor, then crying out, "Good God, powerful God, saving God! That there should be such a man and that you should let him act! Don't you see him, then? Don't you hear him?" To which Scarpia, who recognizes a fellow hypocrite, replies, laughing: "If He is all you're counting on . . . !"[60]

The operatic heroine, on the other hand, insists repeatedly on the sincerity of her faith, and in this aria cites classically Catholic good deeds to prove her case: not only has she given to the poor, she has done so generously and anonymously, "with a furtive hand"; she has dedicated her talent to the greater glory of God, *ad majorem dei gloriam*; like women in every village in Italy, she has given her jewels to decorate the image of the Virgin. The aria is an expression of Tosca's characteristically immature Catholicism in which she is puzzled to find that her investment of piety and good works has drawn such bitter dividends. It is here, along with a few of her more kittenish moments in Act I, where we see Tosca as one of Puccini's "little women," simple, vulnerable, and defined by love.

"I never harmed a living soul," she almost sobs, on a falling phrase. If we believe her, we realize that this is Puccini at his most Neronic. It recalls the image of the child saint Agnes, naked except for her long hair, led by Roman soldiers to the brothel where she is to be raped as punishment for her Christianity. It also recalls a particularly repellent piece of Edwardian pornography, an etching that shows a barely adolescent girl, decked with flowers but otherwise naked, seated spread-legged in the sand of the arena, a look of numb, confused horror on her pretty face; the ropes tied to each wrist and each ankle lead to four wild horses, which are on the point of being lashed into a gallop that will literally tear her limb from limb. Floria, like the child in the picture, is on the point of being torn apart. The aria ends and the Scarpia/Tyranny motif returns, but transposed down a fifth. The baron demands that she make up her mind, and her response is a defeated whimper: "Do you want me begging at your feet?" *(Mi vuoi supplice ai tuoi piedi?)* (The familiar, which Tosca uses here, is also a sign of absolute submission—one uses it when addressing God.) This exchange, which is all too often cut to make room for applause, is followed by a coda in which she pleads for mercy. Scarpia cannot resist a particularly vicious trick. He pretends to yield— "You're too beautiful, Tosca, and too loving: I give in!" Hope leaps up only to be dashed: "It's a cheap price—I'm giving you a life, I only ask you for a moment!"[61]

> *Spoletta interrupts with news that Angelotti has been found but has killed himself. Time has run out, and Floria agrees to the bargain. She insists on hearing the orders for a simulated execution, and then, delaying the coming ordeal, demands a safe conduct out of the state.*

Spoletta's round trip to the villa is the most obvious point where the time frame of the opera is out of synchronization with the real world. Sardou's play offers a much more realistic outline of the movements of the characters. In compressing the action for the opera the librettists have made impossible demands, intellectual as well as physical (such as Scarpia's hyper-speed deductions in Act I; Floria's instant rehearsal; the remarkably short cantata, and the diva's rapid escape from the royal presence). These culminate in Spoletta's jet-age dash from the Farnese to the outskirts of the city, and back, in something under fifteen minutes; a difficult feat in a fast car with a police escort if you don't bother to get out at the villa. (An updated version of the opera developed for the Maggio Musicale in Florence, later produced at the English National Opera, set the action in 1944 and had Spoletta in charge of a radio-directed dragnet of the city, which brought this part of the operation back into the realm of the physically possible.)

Scarpia's order that Angelotti's corpse be hung on the gallows is unelaborated in the opera, but the play offers a sort of explanation. The chief of police does not want it known that Angelotti has escaped hanging by committing suicide; as he remarks jovially to Sciarrone, "Angelotti having been condemned to the gallows, certainly has the right to a hanging."[62] In the play this is a private bit of ghoulishness on Scarpia's part, and is arranged before Floria enters the room. Puccini's use of the moment is far more serious, and far more dramatically telling: the revolting idea that the corpse of her lover's friend will be hanged brings home the fact that Mario himself will soon choke to death at the end of a rope—"Everything is ready [for Cavaradossi's execution], Excellency," Spoletta reports. Floria, balanced on the knife-edge of the decision that now can no longer be avoided, wavers as the orchestra wavers between B♭ and A♭ (bass notes of the first two Scarpia/Tyranny chords), then resolves to a bare E. The ensuing orchestral phrase (ex. 8.6) reiterates and expands on this sign of her hesitation, but now with major chords on B♭

and A♭ (II, 904–7), again closing on a single note, E♮, in octaves (908–9). Scarpia's next words (*Ebbene?* at II, 910–11); ending on G♮, have the effect of turning that solitary E into an E-minor chord. This is the only instance before Scarpia's death scene that this particular transformation from major to minor occurs, prompting one to ask if perhaps the baron's next action seals his fate. He demands that she make up her mind; after she nods, agreeing to whatever Scarpia demands of her, the orchestra (II, 912–13) seems to allude to Beethoven's quartet in F major, at the point where the music asks, "Must it be?" (see ex. 8.6, the two measures after Scarpia's question, "Ebbene?").[63]

Ex. 8.6. Decision (II, 903–14)

Tosca still has the presence of mind to insist that Cavaradossi be freed at once, but Scarpia, as we have already noted, assures her that it is beyond his power to issue a public pardon. Instead, he offers to arrange a mock execution. She is still suspicious, but he assures her that she can listen while he gives Spoletta his orders. "I've changed my mind. The prisoner is to be shot—pay attention! As we did with Count Palmieri." "An execution . . ." "Faked! As we did with Palmieri, do you understand me well?" Spoletta, of course, immediately recognizes the references to what was, no doubt, a real execution. Tosca, blind to what is going on right in front of her eyes, presses what she believes to be her advantage by demanding to warn Cavaradossi herself, and that is quickly granted. "Remember," Scarpia emphasizes: "At the fourth hour" (this "fourth hour" reference will recur in the next act; see p. 247). And Spoletta replies, "Yes, just like Palmieri." Then he slips quietly away, leaving Tosca alone with Scarpia.

As Scarpia turns to her, Tosca puts him off with another demand. She wants a safe-conduct. Scarpia, with exaggerated courtliness, agrees. It was vitally important that one have not just a pass, but the right pass: in the fall of 1799 four *vetturini*, or travel expediters, were shot by the French for having passes issued by the insurgents.[64] In December 1798 after the Duphot incident, Joseph Bonaparte could not leave Rome until he and his party had secured their passports from the pope.[65]

A modern national passport is quite different from the sort of passport one needed to travel in Europe in the Napoleonic era. A traveler had to have a specific pass from the local ruler, be he pope, duke, king, commanding general, or bandit chief. These were not blanket permits or identifications, but dated passes to go to a specific place within a specific time period. They could be either entirely handwritten, or printed with blank spaces for the required information. There was of course no photograph, but there was a physical description giving age, height, build, color of hair and eyes, features, and distinguishing marks. So Tosca's might read, depending on one's concept of the character: Floria Tosca; age 23; height average, slender build, black hair, high forehead, skin unblemished [that is, not pockmarked from disease], nose regular, mouth large, eyes black, no visible scars or deformities. "The Cavalier who accompanies her" is an unlikely description and sounds rather like something out of a Dumas novel. Unless Cavaradossi is traveling as a servant (and no servant would be described as "the Cavalier") he would require a new name, with his own (accurate) description.[66] Perhaps: Nicola Castron [according to Sardou, his father's given name was "Nicolas" and his mother had been Mlle de Castron before her marriage: Scarpia would have both of these in the dossier to hand]; age 26; height above average; average build;

chestnut hair; high forehead; skin unblemished; nose regular; mouth average; eyes hazel; mustache (brown), not bearded.

The baron asks by which road Tosca plans to leave the city because this must be on the document, along with the gates she plans to use, and the time period for which the passport is valid. As chief of police, Scarpia may or may not have been competent to issue an actual passport; such a document might have required the countersignature of the governor, Diego Naselli. But he could offer what Floria demands, a safe-conduct *(salvacondotto)*.

As Scarpia writes, the orchestra, very softly, begins a twisting, dark minor theme that tells us that a murder is about to be committed (see ex. 8.7). (The same theme will recur when Tosca gives her hysterical description of the event in Act III.)

Ex. 8.7. Murder (II, 968–71)

Scarpia writes out the safe-conduct, and while Tosca reaches for a glass of wine she sees a knife. When he approaches her she stabs him to death.

Then as now, stabbing a full-grown and fully clothed man to death with a single knife thrust is a great deal more difficult than it sounds. In this case it would require an underhand thrust that slipped a thin, very sharp knife between the ribs to rupture the heart. While Tosca is unlikely to have the medical knowledge to explain this sort of precision, she might well be familiar with the technique. Stabbing was the method of choice in the vast majority of

Roman murders (noted in chap. 5). Further, Roman women had a well-established reputation for wearing stilettos as hair ornaments, and for not being reluctant to make use of them.[67]

If Tosca was faced with a moral dilemma over allowing herself to be raped, she has resolved it by opting for another, even more terrible one: she has killed a man, with her own hands; and not only killed him, but (much more serious) has almost certainly damned him. He has died in the very act of committing a particularly vile sin, and not a word or a hint of repentance has been uttered in his brief and violent death agony. In a culture where death and pain were acceptable, but damnation was a supremely serious matter, this would create a psychologically intolerable situation that must be resolved. The method that Tosca instinctively chooses to resolve it strikes modern audiences as bizarre, but in fact makes perfect sense in the historical context of Rome in 1800. The end of the second act of the opera, even more than the parallel scene in the play, is a ritual patterned on formal religious ceremonials; it is an impromptu requiem, without benefit of clerical assistance.

As soon as Scarpia ceases to struggle and cry out, Tosca performs the first part of her ritual: forgiveness. ("He is dead. Now I forgive him.") Sardou's heroine, like Bernhardt a tougher customer than the Floria of the opera, says, "Now we're even" *(A present, je te tiens quitte)*—a very different sentiment. But as we have noted before, Puccini, anti-cleric though he certainly was, understood the Roman Catholic psyche much better than did Sardou, the Parisian secularist.

Next Floria washes her hands. (This too is part of the Catholic Mass, where the priest ritually purifies himself by washing his hands.) Reminded of the present world by the blood on her hands, she searches for the safe-conduct, first on the table and then, frantically, in the rest of the room; she finds it clutched in Scarpia's dead hand, and tries to free the paper from his grasp without touching him. At this point she speaks perhaps the most dramatically effective line in the opera: "And before him, all Rome trembled" *(E avanti a lui tremava tutta Roma)*. This line (which Giulio Ricordi wanted to cut) replaced a banal and peevish comment written by Sardou, "And it is in front of that that a whole city trembled" *(Et c'est devant ça que tremblait toute une ville)*. Puccini may have taken the cadence of his line from a story about Parma and the statue to Count Neipperg, the lover and then second husband of the Archduchess Marie Louise, Napoleon's second wife and widow. Count Neipperg's job was very similar to Scarpia's, and he carried it out with an enthusiasm and skill that at least matched those which gained him renown in the royal bedchamber. The mayor of Parma pointed Neipperg's statue out to Puccini, commenting that "There is a remembrance in marble of the man be-

FIGURE 45. In one of the emblematic scenes from the opera, Tosca places a crucifix on Scarpia's chest. Dr. Girvice Archer

fore whom trembled all of Parma."[68] The phrase immediately struck the composer's ear, and at the appropriate time it emerged as one of the most effective lines in opera. Not only is it dramatic, the line is a pungent comment on the passing of earthly power in the tradition of the liturgical formula, "Remember, man, that thou art dust, and unto dust thou shalt return."[69]

Floria completes the ceremony by setting lighted candles by the body, and laying a crucifix on the chest (see fig. 45). This all looks so odd that directors often ascribe it to mental unbalance, neurotic religious scruples, or a flair for the theatrical that must play itself out even if only for the private audience of a corpse.[70] In fact what she does bears a very close resemblance to the normal funerary rites that preceded burial in eighteenth-century Rome; and it seems likely that much of its subliminal power comes from just these associations.

In the Roman tradition, corpses were carried through the street with their faces uncovered, and laid out in state in the churches, surrounded by candles (the number is often specified in the *defunto*'s will—eight or ten, if he wished to strike a note of modesty; dozens, if he wanted to go out in style). After lying in the church for the prescribed time—and in the summer heat with the added heat of the candles, this could have perfectly hideous consequences for the unembalmed corpse—the dead person was interred either in the church or near it.[71] This was usually done at night. Robed and cowled attendants, often members of a confraternity devoted to this service, kneeling, made a

circle around the body and the light of their candles and torches fell on the
dead person's face for the last time.[72]

Less than a year after Bernhardt's *La Tosca* opened in Paris, Fanny Davenport presented an English-language version in New York. The audience
was predictably shocked by the "foul horrors" of the plot, but the sticking
point was this funeral scene, which was denounced as sacrilegious. There was
such an uproar that the candles and the crucifix were eliminated, and Tosca
merely slipped quietly from the room. The scene that so shocked New York
is described this way in the 1909 published version of Sardou's play:

> She starts to leave then, noticing the lit candles, goes to extinguish them,
> then thinks better of it, takes a candle in each hand and slowly goes to place
> the one she holds in her left hand at Scarpia's left hand; she passes in front
> of the body, turning her back to the audience, and places the other at his
> right hand. Looking around and moving towards the door, she sees the
> crucifix at the prie-dieu. Removing it, she takes it by the base and, showing
> the head of Christ to the audience she kneels in front of Scarpia and places
> the crucifix on his chest. At this moment there is a third drumroll in the
> citadel. Floria rises and goes to the door at the back of the stage, pulls the
> bolt and opens it. The antechamber is dark. She listens, putting her head
> forward, then, very cautiously moving through the door, she disappears.[73]

The only notable difference between this and the rather more abbreviated
directions in the opera has to do with the crucifix. There is no mention of her
taking it by the base and displaying it to the audience. The Italian text speci-
fies that she carries it "reverently" or "religiously." As she kneels to place the
crucifix on the corpse Puccini the master dramatist startles both her and us
with a "very distant" drumroll as the dynamics shift suddenly from *ppp* to *f*
(II, 1066). It sounds, and is probably meant to sound, like the sudden long
drumroll that traditionally accompanied the release of the trapdoor under a
hanged man, meant to cover the often extended and horrible sounds of a man
choking to death. As death offstage parallels and emphasizes death onstage
Tosca silently and cautiously slips away. As she does so, the Scarpia/Tyranny
motif—now that Scarpia is dead, with a final E minor chord—dies away
slowly to *pppp*—the nearest thing to silence—and the curtain falls rapidly.

9 *Act Three*

*B*etween midnight and dawn, 18 June 1800

The platform of Sant'Angelo, just below the great bronze statue of Michael the Archangel. Beyond the ramparts of the castello is the flat plain of the Tiber and the Bridge of the Angel leading to the execution square and the city. Behind the fortress rise the basilica of St Peter and the Vatican palace.

Hadrian, third of the Five Good Emperors, ordered the construction of his tomb between A.D. 135 and 139. The monument began as a huge drum-shaped structure some sixty feet high, resting on a massive square podium, a man-made mountain rising on the sloping banks of the Tiber opposite the city of Rome (see fig. 46). The top of the great mound was planted with cypress trees and other greenery, and a monumental statue rose over the whole. The base, which contained the funerary chamber, was built of concrete, tufa (volcanic stone), and brick; it was faced with marble, and the whole monument was enclosed by a railing in the middle of a park. As the empire declined the function of the mausoleum gradually changed. The hollow space inside became a fortress, and the square base was extended to enclose ramparts and battlements. In this form it served first as a refuge from barbarians, and then as the main defense of Rome, a role it fulfilled for over a thousand years. It acquired its angel, and its present name, after 590, when Pope Gregory the Great saw the apparition of the archangel at its summit, announcing the end of a plague that had been devastating the city. By the Middle Ages the metamorphosis of the tomb of Hadrian into the Fortress of the Holy Angel was complete. Air shafts leading to the emperor's tomb had become dungeons; Hadrian's ramp was extended by a vast, gently graded stair that spanned the funerary chamber. The middle section of this stair was a wooden drawbridge that could be raised, leaving attackers to scale the steep walls of the inner chamber under a rain of arrows. In 1800, the time of Angelotti's and Mario's supposed involuntary residence there, the drawbridge could still be raised, isolating the papal rooms in the upper levels of the fortress.[1]

FIGURE 46. View of the Castel Sant'Angelo from the river in an engraving by Piranesi, showing how the fortress appeared in the eighteenth century. Author's collection

The great bronze figure of the warrior archangel Michael that now dominates the monument stands almost twelve feet (4 meters) high, with a fifteen foot (5 meter) wingspan, and weighs 9,228 pounds, or 3.2 tons.[2] It was relatively new in 1800: forty-eight years earlier Benedict XIV had ordered Francesco Giardoni to cast the great statue on a design by Peter Anton Verschffelt. The new Michael replaced the battered stone angel by Raffaello da Montelupo that now stands in the courtyard of the cannonballs. True to the medieval vision of Gregory the Great, Michael is sheathing his sword, his gentle, almost pretty face expressing a cool, detached sympathy for the human suffering he witnesses. Such detachment must have been tested when, two years before the events of the opera, the angel suffered the indignity of being renamed "The liberating genius of France," painted red, white, and blue, and having a liberty cap stuck onto his head. (To be fair, the French probably got the idea from the Roman custom of dressing the basilica's bronze statue of St Peter in papal robes, with the triple crown and the fisherman's ring.)

The men and women associated with the Castel Sant'Angelo have been as eccentric, and as multifaceted, as the fortress itself.[3] The goldsmith and adventurer Benvenuto Cellini helped defend the fortress during the siege of 1547. Later he spent some time in one of its least desirable cells before he escaped, jumping from the rampart and breaking his leg. In the eighteenth century Cagliostro (Giuseppe Balsamo) was held for a short time at the Castel Sant'Angelo. Eight parts charlatan, one part mystic, and one part madman, Cagliostro made the mistake of returning to Rome in 1789. The Holy Office had him arrested and sentenced him to life in prison.[4] The rooms in the fortress that bear his name today are decorated with bizarre, cabalistic figures. Although it probably saw less in the way of vileness than most medieval fortresses, the Castel Sant'Angelo inevitably attracted horror stories, some more or less true (like the fate of the unfortunate Beatrice Cenci), some generated by political enmity (like the tales of Borgia poisonings), and some simply titillating, made up by people who like that sort of thing. The Marquis de Sade used Sant'Angelo as a setting for part of his novel *Juliette, or the Prosperity of Vice:* the sheer weight of the abuse that the place offered to his imagination must have made his pulse race. Madame de Staël's *Corinne, ou l'Italie,* also mentions Sant'Angelo, this time in the more respectable guise of a monument to Roman liberty and to the dignity of a noble death.[5] During the Roman Republic of 1848–49 Garibaldi's Red Shirts toured the fortress by the light of torches, guided by cagey old Romans who fed them hair-raising fictions about tormented Inquisition victims, their shrieks for mercy unheard, their mangled corpses piled into mass graves.[6] By contrast, for the people of Tosca's Rome the fortress was almost cosy. Its reassuring bulk rose above the city like a squat, protective talisman, casting an imposing reflection in the slow-moving Tiber. It was the headquarters for the 3,000-man papal military, who were identified more with parades than with repression. It was the site of the splendid annual fireworks display in June, on the feast of Rome's patron saints Peter and Paul; it was the home base of an aging military band; and if it was a prison, it was a prison only for very rich, very important persons who were unlikely to excite much sympathy in the people at large (ordinary folk got sent to the Carceri Nuove; see chap. 5). In 1798 and 1799, however, the occupying forces and the local republicans made a calculated attempt to change the reputation of the papal fortress, perhaps in an effort to make Sant'Angelo fill for Rome the symbolic role that the Bastille filled in the mythology of revolutionary Paris.[7] Romans were convinced that the French commander was given strict instructions to make the lives of prisoners as unpleasant as possible. An officer named Communeau, they said, was court-martialed for kindness to prisoners, a charge against which he stoutly defended himself.[8]

While it is still dark, the bells of a city filled with bells begin to ring, signaling the first prayers of the day. Below, in the marshy fields where sheep and goats roam, a boy sings a sad tune, unconscious of the tragedy about to take place high above him.

The prelude to Act III was the last part of the opera that Puccini wrote.[9] Before the curtain rises four unaccompanied horns sound a dawn call (III, 1; see ex. 9.1). Sieghart Döhring has noted that this phrase stands outside the action like a motto imposed over the act as a whole. It can be seen as a theme of illusory hope: clear, bright, sure—and totally unfounded. We will hear this same bright, unmistakable melody again, as the lovers seem to rejoice in their coming freedom (III, 394). This time the hope will be even more obviously "unfounded" as their unison, unaccompanied voices soar out into the void— as Döhring has observed, as if the rug were pulled out from under them.

Ex. 9.1. Illusory hope (III, 1–9)

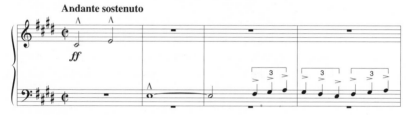

The opening theme begins fortissimo, and decreases to pianissimo as the curtain rises and the glittering orchestration (descending triplets, reminiscent of the winter morning music of Act III of *La Bohème*) paints a picture of a clear, starry night. Soon (III, 44) we hear the first of the bells that run through the Prelude like a connecting thread. These begin in the humble form of sheep bells, which jingle in the distance and gradually grow nearer. Although today the Castel Sant'Angelo is besieged by Roman traffic, in 1900 it stood alone in a rural setting; in 1800 it was a lonely outpost on the banks of the Tiber, and a shelter for shepherds, fishermen, and boatmen.

Act III is set in the military base where the power of Church and State are combined. But the musical imagery at the start of the third act, though it contains military and religious references, is primarily about Nature, and about Love; it transcends worldly power, as the lovers will transcend it by death.

Here Puccini evokes an orthodox set of Romantic visions of Nature: the shepherds, the milky dawn, the church bells abstracted by distance so that they no longer recall the institutional Church so much as a vague, private religiosity.

As part of this appeal to Nature, Puccini wanted an offstage song in the folk style and for this he required a short verse in Roman dialect in a very specific meter. At the end of September of 1899 (only about three months before the premiere of the opera) he wrote to his friend Alfredo Vandini asking him to find a "good *romanesco* [Roman dialect] poet" to compose some appropriate words and provided dummy verses to show the metric system he required:

> *Ho pianto tanto*
> *e n'ho fatto una boccia*
> *perché nel core*
> *io no t'ho fatto breccia*
> *o fiori belli*
> *che state al sol*
> *chinate il capo,*
> *passa il mio amor.*

The request was passed on to Don Pietro Panichelli, who turned to a famous Roman poet and folklorist, Giggi Zanazzo.[10] That same evening Zanazzo dashed off the required words:

> *Io de sospiri*
> *te ne manno tanti*
> *pe quante foje*
> *smoveno li venti;*
> *tu mi disprezzi,*
> *io me ciaccoro,*
> *lampena d'oro*
> *me fai morir.*[11]
>
> (I have given you
> so many sighs,
> as many as the leaves
> that move in the breezes;
> you despise me,
> I suffer for it;
> golden lamp,
> you make me die.)

Puccini changed the words very little to fit his rhythmic pattern ("manno" became "rimanno"; "ne" was inserted before "smoveno") and happily included them in the score. He did not, however, put them into the libretto, and on that basis Ricordi tried to avoid paying royalties to Zanazzo.

The song, and the search for it, offers a good example of Puccini's well-known mania for local color.[12] If we turn to folklore sources we can see how authentic it is. William W. Story, an American who lived in Rome in the first half of the nineteenth century and wrote evocative word-pictures of popular life there, describes the raw music of the shepherds and country folk:

> [it is] rude enough, and seems in measure founded upon the Church chant. It is in the minor key, and consists ordinarily of two phrases, ending in a screaming monotone, prolonged until the breath of the singer fails, and often running down at the close into a blurred chromatic. No sooner is one strain ended than it is suddenly taken up again in prestissimo time and "slowed" down to the same dismal conclusion. Heard near, it is deafening and disagreeable. But when refined by distance it has a sad and pleasing effect, and seems to belong to the place.

Story offers in example a song he heard from a distant carter, just at nightfall. The simple words have the same sort of lovesick melancholy of Zanazzo's more polished verse:

> *E, bella, tu non piangera-a-a-i*
> *Sul giorno ch'io sarò mor-or-or-to-o-o-o-o*[13]

Puccini has come close to this effect. His use of the Lydian mode gives his tune the sound of an authentic folk song and, as in the Roman songs reported by Story, each phrase of the shepherd's song ends with a long, sustained note, followed by a return to the livelier movement.[14] It consists of six phrases in the folk style, the first four following a quick/slow pattern, and the final two falling and dying out, lost in the distance. The use of a boy soprano voice makes it sound even more authentic, though usually not to the point of dying out on a "screaming monotone."

As the sounds of the shepherd and his flocks die away, the sky begins to lighten to the "gray light that precedes dawn" and the sounds of the church bells begin. Puccini was determined to begin his last act with a tone poem based on the bells of Rome, and as early as 1897 he set about precisely defining the sounds that could be heard from the battlements of the fortress. Later he would make a special trip to hear them for himself, going so far as to sleep in the upper casements to get the full effect of the dawn. Meanwhile he tormented his Roman correspondents, Don Meluzzi and Don Pietro Panichelli, for details; in particular he was determined to get exactly the right note for the great bell of St Peter's, colloquially known as *er campanone* (it is E natural—the same note that serves as the bass for the third Scarpia/Tyranny chord). Not only the tone, but the distance had to be just right, so the composer could direct the placement of the backstage bells, some close, some more distant, some very far away. Don Panichelli was given the job of discovering the tones of each of the church bells in the vicinity of the fortress. Puccini, his passion for detail at its height, set an instrument-maker to the task of reproducing the sounds. The whole business is complex and expensive enough to create problems for opera houses even today.[15] After the premiere of *Tosca*, Luigi Illica wrote a peevish letter to Giulio Ricordi complaining bitterly about Puccini's high-handed treatment. The librettist particularly resented the suppression of the text of his "Description of the Dawn" from the stage directions for Act III, the absence of which in his opinion rendered the prelude to that act "long and monotonous, and the great fuss and the great expense over the bells was yet another folly because they [the bells] passed completely unobserved."[16]

Until recently the only working papers that had come to light for the opera's libretto consisted primarily of versions of Act I. This left us with almost no record of the last act's lyric poetry so regretted by librettists. Very recently, however, working papers for Act III were discovered in the private archives of the Giacosa family. These papers include lost Act III material such as Cavaradossi's moving letter of farewell (entirely scrapped in favor of Puccini's own concept); a Latin hymn (traces of which may remain in the second half of the last act duet); and a closing scene which, as Rescigno speculates, eliminated the suicide and has Tosca end the opera with a lament over the body of her lover. [See Appendix 3]

Act III seems to have been a sticking point for virtually everyone but Puccini. His librettists were furious at his eviscerating their poetry. Illica wanted Tosca to go mad instead of killing herself. His publisher, Giulio Ricordi, was disappointed in the music, which he described as "fragmentary" and "scrappy," and in general he considered the whole act a "grave error of conception and workmanship." And Sardou gleefully insisted that Tosca should fling herself into a Tiber transposed to the wrong side of the fortress.

The onstage action begins when a jailer enters—and lest we forget whose fortress this is, his first act is to light the lamp under the crucifix. The orchestra (III, 113 ff.) whispers "sweetly" of Tosca, and of love; and at the end of the Prelude, connected by the bells, the soft, distorted, but still menacing Scarpia/Tyranny chords drift by. Cavaradossi is escorted in by a picket of soldiers, and the treble bells die away. Very softly we hear the first direct quotation of the motif that will get its fullest expression in the tenor aria "E lucevan

le stelle" but which will also end the opera (whether appropriately or not is
a hotly debated topic) (III, 127; see ex. 9.2).

Ex. 9.2. Cavaradossi's aria (III, 128–29)

After a tentative beginning the melody, underscored in the bass by an E♮
an octave below the staff—in fact, the E of the great bell of St. Peter's—ac-
quires a majestic, almost ritual power that contrasts with the routine shuffling
of the bored officials and the stunned and battered prisoner. This is a simple
custody transfer, signatures and ID required, carried out at an inconvenient
hour by men who would rather be doing something else; it is accompanied by
perhaps the most achingly beautiful melody and orchestration in the Puccini
repertoire. Here the theme seems to act as a graphic comment on the impo-
tence of the individual caught in the machinery of the State, and an ironic
revelation of interior human anguish that can underlie what seem on the surface to be simple, routine actions.

> *While Mario waits for execution, Floria slips away from the
> Farnese palace with the safe-conduct. Spoletta has been given
> verbal orders to admit her to the Castel Sant'Angelo; between
> midnight and dawn she must arrange the details of their escape
> from Rome.*

Tosca leaves the Farnese palace after midnight, walking down the great
staircase, where a footman stands lookout to call for her coach as soon as she
appears. The guards would have no reason to stop her: they would instantly
recognize her as an honored guest of the Queen of Naples, with freedom to
come and go as she pleases unless other orders are given; and we know that
Scarpia gave no such orders ("Sei libera; va pure"). Spoletta is busy arrang-
ing two executions (Angelotti must be hanged despite his suicide), and the
sbirri, who have had a busy day, are unlikely to interfere in their employer's
routine personal business.

Floria has little time to waste. Time is passing, dawn only a few hours away,
and a great deal must be done. As she will later explain to Mario, she collects
her gold coins and jewelry, and arranges with a *vetturino* to bring her and her
companion from Rome to Civitavecchia; once there, she plans to find a small
coastal trading vessel, a *tartana*, and escape by sea. She doesn't specify their
final destination, but either the neutral state of Tuscany or the French-held

island of Corsica would suit their purposes and both would be relatively easy to reach by boat. Floria Tosca, who began the opera as a featherbrained, spoiled diva, is now functioning under pressure as a highly efficient manager.

First, she must return home, leaving her guard and driver on alert, and make her way to her apartments. There she wakes her servant, who helps her change into country clothes, rough and inconspicuous garments like those she would normally wear for a stay at the villa. Continuing to wear court dress would be rather like setting out on a morning bus trip through a bad neighborhood in your inaugural ball outfit. The elaborate dress, mantle, and jewelry would be too rigid and uncomfortable for the journey ahead; they would be far too expensive to risk damaging, even for a wealthy woman; and perhaps worst of all, they would be wildly conspicuous in a time when people wore their oldest, shabbiest clothing for travel so as not to attract the attention of thieves and bandits.

The late eighteenth century was not an age of banking and ready cash, at least not for the individual. Great families invested money in land, in bonds, and in business. Tosca, however, is neither a noble nor a member of a great family; she is a successful professional woman and, as an opera singer, she is used to traveling. While she might invest in land or bonds at home in the Veneto, much of her wealth would be readily transportable in the old-fashioned but still reliable form of gold and jewelry. This would be especially true in wartime, when states and institutions were dissolving at an alarming rate. The financial vicissitudes of Tosca and Cavaradossi are fairly typical for the revolutionary decades: her liquid assets can be packed in a small case and carried anywhere; his landed property, confiscated by the State, is wiped out at a blow by an unexpected turn of fortune in politics and war.

Of course having one's wealth in a small, portable case had one obvious drawback: the usual problem of bandits, in the summer of 1800 worse than ever. About a month before the events of the opera are set, Galimberti noted: "All of the roads outside of Rome are unsafe, and every day murders occur even on the most frequented." [17] Even the bold British officer Sir Robert Wilson was annoyed by bandits that year. Wilson passed through Rome in early December 1800, collecting dispatches from the Neapolitan commander Damas, to bring to the Viceroy in Naples. He arrived in the city around midnight and stayed for less than a day. On his way to Rome Wilson and his servant, Samuel, saw five men armed with "long rifles" (no doubt military issue, liberated by deserters setting up in business for themselves). The two Englishmen took out their pistols and Wilson drew his sword, but the bandits were not interested in fighting two armed men ("these were, after all, Italians") and so the travelers arrived safely in Rome. After seeing Damas the following day they left for Naples "around six, despite the fact that I was advised against it": only a few days earlier three officers had been set upon by thirteen bandits, robbed and maltreated.[18]

Tosca says nothing about guns in the opera, but in the play she brushes aside criticism of her venturing alone to the villa, telling Mario that her coachman Ambroise (Ambrogio) is armed.[19] One may assume that she would take similar precautions with the hired carriage. To find this vehicle she has to go from the Piazza Venezia to the Piazza di Spagna—always moving away from the fortress, and in a desperate hurry to beat the sunrise and warn her injured and angry lover of the dangerous role he will have to play. But she must complete her preparations before going to him: time will be even more precious, once the trick is carried off.

Horse-drawn coaches are not directly comparable to modern automobiles: the vehicle one used in town was not at all the same sort of vehicle one used for travel. Town carriages were rather like portable salons, used for cruising during the hour of promenade, or riding up and down the Corso at carnival time, or splashing through the flooded Piazza Navona on August weekends. Traveling coaches were very different vehicles, and ordinary people generally hired them, along with the necessary horses or mules and the postilion to take charge of the animals. The estimable Mrs. Stark, whose popular guidebook appeared in 1799, advises the discriminating traveler to bring his own coach:

> Those persons who design to travel much in Italy should provide themselves
> with a strong, low-hung double-perched English coach or post-chaise, with
> well-seasoned corded springs, and iron axle-trees, two drag-chains with iron
> shoes, two drag-staffs, a box containing extra linch-pins, nails, and tools for
> repairing, mounting and dismounting a carriage (this box should be made
> in the shape of a trunk, padlocked and slung to the iron-work of the car-
> riage), a well, a sword-case, a very light imperial, two moderate sized trunks,
> the larger to go before, with a padlock and chain for the smaller; lamps, and
> a stock of candles fitted to them; the bottom of the carriage should carry
> your own sheets, pillows, and blankets; when you travel, I would advise
> doubling them up daily of a convenient size, and then placing them in the
> carriage by way of cushions, making a leather-sheet the envellope [*sic*].[20]

Roads outside of cities were notoriously difficult, even in Italy where the Romans had left their legacy of highway building. The Président de Brosses was regularly inconvenienced by his carriage turning over.[21] Unless an individual planned to do a great deal of traveling, he would not own a vehicle that could stand up to that sort of punishment. Instead, he would hire one from a professional who arranged journeys—a *vetturino*, the owner/driver of a *vettura,* or travel coach. In Rome, one found these men at the Piazza di Spagna (as today you find the American Express offices there).

The Abbé Richard, in one of the most popular of the travel guides to Rome, advises the tourist to deal with these men, "who will agree to convey the traveler in a certain time, for a certain sum, to any place which he may desire." The *vetturino* generally provided a compact vehicle drawn by one or two mules or horses, capable of carrying two passengers and thirty pounds of baggage about thirty or forty Roman miles a day. Richard advises that "one should always get a written agreement with the *vetturino* as to price, etc, witnessed by two witnesses and stamped at the police station"(!)[22] Tosca, rousing the driver out of his bed in the dark hours before dawn, probably does not follow this last bit of advice. She would in any case be well advised to be cautious. Trebelli, the guard bribed to help Angelotti escape (see chap. 6), was betrayed by the carriage driver he had hired.

Civitavecchia is described as being twenty leagues from Rome, a journey of about five and a half hours in 1800. If all went well the refugees would be in the port town and negotiating for passage on an appropriate vessel well before midday.[23] The distance indicated by a "league" could vary considerably, but twenty leagues was normally an easy journey. Pierre Bergeret de Grancourt, an elegant French visitor of the 1770s, begins his *Voyage d'Italie* by saying that he and his friends arrived in Rome without the least fatigue, having taken two months to get from Paris to Rome because they traveled at the leisurely pace of fifteen or twenty leagues a day.[24]

Richard's book divides Italy up into "Routes," rather in the fashion of a modern automobile club trip map. Route 50 describes the trip from Rome to Civitavecchia, breaking it down into four stages each five leagues apart.

> All of the relays on this route [Mala Grotta, Monterone, and Santa Severa] are at isolated houses, as there are no villages. At various places the road runs along parts of the Roman Way. Santa Severa is a small fort, near the road and the sea, at a short distance from which the traveler passes as far as CIVITAVECCHIA (Centumcella), which is a small and tolerably well-built town, laid out in straight but narrow streets, and surrounded by weak ramparts. In times of peace the English bring codfish to this place, and the French cloths, linen, and other products of their manufactories.

But 1800 was not peacetime and "Floria Tosca and the gentleman who accompanies her" were clearly not ordinary tourists. And for them to go by way of Civitavecchia was a bad joke perpetrated by the chief of police: this was not only the port of papal Rome, guarded by a recently refurbished and well-garrisoned fort, it was also the destination of the convoys of prisoners that regularly left Rome for exile or the galleys.[25] While it was probably true that the "galley slaves" who filled the town experienced little actual confinement or forced labor, Civitavecchia was nevertheless not a good destination or port of departure for two persons fleeing Rome on charges of high treason and (soon) the murder of a police official.

By the time Floria has completed her business at the Piazza di Spagna it would be after the seventh hour, or nearing 4 A.M. modern time. Normally the streets would have been deserted; as dawn approached on 18 June, however, the streets and squares of Rome were still populated with little knots of men arguing over, lamenting, or celebrating the news from the north. Since the first news from Marengo had arrived, rumors about the battle had spread throughout the city. On Tuesday the seventeenth the forces of law and order had seemed to triumph:

> . . . the French are beaten by General Melas, who has retaken Milan, and the [French army] now finds itself caught between three fires with no line of retreat. General Lauden has come from Bergamo after smashing the Jacobins there . . . ; a very large body of Austrian troops has also come from the Tyrol, commanded by the Prince of Condé.[26]

Whether from bravado or confidence, the patriots had refused to believe the news.

> The Jacobins laughed and behaved insolently on hearing this news. . . . A group of carriage drivers heard this . . . and beat up two of them; the others were arrested.[27]

But during the night, the amazing truth about Marengo began to circulate. Perhaps a courier told his mates at the barracks, a secretary or a servant overheard the message for a military or civil official. Before dawn the news had spread from the palace and the castle to the street. The anti-French lawyer Galimberti, about to retire for the night, added a coda to his diary entry of 17 June: "The official notices about Austrian victories over the French in Italy and on the Rhine have been amended." The following day the truth was obvious to everyone.

> A huge number of Jacobins gathered today in the Piazza del Popolo to ridicule the triumphal arch [built to welcome the new pope]. . . . Tonight the Jacobins gathered in the fields around the Castel Sant'Angiolo [*sic*], dancing the Carmagnole, playing and singing. They got nearer and nearer to the fortress; a sentry on the walls challenged them but they just kept singing, so he fired on them, and they moved away.[28]

Had he been on the platform of the fortress one night later, Mario Cavaradossi would have heard not the melancholy song of a shepherd but the rowdy
celebrations of his friends and the angry protests of his guards.

**In the crowded state prison in the upper levels of the fortress,
Mario Cavaradossi listens to the sounds of the summer night,
remembers, and tries to come to terms with his imminent death.**

Stendhal, who visited Rome in the early years of the nineteenth century,
wrote of the Castel Sant'Angelo in his *Promenades dans Rome:*

> the jailer would never answer our questions on the Carbonari [nationalist
> revolutionaries] who are locked up there. Aside from the fever, which can
> afflict them in the summer, they are not badly off. Almost all have fallen into
> an excessive devotion. The view that they have from the height of their prison
> is magnificent and of a nature to transform the most intemperate gloom into
> a gentle melancholy. They hover over the city of tombs; this view teaches
> them how to die.[29]

Looking out over "a city of tombs," Mario hardly has time to move from
despair to gentle melancholy, or to fall into an "excessive devotion." Sardou,
who prided himself on a well-made play, designed *La Tosca* to fit within the
Aristotelian unities, one of which demands that the action unfold within a
twenty-four-hour period. Puccini made the process appear even faster with
his insistence on compressed, rapid action. From the point of view of the
characters, their world dissolves between noon of one day and dawn of the
next. At the start of the opera Cavaradossi is confident to the point of arrogance, humoring Floria but clearly running the affair on his own terms, and
making life-and-death decisions with no thought of consulting or even in-
forming his mistress. In the last act he behaves (appropriately enough) like
a man in shock, struggling to respond to the situation in which he finds himself. When he is brought to the platform of the fortress the music tells us that
he is overwhelmed by grief and regret. As we have seen, he is accompanied by
the first clear statement of the theme that will become his final aria. After being transferred to the custody of the jailer, he is offered the services of a priest,
and refuses with a single, unelaborated "No." He is thinking only of the woman
he believes he will never see again, and bribes the jailer to deliver a letter to
her, giving him a ring, "the only thing that remains of my wealth."[30] While
this transaction is taking place, the orchestra throbs with the Love music from
Act I (III, 168, referring back to I, 153–56). As the Love theme shimmers,
Cavaradossi sits and tries to write, but soon the music falls in chromatic

FIGURE 47. Cavaradossi, awaiting execution, tries to write a letter of farewell to Tosca. One of the publicity pictures by Metlikovitz. © Archivio Storico Casa Ricordi. Reproduced by permission

intervals and gradually slows and grows quieter as he gives up the struggle to find words, and falls instead into memories of sense impressions (see fig. 47).

"Very sweetly" *(dolcissimo, vagamente rubando)* the warm voice of a solo clarinet plays the melody, and at the end of the first long, slow, passionate phrase Cavaradossi, as if thinking aloud, speaks in a monotone. He begins as if in mid-thought, with the word "and": ". . . and the stars were shining." As

the clarinet continues with the simple, yearning melody, the painter continues with his thoughts, his voice gently rising, and then falling: ". . . and the
earth smelled sweet . . . the orchard gate creaked . . . and a footstep brushed
the sand . . . she came in, fragrant . . . she fell into my arms."

The aria proper is quite short, only fifteen measures of vocal line, and the
text is frankly erotic, an intense and economical statement of the characteristic Puccinian blend of Love and Death.

> Oh! sweet kisses, oh languid caresses,
> while I trembling
> freed her beautiful shape from its veils!
> My dream of love is vanished forever . . .
> time has fled past . . .
> and I die in despair!
> And never have I loved life so much![31]

This aria is much debated in the literature. Its lush emotional impact in-
spires loathing in commentators like Joseph Kerman, who seem convinced
that anything this powerfully moving, this plaintive and beautiful, must be
meretricious. Like Tosca's "Vissi d'arte" (which, though her best aria, is arguably not so effectively visceral), Cavaradossi's aria is sometimes dismissed
as a sob of self-pity, a "tragic hiccup."[32] At the other end of the critical scale,
Döhring sees the melody of this aria, not as the facile "hit tune" that Puccini
repeats as often as possible for pathetic effect, but rather as the "organizing
principle" of the act, on a par with the Scarpia/Tyranny chords that he believes organize the first two acts.[33]

With this tightly controlled palette, Puccini has created portraits of three
distinct mental states: erotic passion, the realization of mortality, and finally
the collapse of all hope. For Döhring this is disillusion made concrete in music, a disillusion that will provide the focus for the entire third act. However
we interpret its meaning in the overall scheme of the opera, "E lucevan le
stelle" is an almost clinically accurate representation of a man struggling to
come to terms with the sudden and absolute loss of the physical love and
beauty that have given his life meaning. If the central meaning of *Tosca* is
the illusory nature of happiness, this is the moment of shattering insight into
that illusion, at least for the character Mario Cavaradossi. Floria Tosca's realization will come later, in the last moments of the opera, and will be accompanied by the same music.

The creation of text for this aria was more than usually fraught with
conflict.[34] Illica wanted the hero's last-act aria to be a political credo in praise
of revolutionary liberty. It seems from the librettist's letter of January 1900
that the aria had originally been planned as a direct quote from the text of

Cavaradossi's letter, rather than the "stream of consciousness" of a man unable to write. Little if anything of this text remains in the opera, though we know that the elderly Verdi was deeply moved by it.[35] That is as it should be. Verdi, something of a Risorgimento hero himself, might well have seen Cavaradossi as a martyred defender of Italian liberty, unlike Sardou (who saw him as a Frenchman) or Puccini (who saw him in almost existential terms). At Puccini's insistence, the text of the letter was replaced with a brief lament for lost love, but even this version saw a great deal of shifting and changing before it arrived at its final shape. Giacosa first prepared a text similar to the current one but more discursive and poetic. Another version, substantially the same as the final version, still included bits of remembered conversation between the lovers. Immediately after the line "she fell into my arms" *(mi cadea fra le braccia)* we are told that she "told me all about her day" *(mi narrava tutta la sua giornata)*—a mixture of chat and love-making, realistic enough in a domestic sort of way but hardly appropriate to Puccini's vision of the mental state of his hero.[36] The composer sensibly rejected the lines in favor of a version that is all trembling passion and despair. As he intended, the aria is a memory of love described in sensual terms so evocative and powerful as to raise physical passion to the status of a religion. Puccini was absolutely certain that a young man, in love and facing death, would be thinking not about politics or even about art—and certainly not about the destination of his immortal soul?—but about love. Puccini sketched out his own words for the aria, and battered his librettists into compliance. His plan was that the painter would remember his lover through his senses, one by one: the sight of the stars, the sweet-smelling earth, the creak of the garden gate, and the sound of her footstep on the sandy path. Then his thoughts move from the place to the woman as she falls into his arms. He remembers her fragrance, her kisses and long, unhurried embraces, remembers trembling as he uncovers her body, touches her skin. The image is too intense to be borne, and it forces him abruptly to face the truth: all of this is suddenly and irrevocably lost; he will die at the moment when he loves life more than he had ever dreamed possible. The words "e muoio disperato" (and I die, despairing) were Puccini's own and he insisted they be retained in the final version of the aria, where they are strongly accented (III, 204).[37]

There is no hint of any of this emotion in the Sardou play, where Mario has very little to say at the end. He consistently treats his captors with cool, contemptuous irony, to the point of taking a nap at the precise point when the operatic Mario is pouring out his soul in the wrenching, passionate aria. The curtain rises on scene i of the short last act of the play to find Cavaradossi sleeping on a bench, having already chased away his religious would-be com-

forters. Floria enters with Spoletta and Mario politely apologizes for having
lost his temper with her under the stress of their previous meeting. At the news
that she has secured a safe-conduct for them to leave Rome he is noncom-
mittal until they are alone and then (according to the stage directions) "seizes
her hand violently" and demands to know what she has given in exchange.
On hearing of the murder he compliments her, not on the softness of her hands
(as in the opera) but on her "ancient Roman" courage. She tells him to "fall
down at the shots, and play dead well"; he replies, "Don't worry," and leaves
with the soldiers. When the curtain rises on scene ii he is already dead.[38]

> *Floria, her preparations completed, hurries to her lover to tell*
> *him that his life has been saved. He is incredulous when he sees*
> *the signature on the safe-conduct; she tells him that she has*
> *killed Scarpia.*

While Mario is still weeping, his face buried in his hands, Floria arrives.
The music here, as elsewhere in this opera, is cinematic, describing the actions
of the characters. First, the love theme begins softly, then builds in rapidly
rising agitation until it explodes as the lovers embrace. Without speaking she
shows him the safe-conduct.

As soon as Cavaradossi sees the signature on the pass he is suspicious:
Scarpia does not grant pardons. (The third Scarpia chord, transmuted from
E major to E minor, occurs at the mention of his name; III, 232–33.) This,
Tosca assures him, is his first, and his last. He asks what she means ("Che
dici?"). And suddenly *(scattando, agitando)* it all pours out, in jumbled order and underpinned by fragments of the music that accompanied the events
she describes, a kaleidoscope of emotions.[39] Her account is the description of
a nightmare. It is full of shards of crystal-clear memories: her desperate and
unanswered prayers, the sound of the drum, Scarpia's laughter, the glitter of
a knife blade in candlelight; and then revulsion at the blood on her own hands.

Floria's hysterical account of the murder, like her ritual funeral ceremony, is often seen as mere theatricality on the part of an actress who can't
get off the stage even during a personal tragedy. This hardly seems a reasonable criticism. It is not necessary for one to be an actress to feel the need to
relive and thereby exorcize the horror that an essentially childlike woman
would feel at having killed a man with her own hands. But Floria's detailed
account suggests something else as well: the Roman Catholic rite of confession.[40] Catholics conscious of serious sin are urged to confess and receive absolution as soon as possible or face the danger of damnation. Telling Mario
would certainly have no sacramental value, but Floria's theology is a bit shaky
at the best of times. In any case she has little option: waking her confessor,

or stopping to tell any priest, is clearly out of the question. Even if she still trusted absolutely to clerical reticence—and after the events of that night she may no longer be sure—there would simply be no time.[41] Still, she would have a great psychological need to clear her conscience, all the more so as she must realize that she is still in acute physical danger. Even in the playful banter of Act I, with no menacing clouds on their horizon, she is aware of the implications of failing to confess a serious sin.

Tosca finishes her description of her near rape, and the murder with which she responded, on a high C (III, 276)—her third—that within three measures falls as much as two octaves (traditionally singers have the option of going down to middle C). The music, like the characters, seems stunned by the violence and suddenly becomes simpler, and quieter. Cavaradossi wraps her in the protective mantle of a gentle little arioso that has some of the lilt of a cradlesong about it (III, 281–83; see ex. 9.3).

Ex. 9.3. "O dolci mani" (III, 282–83)

Puccini was determined to keep the pretty melody of "O dolci mani" despite the fact that it did not strike his publisher as a stern enough response for an aristocratic Risorgimento hero. But Puccini's instincts were right. This is a man who has grown past arrogance, and facing his own mortality has made him kind. It is here, as we noted in chapter 1, that Cavaradossi makes his most consistently positive reference to religion. As late as the first published libretto, this arioso was preceded by the exclamation "O salvatrice!"— Oh, saviour! (feminine). This was cut, but the passage as it stands is filled with religious and quasi-religious language: her hands are "pure," destined for "good and pious works" (the word for "destined" here is *elette*, "elect"). And the works to which her hands are elected? To gather roses, to caress children, and to "pray for the unfortunate." It is into these gentle hands that "justice has placed her sacred weapons." It would of course be difficult to argue that Cavaradossi is expressing any sort of orthodox Christian religious views. Instead, he is combining neoclassical paganism ("justice" is a female divinity) with a nineteenth-century view of woman as Household Goddess.

This exchange, and the scene that follows, make up the mirror image of the Act I love scene (according to Carner's schemata—see chapter 6, pp. 133–34). Here the love music of Act I, transported and refined by the violence of Act II, glitters fitfully with the illusory promise of safety and love. This "duet" proved to be the cause of a major difference of opinion between Puccini and his editor, Giulio Ricordi, a difference that fortunately for us is clearly documented in an exchange of letters.[42] Ricordi wrote from Milan on 10 October 1899 (less than two months before the premiere), distressed by what he saw as a serious error in concept and execution: the duet between the lovers that he had expected to be "the true, luminous center of this act." Instead of the transcendent love music for which he had hoped he found fragments, little lines that in his opinion reduced the characters to pygmies, a scene chopped into three interrupted chunks, with music cribbed from an early (and unsuccessful) Puccini opera, *Edgar* (fine music for a Tyrolese peasant girl, Ricordi lamented, but completely out of place "for a Tosca, for a Cavaradossi").[43]

The letter seems to have astonished Puccini. He defended his concept hotly, trying to explain that the librettists had given him nothing but "amorous slobberings" while he was searching for a psychological truth. These characters, he insists, are in no condition to sing the usual tranquil love duet; instead, their exchange must be fragmentary: Tosca is constantly distracted by her worries about the "fake" execution. Absolutely convinced of the correctness of his concept, Puccini insisted that he was right to avoid "academic" sterility and instead serve the drama, and the characters.

For a long time critics agreed with Ricordi. More recent scholarship, however, tends to accept Puccini's opinion that the psychological reality of the scene outweighs any lost lyricism. Lyricism, as we have noted above (pp. 185–86), sets the music of the lovers apart from Scarpia's music. It is possible to read this interrupted lyricism of Act III as an indication that Scarpia continues to thwart their plans and their love (see p. 255 below for the implications of this statement for Puccini's musical choice at the end of the opera).

The first of the two interruptions that so bothered Giulio Ricordi comes at the end of "O dolci mani." Tosca frees her hand and hurries to explain what she has done (collected her money, hired a carriage), and what *he* must do: "first, you'll be shot" *(prima sarai fucilato)*. The orchestra hints at deception (III, 310; see ex. 9.4) as she explains that it will all be pretend, simulated, with blank cartridges. Although she assures him that it will not be a real execution, the music has already made the unequivocal statement that it will indeed be real. This may simply be Puccini inviting the audience to share in knowledge that is hidden from the characters. Or it may represent a cold shudder of apprehension that crosses Cavaradossi's mind as soon as he hears these words. (Or, arguably, it may be both.)

Ex. 9.4. Deception (III, 310)

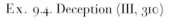

Illica and Giacosa struggled to provide Puccini with a text for this section of the libretto that would meet with his approval. Traces of that struggle remain among Giacosa's notes:

> Tosca: Listen . . .
>   Cav: No. I want to read
>   this paper again—Scarpia has granted a pardon
>   at what price?

and

> Tosca: But first you must submit to a grim
>   comedy.

and

> Tosca: I have understood the order clearly;
>   Scarpia [gave?] it to Spoletta
>   in my presence. It is necessary that the Holy Office
>   see you dead.
>   It must watch your execution
>   It is up to Spoletta to see to it secretly
>   that the guns are loaded only with powder
>   Everyone must believe you dead.

and

> Tosca: Let's go to the open . . .
>   Cav: Yes, let us fly from this
>   deadly city!
> Tosca: At Ostia [*sic*] we'll rent a *tartana*
>   and go by way of the great, free sea.
>   Cav: I see you.
>   I speak to you, and it is not an illusion. Oh, how cowardly
>   the thought of you made me.
> Tosca: Who suffers
>   on earth any longer? Smell the perfume of roses.

> Does it not seem to you that every thing
> smiles, in love under the sun?
> CAV: Even in anguish your face was lovely to me.
> (It was bitter to me to recall your face.) [44]

These fragments of dialogue seems to have less to do with "amorous slob-berings" than with attempts to resolve certain plot considerations: Cavaradossi's acceptance of the apparent reprieve; the still unresolved question of his doubts about the way in which his life has been saved; and a plausible explanation for the fake execution—Giacosa thought of dragging the Inquisition (the "Holy Office") into the plot, an idea that was mercifully forgotten. Tosca is concerned with practical travel plans, such as renting a *tartana*, at Ostia. (In fact, Ostia is a much more reasonable choice for a embarkation port, though the name lacks the sonorous appeal of Civitavecchia.)

Only bits of the draft were salvaged for the final version, notably the references to freedom on the sea, and Tosca's reverie about the scent of roses. Cavaradossi's last two lines evolved into a sonnet beginning "Death was bitter to me only because of you" (*amaro sol per te m'era morire;* see below). The scene as it finally emerged consists of twelve economical lines (plus the sonnet):

> TOSCA: Listen . . . the time is near; I've already collected
> gold and jewels . . . a carriage is ready.
> But first . . . laugh, love . . . first you will be
> shot—a sham—with blank guns . . . —
> a fake execution. At the shot . . . you fall.
> The soldiers go away . . . and we are saved!
> Then to Civitavecchia . . . a *tartana* . . .
> And away by sea!
> CAV: Free!
> TOSCA: Free!
> CAV: Away by sea!
> TOSCA: Who suffers
> Any more on earth? Do you smell the scent of roses?
> Doesn't it seem to you that all things
> lovingly await the sun? [45]

Cavaradossi makes his first comment, "Free!", against a gentle, wave-like accompaniment (played softly, *ondeggiando*). But the music, mimicking the rhythm of a boat at anchor, tells us that in fact they will not be going anywhere. [46]

The libretto does not tell us if Cavaradossi knows that he is going to die, but there are several points that can be interpreted as indicating that he does indeed know or at least suspects. The tenor Beniamino Gigli, a great Cavaradossi of the 1930s and '40s, was one of the first interpreters of the role to

decide that the painter is not deceived by Floria's assurances that the execution will be a mere charade. In his autobiography, Gigli wrote of the character, "he is certain that these are their last moments together on earth, and that
he is about to die."[47] Placido Domingo, the dominant interpreter of the role
in the 1980s and 1990s, makes it quite obvious that Cavaradossi knows the
truth. In a televised interview in connection with the 1985 Metropolitan Opera
production, Domingo stated that he has long performed the role "as though
Cavaradossi knows perfectly well that he is going to be dead." And Tito Gobbi,
the distinguished interpreter of the role of Scarpia who often directed the
opera in his later years, agrees: "Unlike Floria, Cavaradossi knows that Scarpia never yields, though he pretends to believe in order to delay the pain for
Tosca."

In practical terms the scheme Floria presents to her lover is one in which
only a half-crazed opera singer could believe. No one who had watched such
executions could have entertained much hope of surviving one unharmed.
And firing-squad executions were common with the French army wherever
they went: hardly a week passed under the Roman Republic without at least
one man shot in one of the public squares of the city. The procedure looked
less like a stage production of *Tosca* than like Goya's horrific *Third of May*
(see fig. 48), or like a gangland killing. When twenty-two men from Rome's
Trastevere district were shot in February 1798 they were marched to the Piazza del Popolo, forced to kneel down in a row, and one by one shot in the
head.[48] One survived, but other soldiers arrived and fired five rounds into him.
The method used for military executions was somewhat different, but no more
survivable. Soldiers surrounded the kneeling or seated victim on three sides,
and fired downward at point-blank range. While a successful artist like Cavaradossi, unlike most of his generation, might have avoided service in the
armies of the French Revolution (David's students were exempt from con-
scription), neither he nor any other man would have found it easy to avoid
seeing the results of military discipline. The harrowing fact that firing-squad
victims were shot in the head could hardly have escaped him.[49]

Mario's first comment after hearing what Floria has to say about the simulated execution is the single word "Free!" *(Liberi)*. Although there is an exclamation point after the word in the score, it would be easy to read it as a
question rather than a statement, especially when she replies with the same
word, as if reassuring him. He then says, "We'll go by sea" *(Via pel mar)*, repeating the last words of her excited account, again in a way that can easily
be interpreted as a question. (In the live telecast of the opera, Domingo at this
point grimaced and crushed the safe-conduct in his fist in mute anguish.)[50]

Mario then returns to the love scene as his next passage is sung, as the

FIGURE 48. A chillingly realistic portrayal of a military execution of civilians by firing squad, showing the grisly reality of the procedure. Goya, *The Third of May* (detail). Museo del Prado, Madrid. Art Resource

directions tell us, "with the most tender emotion." "Death was only bitter for me because of you" *(amaro sol per te m'era il morire)*, he begins. If his aria at the start of the act was the character's breakthrough from denial into grief in the face of death, this scene is the beginning of reconciliation and acceptance. Is this message—that he will continue to live through her—the one that he had tried, and failed, to write in his letter? "I will see the blazing of the sky, and its decline into darkness, in your revealing eyes, and the beauty of all things will have voice and color only through you."

Tosca's response can be read as an unconscious continuation of the same theme. It begins as a statement of her faith that the love that saved his life will make the world seem beautiful for them, but she soon drifts off into an essentially transcendent concept, that they will be joined together in heaven like clouds that float over the sea at sunset.

Despite Puccini's dislike of "academic" poetry, this exchange taken together makes a perfect classical sonnet. It consists of fourteen lines, octave and sestet, each with the requisite number of syllables, and with the traditional rhyme pattern: *abababab cdcdcd.*

> CAV: *Amaro sol per te m'era il morire,*
> *Da te la vita prende ogni splendore,*
> *all'esser mio la gioia ed il desire*
> *nascon di te, come di fiamma ardore.*
> *Io folgorare i cieli e scolorire*
> *vedrò nell'occhio tuo rivelatore,*
> *e la beltà delle cose più mire*
> *avrà sol da te voce e colore.*
> TOSCA: *Amor che seppe a te vita serbare*
> *ci sarà guida in terra, in mar nocchiere*
> *e vago farà il mondo a riguardare.*
> *Finché congiunti alle celesti sfere*
> *dileguerem, siccome alte sul mare*
> *a sol cadente, nuovole leggere!* [51]

If transcending death is possible at all, for the unbelieving artist (Cavaradossi, and also Puccini?), it is only possible through the forces of art, and of human love. So Cavaradossi, referring to visual and musical beauty, says that he will see "the brightening of the skies and their loss of color" in her eyes; that beauty will have "voice and color" only through her.

There is a moment of stillness, and then Floria, worrying about his ability to fall convincingly, tries to bring the conversation back to a rehearsal for the execution. The musical structure here (III, 370) is the same as that of the first interruption, but now it is distributed over both voices. He replies to her prompting with the blackest sort of gallows humor:

> TOSCA: Be careful! It's essential that you fall immediately.
> CAV: Don't worry, I'll fall right away, and "al naturale."

The libretto stage directions call for him to say this "reassuringly" and the working papers were even more clear: "smiling, reassuring her." In the score the directions consist of one word: "Sadly" *(triste).* As he makes this grim joke the warning chords (ex. 9.4) sound again—more irony? or Cavaradossi's inner conviction that his words are more true than she knows? [52]

She wants to continue with her short course in stage technique, fussing over him like an Italian mother ("but pay attention to me so you don't hurt yourself . . ."); he interrupts her, pulls her to him, and begs her to "talk to me again the way you just did"—that is, to talk not about the shooting but about the way in which their love will transcend death, "like clouds over the sea at sunset."

If he does *not* know that he is going to die, the situation is merely pitiful and ironic, a particularly heartless example of Puccini's bringing the audience in on a secret so that together we can watch this helpless, deluded young couple walk blindly into the final trap.[53] The situation is quite different if Cavaradossi knows the truth but is forcing himself to pretend in order to give her a few more moments of hope and happiness rather than telling her about the terrible reality that neither of them can change.

The third segment of the "fragmentary" last duet begins "sweetly" as Mario interrupts her interruption and pulls her close *(la interrompe, attirandola a sé)*, telling her to speak to him again as she did before, "the sound of your voice is so sweet" (III, 385)—is there a flicker of the motif of "O dolci baci" here? Her response is "almost ecstatic" *(quasi estasiata);* he joins her and their unison voices soar to a high B♮ while speaking of "harmonies of color, harmonies of song."[54] A crescendo leads them to the brink of the precipice, and their voices soar in unaccompanied unison phrases. This hymn to triumphant (and illusory) hope is sung to the same notes (an octave higher) that the horns played before the curtain rose on this act.

As late as the 1899 printed libretto, and the full score of the opera from 1900 (the year of the premiere) this duet was followed by this exchange:

> TOSCA: Our country is there, where love leads us.
> CAV: Everywhere we will find Latin traces
>   and the ghost of Rome.
> TOSCA: And if I see you,
>   remembering, looking toward the heavens,
>   *I will close your eyes with a thousand kisses,*
>   *and call you by a thousand loving names.*[55]

Eduardo Rescigno surmises in his preface to a recent Ricordi edition of the libretto that this passage is probably what survived from the famous Latin hymn. The current version of the opera includes only the italicized lines. The Latin hymn was not the only victim of Puccini's ruthless drive for clarity in this scene. He did not want any reflection or character development to interfere with the nervous haste with which these two rush toward death. Giacosa had sketched out several bits of dialogue designed in academic fashion to complete his characterizations. Floria, who began the opera as a featherbrain, has changed and matured by this point, and the poet wanted to make

some clear statement of her new frame of reference. Several attempts were
recorded, and discarded:

> O Mario, does it not seem to you
> that we now love each other
> for the first time?

and

> Tell me if you remember
> our past love

and

> My Mario, does it not seem to you
> that our love is born today?
> If you remember any
> of the joyful times past
> does it not seem to you well
> to forget

and

> Mario, Mario and only yesterday
> I was ignorant of evil.
> I have learned so much.

and

> Listen, was our love real
> up to yesterday?
> We were was never so steadfast and proud.[56]

Puccini seems to have classed lines such as these either with the "academic, academic" or the "amorous slobberings". In either case, he had no interest in such speculations, but only in the rapid forward movement of the
plot. In the final version all of these poetic efforts were scrapped, and only the
poignant lines that begin "I will close your eyes with a thousand kisses" now
appear in the opera. Puccini may have deleted the rest of them for purely musical reasons, but in removing the extraneous dialogue he also removed references that would have brought the lovers' last scene down from the transcendent to a concrete future on this earth. In fact, their love will not change, they
will find no new country, they will not be troubled by nostalgia for Rome. In
a few minutes she will close his eyes with kisses, and join him in death.

> ***Exhausted he sinks back against the parapet, his arms around
> her, and she bends over him, gently brushing his hair back***

away from his face and kissing his closed eyes. The jailer and
the officer commanding the firing party find them clinging to
one another.

The libretto has already told us (Scarpia and Spoletta, Act II) that the execution will take place at "the fourth hour" *(a l'ora quarta),* and at this point
the score reminds us by having a bell chime four times. The phrase "the
fourth hour" suggests that this is "Italian time," but in fact that would have
been far too early, closer to 2 A.M. than to dawn. Rather, the librettists seem
to be indulging in the usual dramatic fiction of firing squads and death at
dawn, which comes around 4:30 A.M. in Rome at this time of year. Although
executions by firing squad were the rule under French domination (the guillotine was not introduced in Rome until after 1808), they were rare under the
Allies and under the papal government, both of which much preferred hanging. The following is an account of a typical firing-squad execution that took
place under the Roman Republic. At noon on the penultimate day of 1798 the
young Neapolitan partisan Don Gennaro Valentino (another of Maria Carolina's pets, and perhaps a lover) was brought to the Piazza Montecitorio to be
shot. Valentino, who was in his early twenties, had served as commander of
the urban militia during the brief Neapolitan occupation of Rome, and when
the city fell again to the French he had remained behind on the promise of a
safe-conduct, to help keep the peace.[57] Although the civilian authorities tried
to save him, the French commander Championnet was determined that he
should die, and the execution was designed as a propaganda spectacle. Fortunati tells us that the weather was unusually cold that week.[58] Valentino, who
had been held in the Castel Sant'Angelo, was marched through the city in the
midst of a large troop of reserves, preceded by a military band and followed
by a picket of French cavalry. Galimberti describes the execution:

> When he arrived at the Piazza Montecitorio the square *[quadrato]* of reserve
> troops opened, and he entered to undergo the execution. . . . Then the pa-
> triots howled at him, shouting "Death to the tyrant." He was quite fearless,
> and without a blindfold [even the official republican newspaper, the *Moni-*
> *tore,* agreed that he "faced his death with insane courage"]. He knelt and
> took off his hat himself, and prepared for the blow, holding a crucifix in his
> hand. At the first volley of shots he fell, struck in the forehead; a second vol-
> ley was fired into him as he lay on the ground.[59]

It was not uncommon for a firing squad to have to fire two or more volleys.
The Trasteverino who survived the first volley in the February execution was
then hit with five more rounds. Andreas Hofer, the Tyrolese partisan leader

executed by the French army in November 1809, was hit by five volleys for a total of about forty rounds. Fortunati's account of Valentino's death is even more harrowing than Galimberti's. According to him the young general was injured by the first volley, "but was immediately carried on a stretcher into the Church of the Orphans where they finished murdering him with bayonets."[60]

The chronicles of the confraternity of St John the Beheaded record only one execution by firing squad under the papal government during this period, when Antonio Arrisa, or Avvisa, a young soldier from Treviso in the Veneto, was shot for desertion in 1795.[61] The procedure was so unfamiliar that the confraternity members were offered, and gratefully accepted, the opportunity to walk through a "dress rehearsal" for the "formation of the square".

The confraternity's account of this execution is reproduced below. It is worth extensive consideration, not only because it parallels the killing in the last act of *Tosca* but because it shows how very seriously the old regime took death. The so-called "Terror" of 1793–94 in France was terrible precisely because it introduced a new efficient sort of State-inflicted death in place of the elaborate and victim-centered ceremonial of earlier times. Modern historical mythology holds that with the liberal revolution, individual human life gained a value and a dignity that it had lacked under the old regime. But along with a faster, more sanitary, and (perhaps) less painful process of execution came a de-emphasis on the individual whose death it was. Antonio Arrisa was certainly distressed by the procedure. But there was no doubt at all about the tremendous importance of the life that was about to be taken from him, and the even greater value of the spiritual life upon which he was presumed to be entering.

On 15 September 1795 the confraternity brothers gathered at the second hour of the night (around 8:45 P.M.), prayed together, and proceeded by carriage to the gates of the Castel Sant'Angelo. Accompanied by officers and soldiers, they were brought to the chapel in the central tower that had been prepared for their use. The chaplain gave the usual benediction, and the brothers began to recite the penitential psalms.

At the third hour (about 9:45 P.M.) the sentence was given to the notary, and at half past the third hour the condemned man was brought to the *confortoria* surrounded by soldiers and the sentence was read to him with two sergeants acting as witnesses. Arrisa wept and sobbed, lamenting his evil past and the fact that his poor mother would have to hear such news. After about an hour he began to calm down. He was given water and wine.

At half past the fifth hour he was taken into the chapel. Together the condemned and his comforters recited the Litanies of the Blessed Virgin and three Aves; then he knelt at the altar and put on the habit of a Carmelite monk, which he kissed, but still did not speak.

At three-quarters after the sixth hour "his tongue was finally loosened, and he began to weep and plead for God's mercy and forgiveness."

Between the seventh and the ninth hour he made his confession, finishing at about four in the morning. At the ninth hour the confraternity member Canon Giubileo celebrated Mass, "which the delinquent heard on his knees, with great devotion."

At three-quarters past the ninth hour he left the chapel to make his will. He said that his name was Antonio Arrisa, from Treviso, and that he was twenty-two years old. He had a mother, five brothers, and four sisters, three married and one unmarried. The confraternity traditionally offered a dowry for the female relatives of condemned men, and he wanted that dowry to go to his unmarried sister—but she was not to know where it came from, or why. He was extremely anxious that his mother should not hear that he had died such a shameful death, and went to great lengths to see to it that she thought he had died in the hospital, sending word to that effect through his brother Francesco. He left some money to Giuseppe Bernardinelli, a soldier who deserted with him but who was not to be executed, begging him that, should he return to Venice, he should not tell Arrisa's family about the way he died. The condemned man expected a small legacy from his mother, and wanted it distributed in the following fashion: his brothers were to use part of it to pay his debts; part was to go for alms, asking the recipients to pray for his soul; the rest was to be divided among his brothers. Monsignor Priuli, a lawyer in Venice, was to be asked to carry out the provisions of the will.

Arrisa finished his testament at a quarter past the tenth hour and returned to the chapel for communion; a second Mass was then offered, then a third, and finally a fourth, celebrated by the chaplain of the fortress. At a quarter past the eleventh hour he began to weep again, but the brothers gave him some chocolate and he seemed to recover his spirits.

At the twelfth hour (about 8:45 in the morning) the sacristan sent to see if the execution party had gathered. At the thirteenth hour the brothers proceeded to the courtyard of the rampart, carrying the crucifix. The *paziente* was brought out from the chapel and, supported by two brothers, began the walk to the courtyard. At the end of the *cordonata* (that is, the shallow staircase leading from the upper part of the fortress) the boy's strength failed him, so he was seated on a chair carried by two convicts. Before leaving the chapel the *paziente* had asked to be blindfolded and this was done. He was then carried to the *piazza d'armi*, still seated in the chair; he received absolution again,

and was carried into the square, to the arranged place. He asked for, and received, a final absolution; the two brothers who were with him withdrew to
stand by the six soldiers, who fired. At half past the thirteenth hour the unfortunate lad, "calling loudly on the names of Jesus, and Mary, gave his soul
up to God." The brothers then returned to the chapel where they heard Mass,
and, after waiting a while for the blood of the dead man to congeal, brought
the corpse to the church of St John the Beheaded. He was buried in the confraternity graveyard after the usual intercessions. "And so it ended, to the
glory of God and of St John."

Cavaradossi's death is profoundly different from this real eighteenth-
century execution. Like the man himself it is modern, unsuited to the city and
the time. Nowhere else is it so obvious that this is a man from a new, northern world, a true child of the revolution. He brushes aside the Roman way of
death in favor of the isolated, impersonal death of the modern era as inau-
gurated by the efficient killing machine in the Place de la Révolution. Cavaradossi, who according to Sardou spent his boyhood in the shadow of the
guillotine, looks on death as a private, secular affair; he considers that the
destination of his immortal soul, assuming that he has one, is no one's business but his own. It is unlikely that any condemned man in Rome in 1800
would have been allowed to continue in this attitude, not out of spite but because the idea of dying without making one's peace with this world and the
next would have been incomprehensible to the men in charge of execution in
that time and place. On the rare occasion when a hardened criminal refused
reconciliation, the proceedings ground to a halt while priests, guards, confraternity brothers, and government officials pleaded, bullied, and cajoled.
Only when it was absolutely clear that no repentance would be forthcoming
would the execution proceed, to the great distress of all concerned.

> *Floria, nervous but unsuspecting, watches and comments on
> the tedious business of the firing squad. Finally, they fire and
> Mario falls to the ground. When the soldiers leave she discov-
> ers that Mario is dead. While she laments over his corpse, Spo-
> letta and Sciarrone rush in with news of Scarpia's murder and
> try to arrest her. Floria pushes them aside, and throws herself
> to her death in the courtyard below.*

The firing squad's preparations, and Tosca's comments, are carried out
against the background of a eerie march tune (Carner calls it a "march to the
scaffold") (III, 428; see ex. 9.5).[62] Its jaunty, almost cheerful sound makes the
firing squad seem like toy soldiers. The music that accompanies the actual execution is cinematic in the extreme. The march is interrupted, almost frozen,

by a drumroll and a tremolo in the cellos and basses (III, 458–60). Then, the march theme crashes back fortissimo, enlarged to the entire orchestra. Spoletta prevents the sergeant delivering the coup de grâce and Tosca watches the soldiers leave, in an agony of concern that Mario might get up before they are safely out of sight.

EX. 9.5. Execution (III, 428–29)

In the moment of truth, when she discovers that her lover is dead, all illusion collapses—and the music seems to dissolve into chaos. At this point Illica and Tito Ricordi (who had become involved at this point), yearned to put in a "lament" in the classical operatic style. They were particularly determined to add it when it seemed possible that Tosca would not commit suicide at all, but go mad. Not only was suicide "antipatico," they feared that it would be the final straw for an audience that had already been asked to sit still for extramarital sex, a strong dose of anti-clerical imagery, torture, attempted rape, murder, and one offstage suicide (male). When the play was produced in English in New York within six months of its Paris premiere, it was Tosca's suicide that called for the loudest condemnations—so much so that the first American Tosca, Fanny Davenport, changed the end. After the first week or so of the production, the play ended with the hapless Tosca falling dead on the body of her lover, shot by the soldiers.[63]

Puccini seems to have realized from the start that a lament by Tosca after she discovers Cavaradossi's death was a bad idea. Describing a meeting with Sardou, he quotes himself as telling the French writer that "this" (the lament scene) is the "overcoat aria"—that is, the place where the audience begins to get up and put on their overcoats.[64]

Instead of an "overcoat aria," Puccini decided on a finale that sweeps past at dizzying speed, barely pausing for breath, and accompanied by pure "action" music. No sooner has Tosca discovered the dreadful truth than Sciarrone's voice is heard shouting offstage, "I tell you, stabbed!" *(Vi dico, pugnato!)*. Scarpia's henchmen, with soldiers in tow, dash in, intent on arresting the murderess.

Sardou, who hated loose ends, does not leave us wondering how the police managed to discover their chief's body so quickly, after he has given specific orders that he should not be disturbed.[65] In the play Tosca, sobbing over her dead lover, actually tells them that she has killed Scarpia:

> FLORIA: Oh, the tiger! And I can't kill him again! . . . Yes, I've killed
>   him, your Scarpia! Killed, killed, do you understand? I drove
>   a knife into his heart, and I want to plunge it in again and
>   twist it![66]

Spoletta does not believe her but she insists, telling them to go and see for themselves (they can do this quickly because in the play Scarpia's offices are in the Castel Sant'Angelo, not the Farnese palace). Spoletta sends two men to check; only when they return with confirmation of the story does he tell her that she will pay for the murder with her life:

> FLORIA: *(rising)* Take it [my life], so I won't have the horror of looking
>   at you any more, bandits who do things like this, a rotten
>   people who accept them, a shameless sun that shines on
>   them!
> SPOLETTA: Devil! *(to Floria who, during this time goes to the parapet)*
>   I'll send you to join your lover!
> FLORIA: *(standing on the parapet)* I'm going there, scum![67]

The Floria of the opera is (as we have seen) a very different person from the brittle, vindictive Parisienne of the play. The librettists tried to soften Floria Tosca, an effort that included giving her hints of madness throughout the last act, though by the time the final text emerged these had become so subtle they are easy to miss. One hint might be her odd reverie about floating away, like light clouds in the sunset; a comment that is accompanied in the score by the directions "staring fixedly, singing, as though in a vision."[68] When she discovers that Mario is dead she can only sob out broken phrases of uncomprehending grief (see fig. 49).

She has only a few moments before Spoletta and Sciarrone arrive with the news that Scarpia's body has been found: "Tosca is the woman!" *(La donna è Tosca!)* Sciarrone shouts. From III, 498—as Tosca, sobbing, calls out Mario's name—until the end of the opera, there is a single, crescendo wave of forty-four measures (taking some twenty to twenty-five seconds to complete), with almost all of the vocal parts shouted or sobbed. Floria pushes the police and soldiers aside, runs to the edge of the platform, and appealing to divine justice, throws herself to her death in the courtyard almost 150 feet below.

Given Puccini's preference for madness over defiance, it seems clear that it is the horror of Mario's death that drives her to throw herself from the battle-

FIGURE 49. "Tu? Così?" Tosca discovers that the "simulated" firing squad has been all too real, and Cavaradossi is dead. © Archivio Storico Casa Ricordi. Reproduced by permission

ments, not outrage or fury, or even fear. Although her last words are "Scarpia, before God!" *(O Scarpia, avanti a Dio!)*, the music that ends the opera is that assocated with the man she loves, not the one she hates. The conflict between the verbal and the musical clues gives the end of the opera a twist of controversy that, barring some unexpected discovery among Puccini's papers, can never truly be resolved. Joseph Kerman's vitriolic dismissal of the closing phrase ("Tosca leaps, and the orchestra screams the first thing that comes into its head") is the most famous statement of the opinion that Puccini mishandled the end of the opera, but it is not the only one.[69] Even Mosco Carner, who is generally sympathetic to the opera, has said that he regrets that Puccini did not see fit to end *Tosca* with Scarpia's theme.[70]

Much of the condemnation of the use of the theme from Mario's aria stems from the argument that Floria never hears it. While this is true of the score as it now stands, as late as the first printed edition of the score the theme was briefly quoted at the point at which she discovers that Mario is dead.[71] It seems possible that Puccini may have considered using this theme as part of the "overcoat aria" lament that would have been sung at this point had the "mad scene" idea survived.

Since the quotation, along with the lament, was ultimately rejected, does the opera now end on an inappropriate note, the hit tune of the act plugged in for the finale with crass disregard for dramatic truth? There are any number of possible alternative arguments. Has Floria finally succumbed to despair just as Mario did, so that the repetition of the phrase from his aria is a fitting accompaniment for the final act of two wasted lives? A variation on the theme of shared despair would argue that Mario, as a modern secular man, has no religious faith to turn to, and instead (like Puccini himself) he has found meaning through the aesthetic values of art and human love. For him there is nothing else to life, and he works out his destiny within this framework. Floria, on the other hand, begins the opera with an unquestioning faith in her childish vision of religious truth: she clings to the hope that if she trusts and acts as she should, all will be well. After she has been cynically manipulated by a triumphantly evil man, after she has been forced to betray the man she loves in an attempt to save him, after she has been left alone with no help from angels or saints, and only the knife in her hand to protect her from violation—after all of this, her faith begins to crumble. When she turns her lover's body over and sees that he is dead, all of her hopes are crushed and she is faced with the unbearable insight that Mario was right all along, that there is no meaning in life beyond beauty and human love. And she cannot bear to live in such a world without him. The problem with this interpretation, of course, is her final appeal to God.

More simply, the repetition of the theme may be taken as a particularly bitter form of irony. Cavaradossi's lament for his own death is expanded to include hers: Floria, so recently filled with an insane hope, dies at the time when, like Mario, she has never loved life so much.

Eric Plaut, an opera-lover who is also a psychiatrist, offers a Freudian interpretation of the end. In this interpretation, Scarpia and Cavaradossi are both aspects of Puccini's character: Scarpia the ruthless womanizer, Cavaradossi the loving but weak artist. Not only do both men provide the motive for Tosca's suicide, both men are in fact the same man, the composer himself, and so they must be combined in the cathartic finale.[72]

Another psychological analysis, this time in the feminist tradition, comes from Catherine Clément.[73] In her brilliant if idiosyncratic essay Tosca's flinging herself into the void is the final vertiginous act of a woman, hurried, breathless, driven by a male world that she can neither control nor understand. It is an act that encompasses all of opera as "the undoing of women," the fatal burst of freedom, self-immolation as the price of exceeding the bounds of a gender-defined culture. Although Clément does not specifically address the question of the music that follows the heroine's suicide, one might surmise that Floria's "undoing" is brought about less by Scarpia's malevolent lust than by the fact that Mario, who now lies dead in her arms, loved her. That love not only involved her in the fatal world of masculine aggression, it made her vulnerable and unable to live without him.

While psychological interpretations favoring Puccini's choice of a final theme have been fairly common, it is only recently that musical analysts have begun to concur. Michele Girardi, writing in 1995, observed: "It is only in this moment, after the drama of politics and bigotry is concluded with an impossible challenge [that is, Tosca's call on Scarpia to meet her before God] that Cavaradossi's despairing melody can conclude the opera with the sign that sensual love is the only real and certain Good."[74]

For Sieghart Döhring, the end of the opera is appropriate because it combines the three central factors in Tosca's dilemma: Cavaradossi, Scarpia, and religious faith. In Döhring's view the third act of *Tosca* does not end with Scarpia's theme because, unlike the first two acts, the third act is not primarily about the malignant power of the Church-dominated State.[75] He argues that the meaning of Act III has shifted to something more personal, and more typically Puccinian: the illusory nature of happiness. At the final curtain, as all illusion collapses, the music of disillusion, most clearly stated in Cavaradossi's aria, proclaims the meaning of the act.

Puccini certainly used themes to indicate the thoughts of his characters; if he rejected the Scarpia/Tyranny theme as a closing motif he did so for reasons of his own that he did not see fit to explain. Perhaps Puccini, a master of theatrical effect, would not have been above reiterating a hit melody for the sake of an exciting ending. Since he did not explain his choice, we must simply accept it (though some critics have felt that we do not have to like it). But *Tosca* would be a very different opera if it ended, as Charles Osborne, Spike Hughes, Mosco Carner, and others have urged that it should, with the three harsh chords associated with Scarpia and tyranny rather than with Cavaradossi's lament.[76] In spite of despair and disillusion, the painter's legacy is a passionate cry that life *does* have meaning, a meaning that can be found in love and beauty—even if love and beauty are fragile and temporary. To end the opera with the Scarpia/Tyranny chords would have conveyed the ultimate triumph of meaninglessness and evil. In 1900 Puccini could stress disillusion, could reject the idea that patriotism or religion give meaning to life, but it was still early in the century for a truly popular work of art to offer the nihilistic message that life has no meaning at all.

Part of the message of *Tosca* is that happiness is an illusion, inexorably destroyed by tragedy. Another part is that the great world of politics and institutions is indifferent to that happiness, or that tragedy. Scarpia has no particular desire to ruin two young lives—he is not interested enough to care. They have simply become enmeshed in his machine, annoyed him, caught his eye. Yesterday it was Angelotti and his sister, the day before that, Count Palmieri and perhaps some woman who cared about him; tomorrow, *diverse beltà, vini diversi*. This is a twentieth-century story, and part of its power lies in its preview of totalitarianism. The omnipotent twentieth-century State that would give us Mussah Dagh and Verdun, Buchenwald and the Katyn Forest, and the massacre of Roman civilians in the Ardeatine caves, was already flexing its muscles when *Tosca* was being written.

Puccini—cynical, loving, vain, with all the psychological baggage of the fin de siècle—manipulates our feelings because he shares our crippling little secret and amplifies it: those of us not immune to the opera's power care about his puppets; we care about those tormenting passions, those hopes and terrors, those illusions. At least the last notes of *Tosca* allow us the catharsis of mourning them.

Appendix 1

Sardou's _La Tosca_ and Puccini's _Tosca:_ Plots and Parallels

CHARACTERS

Sardou's _La Tosca_

FLORIA TOSCA, a famous singer
MARIA CAROLINA, Queen of Naples
LUCIANA, Tosca's maid
GENNARINO, Mario Cavaradossi's servant
(at the church)*
PRINCESS ORLONIA, a Roman aristocrat
A MONSIGNOR, a Roman cleric*
BARON SCARPIA, Regent of Roman Police,
from Naples
MARIO CAVARADOSSI, a French painter
and Tosca's lover
CESARE ANGELOTTI, escaped prisoner,
former Consul of the Roman Republic
THE MARQUIS ATTAVANTI, courtier and
husband of Angelotti's sister
EUSEBE, sacristan at the church of Sant'
Andrea des Jésuites, i.e. al Quirinale
VISCOUNT TRÉVILHAC, a French royalist
émigré
CAPRÉOLA, a noble guest at the Queen's
reception
TRIVULCE, the Marquise Attavanti's
gentleman companion
SPOLETTA, a Neapolitan captain of
carabinieri
SCHIARRONE, a police agent
CECCHO, Mario Cavaradossi's servant
(at the villa)
PAISIELLO, Neapolitan composer
DIEGO NASELLI, Prince of Aragon and
Governor of Rome
A HUSSAR, courier from the army at
Marengo

COLOMETTI, Scarpia's servant
A SERGEANT
THE PUBLIC PROSECUTOR
ALBERTI (or ROBERTI), the executioner
Police Spies and Agents; offstage Choir,
onstage Orchestra and Chorus; Guests,
Courtiers, and Servants of the Queen of
Naples; Scarpia's Servants; Jailers, and
Soldiers

Puccini's _Tosca_

FLORIA TOSCA, a famous singer
MARIO CAVARADOSSI, a painter, Tosca's
lover
THE BARON SCARPIA, chief of police
CESARE ANGELOTTI, an escaped political
prisoner
SACRISTAN at the church of Sant'Andrea
della Valle
SPOLETTA, a police agent
SCIARRONE, a policeman
A JAILER at the Castel Sant'Angelo
A SHEPHERD
A Cardinal, a Judge, Roberti (the execu-
tioner), a Clerk, an Officer, a Sergeant;
Soldiers, Police Spies, Ladies, Nobles,
Citizens, etc.

*In the 1887 and 1909 productions, these
parts were played by women.

PLAY	OPERA

Act I: Jesuit church of Sant'Andrea al Quirinale

Act I: Church of Sant'Andrea della Valle

i: *Gennarino, Eusebius*
The Painter's servant and the sacristan discuss Mario Cavaradossi and the news from the front; Eusebius samples the wine from the lunch basket.

i: *Angelotti, alone*
Angelotti staggers in, finds the key his sister has hidden for him, and hides in the Attavanti chapel.

ii: *Gennarino, Eusebius, Cavaradossi*
Mario returns, having been on a shopping expedition, and sends the boy and the sacristan away.

ii: *Sacristan, alone*
The sacristan bustles in, complaining about dirty paint brushes. He is surprised not to see the painter. He looks at the lunch basket, then pauses to recite the Angelus.

iii: *Cavaradossi, Angelotti*
Angelotti introduces himself and is welcomed by the painter. He explains his escape, how he earned the enmity of Lady Hamilton, and his current predicament. Mario introduces himself with a brief biography, and talks about his affair with Tosca.

iii: *Sacristan, Cavaradossi*
Mario enters, unveils his mural, which includes a portrait of the Marchesa Attavanti as the Magdalene. He begins to paint [Aria: "Recondita armonia"].

iv: *Cavaradossi, Tosca*
Tosca arrives and teases Mario about the Attavanti woman; they chat and flirt.

iv: *Cavaradossi, Angelotti*
Angelotti emerges from hiding, and Mario agrees to help him. On hearing Tosca's voice, Angelotti hides again, taking the lunch basket with him.

v: *Cavaradossi, Tosca, Luciana*
Tosca's maid brings news of the supposed royal victory at Marengo. Tosca asks that Mario paint the eyes of the portrait black, and leaves to rehearse the cantata.

v: *Cavaradossi, Tosca*
Tosca is suspicious of the delay, but plans an evening rendezvous [Aria: "Non la sospiri"]. Recognizing the portrait, she is jealous but is placated in a love scene [Duet: "Qual'occhio al mondo?"] and leaves, asking him to "make the eyes [of the Magdalene] black."

vi: *Cavaradossi and Angelotti*
The two men decide to risk leaving the city in the confusion of the victory; a signal shot from the Castel Sant'Angelo announces Angelotti's escape. He goes into the chapel to don his disguise.

vi: *Cavaradossi, Angelotti*
The men discuss Angelotti's escape. Cavaradossi, learning that Scarpia is Angelotti's pursuer, swears to save the escaped prisoner even at the cost of his own life. Giving Angelotti the key to his suburban villa, Cavaradossi tells him of a hiding place in the well where he will be safe in case of urgent danger. A cannon shot gives the news that the escape has been discovered. Angelotti snatches up the disguise his sister has left for him, and the two men hurry out together.

vii: *Cavaradossi, Eusebius, then Gennarino*
The sacristan hurries in to gloat over the news of the supposed victory over Bonaparte. The boy brings news of how the escape was discovered; Angelotti slips out the side door, and Mario leaves to join him.

vii: *Sacristan, choir, students and acolytes, penitents and townspeople*
The sacristan enters with (mistaken) news of victory at Marengo, and assembles the excited choirboys for the Te Deum.

viii: *Eusebius, Scarpia, Schiarrone,*
  Colometti, agents, then Gennarino
Scarpia arrives with his agents. They have
missed Angelotti, but discover the fan. The
sacristan informs them that Cavaradossi
was alone in the church during the midday
break. They find the empty basket and the
portrait, and learn that Tosca has been
there, and left flowers. They kneel as the Te
Deum begins.

viii: *The same, plus Scarpia and police*
  agents
Scarpia's entrance throws the Sacristan and
his audience into panic. Scarpia questions
the Sacristan and learns that Cavaradossi,
whose name he recognizes, has painted the
portrait of Angelotti's sister as the Magda-
len. The police search the chapel and find
the empty lunch basket, and the fan belonging to the Marchesa Attavanti, part of the
disguise that was inadvertently left behind.
Seeing Tosca, whom he knows to be Cavaradossi's mistress, Scarpia forms a plan to use
the painting and the fan to trick her into
betraying her lover's whereabouts.

ix: *The same, plus Tosca*
Tosca has returned to the church to tell
Mario that she has to sing for the court that
night, and so cannot meet him. Scarpia uses
the fan to convince her that her lover is with
the Marchesa Attavanti. She hurries out,
and is followed.

x: *Scarpia alone*
As the Te Deum begins, Scarpia plans the
capture of the rebels and his conquest of
Tosca [Te Deum and "Va, Tosca"].

Major differences: in the play there is much more exposition; Angelotti and Cavara-
dossi are strangers; there is much less stress on the portrait of the Marchesa; Scarpia
has a great deal less to do. Tosca does not return to the church, having agreed with
Mario that he will wake her up the following morning, after her court appearance,
which he refuses to share.

Act II: Great Hall at the Farnese palace

i: *Trévilhac, Capréola, Marquis Attavanti,*
   Trivulce, plus ladies, gentlemen, an
   orchestra, and gambling tables
At the Queen's reception, a French émigré
(Trévilhac) is introduced to Roman society.
Attavanti explains the role of Trivulce, his
wife's gentleman companion. The bandit-
commanders of the royalist army are discussed.

ii: *The same, plus Scarpia, then Schiarrone*
Scarpia learns that Cavaradossi's town
house has been searched; the Marquise Attavanti is at Frascati; Scarpia decides to
watch Tosca.

iii: *The same, with Tosca*
Tosca makes a grand entrance surrounded
by admirers; she speaks briefly with Scarpia, and expresses sympathy for Angelotti.

iv: *The same, with Queen Maria Carolina;*
   Diego Naselli, Prince of Aragon; Gen-
   eral Froelich; English, Neapolitan, and
   Austrian officers; the Duke of Ascoli;
   Paisiello; cardinals, monsignors, musi-
   cians, singers, etc.
The Queen greets Tosca graciously, then
threatens Scarpia with disgrace if he fails to
find Angelotti; in a monologue, Scarpia decides to use the fan to trick Tosca.

v: *Tosca and Scarpia, other characters in*
   background
After a flirtatious exchange, Scarpia questions Tosca's wisdom in trusting Cavaradossi, then gives her the fan; Trivulce iden-
tifies it as the Marquise's; Tosca throws a
tantrum, and must be forced to remain and
sing. The cantata is interrupted by news
from Marengo which the Queen reads out,
and then faints. Tosca hurries out, Scarpia
orders his agents to follow in his carriage,
and he leaves with Attavanti.

This scene, modified, appears in Act I of
the opera (above), as Tosca returns to the
church to find Cavaradossi gone.

The news from Marengo arrives in the
middle of Act II of the opera.

*Although Franchetti was attracted by this setting, the court scene appears in the
opera only as offstage parallel to the events of Act II. The two essential plot devices
described above were moved from the play to the opera. There is more extensive exposition in the play, and different characterizations. Tosca is portrayed as more
worldly-wise, more temperamental, and more brazen; Scarpia is shown as a courtier
rather than as an independent and all-powerful villain.*

Act III: THE GROUND FLOOR OF CAVARADOSSI'S VILLA

i: *Mario, Angelotti, Ceccho*
The men arrive at the villa, discard the woman's disguise, and send Ceccho, the servant cum tenant farmer, to prepare a meal.

ii: *Mario, Angelotti*
Mario describes the history of the villa, and how he came to rent it; he tells Angelotti about the well and sends him to familiarize himself with it.

iii: *Mario, Tosca*
Tosca arrives and accuses Mario of disloyalty, especially after finding the discarded dress, but sees Angelotti (offstage) and apologizes. They realize that Scarpia has tricked her, and must be close behind.

iv: *Mario, Tosca, Ceccho, Angelotti*
The servant Ceccho hurries in to announce the arrival of the police; Angelotti goes to hide in the well; Mario orders Tosca to be calm.

v: *Tosca, Mario, Ceccho, Scarpia, the Marquis Attavanti, Schiarrone, Spoletta, Alberti (or Roberti), a clerk, and agents*

After a brief pretence of looking for the Marquise, Scarpia accuses Mario of harboring Angelotti, and sends the Marquis back to inform the Queen that the fugitive will soon be found.

vi: *The same, minus the Marquis*
Mario denies Angelotti's presence and is sent into the next room for questioning.

vii: *The same, minus Mario*
The magistrate is told to take his orders from Scarpia, and follows the agents and Mario into the next room.

viii: *Tosca, Scarpia, Schiarrone, police*
As in the opera, Tosca is questioned, becomes aware that Mario is being tortured, and gradually (very gradually) breaks down and give away the secret.

Act II: SCARPIA'S APARTMENTS AT THE FARNESE PALACE

i: *Scarpia*
Eating his dinner, Scarpia waits for news of the search for Cavaradossi and Angelotti.

ii: *Scarpia, Sciarrone*
Sciarrone opens the window to the sound of dance music from the royal apartments, and is sent with a note for Tosca.

iii: *Scarpia, alone*
Scarpia looks forward to a violent conquest of Tosca [Aria: "Ha più forte sapore"].

iv: *Scarpia, Spoletta, Sciarrone*
Spoletta brings news that he has failed to find Angelotti, but has arrested the painter.

v: *The same, plus Mario and agents, Roberti, judge, and clerk*

The interrogation begins politely as Tosca's voice is heard from the royal apartments below. Mario denies all charges.

vi: *The same, plus Tosca*
Tosca enters and is surprised to see Mario; he whispers to her to keep silent as he is taken away.

vii: *Scarpia, Tosca*
As Tosca becomes aware that Mario is being tortured, she tries to keep the secret.

viii: *Scarpia, Tosca, Mario (offstage), Sciarrone*
Despite Mario's forbidding her to talk, Tosca cannot bear his screams of pain, and tells Scarpia where Angelotti can be found.

ix: *The same, plus Mario and then Colometti*
Mario is brought in, collapses, and is revived in time to overhear word of Angelotti's capture and suicide. Mario and Tosca are taken away to prison.

ix: *The same, plus Mario and agents*
Mario is carried in; Tosca tries to comfort him, but he pushes her away when he hears Scarpia tell Spoletta where to find Angelotti.

x: *The same, plus Sciarrone*
Sciarrone hurries in with news that Bonaparte has won the battle at Marengo. Mario shouts "Victory!" and attacks Scarpia; he is dragged away to be hanged for treason.

Act IV: A ROOM IN THE CASTEL SANT'ANGELO

i: *Scarpia, Schiarrone, a waiter, a lackey, and Colometti*
It is almost dawn. Scarpia dines, and is told about conditions in the city, and Cavaradossi's refusal of religious comfort.

ii: *The same, plus Spoletta*
Spoletta brings the governor's order for Cavaradossi's execution. Scarpia orders Angelotti's corpse to be hung and then denied Christian burial, and sends for Tosca.

iii: *Scarpia, Tosca*
Tosca is brought in and, as in the opera, is called upon to submit to Scarpia in exchange for Mario's life.

xi: *Scarpia, Tosca*
Tosca offers Scarpia a bribe, and he tells her that his price is rape [Aria: "Già, mi dicon venal"]. She tries to resist, but on hearing the drums escorting the prisoner to execution she collapses in despair [Aria: "Vissi d'arte"].

iv: *The same, with Spoletta*
Tosca agrees to the bargain, and the simulated execution is carefully arranged.

xii: *The same, plus Spoletta*
Spoletta brings news of Angelotti's suicide. Tosca nods her agreement to the bargain, and Scarpia gives orders that Cavaradossi will not be hanged but shot, with blank cartridges.

v: *Scarpia, Tosca*
Scarpia makes out a safeconduct. Tosca stabs him, as in the opera. She places candles and a crucifix near the corpse, and slips away.

xiii: *Scarpia and Tosca*
Tosca asks for a safeconduct and as Scarpia is writing it she finds a knife. He approaches her, and she stabs him. When he is dead she takes the safeconduct, arranges candles and a crucifix around him, and slips away.

Act III of the play contains much of the action of Act II of the opera, with the major difference that the interrogation and torture scenes take place (more reasonably) at Cavaradossi's villa. The action of Act IV of the play is almost identical with that of the second half of Act II of the opera, with the exception of the governor's order (which has no parallel in the opera), and the fact that Angelotti's capture and death have already occurred in the previous act. Act IV of the play is set in the Castel Sant'Angelo rather than at the Farnese palace.

Act V, First Set: CHAPEL OF THE CONDEMNED IN THE CASTEL SANT'ANGELO

Act III: PLATFORM OF THE CASTEL SANT'ANGELO

i: *A shepherd boy (offstage)*
Before dawn, a shepherd sings, matins bells ring, and the sky slowly lightens.

i: *Mario, Spoletta, a guard and his assistant, a sergeant, and two soldiers*
Spoletta wakes Mario to tell him Tosca has arrived.

ii: *A jailer, soldiers, Cavaradossi*
Mario is brought to the platform to await execution. He gives his ring to the jailer in exchange for the man's promise to deliver a letter to Tosca. But, overwhelmed by memories, Cavaradossi cannot complete the letter [Aria: "E lucevan le stelle"].

ii: *The same, plus Tosca*
Tosca hurries in and, once the soldiers and guards have left, tells Mario that the execution will be a sham. Spoletta goes to make final arrangements.

iii: *Cavaradossi and Tosca*
Tosca arrives and tells him how she has killed Scarpia after he ordered a fake execution [Aria: "Il suo sangue e il mio amore"]. He comforts her [Arioso: "O dolci mani"]. They cling to one another, planning a new life [Duet: "Amaro sol per te"].

iii: *Tosca and Mario*
Mario angrily demands to know what Tosca has paid for his life, and she tells him that she has killed Scarpia.

iv: *The same, with Spoletta and soldiers*
Spoletta and the soldiers escort Mario away.

v: *Tosca, alone*
Tosca waits, nervously rehearsing their flight to Civitavecchia. At the sound of the shots, she hurries out.

iv: *The same, with jailer, soldiers, and Spoletta*
As the bells ring 4 A.M., the firing squad arrives. The lovers are parted. Mario goes with the soldiers, refuses a blindfold, and, as the soldiers fire, falls to the ground.

Second Set: PLATFORM OF THE CASTEL SANT'ANGELO

Spoletta, Mario, soldiers, then Tosca
Mario lies motionless, Spoletta sends the soldiers away. Tosca arrives, and tells Spoletta to see that the way is clear. A sergeant comes for the corpse, but is dissuaded. Tosca discovers that Mario is dead, and tells Spoletta and Schiarrone that she has killed Scarpia. This is verified, and Tosca throws herself from the parapet.

v: *Tosca, then Spoletta and Sciarrone*
Tosca waits impatiently until they are alone, then calls to Mario. He is dead. Spoletta and Sciarrone arrive, having found Scarpia's body. Tosca pushes them aside and leaps from the parapet.

Act V of the play consists of two very short tableaux in which the action is similar to the opera, though the characterizations are very different.

Appendix 2
Libretto-making

There is no systematic collection of working papers to show the complete process of transition of *La Tosca* from play to opera, but a number of sources exist that can be used to disentangle some of the skeins.[1] Except for the first published libretto and the autograph score, most of these versions are written out by a professional copyist, with only the occasional notation by one or other of the libretto team. They are difficult to date precisely, and Act I is heavily overrepresented. Acts II and III do not appear until relatively late in their evolution. These sources are, from the most recent to the oldest:

The *first published libretto* of *Tosca*, issued in 1899, before the premiere of the opera.[2] This libretto contains a number of (generally minor) variations in the text, and several early versions of dialogue that indicate a fluid stage of character development.

Puccini's *autograph full score*, at the Ricordi archives, is dated between January 1898 and 28 September 1899 ("4:15 A.M."). This shows a literary text very similar to the first published libretto, some differences in the music, and numerous textual variations in the first- and third-act love scenes between Tosca and Cavaradossi.

The *libretto drafts* at the Ricordi archives, comprising some 150 manuscript pages, represent the most substantial holding and include versions of all three acts of the opera. These libretto drafts include a complete version of Act III, written out by a professional copyist with a few notes by Puccini. There is also a complete version of Act II, also copied out by a professional copyist (though not the same one who wrote Act III), with comments and changes by Puccini and by Ricordi. This manuscript dates to some time after July 1898, as it includes changes made at Puccini's own suggestions, such as the change from "Tu m'odii?" (You hate me?) to "come tu m'odii" (how you hate me), according to Puccini's instructions of July 1898. It also includes stage directions that were suggested by Sardou.[3]

The bulk of the libretto drafts in the Ricordi archives relates to Act I, of which there are three distinct versions, along with scattered notes and stage directions:

Document A, the earliest and also the most interesting version of Act I in terms of the opera's genesis, includes several expanded stage directions that Illica has scribbled on bits of paper. This version includes a now-vanished scene between Tosca and the Sacristan and two versions of the Act I finale, one close to the Te Deum scene as it is now performed and the other quite different, probably dating to before February 1898 (see New York Public Library collection, below). There are fragments of other scenes, most notably between Scarpia and Tosca.

Document B incorporates the stage directions, separate in A, into a professionally copied transcription. This consists of two parallel versions of the text, one by the professional copyist, the other by Giacosa incorporating suggested modifications.

Document C is a copy of Act I that is almost identical to the 1899 first published libretto version. But among these pages is a complete text, by Illica, for an extremely interesting trio intended for Act II. Act III is represented in Document C as well, basically in its 1899/1900 form.

A fourth major source are the *working papers* held in the New York Public Library. These thirty-eight pages seem to date from 1 February 1898, both from internal evidence and because Puccini has dated one of the pages: "Tosca / quella vera! / Ma... / convien ritornarci / 1. febb 98" (Tosca, the real one! But . . . we'll have to go back to it. 1 February 1898). The manuscript pages include a nearly complete professionally copied draft of Act I with notes by Puccini and Illica, plus about twenty-five pages written out by Illica and by Giacosa.

Act I in these working papers seems to represent a stage after Giacosa submitted a version of the complete text at the end of 1896. Puccini, already composing the music, was not satisfied with the text or with the characters. He complained to Illica that Giacosa's libretto lacked "emotional directness," and insisted that "La Tosca needs your help in an extraordinary way!"[4] There are still major plot wrinkles to be ironed out at this point and a two-page memo (in a secretary's hand) outlines problems that must be solved.[5]

Finally, perhaps the oldest of the *libretto fragments* is a passage reproduced in facsimile by Richard Specht and identified only as "a passage from the first version of the libretto of *Tosca*." This tantalizing fragment now exists only in Specht's book, as the original has been lost. This is a quartet to be sung by Tosca, Cavaradossi, the torturer (!), and Spoletta, while Scarpia stands by, silent.[6]

These collections of working papers, along with papers reported by Deborah Burton, have been used throughout this book to illuminate the process of character development.

Appendix 3
1896 Working Papers for Tosca

A *Tosca* that ends without the leap from the parapet? The text of Mario's letter that reduced Verdi to tears? Scholars have long been aware that such scenes once existed, but until now we could only extrapolate and guess about their specific contents. Now, more than a century after Luigi Illica, Giuseppe Giacosa, Giacomo Puccini, and Giulio Ricordi hammered out the first version of a Puccini libretto for *Tosca*, some of this precious material has come to light, in the private archives of the Giacosa family at Colleretto in Canavese.[1] They were found in a 112-page lined notebook, in which the libretto was copied out in a fine hand (probably by one of Ricordi's copyists), interspersed with printed stage directions (possibly from the 1894 libretto prepared for Franchetti). The notebook and associated papers include priceless marginal notations made by the four men as the text made the rounds among them during 1897. It seems possible that more treasures may still exist, perhaps buried in the vast Ricordi archives: even the original version of the libretto prepared for Franchetti in 1894 may yet emerge.

A paper describing the Colleretto materials was presented by Pier Luigi Gillio during **Tosca 2000,** an international interdisciplinary conference held in Rome under the auspices of the Teatro dell'Opera as part of the celebrations of the centennial of the opera, and the bicentennial of the historical events the opera depicts.[2] This appendix is based on Prof. Gillio's presentation, with the kind permission of Dott. Paolo Cattani, grandson of the librettist Giuseppe Giacosa.

The outlines of the story of the making of the *Tosca* libretto are well known (see pp 17–18 above, and Appendix 2). Puccini was first attracted to Sardou's *La Tosca* in 1891, and shortly thereafter convinced Ricordi to secure the opera rights to the property. However, he lost interest and Ricordi, who had already asked Illica to prepare a draft for the libretto, transferred the composition rights to Baron Alberto Franchetti. In 1894, Franchetti, Ricordi and Illica presented a detailed plan to Sardou and got his approval (as of January 2001, this plan and the libretto prepared for Franchetti remain lost). However, the following year (1895) Puccini again became interested in *La Tosca* and Franchetti, who had not found the piece to his liking, gave it up. Giacosa then agreed to prepare a libretto for Puccini, but it was not until July of 1896 that he responded to pressure from Ricordi and completed a version of the first act; by December, his draft of the entire opera was in the publisher's hands. There would be three more years of labor before anything like a final version of the text would be made.

266

Puccini, of course, was given to fussing over his librettos, but the text of *Tosca* in fact shows fewer changes than most. For one thing, the play on which *Tosca* is based was a very polished work; for another, Sardou retained tight control of the rights to his play and refused to allow drastic changes from his original: most notably, it was Sardou who insisted on Tosca's suicide, over the objections of the librettists and the composer, who, in agreement with early audiences, found it "antipathetic."

The Colleretto papers seem to represent a period in which the Italian team was trying to move away from Sardou's ending to a new one in which Tosca would go mad rather than commit suicide. There are also some rather confusing references to Floria Tosca as a Venetian, an identity that disappeared completely from the final text.

The versions of Acts I and II represented in these papers are not very different in outline from those already discussed in this book and in Deborah Burton's dissertation. They include the unappealing scene between Tosca and Scarpia in which she, more enraged than heartbroken, imagines Cavaradossi's treachery (see pp. 153–55, above), followed by a skeleton version of what would become the closing scene of Act I, already envisioned as a counterpart between Scarpia's lust and the ritual of the Church (see pp. 155–61, above).

Scarpia's apartments

The descriptive notes at the beginning of each act are extremely detailed. While not markedly different from the material which would appear (in abbreviated form) in the printed libretto, these notes tend to give much more information about character development and atmosphere. For example, the printed directions for the setting in Scarpia's apartments in Act II are very similar to the definitive description of the scene, but Illica, who apparently thought it insufficient, has added the following, rather heavy-handed, amplification which stresses Scarpia's bigotry and ties with the Church:

Scarpia's room on an upper floor of the Farnese Palace
The cheerfulness of the architecture makes a strange contrast with the hieratic majesty of Caracci's paintings. It is a salon yet seems to be a church; there is an affected ostentation of religious severity to the point of bigotry, of superstition, in the prie-dieu with reading shelf placed under the red monastic-style [a certosina] *crucifix, and an obvious worldly sensuality in the magnificent alcove decorated with a display of adoring cupids* [amorini], *in the great mirror over a white lacquer buffet, with its gilded ornaments and scrollwork, the elegant little table, divan, arm chair, writing desk, and identical chairs of the same style upholstered in azure silk damask. Also of azure silk damask are the extremely rich curtains of the alcove and the drapes of the large window on the right that overlooks the Piazza Farnese. To the left, on the opposite side, a small door set in the great wall is almost invisible, so skillfully done and so perfectly does it fit together with the wallpaper and the molding of the high wainscoting that completely encircles the room.*

And to complete the contrast, on the reading shelf [of the prie-dieu] *a large
book of psalms, open, and a table sumptuously set for dinner with a profusion
of silver and crystal and above all many different wines, under the bright light
of two double candelabra.*

Scarpia's monologue

Scarpia, seated for his dinner, has a long opening monologue here, apparently
conceived of as being in addition to "Ah, più forte sapore" as it now exists. This opening monologue is lengthy and elaborate, a contemptuous description of the courtly
fashion of love-making of the day:

> SCAR: So, Tosca, are you mine if I wish?!
> *(Drinks again)*
> The lovely woman, mine? If I wish it, yes! / Faithful friend of
> my queen . . . *(interrupts himself)* / Well? What does it matter?
> She is a divine woman! / Shall I make tender rhymes, or raise
> songs, / draw forth amorous chords from instruments, / or sighs
> from my heart? . . . Murmur / eclogues to the meadows and rat-
> tle off thousands / upon thousands of silly tales by moonlight /
> or by sunrise? Interpret / the perfume of flowers or walk back
> and forth / under a dark balcony with my hand to my breast? /
> With soft and ardent eyes / sketch in chalk or paint on canvas? /
> Make love like an artist or a gallant, / scratch on a lute, coo like
> a dove? / Of a loving nature, no, I am not, / like a lover who
> only for a thrill / throws flowers to Tosca on the stage, / accom-
> panies her home in torch-light parades, / and wastes half the
> night serenading. . . . / I am not a man for that. I am Scarpia. /
> The good Lord created many women / and many wines . . . and
> I taste and sample. / Now, O Floria, destiny has brought you to
> me, / and I take you, and am grateful for my destiny! / Yes, I
> want her. I want you, Tosca! It's the truth!

"Vittoria!" scene

The papers contain several ideas for Cavaradossi's Act II "Vittoria!" scene and the
succeeding ensemble. Puccini had apparently already composed the music and various texts were tried out and rejected. There is also text for Tosca and Scarpia, some
of it slightly different from that quoted on p. 206 (above). Almost all of this section
was eventually cut:

> TOSCA: *(trying to pull Mario away, to make him put on his overcoat
> and bring him towards the door)* Mario, don't curse, Mario, let
> us flee, / Give in to my pleas! / What do victor and vanquished
> matter? I adore you, / all the rest is madness! / Come, it's the
> night for love. / Hush! . . . / Calm your pitiless anger! / I want,
> with my tears and with my kisses, / to heal your injuries!

Scarpia, rather than bellowing, "Take him away from me!" [*Portatemelo via!*] as
he does now, gives specific instructions to Spoletta with regard to Cavaradossi:

> SCAR: Take this man bound to the Castel Sant'Angelo, / your head will
> answer for it!

Recalling the promise that Sardou's Scarpia makes to free her lover if she speaks,
Tosca objects to Mario's being dragged away :

> TOSCA: No . . . you said he would be saved . . . you promised!

Puccini's Scarpia, of course, never promised any such thing, and this reference
is cut.

Act III prelude

It is in Act III, however, that the most dramatic differences between the working
papers and the final version of the opera emerge, starting with the poetic description
of the Roman dawn that was later cut, much to Illica's disgust (see pp. 226–27 above).
The third-act setting is substantially as it now appears, but described in more detail.
The curtain rises on the upper platform of the Castel Sant'Angelo, a parapet in the
back of the stage overlooks the city from the Colosseum to St. Peter's basilica (a wider
panorama than indicated in today's libretto, where only St. Peter's is specified). At
stage left, elevated three steps, there is a small prison room with a barred window
opening onto the platform; inside, along with the bench, the rough table (with a heavy
calfskin-bound registry, a wooden inkstand, and a pen), the crucifix, and the lamp
now indicated, there is also a prie-dieu. It is just dawn. The platform area is barely
illuminated with an uncertain, gray light; the prison room, on the other hand, is immersed in the deepest darkness.

The instrumental music introducing the act is given the following scenario:

> The prelude consists of two parts, *the first* recalling scenes from the drama,
> and *the second*, descriptive.
> *(The curtain rises gradually, at the end of the* first part, *so that the second
> part of the prelude, from the description of the first light of dawn that gradu-
> ally illuminates the scene, encompasses and unites the different scenic episodes
> that occur on stage until the bell from the Church of the Miracles [which re-
> mains hidden, but which one supposes is to the left] strikes five.)*

The curtain rises on the following scene:

> The trembling light of dawn gradually spreads over the platform of the Castel
> Sant'Angelo. Still a huge, indistinct mass on the right, the great cupola of St. Pe-
> ter's rises in the immediate foreground, becoming ever more clearly distinguished
> from the surroundings as daylight grows stronger.
> Everything around St. Peter's and the Castel Sant'Angelo is immersed in a
> heavy, leaden fog. Far away, at the extreme background, from San Pietro Monto-

rio there comes ever so faintly the sound of the bell calling to matins; immediately, after a short interval, the little bell of the convent of Sant'Onofrio responds, in the middle distance, to the right; then, still alone and faster, the bells of the Church of the Miracles, very close, to the left, chime matins.

Resounding from the barracks at Aracoeli, the reveille trumpet; a single trumpet blast responds from the Castel Sant'Angelo.

A Jailer with a lit lantern enters climbing up from the spiral stairs to the right, crosses the platform, searches among a heavy bunch of keys and opens the door of the room to the left, enters and lights the little lamp suspended before the Crucifix which hangs above the prie-dieu.

In the rough little room there is only the prie-dieu, a bench, and a little table upon which is a register, an inkstand, and a pen. It is the register in which the Jailer writes his declaration of having "received from the hands of the Sergeant the person of ...., the condemned man destined to be executed by firing squad, to be carried out on the platform of the Castel Sant'Angelo."

Having lit the lamp of the Crucifix, the Jailer also lights the oil lamp on the table, and sits waiting, yawning, still half asleep.

In the middle ground Rome is now becoming clearer; there, outlined, is the bell tower of Sant'Onofrio, and farther away the spires and facade of San Pietro Montorio.

The roll of a drum sounds lugubriously. A little later a picket commanded by a Sergeant of the guard enters from the right and crosses the stage, escorting Cavaradossi. A soldier holds a lighted barracks lamp high, attached to a rifle.

At the sound of the cadenced footsteps of the picket the Jailer rouses himself, rises, and opens the gate; the soldiers line up and make way for Cavaradossi who enters followed by the Sergeant, who immediately gives the transfer order to the Jailer.

Cavaradossi's letter

The story about Puccini rejecting the academic verses presented by his librettists in favor of the brief, sensual text of *E lucevan le stelle* is well known. Thanks to this collection of papers it is now clear just what was rejected. The earlier text is indeed wordy and formal, but at the same time, rather touching. What we have is the text of the letter that (in the opera today) Mario begins to write, and then discards, unable to put his feelings into words. Here we have him composing what he hopes will be comforting lies about a resignation and courage he does not feel, and an immortality in which he does not believe. He gives up the effort, and begins to recall what is essentially the subtext of the aria as it now exists. If nothing else, this subtext should be useful to singing actors trying to understand the character's train of thought.

JAILER: Write.
MARIO: *(writes)*: "'My life!' Remember? In the happy hours / when
        I adored you, I often called you "mia vita."[3] / But by now the

drama of my life is almost played out, / and love will last longer
than mortal days. / 'Love' is what I want to name you in this
hour, / and the name of Love I will repeat, dying. / Do not
weep, my darling: death is a dawn. / Love is the promise of
an eternal future."
(Stops writing)
No, no, in vain do I feign courage / that is not in my heart. To
the imminent / fate I am not resigned. / Even in this bitter hour,
her dear voice / still whispers sweet illusions. / Oh, her kisses!
Oh, the intoxication / of our nocturnal trysts! / Oh, longed-for
bodies, / known yet ever new in reborn / desire! How short
were the beautiful days! / She came, soft footsteps / pressing
the grass. / Her cheek blushing with the night air, / from within
her cape, laughing, she offered me. / Then, on my knees, /
all curled up, to my lips – her eyes, / her mouth, her neck,
and the ocean waves of her hair, / she gave up to my pleas. /
It is over, it is over. / I die in despair, / and never have I loved
life so much.

"Latin Hymn" and duet

The so-called Latin Hymn was also cut, over Illica's fierce opposition. It was
no doubt inspired by Sardou's lines, "Ah, courageous woman. You are indeed a Roman . . . a true Roman woman of the old days!" (*Ah, vaillante femme. Tu es bien une
romaine . . . une vraie romaine d'autrefois!*) As Gillio notes, the years at the end of the
nineteenth century were, especially in Italy, years of an increasing "cult of *romanità*
(Roman-ness)." Not so long after the premiere of *Tosca*, this cult would find concrete
political expression as Mussolini began his attempt to recreate the power and confidence of the Roman Empire. Fascination with *romanità*, interestingly enough, was
also at a peak in the century before, at the time when the action of the play and the
opera is supposed to be set. The French Revolutionary cult of antiquity especially
looked to the masculine virtues of the Romans, and away from the feminine sensibilities of the Old Regime and of nascent Romanticism. Curiously, in this text we have
both a clear statement of *romanità*, and an emphasis on Tosca's Venetian origins (Sardou placed her in the care of the Benedictine nuns of Verona).

The very formal and rhetorical text includes the following dialogue, originally
planned to follow the point in the duet where the lovers sing of "harmonies of color,
harmonies of song" (*armonie di colore, armonie di canti*). Surely this sort of dialogue
is what Puccini had in mind when he complained about "academic, academic, academic!" and "amorous slobberings":

> TOSCA: Our homeland is wherever love leads us.
> CAV: *(Exultant)*
> Everywhere we will find Latin traces, / and the ghost of Rome!

TOSCA: *(at Mario's words she too becomes exultant)*
    And if I see you, / remembering, looking far away at the heavens
    / I will close your eyes with a thousand kisses / and call you by
    a thousand loving names / Until, at the sweet recollection, /
    You will forget, and respond. . . .
CAV: . . . I love you.

After the point where Cavaradossi now sings "Speak to me again as you did before, the sound of your voice is so sweet" (*Parlami ancor come dianzi parlavi: è così
dolce il suon della tua voce*), the following section was proposed:

TOSCA: *(Smiling)*
    Much sweeter music, / Mario, my lips will utter / Of every differ-
    ent people / I know the loving rhymes / My song will assemble /
    like a crown of flowers, / the lullabies of the cradle / and the
    hymns of love.
CAV: Every palpitation of yours will resound / like an aeolian harp in
    the breeze, / every thought the sweet accent / of a harmonious
    string. / Noble Latin blood / lifts your heart. / In you a new
    April / will sing and be fragrant with love.

After more of the same sort of dialogue, Spoletta and the firing squad arrive on
the scene. The lovers, ignoring them, continue with their billing and cooing.

CAV: Dreaming lovers / by flowery fields, / our two lives / will be filled
    with enchantment.
TOSCA: My fate / will be in your fate.
CAV: And we will sail the oceans / under skies never seen / And we will
    climb the bitter peaks / of the eternal snow .
TOSCA: You will share with me equally / in life and in art.
CAV: Our wedding bed / will be a quivering gondola.
TOSCA: I will be your wife / I will belong to you.
CAV: The waves of the shimmering / canals will kiss, / the old stories, /
    the old glories. . . . [4]
    (the hour of six sounds)[5]
TOSCA: Here they are . . . now kiss me / Despite your solemn, mournful
    reserve, / Your eyes are laughing . . . imitate me / see how I dis-
    solve in tears.[6]

Tosca's mad scene

All of the above would be of some interest, but the greatest discovery of the
newly recovered libretto pages is the final scene, which differs so dramatically
from the opera as it now stands as to transform it completely, from a satisfactorily
old-fashioned nineteenth–century melodrama, to a grotesque piece of art nouveau
decadence.

One's first thought is that Puccini would never have considered such an ending, but in fact, from the letters it appears that he did indeed do so, even preferring it to the leap from the parapet, and giving it up only when Sardou categorically refused to countenance such a change when the composer went to see him in January of 1899. ["He wants that poor woman dead at all costs. . . ."]

In place of the breathless rush toward suicide that we now find in the opera, the Colleretto papers offer an extended and bizarre mad scene, in which Tosca quickly moves from horror at the discovery of Cavaradossi's death, to an immediate refusal to accept the fact that she has lost him. Instead, she transposes Mario's death into Scarpia's. She first relives Scarpia's murder, then goes on to imagine his funeral, with all the religious panoply that she had tried to provide with the cross and candles of Act II. From there she imagines a crowd of women (presumably, like herself, victims of Scarpia) burdened with their dead. In an image reminiscent of Dante, she thinks that they are trying to pull her and her lover from their gondola (this seems to be a reference back to the Mario/Tosca duet, and the "wedding bed will be a quivering gondola" image). She sings a snatch of what is presumably the song of the gondolier, words sung by Mario in the love duet; and finally, to complete the religious imagery with a secular *Pietà*, Tosca remains alone on the stage, her lover's corpse in her lap as the curtain falls.

Here is the text:

> TOSCA: *(Seeing him immobile she bows, touches him, lifts the cloak, looks at her hands, and gives a terrible cry)*
> Ah! Dead! They've killed him! The murderers! / Killed? Who? Tosca has killed Scarpia, / then placed a crucifix on his chest / And fled with her lover. It is Scarpia who is dead, / What a crowd . . . priests, monks, choirboys, / Praying women . . . He died in sin . . .
> *(throwing gold and jewels)*[7]
> Bury him in hallowed ground / And say for him many Masses *(looks around)* Women, and more / Women . . . they are all women . . . their loosened hair / Falls to the ground like black mantles / And they are dragging reluctant children . . . / One weeps for a husband . . . one for a lover / Another for a son . . . all of them are weeping and each one / Has a corpse across her shoulders like a cross
> *(throws more gold and jewels)*
> For you, take it . . . for you – but with your hands / Don't grasp hold of our gondola!
> *(with a terrible cry)*
> They want to take my Mario away from me. Push them away / with the oar, gondolier. He is not dead / you know it. He's sleeping . . . he is tired. All of you away, away! / The waves of the shimmering / canals kiss / The old stories / the old glories . . . /

Don't sing, gondolier . . . soft, soft . . . / I want a great silence
around us / Eternal silence, and eternal love.
*(And Tosca, with Mario's corpse in her lap, remains motionless
with her finger against her lips in the act of pleading for silence
from the imaginary gondolier whom she sees only in her mind.)*
(The curtain falls.)

Notes

Works and sources frequently cited have been identified by the following abbreviations.

Burton   Deborah Burton, "An Analysis of Puccini's *Tosca:* A Heuristic Approach to the Unifying Elements of the Opera." Ph.D. diss., University of Michigan, 1995. UMI: Ann Arbor, Michigan, 1995

Fortunati   Francesco Fortunati. "Avvenimenti sotto il pontificato di Pio VI, dall'anno 1775 al 1800." I-Rvat, MSS Vat. lat. 10730–10731

Galimberti   Antonio Galimberti. "Memorie dell'occupazione francese in Roma dal 1798 alla fine del 1802." I-Rn, MSS 44 and 45

Gara   Eugenio Gara, ed. *Carteggi Pucciniani.* Milan: Ricordi, 1958

GB-Lbm   British Museum

Girardi   Michele Girardi. *Puccini: His International Art.* Chicago: University of Chicago Press, 2000

I-Mr   Milan, Archivio Ricordi

I-Ras   Rome, Archivio di Stato

I-Rca   Rome, Biblioteca Casanatense

I-Rmr   Rome, Museo di Roma

I-Rn   Rome, Biblioteca Nazionale

I-Rvat   Biblioteca Apostolica Vaticana

Pintorno   Giacomo Puccini, *276 lettere inedite*, ed. Giuseppe Pintorno. Milan: Nuove Edizioni, 1974

Sala   Giovanni Antonio Sala, *Diario romano degli anni 1798–99*, ed. G. Cugnoni, 3 vols. Rome: Società Romana di Storia Patria, 1882–86.

US-NYp   New York Public Library

INTRODUCTION

1. Anonymous; it appeared in *La vera Roma*, 12 January 1900. Quoted by Michele Girardi in his discussion of "local color" in his chapter on *Tosca*, "Rome between Faith and Power," in *Puccini: His International Art*. Chicago: University of Chicago Press, 2000.

2. Rome as it was ruled by the popes until the Papal States were conquered and the city became the capital of the Italian state in 1871.

3. Girardi, 165.

4. Ibid.

5. There are enough "historical" operas to provide material for a charming book. See Jellinek, *History through the Opera Glass*.

6. This movement has generated a vast literature. One might begin with the works of Steven Greenblatt, the man who coined the term: "Fiction and Friction"; *Shakespearean Negotiations*, based on the original essay; and *Learning to Curse*. Major surveys of the movement are found in two books edited by Harold Aram Veeser, *The New Historicism* and *The New Historicism Reader*, a collection of essays, including one by Greenblatt himself, "Towards a Poetics of Culture"

(the term he now prefers to "New Historicism"), 1–14; Judith Lowder Newton, "History as Usual? Feminism and the 'New Historicism'," 152–67; Hayden White, "New Historicism: A Comment," 293–302; and Frank Lentricchia, "Foucault's Legacy: A New Historicism," 231–42. Of related interest are works by cultural historians, such as Foucault himself, and Lynn Hunt, *The New Cultural History*, and Robert Darnton, such as *The Great Cat Massacre.*

CHAPTER ONE

1. "Nel farmi schizzo poi del panorama, voleva che si vedesse il corso del Tevere passare fra S. Pietro e il Castello!! Io gli ho detto che il *flumen* passava dall'altra parte, sotto, e lui tranquillo come un pesce ha detto: 'Oh, questo non è niente!' Bel tipo, tutta vita, fuoco e pieno di inesattezze storico-topo-panoramiche." Puccini to Giulio Ricordi, from Paris, 13 January 1899; Gara, no. 200, 172.

2. Puccini was in the act of composing *Tosca* when he made the famous comment about his "Neronic instinct," in a letter to Alfredo Caselli, 18 August 1898; Adami, *Letters of Giacomo Puccini*, no. 61, 124.

3. Introduction to Barrett Harper Clark's edition of Victorien Sardou's *Patrie!*

4. Mouly, ed., *Les Papiers de Victorien Sardou*, 81–94.

5. Zeldin, *France, 1848–1945*, 711; Clark, introduction to Sardou, *Patrie!*; Hart, *Sardou and the Sardou Plays*, 24–32. See also Marek, "The Well-Made Play."

6. Sardou had a weakness for titles that ended in "-dora," starting with a play simply titled *Dora* (1877), which was translated into English as *Diplomacy.* This inspired G. B. Shaw, who despised everything Sardou stood for in the theater, to the following: "Up to this day week I had preserved my innocence as a playgoer sufficiently never to have seen *Fédora.* Of course I was not altogether new to it, since I had seen *Diplomacy Dora* and *Théodora* and *La Toscadora* and the other machine dolls from the same firm." Shaw, "Sardoodledom," reprinted in *Bernard Shaw: The Drama Observed*, 2: 353–59.

7. General Georges Boulanger, a charismatic military leader, for years served as a focal point for widespread discontent with the regime. Boulanger seemed on the point of seizing power in a coup in January 1889, but fled to Brussels, and two years later committed suicide on the grave of his mistress. The Wilson scandal, which took place around May of 1887 while the Boulanger troubles were at their height, shook the pillars of the Republic.

8. The 200th anniversary of the French Revolution and Napoleon, which began in 1989 and will continue until 2014, has been characterized by controversy. The first and greatest of the modern Western revolutions could not avoid being seen in the light of the collapse (precisely 200 years later) of its most successful heir, the Bolshevik Revolution (1917–89). The first centennial, on the other hand, was orchestrated as an orgy of self-congratulation despite undercurrents of serious discontent in France. See Angenot, *1889: Un état du discours social.*

9. "L'esprit clerical, c'est la négation des conquêtes de la science moderne, la haine de la dignité humaine, le retour aux sanglantes ténèbres du moyen âge, en un mot le contrepied de la Révolution." Larousse, *Grande Dictionnaire universel du XIXeme siècle* (1868), vol. 4, s.v. "clericalisme."

10. The law, promulgated on 9 December 1905, provided for (1) complete liberty of conscience; (2) the severing of all church connections with the state; and directed that (3) all church property was to be taken over by private corporations.

11. See Zeldin, *Conflicts in French Society.*

12. Angenot, *1889*, 757.

13. Eugen Weber, the grand old man of Third Republic studies, turned his attention to Sardou's play in "About *Thermidor:* The Oblique Uses of a Scandal."

14. Sardou, *La Tosca*, I, iv: "Je n'ose plus me confesser et lui avouer que les moustaches sont toujours là, parce que j'ai plaisir à les fréquenter. . . . Mais mon compte est bon, va . . . Je suis en état constant de péché mortel, et si je venais à mourir subitement . . . [L'enfer!] Encore si

c'était avec toi!" Unless otherwise noted, quotes are taken from the 1909 edition of the play in *L'Illustration théâtrale* and the translations are my own.

15. Jules Michelet, *Le Prêtre, la femme, et la famille*. His rallying cry was "May the religion of the home replace religion." See Zeldin, *Conflicts in French Society*, 13–50.

16. Burton, 419.

17. "Quando seppi che tu prendevi a trattare *La Tosca*, speravo che ti rivolgessi a me, poichè, a saputa di tutti—il Puccini per il primo—quell'argomento era stato da me primissimamente indicato, e già erano corse lettere fra me e Sardou . . . Invece, scegliesti Giacosa!" (When I learned that you were starting to deal with *La Tosca*, I hoped that you would turn to me, because, as everyone knows—Puccini first of all—that plot was first suggested by me, and letters had already passed between me and Sardou . . . Instead, you chose Giacosa!) Letter of Fontana to Luigi Illica; Morini, "Illica e Fontana," reprinted in Gara, 32.

18. A recent thorough examination of the negotiations appears in Burton, 418–62. See also Burton, "The Creation of *Tosca*."

19. Gara, 57.

20. I-Mr, Copialettere, 29 December 1891.

21. Morini, "La Tosca all'anagrafe della storia," 63; Fondo Illica, Biblioteca Passerini-Landi, Puccini–Illica, 15 December 1892, cited by Burton, 455; Gara, 78; I-Mr, Copialettere, 29 July 1893.

22. Gara, 96.

23. Ibid.; I-Mr, Copialettere, 17 May, 27 July, 9 August, and 30 September 1894.

24. Morini, "La Tosca," 63.

25. I-Mr, Copialettere, 19 November 1894, 5 May 1895; Gara, 113 and 117; Morini, 64. Morini quotes a Franchetti letter to Illica, written 16 June 1916, in which the composer says that he gave the libretto up because he did not hear ["sentire"] the music in it. Franchetti's son Arnaldo insisted that there were no hard feelings between the two composers, described by Burton, 456.

26. Pintorno, 68–70.

27. A discussion of the evolution of the libretto is found in appendix 2.

28. "Ah, there is an avenging God" *(ah, c'è un Dio vendicator)*, and "Atheist, I believe in God!" *(Ateo, credo in Dio!)*, both projected for Act II.

29. "O dolci mani mansuete e pure, / o mani elette a bell'opre e pietose / a carezzar fanciulli, a coglier rose, / a pregar, giunte, per le sventure"; *Tosca*, III, ii.

30. "Pieno è il paniere . . . fa penitenza?" *Tosca*, I, ii.

31. Santi, "Tempo e spazio ossia colore locale in *Bohème, Tosca, e Madama Butterfly*," 86–87. The only extensive consideration of Puccini and religion has been in John DiGaetani's *Puccini the Thinker*, in which a section (Part II) has been devoted to "God, religion, and the Roman Catholic Church," 50–80.

32. DiGaetani, *Puccini the Thinker*, 71. Puccini was by no means the only anti-cleric on the *Tosca* team. While Puccini's anti-clericalism seems to have been a personal feeling, for Luigi Illica it was apparently a matter of intellectual and social conviction. "Illica, as a fervent anti-cleric, took every opportunity to stress the negative aspects of clerical dominance in Rome." Girardi, 194.

33. Del Fiorentino, *Immortal Bohemian*, 64. San Giacomo (or James) was martyred by being thrown from the roof of the temple at Jerusalem.

34. Ibid., 110.

35. Del Fiorentino, *Immortal Bohemian*, and Panichelli, *Il "pretino" di Giacomo Puccini racconta*.

36. The elderly country priest who performed the ceremony, Father Michelucci, wrote in the church records: "Maestro Giacomo Puccini, son of Michele and Albina Magi, and Elvira Bonturi, widow of Narciso Gemignani, . . . having obtained the dispensation of the three canonical banns, being free of the impediment of crime and with no canonical impediment now existing against

the valid and lawful celebration of their marriage, having been questioned *in facie Ecclesiae* and their consent *per verba de praesenti* having been received, were by me, the undersigned, united the third of January 1904 in the holy bonds of Matrimony in the presence of two witnesses, Dr. Rodolfo Giacchi and Giuseppe Razzi." Del Fiorentino, *Immortal Bohemian*, 114.

37. Ibid., 218–19.

38. "Ridammi, caro pretino, la fede che avevo." Panichelli, *Il "pretino"*.

39. Del Fiorentino, *Immortal Bohemian*, 178.

40. Emilia Noether's work on the background to unification, *Seeds of Italian Nationalism (1700–1815)*, is dated, but remains the best single study of the pre-Risorgimento period in English.

41. Hibbert, *Rome, the Biography of a City*, 274–85.

42. The best-known example of this is Mosco Carner's biography of 1959, *Puccini, a Critical Biography*. Many of Freud's conclusions have been questioned recently, and their applicability to Puccini (which has contributed to the devaluation of the composer's work) should be reevaluated.

43. Cited in Sardou, *L'Illustration théâtrale*, 33.

44. A clandestine radio station operated from one of the bell towers of Sant'Agnese. The monument placed in the church reads as follows: "A Maurizio Giglio che fedele, generoso, impavido, la luminosa vita immolò al patrio onore gli amici nel luogo del suo lavoro a perenne memoria posero. Parigi xx.xii.mcmxx Roma xxiv.iii.mcmlxiv." (To Maurizio Giglio, who, faithful, generous, fearless, immolated his luminous life to the honor of his country, his friends, in the place where he worked, have placed this to his perpetual memory. Paris, 20 December 1920, Rome, 24 March 1944.) The events which led to Giglio's death are detailed by Robert Katz, in *Death in Rome*.

45. In Sardou's play, Cavaradossi was born in Paris. Another parallel lies in the fact that Scarpia works, not for the pope but for an Italian state allied to the Austrians (commonly called "tedeschi" or Germans in Italian)—as the Roman fascists were allied to the German Nazis, followers of the Austrian Adolf Hitler.

Chapter Two

1. Giuntella, *Roma nel Settecento*, 55–59; Gross, *Rome in the Age of Enlightenment*, 1–39; Hibbert, *Rome*, 202; Andrieux, *Daily Life in Papal Rome in the Eighteenth Century*, 11–40.

2. Casanova arrived in Rome dressed as a gentleman, but quickly adopted clerical garb, noting that "everybody [in Rome] is either a priest or trying to look like one." See Andrieux, *Daily Life*, 53. When Mrs. Piozzi visited Rome in 1784 she cautioned that "we shouldn't assume that all men are *abates* who dress that way—many wear black as the Court garb, many because it is not costly, and many for reasons of mere convenience and dislike of change." Piozzi, *Observations and Reflections* (1789), ed. Barrows, 207.

3. Gross, *Rome in the Age of Enlightenment*, 202.

4. Hibbert, *Rome*, 202.

5. Charles de Brosses, *Lettres familières écrites d'Italie en 1739 et 1740*; and Tobias Smollett, *Travels*, 112

6. William Hazlitt, *Notes of a Journey through France and Italy*; Robert Thomas Wilson, *The Life of General Sir Robert Thomas Wilson*; and Piozzi, *Observations*, 214.

7. Tackett, "The Civil Constitution and the Oath of 1791," 269–86.

8. Angeli, *Storia romana di trent'anni*, 117. De Bernis was among the most elegant and expansive of the old-regime cardinals (he owed his cardinal's hat to the patronage of Madame de Pompadour; his cook was reputed to be the finest in Europe). He died in 1794 at the age of 80.

9. Holtman, *The Napoleonic Revolution*, 17 and 218–19.

10. Pastor, *Storia dei papi*, ed. Mercati and Cenci; Bokenkotter, *A Concise History of the Catholic Church*, "The Church in a State of Siege, A.D. 1650–1891"; Nussdorfer, *Civil Politics in the Rome of Urban VIII*; Gross, *Rome*; Heriot, *The French in Italy*; Tivarone, *L'Italia durante il*

dominio francese, 63–79; Giuntella, "La giacobina repubblica romana"; McBrien, *Lives of the Popes,* 328–33. The century saw several unusually long papacies, Clement XI (1700–1721), Benedict XIV (1740–58), and Pius VI (1775–99).

11. The reevaluation of eighteenth-century Rome begins with V. E. Giuntella. See his essays "La giacobina repubblica romana" and "Roma nel Settecento: La capitale e i problemi dello stato"; and his 1971 monograph, *Roma nel Settecento.* Giuntella's work is paralleled by the work of Franco Venturi and the reevaluation of the Enlightenment in Italy, most notably his five-volume study, *Settecento riformatore* published between 1969 and 1984: *Da Muratori a Beccaria; La chiesa e la repubblica dentro i loro limiti, 1758–1774; La prima crisi dell'Antico Regime, 1768–1776; La caduta dell'Antico Regime, 1776–1789,* 1: *I grandi stati dell'Occidente;* 2: *Il patriottismo repubblicano e gli imperi dell'Est.* Two volumes of this seminal series have been translated by R. Burr Litchfield as *The End of the Old Regime in Europe, 1768–1776: The First Crisis* (1989), and *The End of the Old Regime in Europe, 1776–1789* (1991). A full bibliography of Venturi's works can be found in *L'età dei lumi: Studi storici sull Settecento europeo in onore di Franco Venturi.* Some of the fruits of Venturi's work have appeared in English in Dino Carpenetto and Giuseppe Ricuperati, *Italy in the Age of Reason, 1685–1789,* part of the Longman History of Italy series published in 1987. For works on the papacy in English, see Hales, *Revolution and the Papacy,* and Chadwick, *The Popes and the European Revolution.* The most extensive and useful English-language work on Rome in the old regime has been Gross, *Rome in the Age of Enlightenment.* Italian-language monographs on the eighteenth century continue to appear, most notably for the purposes of this book a series published by the Istituto della Enciclopedia Italiana: *Orfeo in Arcadia: Studi sul teatro a Roma nel Settecento,* ed. Petrocchi; *Le Muse galanti: La musica a Roma nel Settecento,* ed. Cagli; and the two-volume set, *Il teatro a Roma nel Settecento.*

12. This and other aspects of the social structure in Rome in the eighteenth century are discussed in Gross, *Rome.*

13. Ibid., 196.

14. Giuntella, *Roma nel Settecento,* 60.

15. Richard Duppa, an English painter, stayed in Rome during the French invasion and the establishment of the Republic of 1799. Duppa, "A Journal of the Most Remarkable Occurrences that Took Place in Rome upon the Subversion of the Ecclesiastical Government in 1798," 10–11.

16. A silk merchant's daughter from Marseille, Mlle Clary later married one of Napoleon's marshals, Jean-Baptiste Bernadotte, and went on to help found the present royal house of Sweden. She was the subject of a popular novel and film in the middle of this century.

17. Cited by Heriot, *The French in Italy,* 171.

18. Duppa, "Journal," 34–36.

19. Fortunati, 20 February 1798, 185–91.

20. Renzo de Felice, "Angelucci, Liborio," *Dizionario biografico degli italiani,* 3: 251–53. See also Casini, "Il parlamento della Repubblica Romana."

21. Cited by Giuntella, *Roma nel Settecento,* 204, after C. Trasselli, "Processi politici romani dal 1792 al 1798."

22. At about this time Sardou's Angelotti is supposed to have gone from Rome to Naples with Championnet, and then in the spring of 1798 fled back to Rome. The diarist Fortunati noted a similar event in Rome on 14 May, when "General MacDonald with five carriages arrived from Naples, along with many Neapolitan Patriots (including two dukes, six princesses, and a duchess) heading for Milan, having fled Naples to avoid being shot as subsequently happened to their companions . . ." ("fuggiti da Napoli per non esser fucilati come in appresso segui ai loro compagni . . .").

23. The Constitutional Circle accused him of a membership in a "cabal of ambition, wickedness, and self-serving." Cretoni, *Roma giacobina: Storia della repubblica romana del 1798–99,* 261–67.

24. *"Marforio:* Eh bada bene che non ti senta; perche quando e in collera va bestialmente sulle Furie, e pare un indemoniato, caccia fuori spada, pistole, siringhe, e lanciette." Fortunati, 15 September 1798. The statue of Pasquino stands at the back of the Braschi palace, while Marforio, a river god, is found at the Capitoline.

25. Fortunati, after describing Angelucci as a blood-letter and obstetrician, says that he got rich buying the orchards of San Clemente, the vineyards of the Ecclesiastical College, and the Palace of the Order of Malta, and by manipulating the republican Ministry of National Goods (*beni nazionali*) and buying up bonds on the cheap. Fortunati, 15 September 1798 and Monitore di Roma, 13 September 1798, "Litanie di Pasquino."

26. De Felice, "Angelucci," 253.

27. Heriot, *The French in Italy*, 172.

28. Gori Sassoli, *Della chinea e di altre 'Macchine di gioia.'*

29. Dowd, *Pageant-Master of the Republic: Jacques-Louis David and the French Revolution.* For a recent analysis of the role of the artist in revolutionary France see Crow, *Emulation: Making Artists for Revolutionary France.* When David designed the spectacle for Robespierre's festival of the Supreme Being using the device of burning one figure (in this case, tyranny) to leave another shining triumphantly forth, he was making use of an old Roman technique.

30. For a discussion of the festival *macchine* see Gori Sassoli, *Della chinea.*

31. Fortunati, 23–24 February 1798.

32. See also chapter 8, below.

33. Fortunati, November 1798 and 7 June 1799.

34. Gross, *Rome*, 58–59, based on Bellettin, "L'evoluzione demografica dell'Italia nel quadro europeo del Settecento," in *La popolazione italiana nel Settecento*, 50–52.

35. As did Giuseppe Antonio Sala, a member of the curia, in his account of the events of 1798 and 1799 in *Diario romano degli anni 1798–99.* Republican festivals are also noted with a jaundiced eye by Antonio Galimberti, "Memorie dell'occupazione francese in Roma dal 1798 alla fine del 1802," I-Rn, MSS 44–45.

36. Holtman, *Napoleonic Revolution*, 218–19.

37. Vincenzo Bianchi, writing in the *Monitore Romano*, 16 Piovoso, 355.

38. Cited by Galimberti, 27 September 1798.

39. *Il matrimonio democratico* inspired much condemnation in the *Monitore di Roma*, where it was denounced in terms at least as moralistic and repressive as any the papal censors had ever managed. The farce, the critic wrote, is an outrage to public decency (*lesive del buon costume*), "a triumph of ignorance and lasciviousness, indecent dress, indecent acts, and revolting actors." The government was urged to call the impresarios strictly to account for their productions, and to demand "a respectable silence" without those shouts and loud muttering that disturb honest citizens who have come to hear the show. Predictably, this topical show had caused an uproar in the theater as Romans, who had always considered theater to be an interactive art despite the best efforts of their rulers, shouted out in delight or outrage as they recognized allusions to local characters (the late pope's nephew for one) with showers of whistling, foot stamping, and roaring. Governments can never afford to have a sense of humor; the Republic issued stiff regulations forbidding audiences to "identify personages, or cry out." These were of course ignored. Brigadier General Vial, Commander of the Public Squares, had a notice posted: "There are to be no more performances contrary to good morals, or to the republican government." The papal censors, who had tried and failed to control audience responses in the theater, must have smiled. In the summer of 1798 General MacDonald, the French commander in Rome, ordered that all shows had to be approved by the Police Commissioners at the direction of the Municipality, fifteen days before opening. Productions that disturbed the peace were punishable with a heavy fine on the first offense, and offenders got a year at hard labor for the second.

40. *Monitore di Roma*, 29 Piovoso, Year VII; Sala, 18 June 1799.

41. "Signs of jubilation, feasts, and patriotic songs, which call to mind the fortunate epoch

of our regeneration, irritate the aristocrats and the enemies of democracy. These make every effort to smother that energetic spirit which republican music excites in the soul, they discredit it, they sneer at it. Citizens of Rome, the brave French owe much of their great deeds to their republican music. The same enthusiasm must grow in all free men. No one can be insensible to it, except those who have the souls of slaves, and cowards." Edict of 27 September 1798, quoted by Galimberti on that date. One Giovanni Flori, writing in the *Monitore di Roma* on 9 May (6 Caldifero) of the same year, sternly advised that "the theater in a Republic must be a place consecrated to education" and firmly rejected the old style, saying that "the masculine accents of Cato and Brutus would better shape the heart of the people than the long trills of a *musico*" (that is, a castrato).

42. Cretoni, *Roma giacobina*, 177 and 181.

43. Sala, 1: 350.

44. Thus inspiring one of Pasquino's best quips: "Coi soldati infiniti / Si mosse da' suoi liti / Verso Roma bravando / Il re Don Ferdinando / E in pochissimi dì / Veni, vedi, e fuggì" (With an infinite number of soldiers, King Ferdinand arrogantly set off from the coast toward Rome; and in just a few days he came, he saw, and he fled).

45. Romans would not have missed the reference to the long queues that ordinary citizens had to face. The story is repeated with some relish by Fortunati, 16 June 1799.

46. Fortunati, 23 September 1799.

47. Alexander seems to have been deterred from these plans by the fact that the Order of Malta had chosen him as their Grand Knight—a truly bizarre choice since the tsar was Russian Orthodox rather than Roman Catholic, and a choice that was necessarily opposed by the pope.

48. On the point of exile he had come out to bless the people only to find troops keeping the crowd at a distance. He remonstrated with the commander, saying that "I am accustomed to bless my people, not the stones." Fortunati. Stories like this, true and fabricated, circulated and increased his popularity,

49. Tuscany was then a Habsburg dependency, having come under the rule of the empire on the death of the last Medici in 1737. In 1799 its ruler was Ferdinand III of Tuscany, nephew of the Holy Roman Emperor and one of the four more or less closely related Ferdinands on thrones in Italy at the time. Ferdinand III, grand duke of Tuscany, was the nephew and son-in-law of King Ferdinand IV of Naples, and also the nephew of the king of Naples's brother-in-law the Archduke Ferdinand, viceroy of Milan. Duke Ferdinand of Parma was the uncle by marriage of the grand duke of Tuscany, and a brother-in-law to the king of Naples and the viceroy of Milan. We owe this proliferation of royal Ferdinands to the dynastic and political successes of the rival houses of Bourbon and Habsburg during the seventeenth and eighteenth centuries, as well as to the tangled patterns of intermarriage characteristic of royal houses.

CHAPTER THREE

1. The relevant provisions of the treaty are contained in Articles 12 and 13. According to Article 12, Citizens of Rome and elsewhere who took part in or acted as officials of the Roman Republic were to be free to leave with the French troops under the same terms offered to them, or to remain in the Roman states without being molested in any fashion for their political opinions or for the work which they carried out while they were employed in civil or military functions. In Article 13 Commander Trowbridge, on the part of His Britannic Majesty and his Allies, obligated themselves under English guarantee that no individual in the state was to be disturbed for opinions, nor persecuted; that their persons and property were to be equally respected. They were also to retain every liberty to alienate or otherwise dispose of their property. I-Ras, Miscellanea di carte politiche riservate, busta 27, fasc. 922, as cited by Maria Consilia Buzzelli Serafini, "La reazione del 1799 a Roma: I processi della Giunta di Stato."

2. In the Sardou play, Angelotti's misfortunes have included being sentenced to three years in the galleys. See chapter 5, below.

3. Sala, 30 September 1799: "All'alba cominciò l'ingresso della truppa napoletana in sommo silenzio e senza batter cassa" (At dawn the entry of the Neapolitan troops began in absolute silence, without beating the drum). Galimberti records the events in more detail: "Essendosi saputo che all'avvicinare del nuovo giorno entrar dovea la truppa Napolitana nella città vi fu grandissimo moto di Patriotti e di Francesi, i quali tutti si preparano alla partenza" (Since it was known that toward the start of the new day the Neapolitan troops would enter the city, there was a great disturbance among the patriots and the French, all of whom prepared to leave). And the following day: "Un ora circa prima dell'Alba la truppa Napolitana entrò la Porta S Giovanni, e prese possesso della città di qua dai ponti. Una divisione di cavalleria circondò subbito il Ghetto già miniccinato di saccheggio dal popolo" (An hour before dawn the Neapolitan troops entered the San Giovanni gate, and took possession of the city from there to the bridges. A cavalry division immediately surrounded the Ghetto which the people have already threatened to sack). Galimberti, 29 and 30 September 1799.

4. In one of many incidents, in December 1798 a royal courier was mistaken for a Jacobin and beaten to death in the square in front of the royal palace in plain view of King Ferdinand. The incident is described, along with speculations that Queen Maria Carolina engineered it for her own reasons, by Heriot, *French in Italy*, 209.

5. "Eighteenth-century painting in Rome was, in its own time, considered preeminent in Europe by virtue of its location, its tradition, its extraordinary quality, and the fact that it was, more than ever before, the school which represented the classic yet hosted every change." Clark, *Studies in Eighteenth-Century Roman Painting*, p. xx.

6. The litany of artists who worked in Rome is long, and most of them are recognized only by specialists: Batoni, Cades, Cavallucci, Conca, Tofanelli; Canova, Carstens, David, Grauffier, Fabre, Drouais, Peyron, Saint-Ours, Gagneraux, and Prud'hon; Unterberger, Tischbein, Flaxman, Humbert de Superville, Landi, Camuccini, Costantini, and Agricola; Heckert, Jacob More, Wuitcky and Wallis, Sablet and Ducros, Giani and Coccetti. Among the women painters, Angelica Kauffmann, Goethe's friend, and Elisabeth Vigée-Lebrun are the most famous, but there were many others. Clark, *Studies*, 130.

7. Elisabeth Vigée-Lebrun, *Memoirs of Vigée-Lebrun*, 89; but the idea was a commonplace of the time.

8. Coyer, *Voyages d'Italie et de Hollande*, 276.

9. See also Gross, *Rome*, 231.

10. Goethe describes this in his account of the Roman carnival in *Italian Journey (1786–1788)*, 451–55.

11. Duppa's works include "A Journal of . . . the Subversion of the Ecclesiastical Government in 1798," 1799, as well as books on Michelangelo and Raphael. *Dictionary of National Biography*, ed. Sir Leslie Stephen, vol. 6, s.v. "Duppa, Richard."

12. J. Salmon, in his guidebook published in London in 1800, *An Historical Description of Ancient and Modern Rome*, admires the Sistine Chapel for its "many sublime and accurate figures"; Vigée-Lebrun defends the Last Judgment for the "expression and boldness of its foreshortened figures" and argues that the chaos is justified by the subject matter (84); Goethe admires "the self-assurance, the virility, the grandeur of conception of this master" (142).

13. Goethe, *Italian Journey*, 62.

14. Bryson, *Word and Image*, 204–38.

15. "I would have already had a run-in with [*eu maille à partir avec*] the hideous Scarpia if I hadn't come up with a ruse . . . I asked the chapter of this church for permission to paint that wall, without pay. . . . This devout piety has kept the hounds at bay [*a conjuré l'orage*] and I may owe my safety to it until Floria leaves for Venice where she has an engagement for next season" (Sardou, *La Tosca*, I, iii).

16. Crow, *Emulation*, 232.

17. Salmon, *Historical Description*, introduction.

18. See *L'Accademia di Francia a Roma: Villa Medici*; Navenne, *Rome e le palais Farnèse pendant les trois derniers siècles*; and Vicchi, *Les Français à Rome pendant la Convention*.

19. The 1729 spectacle for the birth of the Dauphin, designed by Pier Leone Ghezzi and paid for by the French minister to Rome, is best known today through Pannini's famous painting.

20. Much of the following material on David is taken from three studies of art and revolution: Crow, *Painters and Public Life* and *Emulation*; and Albert Boime, *Art in an Age of Revolution*.

21. A speech repeated in Jules David's biography, *Le Peintre Louis David, 1749–1825*, 57. It is worth noting that this book was published only a few years before Sardou's *La Tosca* first appeared, and so contributed to the "climate of opinion" within which Sardou created his characters.

22. Crow, *Painters and Public Life*, 251.

23. This monumental work is known only from its cartoon, as the canvas was never finished. Politics moved faster than painting and before the canvas could be completed many of the "heroes" of the Estates-General and National Assembly had been guillotined as traitors.

24. David, who had little respect for the Church, declared himself utterly charmed by the pope's dignity and simplicity. See Anita Brookner, *Jacques-Louis David*, 157–58.

25. Vicchi, *Les Français à Rome*, 167.

26. Sardou, *La Tosca*, I, iii.

27. A letter in Brissot's Parisian journal *Patriote français* in October 1790 discoursed on the virtues of short, straight, unpowdered hair, saying that "[t]his coiffure is the only one which is suited to republicans; being simple, economical and requiring little time, it is carefree and so assures the independence of a person; it bears witness to a mind given to reflection, courageous enough to defy fashion." Quoted in Schama, *Citizens: A Chronicle of the French Revolution*, 525.

28. In Naples in 1799, short hair and boots were seen as evidence of political conviction, and at the height of the White Terror fashionable men were reduced to attaching fake queues to their short hair lest they be mistaken for Jacobins. This hostility was, however, as much a matter of class as of anything else; the Neapolitan mobs took their chance to butcher the upper-class liberals whom they identified as much by their fashionable appearance as by their politics.

29. Official policy is reflected in statements such as the following: "The encouragement which [the Convention] gives to the arts must assure those in every country who contribute to the glory of the name of France and the individual prosperity of her citizens that they will always be the primary object of our solicitude." Minister of the Interior to the banker Moutte in Rome, asking him to continue funding the Academy, 12 November 1792; Vicchi, *Les Français à Rome*, 168.

30. "There were two preliminary trials for the Rome Prize: first, a painted or drawn compositional sketch, then an *académie* or painted image of the half-length model, and if the student survived these he then entered into closed cubicles for almost three months to paint the masterpiece." Boime, *Art in an Age of Revolution*, 164. The entire process is examined in detail in Grunchec, *Le Grand Prix de peinture*.

31. Gérard, *Correspondance* (Rome, 1790), 59 et seq. Letters from Girodet to Gérard from Rome, 1790. Vigée-Lebrun's description of the fireworks is found in her memoirs, 90–91.

32. Vicchi, *Les Français à Rome*, doc. xiii; and Rodocanachi, *Le Château Saint-Ange*, 238–39. See also *Correspondances des directeurs de l'Académie de France à Rome*, 16: 112, and Angeli, *Storia romana*, 204–9.

33. A reconstruction offered by Antonio Simoni and Adolfo Cano in "La pistola a semiretrocarica, un interessante caso giudiziario," 87, as translated by Hughes in "Fear and Loathing in Bologna and Rome: The Papal Police in Perspective," 102.

34. Angeli, *Storia romana*, 204–9.

35. ". . . it seems that for you and Puccini Cavaradossi should be nothing more than a 'signor tenore'"; Giacosa to Giulio Ricordi, 9 September 1898; Gara, no. 196, 169–70.

36. Gay, *The Enlightenment*, 662.

37. If Helvétius and Voltaire were *personae non gratae* in Rome, Rousseau was hardly more welcome. Rousseau's 1776 essay on religion, *Profession de foi du vicaire savoyard* (The Profession of Faith of the Savoyard Pastor), managed to offend even liberal Protestants with its pantheistic feel-good religiosity.

38. Sardou, *La Tosca*, I, iv.

39. The encyclopedists were a group of philosophes whose work clustered around the publication of the *Encyclopédie, ou Dictionnaire raisonné des sciences, des arts et des métiers*, edited by Denis Diderot and Jean d'Alembert. Abate (or Abbé) Ferdinando Galiani (1728–87) was a Neapolitan economic theorist whose work on free trade in agricultural produce was greatly admired in France. He was in Paris between 1759 and 1769 as secretary to the diplomatic mission of the Kingdom of Naples. Claude Adrien Helvétius (1715–71) was a Swiss writer who lived most of his life in France.

40. Sardou, *La Tosca*, I, i.

41. The recently ended occupation of Rome by Napoleon III was a major factor in French and Italian anti-clericalism in the later years of the nineteenth century when Sardou and Puccini were working.

42. *Enciclopedia storico-nobiliare italiana*, vol. 2, s.v. "Caravadossi," 316–17.

43. Salmon, *Historical Description*, 220.

44. Vigée-Lebrun, *Memoirs*, 83–87.

45. Sardou, *La Tosca*, III, ii.

46. We will look more closely at this location in chapter 7.

47. Salmon, *Historical Description*, and Charles Mercier Dupaty, *Lettres sur l'Italie*, letter xviii.

48. Ibid.

49. The Giunta di Stato records include the trial of Pietro Fedeli, a Piedmontese soldier who deserted from the French army and attempted to stay in Rome with his Roman wife. He was arrested and it required numerous affidavits from his in-laws and parish priest to secure his release. I-Ras, Giunta di Governo 2, Busta 1, fasc. 13.

50. Fortunati, 11 November 1799. The Jews were included along with patriots and Jacobins because they were suspected of both financing the new state and profiting from it through buying up looted art works and confiscated properties.

51. Galimberti, 11 November 1799.

52. I-Ras, Giunta di Governo 1799–1800, Busta 10. See chapter 5 for a discussion of this case.

53. In a particularly grisly execution, a Russian and a Neapolitan soldier were flogged to death for attacking and robbing a man and his wife. Fortunati, 2 November 1799.

54. Galimberti, 7 November 1799. See also Giuntella, "I Cosacchi."

55. Galimberti, 13 November 1799.

56. See chapter 4. Under the Republic the theaters had been open virtually all year long, and the Allies followed the same policy. Naselli ordered illuminations and celebrations as early as 2 October, just three days after the Allied entry into the city.

57. Goethe describes the carnival 1786 in *Italian Journey*, 451–55. See also Clementi, *Il carnevale romano*, Parte II (Sec. XVIII–XIX), 220–45.

58. Galimberti, 25 January 1800.

59. Ibid., 28 January 1800.

60. Ibid., 23 February 1800, and Fortunati, 15 February 1800.

61. Galimberti, 18 January 1800.

62. The prisoner had been held at the headquarters of Sig. de Leone, Commander of the Public Squares, and condemned by a military court. His case is detailed in the chronicles of the Confraternity of St John the Beheaded, I-Ras, *Confraternità di San Giovanni Decollato, Giustiziati*, 1772–1810, Busta 2.

63. The first rumor is offered by Fortunati, 18 January 1800; the second comes from Galimberti, 18 January 1800.

CHAPTER FOUR

1. Diarists Fortunati and Galimberti record most openings, and have almost nothing good to say about any of them. Typical entries include: "A new musical farce appeared last night at the Apollo theater, but it fell to earth because of a terrible company even though the music wasn't bad" (Galimberti, 9 November 1799) and "The Valle theater opened with a musical farce, *Lo Spazzacamino*, with old music by maestro Paisiello, which was badly attended and met with shouts and whistles" (Galimberti, 27 April 1800).

2. Galimberti describes this opera as consisting of "old music by Maestro Paer."

3. Pastura, "Legislazione pontificia," 172.

4. The opening date for theaters varied from 26 December (as in 1780, 1785, 1787, and 1788) to 8 January (after Epiphany, as in 1791). The Edicts on Theaters (Editti sopra i teatri) can be found in the Archivio Segreto della Santa Sede, and are cited extensively in De Dominicis, "I teatri di Roma nell'età di Pio VI."

5. Pastura, "Legislazione pontificia," 173–74.

6. I-Ras, Computisteria generale della Reverenda Camera Apostolica dopo la riforma di Benedetto XIV, serie rossa, Reg. 13, fol. 803.

7. A survey by the fourteen city districts, or *rioni*, shows the following numbers of theatrical venues: Monti, 3; Trevi, 14; Colonna, 8; Campo Marzio, 13; Ponte, 7; Parione, 12; Regola, 4; San Eustachio, 4; Pigna, 8; Campitelli, 4; Sant'Angelo, 1; Ripa, 0; Trastevere, 2; Borgo, 8. Cairo, "Luoghi scenici nella Roma del Settecento."

8. Robert Isherwood comes to a similar conclusion in *Farce and Fantasy*.

9. Bauman, "The Society of La Fenice and its First Impresarios."

10. By and large foreigners were unimpressed by the ballets that accompanied Italian operas. A German tourist noted that ". . . [n]otwithstanding the badness of the dances performed on the Italian stage, those of Rome are bad beyond description, on account of the men disguised in women's clothes." Archenholtz, *A Picture of Italy*, 282–83. Anna Miller, writing in the 1770s, had a similar impression, commenting that "the black drawers worn by the danseuses have a very disgusting appearance"; *Letters from Italy*, 151. See Kathleen Hansell, "Il ballo teatrale e l'opera italiana," in *Storia dell'opera italiana*, 5.

11. Pastura, "Legislazione pontificia," 167–68.

12. The most useful secondary sources on the theaters of Rome include Ademollo, *Bibliografia della cronistoria teatrale italiana*; Norci Cagiano, "Un teatro tutto di legno"; Cametti, *Il teatro Tordinona poi di Apollo*; De Angelis, *Il teatro Alibert*; De Dominicis, "I teatri di Roma nell'età di Pio VI" and "Roma centro musicale nel Settecento"; Pavan, "Il teatro Capranica"; Rava, *I teatri di Roma*; Rinaldi, *Due secoli di musica al teatro Argentina*; Severi, *I teatri di Roma*; and Tirincanti, *Il teatro Argentina*. Major sources on Roman theatricality include a series of publications by the Istituto della Enciclopedia Italiana, especially *Il teatro a Roma nel Settecento* and *Le Muse galanti: La musica a Roma nel Settecento*; and a group of conference papers organized by Bianca Maria Antolini, Arnaldo Morelli, and Vera Vita Spagnuolo, eds., *Musica a Roma attraverso le fonti d'archivio*. A most useful study of music in seventeenth-century Rome is Margaret Murata, *Opera for the Papal Court*.

13. Cametti, *Il teatro Tordinona*, 200.

14. Galimberti, 31 January 1800.

15. De Brosses, *Lettres familières*, 311.

16. De Angelis, *Il teatro Alibert*.

17. The theater is named for a tower called the "Torre Argentina" in honor of the hometown of its sixteenth-century builder, Johann Burkhard from Strasbourg (in Latin *Civitas Argentarium*). Rinaldi, *Due secoli di musica*, 3–4.

18. Cazzato, Fagiolo, Giusti, eds., *Teatri di Verzura*.

19. Cited by Rinaldi, *Due secoli di musica*, 317.

20. The subject of the castrati has attracted much attention recently. There has been a virtual explosion in recordings of the castrato repertoire performed by male sopranists and contraltos. Among the more interesting of the recent literature are works such as *En Travesti: Women, Gender Subversion, Opera*, ed. Corinne Blackiner and Patricia Smith, and *Queering the Pitch: The New Gay and Lesbian Musicology*, ed. Philip Brett, Elizabeth Wood, and Gary Thomas. Patrick Barbier, who writes more popular books, has published *Farinelli: Le castrat des lumières*, while his book *The World of the Castrati* has appeared in English translation by Margaret Crosland. See also journal literature such as Catherine Bargeron's "The Castrato as History," Nella Anfuso, "The Vocalism of the Castrati: Fantasy and Reality," and Franca Camiz, "The Castrato Singer: From Formal to Informal Portraiture."

21. Moreschi's seventeen recordings were reissued by Pearl Records with liner notes by John Wolfson and Elsa Scammell (Opal 823). They are now available on compact disc. See Law, "Alessandro Moreschi Reconsidered."

22. 1 Cor. 14:33–35. It is a common theme in most traditional religions to assign highly gender-specific roles and to consider deviation from such roles anathema.

23. The phenomenon of the castrati cannot be understood without recalling the Christian ascetic ideal, which actively values the renunciation of sexual activity. In this context what seems to us a grotesque perversion of nature for seventeenth- and eighteenth-century Italians was a reasonable career choice not all that different from taking religious vows of celibacy. Rosselli introduces this important concept in his 1988 essay, "The Castrati."

24. One might speculate on the popularity of the puppet actors and singers, who carried the abstraction from nature even further. In Rome, the puppet shows—which could be extremely elaborate and realistic—were allowed during periods when live theater was banned, perhaps on the theory that the puppets were more edifying and less harmful.

25. Muratori, in "Della perfetta poesia italiana" (1706). Poets like Apostolo Zeno agreed but blamed the low state of theater on impresarios: "It is true that the modern stage is ruled by an effeminate passion, that is, LOVE, which it is impossible to leave out of any story. The fault lies with the private impresarios, who produce theater in order to gain a profit—so they put on performances which attract the greatest audiences, made up of those with the least understanding, and the softer sex, who are most impressed by the weakest passions." Letter from Zeno to Muratori, quoted in Basso, *L'Età di Bach e di Haendel*. And finally, Count Algarotti's essay on opera summed up the relationship between musical theater and the state: "The state should take an interest in the theater, as did the ancient republics, who . . . made a political use of scenic representations to arouse their citizens to a sense of glory, or to keep them peaceably diverted for the general quiet of the commonwealth . . . Unlike the present day, when theater has fallen prey to . . . the mismanagement of mercenary and interested undertakers whose only object is to realize pecuniary contributions on the curiosity and leisure of their fellow citizens." Algarotti, *Essay on Opera* (1762).

26. Silvagni, *La corte pontificia e la società romana nei secoli XVIII e XIX*.

27. Celletti, "I cantanti a Roma nel XVIII secolo," and Stendhal, *Rome, Naples et Florence*, 294.

28. Gavoty, *La Grassini, première cantatrice de S. M. l'Empereur et Roi*. See also Fétis, *Biographie universelle des musiciens*, s.v. "Grassini." These highly colored and inaccurate accounts would have been Sardou's most probable sources.

29. With regard to Belgioioso, Gavoty cites Commandini, *De l'Italia nei cento anni del secolo XIX*, "Principe Alberico XII di Belgiojoso," vol. 1, p. 651.

30. Crescentini, then twenty-seven years old, was one of the greatest of the castrati. He appeared with Grassini in *Giuletta e Romeo* (Juliet and Romeo), which Zingarelli wrote for her.

31. Arnault, *Mémoires d'un sexagénaire.*

32. *Monitore* review of 19 Piovose (8 February) from issue number XLII; cited by Rinaldi, 327–28. Fortunati was less enthusiastic about the bill at the Argentina. Most of his attention was directed to the companion piece to *Ifigenia,* a farce titled *Ferdinand IV, Conqueror of the Roman Republic.* All of his 1 February 1799 entry is taken up with the anti-Neapolitan farce, which, he noted with satisfaction, was "whistled off the stage." Fortunati, 1 February 1799.

33. Fétis, *Biographie universelle,* 210–13 and Escudier, *Vie et aventures.* See also *Nouvelle biographie générale* (Paris, 1855), s.v. "Catalani"; *Enciclopedia dello spettacolo,* s.v. "Catalani"; and Forbes, "Catalani, Angelica," *New Grove Dictionary of Opera,* 4: 4–5.

34. "A name is a terrible thing. I am haunted day and night. I've gone through every family name in Venice from the Doges down." Roosevelt, *Victorien Sardou,* 49–50.

35. Cherubini's opera *La Lodoïska* (libretto by Fillette-Loraux, based on a novel by Jean-Baptiste Louvet de Couvrai) was written for Paris in 1791 as a celebration of revolutionary activism. Mayr's work, produced in Milan after the arrival of the French, had a text by Gonella; the story was basically the same as Cherubini's but the libretto was quite different. Caruso's version, scheduled for the Argentina theater in the 1797–98 carnival season, was apparently a politically motivated version of the same story composed to coincide with the "revolutionizing" of Italy. It was based on a text by G. B. Ferrari. See Pencak, "Cherubini Stages a Revolution." Cherubini's heroine is a radical modeled on the revolutionary women of Paris. Such a woman would have been unacceptable (even in Paris) a century later. Even the liberal republican Sardou preferred his heroines to be politically naïve, pious, and conservative.

36. *Monitore di Roma,* 14 October 1798.

37. Cretoni, *Roma giacobina,* 178–79.

38. Gross, *Rome,* 10–12.

39. Quirini, *Della beneficenza romana* (1878); Piazza, *Eusevologio romano, ossia Delle opere pie di Roma* (1698); and *Regole del conservatorio pio eretto dalla Santità di Nostro Signore Papa Pio Sesto* (1766).

40. Rousseau, *Confessions,* Part 2, Book 7, p. 291.

41. Monnier, *Venise au XVIIIᵉ siècle,* 115–17.

42. Arnold, "Orphans and Ladies: The Venetian Conservatories (1690–1797)," 33ff. See also Malipiero, "La musica dopo la decadenza della cappella ducale," 475–79.

43. Lanfranchi, *Dizionario biografico degli italiani* (1842), s.v. Cimarosa, 540–52. See also Andrea della Corte, *Disegno storico dell'arte musicale;* Calvatore Di Giacomo, *Paisiello e i suoi contemporanei;* J. L. Hunt, *Giovanni Paisiello; New Grove Dictionary of Music and Musicians,* s.v. "Cimarosa" and "Paisiello."

44. Vigée-Lebrun notes that Emma Hamilton liked to wear flowers in her hair, like the character Nina. Floria might do the same in the first act of the opera.

45. Castelvecchi, "From *Nina* to *Nina.*" See also Giambattista Lorenzi, "Notes on Nina, or the girl crazy with love," liner notes for Bongiovanni recording, GB 2054/55–2, recorded live 22 November 1987.

46. Heartz, "From Garrick to Gluck," and Solomon, "Signs of the Times," citing Giambattista Mancini's 1774 treatise, *Pensieri, reflessioni pratiche sopra il canto figurato.*

47. Galimberti, 22 February 1800.

48. Anecdote related by Galimberti, 18 January 1800.

49. These operas are cited only by Galimberti, on the date of performance, i.e. *Il matrimonio in cantina,* farce with music by Crescini (22 February 1800); *Lo Spazzacamino,* farce with music by Paisiello (27 April 1800); and *Gl'intrighi amorosi,* farce with music by Paer (17 May 1800). The last is probably a reworking of a piece first composed in 1795 as *Saed, ossia Gl'intrighi del serraglio,* redone for Bologna in 1797 as *Il male vien dal buco. New Grove Dictionary of Opera,* 3, s.v. "Paer."

CHAPTER FIVE

1. This is a curious transference to Ferdinand IV of the Two Sicilies of the title traditional to the kings of Spain, among them his father Charles III and his brother, Charles IV, then on the throne of Spain and soon to be ousted by Bonaparte.

2. Andrieux, *Daily Life in Papal Rome*, 100; Norwich, *A History of Venice*, 585. The "Black Legend" of the Inquisition, though still popular, is being eroded by modern scholarship. *Tosca* stage directors who insert cowled clerics into the torture scene of Act II of the opera are appealing to an old but quite ahistorical tradition.

3. Cajani, "Giustizia e criminalità nella Roma del Settecento," 263–312. Steven Hughes, "Fear and Loathing in Bologna and Rome," offers a table showing the employees of the major courts in Rome in 1790. These were: (1) Court of the governor of Rome: city; (2) Court of the governor of Rome: province; (3) Court of the cardinal chamberlain; (4) Court of the cardinal vicar; (5) Court of monsignor auditor camerae; (6) Court of monsignor treasurer general; (7) Court of the Campidoglio and conservators. In addition there were the court of the senator of Rome, the signatory court, and the courts of the congregations of the Immunità and Buon Governo, to say nothing of appeals courts such as the Rota. The records of the courts of the governor are held in I-Ras, Tribunale del governatore.

4. Gross, *Rome*, 221.

5. Ibid. 223.

6. Andrieux, *Daily Life in Papal Rome*, 92.

7. Gross, *Rome*, 225.

8. Cesare Beccaria condemns clemency as "an act . . . contrary to the public good" since it weakens the certainty of punishment, which should be the greatest threat of the law. Beccaria, *On Crimes and Punishments*, chapter 20.

9. In the five-year period between 1796 and 1800 any one day saw an average of 635 persons in the prison population. Few, however, were held for long, and it has been estimated that roughly 16,000 people passed through the prisons of Rome in 1800. Paglia, *La pietà dei carcerati*.

10. Andrieux, *Daily Life in Papal Rome*, 101–2. The *cavaletto* or "little horse" was a portable frame for whipping; the *tratti di corda*, or *strapado*, described below, was a form of the rack.

11. Biblical novels were popular in the late nineteenth century. Lew Wallace's *Ben Hur: A Tale of the Christ* was published in 1880 and widely translated.

12. Gross, *Rome*, 230; Andrieux, *Daily Life in Papal Rome*, 102. See also Moore, *A View of Society and Manners in Italy*, 474–75.

13. Cajani, "Giustizia e criminalità," 283–84.

14. Gross quotes a proverb "Nun dite pover'ômo a cchi mmôre ammazzato; perché si ha ffatto er danno l'ha ppagato" (Don't say "poor man" about the one who was murdered, because he who did the harm has paid for it). Zanazzo, *Tradizioni popolari romane*, 1: 202.

15. *Tosca*, II.

16. Among the first modern police forces were the Paris police organized by Lenoir prior to the French Revolution, and the London police created by the reforms of Sir Robert Peel in 1829. See Williams, *The Police of Paris 1718–1789*.

17. Gross, *Rome*, 220.

18. *Regolamento organico e di procedura criminale*, Article 348, issued by Gregory XVI on 5 November 1831. At the end of October 1800 Pius VII's staff had issued a *Reformatio Curiae Romanae*, of which Article 121 called for "a more appropriate proportion between crimes and punishments to facilitate the system and the relevance of proofs, under which shall also fall the use of torture." Picca, *La tortura in Roma*, 18. As late as 1849 the issue was still under discussion, with the edict that "the use of torture and the punishment of the *corda*, both already banned, remain perpetually abolished." *Bullarium Romanum*, vol. xiv (Roma, 1849), 60, as cited by Fusco di Ravello, "Tra conservazione e ratione," 323.

19. Langbein, *Torture and the Law of Proof,* and Fiorelli, *La tortura giudiziaria nel diritto comune.*

20. Fiorelli, *La tortura giudiziaria,* 1: 131 and 2: 38.

21. Cajani, "Giustizia e criminalità," 273–74. See also the most influential of the anti-torture publicists, Cesare Beccaria, *On Crimes and Punishments,* chapter 12, where he notes that "[Torture] is an infallible means indeed—for absolving robust scoundrels and for condemning innocent persons who happen to be weak."

22. Spoletta's interjection in Act II of the opera has no parallel in the play.

23. Buzzelli Serafini, "La reazione del 1799 a Roma," and Rossi, "L'occupazione napoletana di Roma."

24. For the treaty provisions, see chapter 3, n. 1.

25. Quoted in Buzzelli Serafini, "La reazione del 1799 a Roma," 151, citing Biblioteca di Storia Moderna e Contemporanea Roma, Bandi, A8/24.

26. Cajani, "Giustizia e criminalità," 160.

27. Galimberti notes that on one occasion, when there were more than 900 prisoners in Rome, sixty-two were released to relieve overcrowding, and because no one knew for sure why they were in prison in the first place. Galimberti, 4 April 1800. See also Buzzelli Serafini, "La reazione del 1799 a Roma," 206–7.

28. Rossi, "L'occupazione napoletana di Roma," 706–7.

29. A letter from the Neapolitan Minister of Police, Bonifazio Cataldi, to Cardinal Ruffo, which Ruffo passed on to the court at Palermo. Ibid., 706–9.

30. Buzzelli Serafini, "La reazione del 1799 a Roma," 180, citing I-Ras, Giunta di Stato 1799–1800, Busta 8, fasc. 84.

31. Ibid., 186.

32. Among the many works of historical fiction and fictionalized history that focus on the Nelson–Hamilton affair, see Sontag, *The Volcano Lover: A Romance.* Floria Tosca comes into Sontag's retelling of the Hamilton story, where the fictional singer serves as an echo of Emma as a passionate and loving woman whose political ignorance leads to unintended tragedy. Baron Scarpia is there as well, an uncouth Sicilian recently ennobled by Queen Maria Carolina, a man with a powerful animal sexual magnetism and "perfect manners flecked with rudeness." See also Fraser, *Beloved Emma;* Lofts, *Emma Hamilton;* and Russell, *Nelson and the Hamiltons.* Of particular interest in terms of fiction is the World War II era film, *That Hamilton Woman,* produced by Alexander Korda in 1941 with Laurence Olivier as Nelson and Vivian Leigh as Emma Hamilton. For a less melodramatic treatment of the episode, see Gutteridge, *Nelson and the Neapolitan Jacobins.*

33. As Lady Hamilton, Emma acted as a patron of the arts, sponsoring concerts and performers. She had a considerable reputation as an amateur performer herself, and was especially famous for her "attitudes" in which she replicated figures from antiquity, dressed in costumes that inspired profound changes in the dress of contemporary ballerinas, and actresses, and opera singers.

34. A clause in the marriage contract provided that Maria Carolina would take a seat on the Council of State on the birth of an heir, with equal prerogatives to those of her husband. Habsburg women were not trained to be mere ornaments.

35. Carpanetto and Ricuperati, *Italy in the Age of Reason 1685–1789,* 238; Acton, *The Bourbons of Naples (1734–1825),* 128; and Gutteridge, *Nelson and the Neapolitan Jacobins.*

36. From the name given the colony by the ancient Greek settlers, after Parthenope, a nymph said to have committed suicide by throwing herself into the bay. Typically, the renaming of the state was an attempt to resurrect a classical past and thereby symbolically eradicate 2,000 years of tradition and history.

37. One of the most influential studies of these Neapolitan martyrs was Atto Vannucci's *I martiri della libertà italiana dal 1794 al 1848,* written in the revolutionary year of 1848 and republished in 1887, the same year in which Sardou's *La Tosca* was first produced.

38. For the story of Luisa Sanfelice, see Vincenzo Cuoco, *Saggio sulla rivoluzione napoletana del 1799* (first published in 1801). Cuoco was an active participant in the Parthenopean Republic, and was involved in the Sanfelice case. Another republican historian, Carlo Botta, includes this case in his *Storia d'Italia dal 1789 al 1814;* Benedetto Croce, perhaps the single most influential Italian historian of the twentieth century, also wrote extensively on the history of Naples and the Parthenopean Republic. Atto Vannucci includes La Sanfelice among the martyrs in *Martiri della libertà*, 161–67.

39. In Act I of Sardou's play Floria tells Mario that she will have to stay late at the gala at the Farnese Palace, as she has been specially invited to dine at the royal table ("[the queen] is very good to me"). Sardou, *La Tosca*, I, iv.

40. The depression of the 1870s was particularly devastating in Sicily; a high percentage of the Italian peasants who emigrated to the United States were of Sicilian or Neapolitan origin and came at this time.

41. In Act I Angelotti makes a clear distinction between Scarpia and Naselli, telling Cavaradossi that "the governor [Naselli] is not a wicked man"; in Act II Sardou goes so far as to have both Scarpia and Naselli onstage at the same time; and in Act IV Spoletta delivers to Scarpia a handwritten execution warrant from Naselli, who has spent the evening at the Farnese palace calming the Queen.

42. Spreti, ed., *Enciclopedia storico-nobiliare italiana*, s.v. "Naselli." Nicola, *Diario napoletano, 1798–1825*. Naselli's tenure as royal lieutenant in Sicily came to an undignified end when riots broke out and Naselli had to flee in his underwear.

43. For a profile of this type of local leader see Huppert, *After the Black Death*, 80–100.

44. Pezza remained a loyal supporter of the Bourbons, and was executed in 1806 when Naples became part of the French empire. He made a good end, facing a French firing squad with courage. In an odd post-mortem incarnation, Pezza became the central figure in Auber's popular opera *Fra Diavolo*, where he mutated into a generic gentleman-bandit of the early nineteenth century. For biographies of Michele Pezza, or Fra Diavolo, see: Amante, *Fra Diavolo e il suo tempo (1796–1806)*; Franchi, *Fra' Diavolo*; Jallonghi, *Fra' Diavolo nella storia e nell'arte*; Dell'Ongaro, *Fra' Diavolo*; Gachot, *Histoire militaire de Massena: La troisième campagne d'Italie (1805–1806)*, 220–46; Marco Monnier, *Notizie storiche documentate sul brigantaggio nelle provincie napolitane*. Auber's opera, with a text by Eugène Scribe, is *Fra Diavolo, ou l'hôtellerie de Terracine*, first produced in Paris in 1828.

45. The unusual name "Vitellio" probably appealed to Sardou because it suggested the Emperor Vitellius, who had a reputation for brutality.

46. Riccardi, *La ristorazione del 1799, ossia I martiri di Napoli*, and Cardoni, "Il Te Deum de' Calabresi," 79–85.

47. Accounts of this episode, which Romans found highly amusing, appear in the diaries of Galimberti and Fortunati on and around 20 May 1800.

48. These proclamations are collected into volumes in the Roman state archives, I–Ras, Bandi 416.

49. Ibid.

CHAPTER SIX

The discussion of the music of Puccini's opera draws on recent Puccini scholarship, most notably by Michele Girardi and Roger Parker. I am especially grateful to Dexter Edge, who guided me through the mysteries of the score, and to Deborah Burton, whose unpublished dissertation I consulted extensively.

1. Musical references in the text are to the 1995 vocal score of *Tosca* edited by Roger Parker, with the piano score based on the 1899 redaction by Carlo Carignani; I, 1 refers to Act I, measure 1, etc.

2. Keefe, "The Music of Puccini's *Tosca*," 17. Perhaps the violence, plus the unresolved character of the whole-tone scale, suggest this sociopathic character.

3. Burton, 115.

4. See chap. 8, 195 and 203–4.

5. Girardi, 165–66.

6. Ibid., 172–76. Deborah Burton has identified eighteen appearances of the "Scarpia" chords, only eleven of which occur when Scarpia is on stage, or mentioned. She argues that this suggests the chords refer to evil in general, as well as to Scarpia as a character. Burton, 115.

7. Gilii was also director of the papal botanical gardens, and of the natural history museum. See Giuseppe Lais, "Memorie e scritti di Mons. Filippo Luigi Gilii; *Dizionario biografico universale*, s.v. "Gilii"; and *Biografici degli italiani illustri*, 6: 362. "Memorie e scritti, F. L. Gilii," Biblioteca Apostolica Vaticana.

8. *Tosca*, I.

9. Fortunati tells us that twenty people were killed in the blast, which Romans believed to have been part of a plot that had misfired. It seems more likely that the gunpowder stored there for the fireworks display for the feast of Saints Peter and Paul ignited accidentally. Fortunati, 28 June 1795.

10. In 1800 Roman time was still calculated according to a 24-hour clock and was fundamentally different from modern, so-called French, time. The first hour began half an hour after sunset, and continued around the clock, so that the twenty-fourth hour began half an hour *before* sunset. For a discussion of the Enlightenment implications of this controversy, see Talbot, "Ore Italiane," 51–59.

11. The 1941 Renoir/Koch/Visconti film based on Sardou's play shows Angelotti rescued by friends disguised as workmen who bring him out with them, delayed only by confraternity members carrying the coffined body of Count Palmieri, shot that morning.

12. See Ademollo, "Le giustizie a Roma," 310–31. See also I-Ras, Arciconfraternità di San Giovanni Decollato, 1497–1870, Busta 11 (1772–1810).

13. De Brosses, *Lettres familières*, Letter iii, 44.

14. Ortolani, *Sant'Andrea*, 112, and Pericoli Ridolfini, *Sant'Andrea della Valle*, 1.

15. Draft libretto of *Tosca*, US-NYp.

16. I-Ras, Teatini, 24 XI, Regolari 2203 Libro Mastro.

17. "Era giunto da Livorno Benedetto Greco già servitore del defonto Card. Rezzonico Camerlengo, e celebre Reb.no, e Commissario Francese. Il Bargello avendo avuto l'ordine di carcerarlo in qualunque luogo, lo trovò; esso si potèa fuggire e si rifugiò nella Chiesa di S Andrea della Valle, ove era il Ssimo. esposto per le solite Quarantore. Il Bargello coi Birri l'inseguì, e accostatoglisi in chiesa, gli disse sotto voce, che si uscisse; avendo esso ricusato di ubbidire, il Bargello lo prese in petto, e l'arrestò. Naque gran tumulto: accorierono i Can.ci, e condussero il Greco in Sacrestia. Spedirono quindi al Gen. Naselli per sapere la di lui volontà, e n'ebbero in risposta, che consegnassero il Greco alla Truppa, come fu eseguito. Nel dopo pranzo però il Greco fu rilasciato, si disse, per una Patente della Russia che esso esibiva." (Benedetto Greco, former servant to the late Cardinal-Chamberlain Rezzonico and a well-known Jacobin and French Commissioner, came from Livorno. The Captain of the Guard had orders to arrest him wherever he found him; he was able to flee to the church of Sant'Andrea della Valle, where the Blessed Sacrament was exposed for the usual Forty Hours Devotion. The Captain, with the sbirri, followed him, approached him in church, and said to him, softly, that he should come with them; when he refused to obey the Captain took hold of him and arrested him. A great tumult began; the canons of the church came running up and took Greco into the sacristy. They then sent to General Naselli to see what he wanted done, and he replied that they should turn Greco over to the Troops, which was done. In the afternoon, however, Greco was released, they say because he showed a safe-conduct from the Russians.) Galimberti, 23 February 1800.

18. I-Ras, Teatini, 2140, Chiesa, arredi sacri, libri 1559–1864; 2145/120 Affari teologici, 1625–1849; 2160/52 Affari personali, 1616–1840; 2169 Giustificazioni diverse, 1795–1807; 2142/105 Funzioni Sac. 1786–1869; 2142/107 Introito sacrestia 1780–1806; B. 2104/2 1800 (circa) Indice dell'Archivio di S. Andrea della Valle; Reg. 2203, Libro Mastro della Vte. Casa de RR. PP. Teatini di Sant'Andrea della Valle, 1779–1801.

19. The purchasing power of Roman coins at this time is difficult to establish with any precision. Inflation was rampant, and the price of basic foodstuffs, while subsidized, rose steeply throughout the period of foreign occupation. According to Fortunati, in June 1800 a pound of beef cost six baiocchi, a pound of veal cost between 7 and 14 baiocchi depending on quality. A pound of bread cost 4½ baiocchi in May and June, but when the new pope arrived in early July, he immediately lowered the price to 3 baiocchi. La Guardia (p. 37) gives the following values for common Roman coins at the end of the eighteenth century: 5 copper quattrini made up one copper baiocco; 100 baiocchi made one silver paolo (also called a testone because it bore the head of the current pope); 5 paoli equaled one scudo.

The pay records of Sant'Andrea della Valle between 1796 and 1800 show that singers for the Easter Passion earned one scudo; 15 paoli (or three scudi) went to a painter who colored the crucifix; a deacon and subdeacon each earned an extra 20 paoli for a sung Mass; *festaioli* (decorators) got regular tips of 15 baiocchi "for drinks." In December of 1800, they paid 1½ scudi for a portrait of the new pope (Pius VII Chiaramonti). I-Ras, Teatini, 2142–107: Introito ed esito della Sagrestia, 1790–1806.

20. Mahler to his wife Alma, 20 April 1903. Alma Mahler, *Gustav Mahler*, 225.

21. Carner, *Puccini*, 101.

22. Most stage directors provide Cavaradossi with a freestanding easel, but it makes a great deal more sense for him to be working on a mural. This argument is convincingly presented by Mahon, "A Note on the Staging of *Tosca*," 162–63.

23. The story about Martha's worry over household concerns and her sister Mary's choice to sit at the feet of Jesus occurs in Luke 10:38–42; the raising of their brother, Lazarus, occurs in John 11:1–44. Mary Magdalene is mentioned by name in the Resurrection accounts, and in Luke 8:2 as a follower of Jesus formerly possessed by devils. The story of the unnamed "sinful woman" at the Pharisee's dinner occurs just before this, in Luke 7:36–50.

24. "Il est allé jusqu'au quartier des Juifs, acheter une étoffe pour sa peinture." (He's gone as far as the Jewish quarter to get some fabric for his painting.) Gennarino to Eusèbe, Sardou, *La Tosca*, I, i.

25. Keefe, "The Music of Puccini's *Tosca*," 18.

26. Parker, "Analysis," 141.

27. US-NYp, Draft libretto of *Tosca*. The proposed verses are in Illica's handwriting.

28. Ange: Il carcere me ha dunque assai mutato!

     Mario: *Il carcere!* (Cavaradossi guarda fiso il volto di Angelotti [e cerca; ma a un tratto, rapidamente, in lui l'artista, più pronto, afferra la rassomiglianza fra la ignota Maddalena e il giovane—e da un colpo così Cavaradossi ravvisa Angelotti e nella sua Maddalena, sua sorella la Marchesa Attavanti.])

     Ange: Prison has changed me so much then!

     Mario: Prison! *(Cavaradossi stares at Angelotti's face [and searches; but all at once, suddenly, the artist in him, quicker, recognizes the resemblance between the unknown Magdalene and the young man — and at one blow thus Cavaradossi recognizes Angelotti and in his Magdalene, his sister the Marchesa Attavanti.])*

The section in brackets has been struck out on the manuscript. I-Mr, draft libretto of *Tosca*.

The first printed libretto in 1899 shortened the explication to: "Cavaradossi stares at Angelotti's face, and finally recognizes him" *(Cavaradossi guarda fiso il volto di Angelotti, e finalmente lo ravvisa)*. The directions now read simply, "Recognizing him, he rapidly puts down . . ." *(Riconoscendolo, depone rapido . . .)*.

29. I-Mr:

> Tosca: Dio! Dio! Quante peccata!
> M'hai tutta spettinata!
> E Paisiello che la prova aspetta.

30. "Entra con una specie di violenza, guardando intorno sospettosa." The 1899 printed libretto is more specific, stating that she comes in with a sort of violence, brusquely pushing away Mario, who wants to embrace her, and looks around her suspiciously ("entra con una specie di violenza, allontana bruscamente Mario che vuole abbracciarla e guarda sospettosa intorno a sè"). The manuscript working papers for the libretto add a further descriptive phrase: ". . . avanzandosi a piccoli passi e senza far rumore come un cacciatore che tema di far fuggire" (She enters with a sort of violence, looking around, suspicious . . . advancing with little steps and without making noise like a hunter who fears to frighten away). This second phrase has been struck out with the same heavy pen that Puccini has used in this manuscript for his comments and additions—did Puccini the avid hunter find the image inappropriate for his heroine?

31. This is suggested by Keefe, "The Music of Puccini's *Tosca*," 20 and by Burton, 124.

32. ". . . the whole scene with Mario is a comedy scene. He is debonair, and whistles occasionally, laughing at her jealousy." *New York World*, 4 March 1889.

33. Sardou, *La Tosca*, I, iv. Sardou's heroine is kittenish throughout this scene:

> Floria: *Vous n'avez pas plutôt fait deux grands yeux à cette créature que vous vous dites: "Ah! Les beaux yeux!" Et une petite bouche! "Oh! la jolie bouche! . . . On y mordrait!" Tant qu'à la fin, c'est elle que vous admirez, elle que vous aimez, et ce n'est plus moi!*

> You've no sooner made two big eyes for that creature than you say to yourself, "Ah! What beautiful eyes!" And a little mouth! "Oh! what a pretty mouth! . . . one could take a bite out of it!" Until by the end, it's her you admire, her you love, and no longer me!

34. Draft libretto for *Tosca*, US-NYp.

35. Ibid.

36. Roger Parker, ed., *Tosca*, Ricordi Opera Vocal Score Series, XLI.

37. Autograph Score, Act I, 610–11. I-Mr, reproduced in Parker, *Tosca*, LII.

38. Sardou makes much of this fan. In Act II of the play (set at the Queen's reception) Tosca demands that the Marchesa's husband identify the object; he turns to the lady's *cavaliere servente*, who recognizes it as one he himself has bought for the Marchesa, saying, "I ordered the crown of pearls [part of the Attavanti crest on the fan] at Costa's myself" *(j'ai commandé moi-même la couronne de perles chez Costa).*

39. Sardou, *La Tosca*, II, v.

40. Ibid., III, i.

41. For the text of this exchange, see chap. 7, n. 13.

42. Salmon, *Guide to Rome.*

43. Osborne, *Complete Operas of Puccini*, 139.

44. Girardi, 194.

45. I-Ras, Teatini, Reg. 2203.

46. I-Ras, Soldatesche e galere 3a Num. Busta 90.

47. I-Mr, Draft libretto of *Tosca*, Act I, scene viii:

> (Le loro grida e le loro risa sono al colmo. Allorché una voce ironica tronca bruscamente quella gazzarra volgare di canti e risa. È Scarpia; dietro a lui sta Spoletta e alcune faccie tipiche di birri.)

> Scarpia: *Bravi, si balla in chiesa. Bel rispetto!*

> (Their shouts and their laughter reach a climax. Then an ironic voice

brusquely cuts short this uproar of songs and laughing. It is Scarpia; behind
him stand Spoletta and several typical cop types.)
Very good, dancing in church. A nice sort of respect!

48. The arrest of Angelotti envisioned by Scarpia, though he does not accomplish it, is very similar to the arrest of Benedetto Greco; see n. 17 above. In the Greco case the Captain's clumsy handling caused a riot, something Scarpia clearly plans to avoid.

49. Draft libretto of *Tosca*, US-NYp: "Colei che a Maddalena / Qui ne vien per la posa . . . la modella . . . / A che ora usa venire?"

50. I-Mr, draft libretto for *Tosca*:

SCAR: (si ritira in disparte in ascolto)
TOSCA: (poiché ebbe guardato intorno invano) (al Sagrestano)
         Dov'è?
  SAG: *Chi?*
TOSCA: *Mario.*
  SAG: (seccato) *Ignoto.*
TOSCA: *Come!*
  SAG: *Nel calendario*
              Manca quel nome.
TOSCA   *Il pittor.*
  SAG: *Vedo.*
TOSCA: *Ov'è? domando.*
  SAG: *A voi lo chiedo.*
TOSCA: *C'era pur . . .*
  SAG: *Quando?*
TOSCA: *Dinanzi con me.*
  SAG: *C'era e non c'è.*
TOSCA: *Ei m'aspettava*
         qui per il pranzo.
  SAG: *Pel pranzo? Brava!*
         (raccoglie il paniere che Scarpia ha gettato)
         Ecco l'avanzo.
TOSCA: *Chi lo mangiò?*
  SAG: *Mah! Certo io no.*
TOSCA: *Ah! L'indegno mentì. Sempre mentiva.*
         Io fui presa alla pazzia — e nell'insania
         D'amore, a lui venivo tutta giuliva!
  SCAR: (ascoltando ed osservando Tosca)
         Tosca! Il pittore è suo [illegible]. Ella complice forse? No, no, troppo è devota!
         Farla complice mia piuttosto! Essa è gelosa! Solo che avessi un'arma. Ah, quel
         ventaglio.

51. The idea of the fan went through several verse incarnations. Besides the two we have just seen, and the version in the text as it now exists, there is at least one more:

SCAR: *Nella trama sottil d'un fazzoletto*
         gran gioco ha fatto Jago or io rimetto
         l'anima mia che tal ventaglio segna
         nuova trama sottil di Jago degna.

         In the subtle drama of a handkerchief
         Iago played a great game; now I wager
         my soul that this fan indicates
         a new subtle drama worthy of Iago.

52. *New Oxford Companion to Music*, "Te Deum Laudamus," 1808–9.

53. "Today, whatever our Paris atheists may say, I am going in full state to the *Te Deum* to be sung in Milan Cathedral." *Correspondance de Napoleon Ier*, 6: 469.

54. Galimberti, 4 November 1799.

55. Sardou underlines the tension by having Angelotti hope that the gunshot is merely part of the salvoes for the victory celebration, but Mario, listening for a series of shots but hearing only one, knows better: "No, you see, only one shot. It is certainly your escape they are signaling." Sardou, I, vi.

56. Two letters, each dated simply "August," show Puccini's need for "something to be muttered." In one, to Don Pietro Panichelli in Rome, he sketches out the proposed scene, and says that "Whether the Chapter or the people, I need some muttering, in low and natural voices, without intonation, as if it were real, some little verses. The Ecce Sacerdos is too imposing to be murmured. I already know that it's not usual to say or sing anything before the solemn Te Deum . . . but I repeat, whether it is realistic or not, that I want to find something to mutter . . ." At about the same time he wrote an even more urgent letter to his friend Guido Vandini in Lucca, which begins: "I absolutely need something to be muttered . . . it's necessary for me . . ." and continues, "I've decided on muttering and by God I won't give up the effect." In this hastily scribbled letter, he makes wild mock threats—to get the bishop fired; to write a funeral march for religion; to become a Protestant! Gara, no. 195, 168–69 and Pintorno, no. 46, 79.

57. Canori's letter (below) is in the Ricordi Archives in Milan, I-Mr.

> *Egregio G. Ricordi*
> *Milano*
> *21 8bre 1899*
>
> *Appena tornato in Roma mi misi subito alla ricerca dei Costumi della Corte Pontificia a principio del secolo — di cui Ella mi parlò che le abbisognavano per l'opera* Tosca.
>
> *Nè alla Calcografia Communale (oggi Regia) nè presso i più noti antiquarii mi fu possibile trovarli; finalmente rinvenni tutto occorrente presso un collezionista di stampe.*
>
> *Sono 18 tavole dipinte che egli togliarebbe dalla raccolta dei Costumi della Corte Pontificia sotto Leone XII (1825). Sarebbe proprio quello che a Lei occorre perché da Pio VI, fino ai primi anni del Pontificato di Pio IX, la Corte Pontificia non ha subito variazioni; e di queste 18 Tavole chiede per ristrettissimo prezzo Lire 72 a cioè L4 a figurino colorato.*
>
> *Occorrono tutti questi figurini perchè, non solo nelle solennità religiose il Pontifice inviara la Sua Anticamera, ma essendo St. Andrea della Valle di Patronato Capitolino doveva assistervi anche la rappresentanza del Campidogli (Municipio) quindi il corteggio dovrebbe essere così formato:*
>
> *1°   Sergente degli Svizzeri del Papa*
> *2°   4 Soldati Svizzeri del Papa*
> *3°   4 Domestici Capitolini (Fedeli)*
> *4°   4 Conservatori del Senato*
> *5°   2 Scudieri Pontificie*
> *6°   4 Bussolanti Pontificie*
> *7°   4 Monsignori di Cammerieri Segreti Pontificie*
> *8°   2 Chierici con cotti e turibulo*
> *9°   8 Chierici a torcie accese*
> *10° 2 Mazzieri Pontificie*
>
> *Il Cardinale con il Diacono e il Suddiacono in ricchi parati sacri — Quindi il Gentiluomo del Cardinale — Il Condatorio — il Chierico che per portare la mitra — Il Segretario con bugia accese — il Decano del Cardinale col cappello del Cardinale e i tre Domestici del Cardinale, etc.*

> *Lo svolgimento del corteggio dovrebbe essere come l'acclusa cartina.*
>
> *Questo è quanto occorrerebbe però siccome trattasi di una spesa non indifferente attendo primo da Lei autorizzazione a farla. Si assicuri però che è una vera fortuna aver trovato quanto bisognava.*
>
> *Attendo Sua lettera ed intanto La prego riverirmi la Sua Famiglia e specialmente Suo figlio Tito.*
>
> *Riceva i miei saluti e mi creda suo*
>
> *Guglielmo Canori*
> *Via del Pozzetto 102*

I am grateful to Dottoressa Maria Pia Ferraris at the Ricordi Archives for her assistance with this letter.

CHAPTER SEVEN

1. Gilii, June 1800, "Memorie e scritti," Biblioteca Apostolica Vaticana.
2. Marengo was a pivotal battle in European history, ensuring that France, not Austria, would control Italy until the defeat of Napoleon.
3. Inquisitorial procedure, typically employed in countries using civil or Roman law today, is a method of gathering and presenting evidence (the alternative, typical of countries using common law, is the adversarial procedure).
4. Fortunati, 17 November 1799.
5. The site is "romantic" in quite a different way now, as prostitutes solicit and entertain their customers along the Appian Way.
6. Sardou, *La Tosca*, I, vii.
7. Ibid., III, ii. In his description the playwright seems to have been thinking of the Roman campagna, the wild and dangerous area just outside the city, although the area he describes is in fact within the city walls.
8. Dupaty, *Lettres*, Letter l. In Letter lxix he tells the cautionary tale of a young couple who wandered into the catacombs and were never seen again.
9. Alessandro Verri's *Notti romane al sepolcro degli Scipioni* was immediately translated into virtually every European language and remains in print today. See Angeli, *Storia romana*, 89–97.
10. Colini, "La sistemazione del sepolcro degli Scipioni," 27–32.
11. Galimberti and Fortunati both speak of people being set upon by bandits near the city walls.
12. Cavaradossi seems to have a genetic predisposition to trouble with the Roman government. Luigi had to flee for his life after stabbing a Medici relative of the then-current pope, who had called him a bastard. The exhaustive description of the well, and of his family adventures, is related to Angelotti in Sardou, *La Tosca*, III, ii.
13. Draft libretto of *Tosca*, I-Mr:

> ANGE: *Temo la chiara luce*
> MARIO: *La capella dà uscita*
>   *in un chiostro deserto —*
>   *a mano destra, scavalcato il muro*
>   *il sentier dai canneti alti coperto*
>   *a una mia villa in breve ora conduce.*
> ANGE: *Mi è nota.*
> MARIO: (stacca una piccola chiave che egli tiene ad una catena elegante dell'orinolo, chiave lavorata di finezza, vera chiave di un nido d'amanti)*

*[Stage directions added later by Illica.]

> Ecco la chiave. Innanzi sera
> io vi raggiungo. Recate con voi
> le vesti femminili.

ANGE: *Ch'io le indossi?*

MARIO: *Non monta,*
> non troverete anima viva.

ANGE: *Addio.*

MARIO: *Aspettate! Ove mai*
> fosse urgente il periglio,
> troverete sicuro nascondiglio
> nel pozzo del giardino. Se vi piomba
> una pietruzza, rende
> suon di molt'acqua, ond'è tolto il sospetto
> che alcun v'abbia ricetto.
> Ma a mezzo della canna, a chi vi scende
> (e lo scendervi è lieve)
> s'apre un cunicol breve
> che mette al basso d'una catacomba
> senza passo d'uscita.
> Mio padre v'ebbe un dì salva la vita.
> [Colpo di cannone. I due fanno un sobbalzo di spavento.]

ANGE: *Il cannon del Castello!*
> [Fu scoperta
> la fuga! Ora squinzaglia
> Scarpia i suoi sbirri!] [†]
> Addio!

MARIO: *No, vi fo scorta,*
> Se ci assalgon — Battaglia.

ANGE: *Toccan la porta.*

MARIO: *É il sagrestano*
> via lesti — e piano!

[in a later version, this last line has been struck out, and the following stage directions added:] (Mario fa indossare il suo mantello ad Angelotti—ed entrambi cauti si allontanano perdendosi per le navate della chiesa.)

ANGE: I'm afraid of the bright light.

MARIO: The chapel opens
> onto a deserted cloister,
> to the right, across the wall
> the path covered by tall canes
> will quickly bring you to a villa of mine.

ANGE: I know it.

MARIO: *(He takes off a small key that he keeps on an elegant watch chain, a finely worked key, truly a key to a lovers' nest)* [‡]
> Here is the key. Before evening
> I'll rejoin you. Take with you
> the female clothing.

ANGE: Shall I put them on?

MARIO: Don't bother,
> you won't meet a living soul.

[†] [In a later version these words were given to Cavaradossi.]

[‡] [Stage directions added later by Illica.]

ANGE: Farewell.

MARIO: Wait! If there should
    be urgent danger,
    you'll find a secure hiding place
    in the garden well. If you drop
    a small stone, it will give
    the sound of much water, thus dispelling suspicion
    that anyone could be hidden there.
    But halfway along the shaft, to one who climbs down
    (and the climb down is easy)
    a short passage opens,
    that leads to the bottom
    of a catacomb with no exit.
    My father had it as a life-saver.
    [Sound of a cannon. The two jump with alarm.]

ANGE: The cannon of the fortress! The escape
    has been discovered! Now Scarpia unleashes
    his cops! Farewell!

MARIO: No, I'll be your escort.
    If we're attacked, there'll be a fight.

ANGE: Someone knocks at the door.

MARIO: It's the sacristan,
    go quickly—and quietly!

[In a later version, this last line has been struck out, and the following stage directions added: *Mario puts his mantle over Angelotti — and both cautiously vanish in the nave of the church.*]

14. I-Ras, Giunta di Stato 1799–1800, Busta 10.

15. Sardou, *La Tosca*, I, iv.

16. Ibid., I, i.

17. *Diario di Roma*, 17 June 1800.

18. Fortunati, 6 May 1800.

19. Domenico Puccini, letter to his father, Antonio, from Naples 29 January 1799, Lucca, Archivio di Stato, Legato Cerù 94/19.

20. The libretti to these curious works are now found in the Istituto Musicale Boccherini of Lucca, in the Fondo Puccini. See Guidotti, "La musica per strumenti a tastiera di Domenico Puccini (1772–1815)." See also Biagi-Ravenni and Gianturco, "The Tasche of Lucca: 150 Years of Political Serenatas," 45–56.

21. Among those tried by the Governing Committee or Giunta di Stato in 1800 were many accused of trafficking in goods stolen from churches and churchmen. I-Ras, Giunta di Stato 1799–1800, Busta 2, cases 21, 22, and 31.

22. Gori Sassoli, *Della chinea.*

CHAPTER EIGHT

1. The motif (Ex. 8.1) has been given various labels: "Reflection" (Carner); "Persistence" (Schuller); and "Scarpia's Violence" (Coeuroy). Deborah Burton gives a concise statement of the various motifs and the titles given to them by Puccini, Carner, Coeuroy, Schuller, and Winterhoff. Burton, 112–13. See also her treatment of the Scarpia chords in "Remote Regions and Puccini's Motivic Territory." The question of whether or not Puccini made use of motifs in the Wagnerian sense is controversial. A recent statement that he did indeed do so is found in an article by Schoffman, "Puccini's *Tosca*: An Essay in Wagnerism."

2. These connections have been noted by Carner in *Giacomo Puccini's Tosca*, 34–35; and by Girardi, 184.

3. "Tosca è un buon falco! Certo a quest'ora i miei segugi le due prede azzannano! Doman sul palco vedrà l'aurora Angelotti e il bel Mario al laccio pendere." *Tosca*, II.

4. After Rome became the capital of the Italian state in 1871, the Farnese palace became the French embassy, as part of a trade whereby the Hotel Galifet in Paris became the embassy of Italy. Broglie, *Le Palais Farnèse*, 65–70 and 233–35; Masson, *Companion Guide to Rome*, 132–35.

5. Salmon, *Historical Description*, 167.

6. The Bourbons of Naples later had it moved to that city as part of the Farnese collection now in the National Museum of Naples.

7. Fortunati, 31 January 1799. Minimalist or low-budget *Tosca*-producers, take note.

8. On 22 November 1799, for instance, Saverio Pediconi was arrested and brought to "one of the rooms in this palace [the Quirinale], the residence of the presiding officer" of the Giunta di Stato. I-Ras, Giunta di Stato, Busta 10.

9. This usage is typical of the way composers after the eighteenth century used the gavotte. "Later composers (Richard Strauss, Prokofiev, Schoenberg) sometimes used the title as a neo-classical gesture, but the details of their pieces vary considerably." *The New Harvard Dictionary of Music*, 334.

10. Dieter Schickling ("Giacomos kleiner Bruder") has shown that the gavotte was based on music composed by Puccini's younger brother, Michele.

11. Carner, *Puccini, a Critical Biography*, 373.

12. Sardou, *La Tosca*, II, v:

> (les musiciens accordent leurs instruments)
> PAIS: Si *natural, n'est-ce pas?*
> TOSCA: *No, bémol!* . . .
> PAIS: *Oh!*
> TOSCA: (violemment) *Bémol!*
> PAIS: (retournant à ses musiciens) *Bémol! Bémol!*
> *(The musicians tune their instruments)*
> PAIS: B natural, isn't it?
> TOSCA: No, flat!
> PAIS: Oh!
> TOSCA: *(violently)* Flat!
> PAIS: *(turning again to his musicians)* Flat! Flat!

13. Burton has posited the interesting theory that Sardou, writing within the French classical tradition of tragedy, made all of his characters subject to the workings of a hostile and external fate, rather than allowing Scarpia's evil to operate autonomously. Burton, 46.

14. "E strimpellan gavotte." *Tosca*, II.

15. Ibid.

16. Carner refers to this aria as Scarpia's "erotic credo"; *Puccini, a Critical Biography*, 366.

17. "Bramo. La cosa bramata perseguo, me ne sazio, e via la getto." *Tosca*, II.

18. Carner, *Puccini, a Critical Biography*, 366.

19. US-NYp, draft libretto of *Tosca*:

> SAGR: (a parte) *Mi par vuoto!*
> SCAR: *Che hai detto?*
> SAGR: *Io? Quel paniere . . . in mano*
> *della vostra Eccellenza, mi confonde.*
> *Dov'era? Oh scusi l'Eccellenza vostra*
> *se l'interrogo!*

SCAR: *Vieni!*
   L'Eccellenza risponde.
   In mezzo alla cappella lo ritrovai.
SAGR: *Vuoto?*

20. In the 1909 published edition of the play *La Tosca* the torturer is identified as "Alberti" in the stage directions, although Scarpia addresses him as "Roberti," perhaps because Puccini used that name. There is in the Ricordi archives an indignant letter from a Signor Roberti, protesting that assigning this name to the torturer in Puccini's new opera has brought his own family name into disrepute. Sardou, *La Tosca*, III, v and I-Mr.

21. Jannattoni, "Bugatti, Giovanni Battista (Mastro Titta)," in *Dizionario biografico degli italiani*, 15:11–12. See also Ademollo, *Le giustizie a Roma*, 110–25; Morandi, *Le annotazioni di Mastro Titta, carnefice romano*; Trozzi, *Il boia si confessa*, 81–86.

22. Quartering was carried out after death, and so was no more unpleasant for the victim than hanging, but of course the idea was seriously disturbing. In one case in 1800, the sentence of quartering and exposure was not read to the prisoners, "to avoid unnecessary distress." I-Ras, Confraternità di San Giovanni Decollato, Busta 11 (1772–1810).

23. The guillotine became the standard after 1808 until Rome became the capital of the Republic of Italy in 1871. I-Ras, Confraternità di San Giovanni Decollato, Busta 11 (1772–1810).

24. This and other relevant etchings are discussed by Lyle F. Perusse, "*Tosca* and Piranesi." Sardou, an avid bibliophile, had two sets of Piranesi etchings in his private theater research library.

25. *Tosca*, II.

26. It seems likely that Puccini, faced with the need for an ecclesiastical-sounding text, did the same thing he did with the prayers leading up to the Te Deum—that is, he pasted them together out of a mélange of vaguely pious phrases borrowed here and there from prayers, poetry, scripture, or liturgy. Eduardo Rescigno, *Giacomo Puccini: Tosca*, 57 and 63.

27. It may cast some light on Puccini's attitude toward historical accuracy to note that this song is no more a canticle (a biblical song outside the psalms, such as the Magnificat) than the dance is a gavotte.

28. *Tosca*, II:

Sale, ascende l'uman cantico,
Varca spazi, varca cèli,
Per ignoti soli empirei,
Profetati dai Vangeli,
A te giunge o re dei re,
Questo canto voli a te.
A te quest'inno voli
Sommo Iddio della vittoria.
Dio che fosti innanzi ai secoli
Alle cantiche degli angeli
Quest'inno di gloria
Or voli a te!
Sale, ascende l'uman cantico,
Varca spazi, varca cèli,
A te giunge o re dei re.

29. The second high C occurs as the climax of her resistance during the torture scene, at II, 475. The third (III, 276–77) comes on the word "knife" *(lama)* as she tells Mario that she has killed Scarpia.

30. Galimberti, May 1800.

31. The lawyer in question was Agostino Valle, the public defender or Advocatus Pauperum.

He lost Cappelli, but he did save Saverio Pediconi despite the fact that the court was frankly determined to hang him. For an analysis of the Cappelli case, see De Felice, *Note e ricerche sugli 'Illuminati' e il misticismo rivoluzionario (1789–1800)*. The Pediconi case also features in Buzzelli Serafini, "La reazione di 1799 a Roma." The archival records for the cases against Cappelli, Pediconi, and others are found in I-Ras, Giunta di Stato.

32. I-Ras, Giunta di Stato, busta 10, case of Saverio Pediconi.

33. Fiorelli, *La tortura giudiziaria*, 1: 159–75, and Langbein, *Torture and the Law of Proof*, 4–5.

34. Cajani notes that the *sveglia* was invented to avoid such lawsuits. See "Giustizia e criminalità," 274.

35. It is a misnomer to refer to this room as a torture chamber. Palaces are not normally equipped with such facilities, though prisons may be. A formal "torture chamber" is hardly required, in any case: note that in the Sardou play the torture takes place in Cavaradossi's own house.

36. "Dunque eccoci alle prese proprio con queste benedette scene a due che sono davvero la maledizione della *Tosca*. Orbene sono riuscito ad ottenere un quartetto e sto mettendo insieme un quintetto. Spoletta diventa un curiosissimo tipo." (So, here we are struggling with just these blessed duet scenes that are truly the curse of *Tosca*. Well, I've succeeded in getting a quartet and I'm putting together a quintet. Spoletta becomes a very peculiar fellow.) Letter from Illica to Giulio Ricordi, Milan, 12 January 1895. Gara, no. 120, 113.

37. Evidence of this fragment remains only in a photograph of the script published in Richard Specht's book on Puccini. It is almost certainly by Illica, who was preparing a libretto for Franchetti as early as 1895.

> TOSCA: (sempre verso l'uscio torturandosi le mani dal dolore)
> *Mario! . . . Parlami, Mario!*
> *Ch'io ti senta! . . . Una sola . . .*
> *Una sola parola! . . .*
> (Si ferma alla voce del Procuratore ad ascoltare ancora)
> *L'uccidono! . . .*
> (contro Scarpia)
> > *Ah, sicario!*
> (terribile)
> *T'ha generato madre snaturata!*
> *Ma bada, Scarpia, questo pianto mio*
> *lo segna Cristo nel libro di Dio! . . .*
> *Quel giorno io là saro! . . . Con te e implacata . . .*
> *Tutti i tormenti e la pena d'inferno*
> *là avrai e quel tuo pianto sarà eterno!*
> PROCURATORE: *Così crudel con voi perchè?*
> SPOL: *Parlate!*
> PROC: *Rispondere non vuol! . . .*
> (agli aiutanti)
> > *Stringete ancora!*
> (la voce del procuratore fra i gemiti di Mario spicca concitata e sempre interrogando)
> *Dove? Dove? Dove?*
> SPOL: (borbotta preghiere e invoca nomi di santi)
> *Bella signora de' sette dolori! . . .*
> *Signore Gesù mio! . . . Màrtiri tutti . . .*
> (Cavaradossi esce in un gemito soffocato)
> CAV: (tra gemiti ed urli di dolore)

> *Tu puoi farmi soffrire*
> *mille e mille ferocie . . .*
> *mille e mille miserie! . . .*
> *Tu puoi farmi morire! . . .*
> *Ma le atroci ritorte*
> *non mi trarranno un grido! . . .*
> *A brani fammi! Straziami!*
> *I polsi e il fronte lacera! . . .*
> *La tua tortura io sfido!*
> *Io sfido la tua morte! . . .*
>
> SCAR: (muto, sempre calmo, freddo ed impassibile sta ritto in piedi presso al tavolo, immobile)

Deborah Burton details the texts of several other attempts at versifying this scene, most of them quite similar to the dialogue as it now exists, and none of them approaching the repellent detail of the above. Burton, 493–97.

38. "Judex ergo cum sedebit / quid quid latet apparebit / nil inultum remanebit." Not only does the verse come from the Dies irae, but Spoletta sings it on the correct reciting tone A, repeating the last phrase on the final of the mode, D. See Girardi, Ex. 63.2, p. 175.

39. In the autograph score and in the 1899 printed edition of the libretto, as well as in the first edition of the vocal score and the first printed full score, the question is "Did *I* talk?" *(Ho parlato?)*. Sardou has it both ways. His reviving hero asks, "Tu n'as rien dit, n'est-ce pas? Ni moi?" (You didn't say anything, did you? Nor did I?) to which Tosca replies, equivocally but truthfully, "Non! non! tu n'as rien dit! Rien!" (No! No! You said nothing! Nothing!). I-Mr, draft libretto of *Tosca*, and Sardou, *La Tosca*, III, ix.

40. Harold Acton, *The Bourbons of Naples.*

41. Colletta, *Storia del reame di Napoli*, 319.

42. Acton, *The Bourbons of Naples.*

43. Galimberti, 18 June 1800.

44. I-Mr, draft libretto of *Tosca*:

> MARIO: (*[illegible]* . . . avidamente)
> *E vittoria?*
> (A Tosca con grande entusiasmo)
>   *Vittoria*
> *che fa vile il carnefice*
> *e possente la vittima!*
> *Siam vindicati, Floria!*
> *Trema chi al labbro soave*
> *d'una donna tremante*
> *fa dir l'accusa grave*
> *che le uccide l'amante!*
> (con supremo entusiasmo)
> *Esulto! E vivo! E oblio!*
> *Ateo, credo a Dio!*
>
> FLORIA: *A noi che importa?*
> (va a prendere la levitica di Mario)
> *Indossar e usciamo!*
> (a Scarpia)
> *Non l'ascoltate! . . .*
> (a Mario con voce piena di paura e di *[illegible]*)
>   *Taci! . . .*
> *questa lugubre porta*

> *pria varchiamo!* . . .
> *Nostra vittoria — i baci;*
> *la nostra gloria — amore;*
> *No!* (A Scarpia)
> *Vieni!* . . . (cerca trascinar via Mario)
> (terribile, a Scarpia)
>   *Ah, traditore*
> *è vile!* . . . *Vile!* . . . *Tu mi hai fatta spia,*
> *ed ora* . . .
> (s'interrompe e cercando di aggrapparsi disperata
> a Mario grida disperata verso Spoletta)
>   *Non portatemelo via!*
> SCAR: (sogghinando a Cavaradossi)
> *Vittoria?*
> (corre verso la finestra e la *[illegible]* e sogghinando acenna verso Castel
> Sant'Angelo)
> *Guarda là nell'aer grave;*
> *guarda a Castel Sant'Angelo!* . . .
> *La vittoria è un patibolo!*
> *O moribondo, esulti a gioia breve!*
> *prega piuttosto in ora d'agonia* . . . *!*
> (a Spoletta)
> *Ora sù; la fin! Portatemelo via* . . .
> (E mentre Spoletta e gli sgherri si impossessano di Cavaradossi egli gli dice
> ironico)
> *Ancor qui Scarpia è il forte*
> *e tu ti chiami morte!*

45. In modern Italian, the formal singular is normally *Lei* rather than the old-fashioned *voi*. This has something to do with the Fascist preference for *voi* (*Lei* is the same word used for "she," and was considered effeminate by the manly followers of the Duce). To further complicate matters, God is normally addressed as *tu*. At the end of Act II, as Floria first pleads with, and then stabs, Scarpia, she uses the *tu*.

46. Eric Plaut, opera lover and psychiatrist, notes that a good portion of the fascination with Scarpia lies in the fact that he is frankly a sexual sadist. Plaut, *Grand Opera*, 242–44.

47. Sardou, *La Tosca*, IV, iii.

48. For Scarpia's style of libertinism as an expression of eighteenth-century sexuality, see Porter, "Libertinism and Promiscuity," 1–19. See also Darnton's analysis of the reading habits of the period in *Revolution in Print: The Press in France (1775–1800)*.

49. Ovid, *The Technique of Love*, 46.

50. Sardou, *La Tosca*, II, v.

51. Tomaselli and Porter, *Rape*.

52. The travel diarist Dupaty repeats what he describes as a conversation between himself and a priest to the effect that "if we were more severe about this article [illicit sex], our faith would be abandoned; we have tried strictness more than once and it has been highly unsuccessful." Quoted in Vaussard, *Daily Life in Eighteenth-Century Italy*, 77. On the other hand, eighteenth-century Inquisition casebooks are full of cases where men have been hauled in for trying to convince girls that sex between two people who are not married to other persons is not sinful at all. See Modenese records of the Holy Office, in Orlandi, *La fede al vaglio* and, for example, Modena, Archivio di Stato, Inquisizione 280 and 298, Processi.

53. "Violenza non ti farò; sei libera, va' pure" (I won't force you; you're free, go if you like). *Tosca*, II.

54. Sardou, *La Tosca*, IV, iii.

55. Ibid., I, iv.

56. Argan, *Antonio Canova*, and John Smythe Memes, *Memoirs of Antonio Canova*.

57. ". . . in his use of swift narration, schematic characters, and deftly indicated moods, together with his self-conscious exploitation of familiar conventions, Puccini is a cinematic artist, and some of the most natural comparisons that his works invite are with films . . . with the finest products of the Hollywood studios in their best days—which indeed, like Puccini, learnt some of their technique from more ambitiously innovative works." B. Williams, "Manifest Artifice," 10–11. Döhring's analysis of Act III stresses the idea that the act is made up of a cinematic montage of contrasting shots and shifting focus. Döhring, "Musikalischer Realismus in Puccinis *Tosca*," 249–51.

58. Girardi, 187; and Carner, *Puccini, a Critical Biography*, 276.

59. It is in this blending of the sacred and the profane that Michele Girardi finds her similarities to Scarpia. Girardi, 183.

60. Sardou, *La Tosca*, IV, iii.

61. "Sei troppo bella, Tosca, e troppo amante. / Cedo.—A misero prezzo / tu a me una vita, io, a te chieggo un istante!"

62. Sardou, *La Tosca*, IV, i.

63. Op. 135, Quartet in F major, composed shortly before Beethoven's death. We cannot say whether Puccini was consciously quoting this very appropriate musical question, but Mahler certainly did.

64. Fortunati, August and September, 1799.

65. Heriot, *The French in Italy*, 164–65.

66. The British officer, Robert Wilson, traveled from Rome to Naples in December 1800 on a passport that should have included his servant, Samuel, but it did not. Border guards at Gaeta tried to stop the two men from entering the Kingdom of the Two Sicilies, but Wilson bluffed his way through, along with his passport-less valet. Wilson, *The Life of General Sir Robert Wilson*.

67. Vigée-Lebrun comments on Roman women and stilettos, noting that the Roman wife of one of her painter friends (a middle-class woman) carried one. Vigée-Lebrun, *Memoirs*, 93. Sopranos almost invariably insist on stabbing overhand in a downward motion that would surely bounce off the rib cage.

68. Fratta Cavalcabò, *Mascagni e Puccini*, 12, as cited by Mosco Carner in *Tosca*, 151, n. 22.

69. From the Ash Wednesday ceremony of marking the faithful with ashes as a reminder of mortality.

70. In the English National Opera 1994 production, the backdrop faded into a representation of footlights and an eighteenth-century opera audience, thus not suggesting but stating that in Tosca's mind this is a performance.

71. This was both unsanitary and (by the last decades of the century) illegal in most Italian states.

72. There are many descriptions of such funeral rites. Pier Leone Ghezzi, the eighteenth-century Roman caricaturist, often included notes on the death and burial of his subjects; see for example those on his brother Placido's physician, who died "like an angel" and directed that he should have a simple funeral—with only twelve priests and eight torches, and "no other luxury" (30 October 1739). Or "Antonio Montanari, died 2 April 1737 at 23rd hour, mourned by all Rome, laid out in the church of the Most Holy Apostles with a solemn Mass sung by all the professional musicians, singers as well as instrumentalists, with twelve torches." Ghezzi, I-Rvat, Vat. lat. 3118, no. 175 and 3116, no. 165a. See also Pierre-Jacques Bergeret de Grancourt's description of the funeral of Cardinal Cavalchini in Grancourt, quoted in Andrieux, *Daily Life in Papal Rome*, 133–35, and Story, *Roba di Roma*, 383–86.

73. Sardou, *La Tosca*, IV, v.

CHAPTER NINE

1. The drawbridge was replaced by a permanent bridge only in 1822. See D'Onofrio, *Castel St. Angelo: Images and History; The Angel and Rome: Castel Sant'Angelo;* Masson, *Companion Guide to Rome,* 509–14; E. Rodocanachi, *Le Château Saint-Ange;* and Andrieux, *Daily Life in Papal Rome.*

2. Colalucci, "Report on Restoration"; Contardi, "The Bronze Angel"; and Giuffrè, "The Supporting Structure", in *The Angel and Rome,* 94–102, 33–54, and 117–58.

3. Florence Stevenson offers an amusing survey of some of the women associated with the fortress in "Sant'Angelo's Ladies."

4. Luigi Londei and Neri Scerni, "Giustizia, politica e paternalismo nello stato pontificio."

5. Sade, *Juliette;* and Madame de Staël, *Corinne, ou l'Italie,* 55–56.

6. This anti-papal mythology is the basis of much of Paolo Picca's *La tortura in Roma* (1908).

7. See among others, Simon Schama, *Citizens: A Chronicle of the French Revolution.*

8. Sala, vol. 3, p. 88; and Galimberti, 328.

9. Much of the musicological discussion of Act III is drawn from Sieghart Döhring, "Musikalischer Realismus in Puccinis *Tosca,*" from Girardi, and from Deborah Burton's unpublished dissertation.

10. Letter to Alfredo Vandini from Torre del Lago, 27 September 1899, Gara, no. 205, 175. Panichelli's letter to Vandini is quoted in Gara, 175. Giggi (Luigi) Zanazzo (1860–1911) was the editor of the journal *Rugantino,* a prolific writer of dialect plays and poetry, and the editor of a major four-volume collection of Roman songs and folk tales, *Tradizioni popolari romane.*

11. The dummy verses can be translated: "I have wept so much and drunk a bottle, / because in your heart I have not convinced you; / oh beautiful flowers in the sunlight, / bend your heads, my love is passing by." In standard Italian Zanazzo's verses are: "Io dei sospiri / te ne rimando tanti / . . . per quante foglie / ne smuovono i venti. / Tu mi disprezzi / io me ne accoro, / lampada d'oro, / mi fai morir." See translation by Castel, *The Complete Puccini Libretti,* 2: 215. Letter from Puccini to Vandini with regard to these verses in late 1899 (Gara, no. 211, 180–1): "Grazie dei versi; scelgo il 2° ma il metro non mi torna. Io de sospiri—io te ne manno tanti, Pe' quante foje—che smoveno li venti. L'*io* e il *che* aggiunti sono necessari, dì al gentilissimo Sig Zanazzo (che ringrazio tanto e sarò ben felice di poterlo fare a voce) che sarà un verso dodecasillabo e sarà brutto, ma ci vuole così." (Thanks for the verses; I chose the second but the meter isn't quite right. *Io de sospiri — io te ne manno tanti, Pe' quante foje — che smoveno li venti.* The added *io* and the *che* are necessary, tell the very kind Sig. Zanazzo [whom I thank very much and I will be very happy to be able to do so in person] that it will be a twelve-syllable verse and it will be ugly, but it has to be that way.)

12. See, for example, Santi, "Tempo e spazio ossia colore locale."

13. "Lovely one, you won't weep / on the day that I will be dead." Story, *Roba di Roma,* 24.

14. The Lydian mode also allows Puccini to bring in the Scarpia/Tyranny notes, thus suggesting the continuing influence of Scarpia and the Tyranny he represents over the seemingly peaceful scene of the Shepherd's song. See Girardi, 170.

15. Don Pietro Panichelli: "Io ebbi in quel tempo . . . tutto l'entusiasmo di un amico fedele dall'arte pucciniana per la ricerca dei toni di quelle campane che erano le più vicine agli spalti di Castel Sant'Angelo. Ne feci una nota e gliela mandai subito." (I had at that time all the enthusiasm of a faithful friend of Puccini's art, for the search for the notes of those bells nearest to the ramparts of the Castel Sant'Angelo. I made note of them and sent it to him immediately.) Panichelli, *Il "pretino" di Giacomo Puccini racconta,* 57. "Dammi notizie delle campane Rafanelli e dell'apparecchio—Ho scritto a Ricordi dettagliatamente. Tienimi al fatto di tutto." (Let me know what's happening with the Rafanelli bells and the apparatus. I have written to Ricordi

in some detail. Keep me informed about everything.) Letter from Puccini to Filippo Tronci, instrument maker from Pistoia, dated 6 December 1899; Panichelli, 57–58.

16. ". . . Il libretto presente è così mutilato, antimusicale, che si può dire l'ombra, il programma di quel libretto che aveva entusiasmato Giulio Ricordi. . . . nel mio ultimo atto vi era da cima a fondo la lirica! Vi era la lirica della lettera di Cavaradossi che aveva saputo commuovere un Verdi! Vi era 'l'inno latino' . . . 'l'inno latino' . . . 'l'inno latino' . . . e quel finale la cui abolizione ha costruito o un atto di bestialità o uno di pazzia.

Ma . . . non è stato neppur permessa la più leggera protesta contro codesta mancanza di buon senso che faceva impoverire nella sua essenza musicale non solo l'ultimo atto, ma la poetica della *Tosca* per musica. Dove si appalesa poi la estrema meschinità dell'arte di fare le opere di Puccini è la soppressione della 'descrizione del sorgere dell'alba' a Roma nel preludio-scena dell'ultimo atto. Senza riflettere che la descrizione era non solo necessaria, nel libretto, ma indispensabile per richiamare l'attenzione del pubblico su quel preludio, perché quei dettagli di chiese, ecc ecc erano ragione e perché del brano. Così è sembrato lungo e monotono, e il gran da fare e il gran denaro per le campane hanno constituito una pazzia di più, perché passate completamente inosservate. . . ."

(The libretto now is so mutilated, anti-musical, that one might call it the shadow, the outline of that libretto that so excited Giulio Ricordi. . . . but in my final act there was, from top to bottom, lyricism: there was the lyricism of Cavaradossi's letter that was known to have moved a Verdi! There was the Latin hymn . . . the Latin hymn . . . the Latin hymn . . . and that finale the abolition of which has constituted either an act of stupidity or one of madness.

But . . . it was not even permitted [to make] the slightest protest against this lack of good sense that impoverished in its musical essence not only the last act, but the poetry of *Tosca* for music. Then, where one finds the extreme stinginess of Puccini's style of writing opera is the suppression of the "description of the break of dawn" of Rome in the prelude-scene of the last act. Without reflecting that the description was not only necessary, in the libretto, but indispensable to recall the attention of the public to that prelude, because those details of churches, etc. were the whole reason and rationale for the piece. Thus it seems long and monotonous and the great fuss and the large amount of money for the bells have constituted an additional folly, because it passes completely unnoticed . . .). Illica to Giulio Ricordi, 15 January 1900, Gara, no. 221, 192–94.

17. Galimberti, 12 April 1800.

18. Wilson, *The Life of General Sir Robert Thomas Wilson*. For Wilson's distinguished career after his Roman visit, see "Wilson, Sir Robert Thomas (1777–1849)," in *Dictionary of National Biography*, 21:597–602.

19. Sardou, *La Tosca*, III, iii.

20. Stark, *Letters from Italy*, 263–90.

21. See, for example, the disaster between Bologna and Ferrara described in letter viii, De Brosses, *Lettres familières*, 60.

22. Richard, *Nouveau Guide du voyageur en Italie*, 1829 (one of the many reprints of this popular guide).

23. Sardou's Floria, a little optimistic, says, "With the post horses we can find along the way we can be in Civitavecchia in four hours." *La Tosca*, V, v.

24. Grancourt, 15–17.

25. See chapter 5 for the place of these "galley slaves" in the Roman legal system. See also Gross, *Rome*, 230.

26. Galimberti, 17 June 1800.

27. Ibid., 17 and 18 June 1800.

28. Ibid., 18 June 1800.

29. Stendhal [Henri Beyle], *Promenades dans Rome* (1829), republished as *A Roman Journal*, ed. and trans. Chevalier. Stendhal actually visited Rome only briefly, in 1811, and wrote his famous guidebook years later, without leaving Paris. Sardou owned a first edition of *Promenades*

dans Rome, and borrowed heavily from it, for example the fête at the Farnese palace in Act II.

30. *Tosca*, III. Paying for favors of this sort was a normal part of prison life in this period. Prisoners also had to make arrangements to pay for their food, clothing, and furniture.

31. *Tosca*, III.

32. André Coeuroy thus describes the C♯ to F♯ interval at III, 196–97, comparing it with a similar interval at the start of "Vesti la giubba." Coeuroy, *La Tosca di Puccini*, 115.

33. Döhring, "Musikalischer Realismus in Puccinis *Tosca*," 249–96.

34. In October 1899 Puccini, writing to Giulio Ricordi in defense of his Act III, complained the "the librettists didn't know how to give me anything (I speak of the end) good, and above all, true; it was always academic, academic, and the usual *sbrodolature amorose*" (amorous slobberings), Gara, no. 209, 179.

35. Verdi was reportedly touched by the text of Cavaradossi's last letter, a text Puccini rejected in favor of the sensual verses of "E lucevan le stelle." Another intrusion of patriotic fervor was the "Latin hymn." This also disappeared, except for a few words that close the final love scene. See below.

36. The early draft for the aria:

> Cav: *E lucevan le stelle,*
> *E olezzavano l'erbe*
> *A cigolava l'uscio del giardino*
> *Ed il suo passo lieve*
> *Mordea la rena. Entrava*
> *Fragrante ella e cadea*
> *Nelle mie braccia . . . e mi narrava tutta*
> *La sua giornata e di me s'inchiedea*
> *(. . .) Più dolce concerto*
> *Sua volubile impero.*
> *Mentr'io sciogliea dai veli*
> *La sua beltà. Ciò avvenne*
> *E fu ieri e per sempre*
> *La dolce ora è fuggita*
> *E muoio disperato*
> *E non ho amato mai tanto la vita.*

Giacosa's papers, found in the Archivio Familiare Giuseppe Giacosa. Quoted by Burton, 503. The version in the first published libretto in 1899 retained the "lovers' conversation" phrases, inserting after "mi cadea fra le braccia" the words: "e mi narrava / di sé; di me chidea / con volubile impero." All of these conversational references were eventually stripped away.

37. Described in Ricci, *Puccini interprete di sé stesso*, 89–90. Giacosa was given the task of writing new words for the aria, as it now stands.

38. Sardou, *La Tosca*, V, second tableau, scene i.

39. Girardi describes this music as a "thoroughly modern kaleidoscope of emotions, primary among them the yearning for consolation." Girardi, 190.

40. There is nothing in Sardou remotely comparable to Tosca's account of the killing in "Il tuo sangue e il mio amore" (Your blood and my love).

41. Mario indicates in Act I of the opera that Floria, a believer, keeps nothing from her confessor ("ma credente al confessor nulla tiene celato"), but she may well have become more cautious by the morning of 18 June.

42. Gara, nos. 208 and 209, 177–80.

43. Giulio Ricordi to Puccini, 10 October 1899. Gara, no. 208, 176–78. Although many commentators have assumed that the self-borrowing is situated at the arioso "O dolci mani," Girardi has identified it as coming later in the same scene, at the start of the sonnet, "Amaro sol per te."

The quote is from a segment of Act IV of *Edgar*, which has the same accompaniment but a different melody. The original words are perhaps not irrelevant to the subtext to Cavaradossi's thoughts at this point of the opera, when he tells Tosca that loving her has been and will remain the only thing that gives his life meaning. Edgar's words are: "Ah, ne' tuoi baci io voglio tutto dimenticar" (Ah, in your kisses I want to forget everything). See Girardi, 159, n. 15. See also Atlas, "Puccini's *Tosca*: A New Point of View," 266–67, n. 41.

44. Family archive of Giuseppe Giacosa, cited by Burton, 504–05:

> TOSCA: *Senti.*
> CAV: *No. Voglio leggere un'altra*
> *volta questo foglio — Scarpia ha fatto grazia*
> *a quel prezzo?*

and

> TOSCA: *Ma prima devi piegarti a una lugubre*
> *commedia.*

and

> TOSCA: *L'ordine ne intesi chiaro*
> *Scarpia ne [illegible] Me presente*
> *al Spoletta. Convien che il Santo Ufficio*
> *ti veda morto.*
> *Ei deve riguardare il tuo supplizio*
> *Dato a Spoletta di curar segretamente*
> *che l'armi sian cariche a salva*
> *Ognun ti deve creder morto.*

and

> TOSCA: *Trarci all'aperto . . .*
> CAV: *Sì, fuggire da questa*
> *città funesta!*
> TOSCA: *Noleggeremo ad Ostia una tartana*
> *e via pel gran libero mar.*
> CAV: *Ti vedo.*
> *Ti parlo e non è inganno. Oh come vile*
> *il tuo pensier me facea.*
> TOSCA: *Chi si duole*
> *In terra più? Senti effluvio di rose*
> *Non ti par che le cose*
> *Sorridan tutte innamorate al sole?*
> CAV: *Vago pur nell'angoscia era il tuo viso.*
> (*Amaro a ricordar mi era il tuo viso.*)

45. *Tosca*, III:

> TOSCA: *Senti . . . l'ora è vicina; io già raccolsi*
> (*mostrando la borsa*)
> *oro e gioielli . . . una vettura è pronta.*
> *Ma prima . . . ridi amor . . . prima sarai*
> *fucilato — per finta — ad armi scariche . . . —*
> *Simulato supplizio. Al colpo . . . cadi.*
> *I soldati sen vanno . . . — e noi siam salvi!*
> *E noi siam salvi . . .*
> *Poscia a Civitavecchia . . . una tartana . . .*
> *e via pel mar!*

> CAV: *Liberi!*
> TOSCA: *Liberi!*
>   CAV: *Via pel mar!*
> TOSCA: *Chi si duole*
>   *in terra più? Senti effluvi di rose? . . .*
>   *Non ti par che le cose*
>   *aspettan tutte innamorate il sole? . . .*

46. I am indebted to Arthur Groos for this insight. We know that Puccini, a keen sportsman who lived on the lakeshore at Torre del Lago, was sensitive to this sort of motion.

47. "I could never understand why tenors generally sing most of the third act in tones of happiness and hope. After studying the part carefully, I decided to break with tradition and interpret the music in the way that I was fully convinced that Puccini intended. Floria brings Mario the safe conduct and tells him that he is free to leave the prison; but—and here my interpretation begins to diverge—Mario is not convinced. He can't succeed in bringing himself to believe that happiness is near; Floria, he thinks, must be the victim of a cruel trick. He therefore tries to cheer her up with hopeful words, but during the whole time, until the end, he is certain that these are their last moments together on earth, and that he is about to die. At no time does he succeed in smiling. To me this interpretation seems absolutely logical; at least in my judgement it is permissible." Gigli, *Memoirs*, 71. See also Gobbi, in Carner, *Tosca*, 86.

48. Fortunati, 29 February 1798: ". . . gli fecero mettere tutti in ginocchio uno a canto l'altro, con la faccia voltata alla detta portiera; e mentre uno dei confortatori andava sostandosi, dandogli l'ultima benedizione, immediatamente arrivò la scarica, e così resero l'anima al Sommo Creatore. Uno dei suddetti fucilati non fu colpito in veruna maniera, accadendo in terra prima che arrivasse il colpo. Sentendo il Med.o che il tutto era terminato, si alzò in ginocchioni nuovamente strillando grazie; ma si resero sordi tutti, non dandogli udienza alcuna, e venuti sollecitamente altri cinque soldati Francesi, gli scaricarono altri cinque colpi, e così terminò anche lui di vivere." (They made them all kneel one beside the other, with their faces turned to the gate; and then while one of the comforters went about helping them and giving them the last blessing, the shot was fired and so they gave up their souls to the Supreme Creator. One of the men to be shot was in fact not hurt at all, falling to the ground before the shot was fired. When he heard that it was all over, he got back up on his knees screaming for mercy; but all were as though deaf and no one paid the least attention; then five more French soldiers quickly arrived, firing five more shots into him, and so even he died.)

49. Fifteen years later when Joachim Murat, Napoleon's brother-in-law and sometime king of Naples, was executed by an Italian firing squad, he asked that they not shoot him in the face. He did not want to distress his family, and besides, he was a vain man. His request was not honored.

50. *Tosca*, in the Settings and Times of *Tosca*, 1992.

51. *Tosca*, III:

> CAV: Dying was bitter for me only because of you;
>   from you my life derives every splendor,
>   the joy and desire of my being
>   spring from you, as heat from the flame.
>   The blazing of the skies and their loss of color
>   I will see in your revealing eyes,
>   and the beauty of the most marvelous things
>   will have voice and color only through you.
> TOSCA: Love which knew how to save your life
>   will be our guide on earth, our pilot on the sea
>   and will make the world lovely to behold.
>   Until, united in the heavenly spheres,

> we will wander, as high above the sea
> the light clouds as the sun sets.

52. Eduardo Rescigno takes this to indicate that Puccini meant that Cavaradossi is aware of the truth of his situation but is trying to comfort Tosca. Rescigno, *Giacomo Puccini: Tosca*, 99.

53. Bernard Williams makes a convincing case for this interpretation in "Manifest Artifice," an essay on the limits of Puccini's stagecraft.

54. *Tosca*, III. Here the librettists have achieved an elegant triple reference to the arts and the love that define these two characters.

55. First published libretto, 1899:

> Tosca: *La patria è là dove amor ci conduce.*
>   Cav: *Per tutto troverem l'orme latine*
>   *e il fantasma di Roma.*
> Tosca: *E s'io ti veda*
>   *memorando guardar lungi ne' cieli,*
>   *Gli occhi ti chiuderò con mille baci*
>   *e mille ti dirò nomi d'amor.*

56. Family archive of Giuseppe Giacosa, cited by Burton, 505–06:

> O Mario non ti sembra
> Che ci amiamo la prima
> volta
>
> . . .
>
> Dimmi se ti rimembra
> del nostro amor passato
>
> . . .
>
> Mario mio non ti sembra
> che amore oggi sia nato?
> Se alcun che ti rimembra
> del gaio tempo andato
> non ti senti come bene
> scorrea
>
> . . .
>
> Mario Mario e sol ier'
> ero del male ignara.
> Quante cose è impara
>
> . . .
>
> Senti, fu vero amore
> il nostro infino a ieri?
> Mai così saldi e fieri.

57. Valentino had come to Rome as an agent of Maria Carolina who, according to Belli, was "extremely fond of him." See Cretoni, *Roma giacobina*, 293–339. Cretoni bases his account on the official Roman Republican newspaper, the *Monitore*, as well as on diarists such as Sala and Galimberti, the contemporary account of Count Alessandro Verri, and on G. G. Belli, *Mia vita non terminata*, a youthful autobiography of the Roman popular poet.

58. Fortunati, 30 December 1798.

59. "Circa le 17 escì dal castello S Angiolo preceduto dalla Banda, in mezzo in molto Truppa Sedentaria, e seguito da un picchetto di Cavalleria Francese. Giunto su la Piazza di Monte Citorio si aprì il quadrato di Truppa Sedentaria, ed esso vi entrò per subire il supplizio. Allora i Patriotti gli diedero l'urlo gridando: 'Morte al Tiranno.' Esso era intrepidissimo, e senza benda. S'inginocchiò, si levò il capello da se stesso, e si preparò al colpo tenendo in mano un Crocifisso.

Alla prima scarica cadde colpito nel fronte, e gli fu replicata la seconda in terra." Galimberti, 30 December 1798.

60. Fortunati, 30 December 1798: "ma immediatemente lo condussero in una barella nella Chiesa degl'Orfani, ove con la bajonette lo finirono di ammazzare."

61. The confraternity of St John the Beheaded accompanied and supported men condemned to death. This, along with feeding the hungry, caring for the sick, providing dowries for poor girls, and other social interventions, was considered an important corporeal act of mercy. Their records are kept at the State Archives of Rome, I-Ras, *Confraternità di San Giovanni Decollato*. The 1795 execution of the deserter Arrisa or Avvisa is recorded in Libro 2do 116 Busta 11.

62. Carner, *Puccini, a Critical Biography*, 377.

63. Sardou, in one conversation with Puccini, suggested that Tosca "swoon and die like a fluttering bird" (Gara, no. 200, 172). And the Davenport production of *La Tosca* in New York in 1889 was modified after the first performances to eliminate the suicide. Odell, *Annals of the New York Stage*, 14 (1888–89): 26.

64. Quoted by Checchi, "Giacomo Puccini," 471.

65. Sardou, *La Tosca*, IV, iv.

66. Ibid., V, tableau ii.

67. Ibid.

68. *Tosca*, III, 364. Rescigno, *Giacomo Puccini: Tosca*, 98, favors this interpretation.

69. Kerman loathed the entire opera, and dismissed it—in probably the most famous operatic critique of all—as a "shabby little shocker." Kerman, *Opera as Drama*, 19.

70. Carner, *Tosca*, 115–16.

71. This is discussed by Atlas, "Puccini's *Tosca*," 269–70, n. 51.

72. Plaut, *Grand Opera*, 245–46.

73. Clément, *L'Opéra ou la défaite des femmes*, 52–53.

74. Girardi, 191.

75. Even sympathetic analysts tend to agree that the third act does not mesh well with the two preceding acts. Atlas argues that the last part of the opera went offtrack at the point at which Puccini borrowed his own music from *Edgar*, that is, at "Amaro sol per te." See Atlas, "Puccini's *Tosca*," 266–67.

76. Osborne, *Complete Operas of Puccini*, 143, finds the ending "wildly inappropriate"; Carner, *Puccini*, 377–78, and Hughes, *Famous Puccini Operas*, 109, regret Puccini's choice and suggest that the Scarpia/Tyranny motif would have been better.

Appendix 2

1. Deborah Burton, who had access to all of these collections and also to a set of papers at the Puccini library at Torre del Lago and a privately held collection of Giuseppe Giacosa's papers, has included a scene-by-scene comparison of the various sources in her dissertation, 463–516.

2. *Tosca, melodramma in tre atti di V. Sardou — L. Illica — G. Giacosa. Musica di G Puccini* (Milan: G. Ricordi and Co., 1899).

3. As a culmination of the torture scene, Sardou suggested that Tosca should collapse, giving Scarpia the opportunity to signal for the torture to begin again. The "horrible scream" that results finally forces her to give the information demanded. ("Scarpia, profittando dell'accasciamento di Tosca, va presso la camera della tortura e fa cenno di ricominciare il supplizio—un grido orribile si fa udire.") This is stated in a letter from Ricordi to Sardou, 3 November 1899, Copialettere, I-Mr, but the idea seems to have been suggested earlier, as Puccini appears to refer to it in his letter of July, 1898, Gara no. 193, 167.

4. Puccini to Illica, 30 January 1897, and summer, 1897, Fondo Illica, Biblioteca Passerini-Landi, and Burton, 437.

5. "Entrata Angelotti, e via
   " Sagrestano
   " Cavaradossi
Prima rapida intervista Angelotti con Mario—paniere portato nella cappella alla chiamata di Tosca.
Duetto Tosca Mario—indicare ritorno di Tosca per pranzare insieme alle 3—Lascia Mario per disporsi pel concerto a corte[.] qualche verso di più a Mario
Seconda scena Angelotti Cavaradossi; inserire descrizione pozzo antico sicuro nascondiglio, colpo di cannone; emozione dei due, anche perché Mario teme ritorno Sagrestano: non v'è più esitazione: Mario deve accompagnare il fuggitivo [a few words, struck out and illegible except for "certo" and "cappella"]
Sagrestano accenna al colpo di cannone, cercando anche Mario segue scena come prima.
Entrata di Scarpia: scena col sagrestano, gran sorpresa ritrovando cesto vuoto nella cappella: sicuro indizio per Scarpia,—ecc.
Entra Tosca: scenetta col sagrestano, dispetto per non trovare Mario: piccola gelosia: Scarpia interviene—ventaglio ecc.—ecc.
Monologo ultimo = meno astrologo: ma occorrono non minori parole, frammezzate dal *Te Deum* detto da Scarpia—gli ultimi versi vanno bene." US-NYpl, draft for the libretto of *Tosca*.
   6. Specht, 208.

Appendix 3

1. A detailed account of the newly discovered Colleretto working papers for *Tosca*, including the dramatically different Act III text, will be found in English in *Acts of the Tosca 2000 Conference*, forthcoming from the University of Rochester Press. Pier Luigi Gillio has also written about these papers in "La gestazione del libretto di *Tosca* e passi inediti della prima stesura" in *Tosca* (Rome: Teatro dell'Opera di Roma, 2000), 35–42; and "Il terzo atto di *Tosca* nella prima stesura del libretto: Documenti inediti" in the program booklet, *Tosca* (Milan: Teatro alla Scala, 2000), 66–83.

2. **Tosca 2000** was organized in the United States by Puccini scholars Deborah Burton and Susan Vandiver Nicassio, and in Italy by Guido Salvetti, director of the Conservatorio di Musica "G. Verdi" in Milan and Agostino Ziino of the Università degli Studi "Tor Vergata" in Rome.

3. At the start of the musical phrase from Act I, identified with the love between Tosca and Cavaradossi, that is how he addresses her: "Mia vita."

4. This text was apparently meant to be set to something like a gondolier's song; it reappears in Tosca's final mad scene.

5. This is a much more reasonable time for dawn if the librettists were sticking to "old time," but they gave up on this idea in favor of "the fourth hour," or 4:00 A.M. modern time.

6. This phrase – "Your eyes are laughing" – clearly indicates that Cavaradossi is treating the execution as a joke; Puccini not only shortened this four-line comment, but changed it to the much more ambiguous, "Don't laugh!" (*Non ridere!*).

7. Money to pay for the Masses; for a possible motive, see page 218.

Bibliography

MANUSCRIPT SOURCES

Rome

Archivio Castel Sant'Angelo. I. Fowell Buxton. "Estratto di rapporto à S. Emm. Rev. Card. Tosi sulle prigioni e luoghi di condanna." Visitati da I. Fowell Buxton nel mese di Gennaio 1828.

———. Giovanni Lazzarini. "Ambienti di Castel S. Angelo nel 1828 dal rapporto di una ispezione passata dal tenente colonello G. Lazzarini del 2da battaglione leggera." XIII Roma, CAS 855.

———. Cerasoli. Storia del Castel Sant'Angelo.

Archivio di Stato di Roma [I-Ras]. Arciconfraternità di San Giovanni Decollato, 1497–1870, Busta 11 (1772–1810).

———. Arciconfraternità di San Giovanni Decollato, Giustiziati 1772–1810, Busta 2.

———. Camerale III, Teatri, Busta 2140

———. Editi e Bandi 416, Editto sopra i teatri, 2 January 1789

———. Giunta di Governo 1799–1800, Busta 10.

———. Giunta di Governo 2, Busta 1, fasc. 13.

———. Giunta di Stato 1799–1800, Busta 2, cases 21, 22, and 31; and Busta 8, fasc. 84.

———. Istituzioni di beneficienza e di istruzione, Buste 2056–62 and 2070–74.

———. Miscellanea di carte politiche riservate, Busta 27, fasc. 922.

———. Soldatesche e galere 3a Num., Busta 90.

———. Teatini, 2140: Chiesa, arredi sacri, libri 1559–1864; 2145/120: Affari teologici, 1625–1849; 2160/52: Affari personali, 1616–1840; 2169: Giustificazioni diverse, 1795–1807; 2142/105: Funzioni Sac. 1786–1869; 2142/107: Introito sacrestia 1780–1806; B. 2104/2: 1800 (circa) Indice dell'Archivio di S. Andrea della Valle; Reg. 2203: Libro Mastro della Casa de RR PP Teatini di Sant'Andrea della Valle, 1779–1801.

Biblioteca Apostolica Vaticana [I-Rvat]. Francesco Fortunati. "Avvenimenti sotto il pontificato di Pio VI, dall'anno 1775 al 1800." MSS Vat. lat. 10730–10731.

———. Scritte e manoscritte, Monsigr. F. Gilii.

———. Pier Leone Ghezzi, "Il mondo nuovo," Vat. lat. 3118.

———. "Regole del conservatorio pio eretto dalla Santità di Nostro Signore Papa Pio Sesto," Roma, mdcclxvi.

Biblioteca Casanatense [I-Rca]. Memorie del cavalier Leone Ghezzi scritte da lui medesimo da gennaio 1731 a luglio 1734. MS 3765.

———. Raccolte di varie satire o pasquinate pubblicate in Roma in diversi tempi e circostanze. MS 3934.

Biblioteca Nazionale [I-Rn]. Antonio Galimberti. "Memorie dell'occupazione francese in Roma dal 1798 alla fine del 1802." Manuscript diary, consisting of two volumes and 1,055 pages, MSS 44 and 45 in the Victor Emanuel collection.

Museo di Roma [I-Rmr]. Caricatures of Giuseppe Barberi. Legato XVIII and XIX, Mat. 3266
     and 3267.

London

British Museum [GB-Lbm]. Department of Prints and Drawings, 197 [P. L. Ghezzi].

Milan

Archivio Ricordi [I-Mr]. *Tosca.* Bozzetto Atto I, II. Scene designs by Salvadori.
———. Giuseppe Canori. *Tosca*, description of Te Deum procession.
———. Copialettere, 1896–1900.
———. *Figurini* for *Tosca*; costumes and sets by Hohenstein and Salvadori.
———. "Minute, libretto *Tosca.*" No. f43/1, Divisione [S] P. P Catalogo 1, Sezione d. Draft
     libretto.
———. *Tosca.* Puccini's autograph score.

New York

Museum of the City of New York, manuscript promptbook of *La Tosca*, 115 irregularly
     paginated leaves, 1888.
New York Public Library [US-NYp]. "Drafts for the libretto of Puccini's *Tosca*, Act One,"
     JOB 86-2.
———. "A Flatbush Tosca: or, Fear the Painted Devil." Typescript, Performing Arts collec-
     tion, NCOF+ 79-992.
———. *Nadjezda: A Modern Tragedy in a Prologue and Three Acts*, by Maurice Barrymore
     (New York, 1884), NCOF+.

SECONDARY LITERATURE

Abbate, Carolyn. *Unsung Voices: Opera and Musical Narrative in the Nineteenth Century.*
     Princeton Studies in Opera. Princeton: Princeton University Press, 1991.
Acton, Harold. *The Bourbons of Naples (1734–1825).* London: Methuen, 1956.
———, and Mario Mitchell. *The Last Bourbons of Naples (1825–1861).* New York: St. Martin's
     Press, 1962.
Adami, Giuseppe. *Letters of Giacomo Puccini: Mainly Connected with the Composition and
     Production of his Operas.* Translated by Ena Makin. New York: Vienna House, 1973.
     Originally published as *Giacomo Puccini: Epistolario* (Milan, 1928).
Ademollo, Alessandro. *Bibliografia della cronistoria teatrale italiana.* Milan: Ricordi, n.d.
———. "Le giustizie a Roma dal 1674 al 1739 e dal 1796 al 1840." Rome: Forzani, 1881.
———. *Il carnevale di Roma nel secolo XVIII.* Roma: Sommaruga, 1883.
Agresta, Maria Francesca. "Il teatro della Pace di Roma." *Studi romani* 31:2 (April–June 1983):
     149–160.
Alaux, Jean-Paul. *L'Académie de France à Rome: Ses directeurs, ses pensionnaires.* Paris:
     Duchartre, 1933.
Algarotti, Francesco. *Essay on Opera.* London, 1762. Translation of *Saggio sopra l'opera in
     musica* (1755).
Alliacci, A. R. "All'Argentina qualche cosa di nuovo." *Capitolium* (Rome) 9–10 (1964): 154–55.
Amante, Bruno. *Fra Diavolo e il suo tempo (1796–1806).* Naples, 1904. Repr. Naples: A.B.E.,
     1974.
Andrieux, Maurice. *Daily Life in Papal Rome in the Eighteenth Century.* Translated by Mary
     Fitton. New York: Macmillan, 1969. Translation of *La Vie quotidienne dans la Rome
     pontificale* (1962).
The Angel and Rome. Rome: Palombi, 1987. Originally published as *L'Angelo e la città.* Cata-

logue of an exhibition at Castel Sant'Angelo, 29 September–29 November 1987. Ministro per i Beni Culturali e Ambientali. Rome: Palombi, 1987.

Angeli, Diego. *Storia romana di trent'anni.* Rome: Garzanti, 1945.

Angenot, Marc. *1889: Un état du discours social.* Longueil, Quebec: Le Préamble, 1989.

Antolini, Bianca Maria, Arnaldo Morelli, and Vera Vita Spagnuolo, eds. *La musica a Roma attraverso le fonti d'archivio: Atti del Convegno internazionale, Roma 4–7 giugno.* Rome: Libreria Musicale Italiana, 1992.

Appleton, William S. "The Stop and Go Talent of Puccini." *Opera News* (29 Dec. 1973 and 5 Jan. 1974): 12–16.

Arblaster, Anthony. *Viva la Libertà: Politics in Opera.* London and New York: Verso, 1992.

Archenholz, Johann Wilhelm von. *A Picture of Italy Translated from the Original German of W. de A., Formerly a Captain in the Prussian Service, by Joseph Trapp, A.M.* Dublin, Printed by W. Corbet, for P. Byrne, J. Moore, etc., 1791, trans. of *England und Italien* (1785).

Argan, Giulio Carlo. *Antonio Canova.* Rome: Bulzoni, 1969.

Argument of the Play of La Tosca: Drama in Five Acts by Victorien Sardou, as Presented by Madame Sarah Bernhardt and her Powerful Company by Arrangement with Fanny Davenport. New York: F. Rullman, 1891.

Armellini, Mariano. *Le chiese di Roma dal secolo iv al xix.* Rome: Edizioni del Pasquino, 1982. Repr. of 2d ed., 1891.

Arnault, Antoine-Vincent. *Mémoires d'un sexagénaire.* 4 vols. Paris: 1833.

Arnold, Denis. "Music at the Mendicanti in the Eighteenth Century." *Music and Letters* 65 (1984): 345–56.

———. "Orphans and Ladies: The Venetian Conservatories (1690–1797)." *Proceedings of the Royal Musical Association* 89 (1962–63): 31–47.

Arundell, Dennis. "'Tosca' Re-Studied." *Opera* (London) 11 (1960): 262–65.

Ashbrook, William. *The Operas of Puccini.* 1968. Repr. Ithaca: Cornell University Press, 1985.

———. "Perspectives on an Aria: A Message of Love (*Recondita armonia*)." *Opera News* (16 Dec. 1978): 26–27.

———. "Perspectives on an Aria: *E lucevan le stelle.*" *Opera News* (19 Jan. 1980): 26–27.

———. "Perspectives on an Aria: *Vissi d'arte.*" *Opera News* (15 Dec. 1981): 49.

———. "Some Comments on Puccini's Sense of Theater." In *Critica Pucciniana*, 9–15. Lucca: Comitato Nazionale per le Onoranze a Giacomo Puccini, 1976.

Atlas, Allan W. "Puccini's *Tosca*: A New Point of View." In *The Creative Process.* Studies in the History of Music 3, 247–73. New York: Broude Brothers, 1992.

Bacchelli, Riccardo, and Roberto Longhi. *Teatro e immagini del Settecento italiano.* Turin: Edizioni Radio italiana, 1953.

Balbi de Caro, Silvana, and Luigi Londei. *Moneta pontificia: Da Innocenzo X a Gregorio XVI.* Rome: Edizioni Quasar, 1984.

Baldick, Robert. *The Memoires of the Chevalier d'Eon.* Translated by Antonia White. London: Anthony Blond, 1970.

Bandini, Carlo. *Roma al tramonto del Settecento (scorci di ambiente).* Naples: Sandron, 1922.

———. *Roma e la nobiltà romana nel tramonto del secolo XVIII.* Città di Castello: Lapi, 1914.

———. *Roma nel Settecento.* Rome: Treves, 1927.

Basso, Alberto. *L'età di Bach e di Haendel.* Storia della Musica 5. Turin: EDT, 1976.

Bauman, Thomas. "The Society of La Fenice and its First Impresarios." *Journal of the American Musicological Society* 39 (1986): 332–54.

Beccaria, Cesare. *On Crimes and Punishments.* Translated by Henry Paolucci. New York: Macmillan, 1963. Originally published as *Delle delitte e delle pene* (1764).

Bellettin, Athos. "La popolazione italiana dall'inizio dell'era volgare ai giorni nostri: valutazioni e tendenze." *Storia d'Italia* 5: *I documenti*, 489–536. Turin: Einaudi, 1973.

Belli, Giuseppe Gioachino. *Mia vita non terminata.* Ed. L. Jannattoni. Rome, 1959.

Benedetti, L. *Dario.* In David Silvagni, *La corte ponteficia e la società romana nei secoli XVIII e XIX.*

Berdes, Jane. "The Venetian Conservatories: A Bibliographic Overview." Paper read at the American Musicological Society, Capital Chapter meeting, UM-BC, 16 April 1983.

———. *Women Musicians in Venice: Musical Foundations 1525–1855.* Oxford and New York: Clarendon Press and Oxford University Press, 1993.

Berlinguer, Luigi, and Floriana Colao, eds. *Criminalità e società in età moderna.* Vol. 12 of "La Leopoldina": Criminalità e giustizia criminale nelle riforme del Settecento europeo. Milan: Giuffré, 1991.

Bernardoni, Virgilio, ed. *Puccini.* Bologna: Il Mulino, 1996.

Biagi-Ravenni, Gabriella. *La famiglia Puccini: Una tradizione, Lucca, la musica.* Museo teatrale alla Scala, Milano, 5 dicembre 1992. Catalogue of an exhibit at Lucca, February 1993. Milan: Museo Teatrale alla Scala/Istituto di Studi Pucciniani, 1993.

———, and Carolyn Gianturco. "The Tasche of Lucca: 150 Years of Political Serenatas." *Proceedings of the Royal Musical Association* 3 (1984–1985): 45–56.

Bianconi, Lorenzo, and Renato Bossa, eds. *Musica e cultura a Napoli dal XV al XIX secolo.* Quaderni della Rivista Italiana di Musicologia. Florence: Olschki, 1983.

——— and Giorgio Pestelli, eds. *Storia dell'opera italiana.* 6 vols. Turin: EDT/Musica, 1987– . Forthcoming in English translation: Chicago: University of Chicago Press.

Biografia degli italiani illustri nelle scienze, lettere ed arti del secolo XVIII. Venice: Tipografia di Alvisopoli, 1838.

Boime, Albert. *Art in an Age of Revolution, 1750–1800.* A Social History of Modern Art 1. Chicago: University of Chicago Press, 1987.

Bokenkotter, Thomas. *A Concise History of the Catholic Church.* New York: Doubleday, 1979.

Bonaccorsi, Alfredo. *Giacomo Puccini e i suoi antenati musicali.* Milan: Curci, 1950.

Boschi, Daniele. "I reati contro la persona a Roma alla metà del Settecento." *Archivio della Società Romana di Storia Patria* 112 (1989): 453–480.

Botta, Carlo. *Storia d'Italia dal 1789 al 1811.* Paris: P. Dufart, 1824.

Bragaglia, Anton G. *Le maschere romane.* n.p.: Colombo, 1947.

Brett, Richard, and John Potter. "Role-Playing: Tosca as Woman and Actress." *Opera News* (1 Jan. 1977): 18–20.

Broglie, Raoul de. *Le Palais Farnèse, ambassade de France.* Paris: Lefebvre, 1953.

Brookner, Anita. *Jacques-Louis David.* New York: Harper and Rowe, 1980.

Bryson, Norman. *Word and Image: French Painting of the Ancien Régime.* Cambridge: Cambridge University Press, 1981.

Buccellato, Luciana, and Fiorella Trapani. *Il teatro a Roma nel Settecento.* Rome: Istituto della Enciclopedia Italiana, 1988.

Burton, Deborah. "An Analysis of Puccini's *Tosca:* A Heuristic Approach to the Unifying Elements of the Opera." Ph.D. diss., University of Michigan, 1995. UMI: Ann Arbor, Michigan, 1995.

———. "The Creation of *Tosca:* Toward a Clearer View." *Opera Quarterly* 12/3 (1996), 27–34.

———. "The Real Scarpia: Historical Studies for *Tosca.*" *The Opera Quarterly* 10 (Winter 1993–94): 67–86.

———. "Remote Regions and Puccini's Motivic Territory." Paper read at the Annual Meetings of the American Musicological Society and Society for Music Theory, New York City, 1995.

———. "A Select Bibliography of Articles and Dissertations about Puccini and his Operas." In *The Puccini Companion,* ed. William Weaver and Simonetta Puccini, 327–34. New York: Norton, 1994.

Bustico, Guido. *Bibliografia delle storie e delle cronistorie dei teatri d'Italia*. Milan: Bollettino bibliografico musicale, 1929.

Buzzelli Serafini, Maria Consilia. "La reazione del 1799 a Roma: I processi della Giunta di Stato," *Archivio della Società Romana di Storia Patria* 91 (3d ser., no. 23), 137–211. Rome: Biblioteca Vallicelliana, 1969.

Cagli, Bruno, ed. *Le Muse galanti: La musica a Roma nel Settecento*. Rome: Istituto della Enciclopedia Italiana, 1985.

———. "Produzione musicale e governo pontificio." In *Le Muse galanti*, ed. Cagli, 11–22.

Cairo, Laura. "Luoghi scenici nella Roma del Settecento." In *Orfeo in Arcadia: Studi sul teatro a Roma nel Settecento*, ed. Giorgio Petrocchi, 273–87. Rome: Istituto della Enciclopedia Italiana, 1984.

———, and Paolo Quilico. *Biblioteca teatrale dal '500 al '700: La raccolta della Biblioteca Casanatense*. Rome: Bulzoni, 1981.

Cajani, N. "Giustizia e criminalità nella Roma del Settecento." In *Ricerche sulla città del Settecento*, ed. V. E. Giuntella, 263–312. Rome: Edizioni Ricerche, 1978.

———. "Pena di morte e tortura a Roma nel '700." In *Atti del Convegno Internazionale "La Leopoldina" Siena 2–6 December 1986*, ed. Luigi Berlinguer and Floriana Colao, 517–47. Milan: Giuffrè, 1991.

Calvi, Emilio. "Il teatro popolare romanesco del Settecento." *L'Italia moderna* 6 (1908): 582–600.

Cametti, Alberto. "Il teatro di Tordinona." *Capitolium* 2 (1926–27): 110–15.

———. *Il teatro Tordinona poi di Apollo*. Tivoli: A. Chicca, 1938.

Cantimori, Delio, and Renzo de Felice. *Giacobini italiani*. Bari: Laterza, 1964.

Capriolo, Paola. *Vissi d'amore*. Milan: Bompiani, 1992.

Cardilli, Luisa, ed. *Feste e spettacoli nelle piazze romane: Mostra antologica a cura dell'Istituto Poligrafico e Zecca dello Stato e dell'Assessorato alla Cultura del Comune di Roma*. Rome: Libreria dello Stato, 1990.

Cardoni, Gian Lorenzo. "Il Te Deum de' Calabresi." In Giustino Fortunato, *I Napoletani del 1799*. Florence: Barbèra, 1884. Repr. Cosenza: Brenner, 1988.

Carner, Mosco. *Puccini, a Critical Biography*. New York: Knopf, 1959.

———. *Giacomo Puccini's "Tosca"*. Cambridge Opera Handbooks. Cambridge: Cambridge University Press, 1985.

Carpanetto, Dino, and Giuseppe Ricuperati. *Italy in the Age of Reason 1685–1789*. New York and London: Longman, 1987.

Casini, Claudio. *Giacomo Puccini*. Turin: UTET, 1978.

Casini, T. "Il parlamento della Repubblica Romana." *Rassegna storica del Risorgimento* 3 (1916): 250 et seq.

Castel, Nico. *The Complete Puccini Libretti*. Geneseo, N.Y.: Layerle, 1993–94.

Castelvecchi, Stefano. "From *Nina* to *Nina*: Psychodrama, Absorption, and Sentiment in the 1780s." *Cambridge Opera Journal* 8:2 (1996): 91–112.

Catalogue de la Bibliothèque de feu de M. Victorien Sardou. (Paris: 1909–10).

Cates, Gary. *Monsieur d'Eon Is a Woman: A Tale of Political Intrigue and Sexual Masquerade*. New York: Basic Books, 1995.

Cavalli, Alberto. "I frammenti pucciniani di Celle." In *Critica Pucciniana*, 16–34. Lucca: Nuova Grafica Lucchese, 1976.

Cazzato, Vincenzo, Marcello Fagiolo, and Maria Adriana Giusti, eds. *Teatri di Verzura: La scena del giardino dal Barocco al Novecento*. Florence: Edifir, 1993.

Cecchini, Riccardo. *Giacomo Puccini: Lettere inedite ad Alfredo Vandini*. Lucca: Edizioni V. Press, 1994.

Celletti, Rodolfo. "I cantanti a Roma nel XVIII secolo." In *Le Muse galanti*, ed. Cagli, 101–7.

Chadwick, Owen. *The Popes and the European Revolution*. Oxford: Clarendon Press, 1981.

Checchi, Eugenio. "Giacomo Puccini." *Nuova antologia* 72:23 (1 Dec. 1897): 470–81.

Chiusano, Italo, Marcello Fagiolo, and Elisabeth J. Garms. *Roma dei grandi viaggiatori*. Rome: Edizione Abete, 1987.

Clark, Anthony M. *Studies in Eighteenth-Century Roman Painting*, ed. Edgar Peters Bowran. Washington, D.C.: Decatur House Press, 1980.

Clément, Catherine. *L'Opéra ou la défaite des femmes*. Paris: Editions Grasset et Fasquelle, 1979. In English translation as: *Opera, or, the Undoing of Women*, trans. Betsy Wing. Minneapolis: University of Minnesota Press, 1988.

Clementi, F. *Il carnevale romano*. Rome: Rore-Niruf, 1938.

Coeuroy, André. *La Tosca di Puccini: étude historique et critique. Analyse musicale*. Paris: Mellottée, 1922.

Colalucci, Gianluigi. "Report on Restoration." In *The Angel and Rome*, 94–102.

Colini, A. M. "La sistemazione del sepolcro degli Scipioni." *Capitolium* 3 (1927–28): 27–32.

Colletta, Pietro. *Storia del reame di Napoli dal 1734 sino al 1825*. 1834. Repr., Torino: UTET, 1975.

Conrad, Peter. "Passion Play." *Opera News* (30 Mar. 1985): 16–17.

Contardi, Bruno. "The Bronze Angel." In *The Angel and Rome*, 33–54.

Correspondances des directeurs de l'Académie de France à Rome. Paris: Anatole de Montaiglon and J. Guiffrey, 1907. Edited by André Chastel, under the title *Corrispondenza dei Direttori dell'Accademia di Francia a Roma*. 2 vols. Rome: Edizione Dell'Elefante, 1979–84.

Courtin, Michele. *Tosca de Giacomo Puccini*. Paris: Aubier, 1983.

Coyer, Gabriel-François. *Voyages d'Italie et de Hollande*. Paris: Veuve Duchesne, 1775.

Cretoni, Antonio. *Roma giacobina: Storia della repubblica romana del 1798–99*. Istituto di Studi Romani, Edizioni Scientifiche Italiane. Bari: Dedalo, 1971.

Crow, Thomas E. *Emulation: Making Artists for Revolutionary France*. New Haven and London: Yale University Press, 1995.

———. *Painters and Public Life in Eighteenth-Century Paris*. New Haven and London: Yale University Press, 1985.

Csampai, Attila. "Folterkammer und Wohllaut—Puccinis *Tosca* und die Krise der Gesangsoper." In *Giacomo Puccini: Tosca: Texte, Materialien, Kommentare*, ed. Attila Csampai and Dietmar Holland, 9–29. Reinbek bei Hamburg: Rowohlt, 1987.

Culshaw, John. "John Culshaw speaks up for 'Tosca'." *Opera News* (8 Apr. 1978): 18–19.

Cuoco, Vincenzo. *Saggio sulla rivoluzione napoletana del 1799*. Milan: Tipografia di F. Sonzogno di G. Batti, 1801, 1820. Repr. Milan: Rizzoli, 1966.

Dall'Ongaro, Giuseppe. *Castel Sant'Angelo in the History of Rome and the Papacy*. Rome: Romana Società Editrice, 1986.

Darnton, Robert. *The Forbidden Best-Sellers of Pre-Revolutionary France*. New York: Norton, 1995.

———. *The Great Cat Massacre and Other Episodes in French Cultural History*. New York: Random House, 1984.

———. "The High Enlightenment and the Low-Life of Literature in Pre-Revolutionary France." *Past and Present* 51 (1971): 79–103.

———. *Revolution in Print: The Press in France (1775–1800)*. Berkeley: University of California Press, 1989.

David, Jules. *Le Peintre Louis David, 1749–1825: Souvenirs et documents inédits*. Paris: V. Havard, 1880.

De Angelis, Alberto. *La musica a Roma nel secolo XIX*. Rome: Bardi, 1935.

———. *Il teatro Alibert o delle Dame, 1717–1863*. Tivoli: A. Chicca, 1951.

De Benedetti, Elisabetta. *Studi sul Settecento romano*. Rome: Multigrafica, 1988.

De Brosses, Charles. *Lettres familières sur l'Italie en 1739 et 1740*. Paris: Garnier Frères, 1839. Vol. 2.

———. *Roma nel Settecento*. Edited and translated by G. Brigante Colonna. Rome: Eden, 1946.

De Dominicis, Giulia. "I teatri di Roma nell'età di Pio VI." *Archivio della R. Società Romana di Storia Patria* 46 (1923): 49–243.

———. "Roma centro musicale nel Settecento." *Rivista musicale italiana* 30 (1923): 511 et seq.

De Felice, Renzo. *Note e ricerche sugli 'Illuminati' e il misticismo rivoluzionario (1789–1800)*. Storia e letteratura: raccolta di studi e testi, 84. Rome: Edizioni di Storia e Letteratura, 1960.

Del Fiorentino, Dante. *Immortal Bohemian: An Intimate Memoir of Giacomo Puccini*. New York: Prentice-Hall, 1952.

Della Corte, Andrea. *Disegno storico dell'arte musicale*. Turin: G. B. Paravia, 1944.

Dell'Ongaro, Giuseppe. *Fra' Diavolo*. Novara: Istituto Geografico de Agostini, 1985.

Diario ordinario or *Diario di Roma*, 1716–1836. Rome: Chrakas.

Diderot, Denis, and Jean d'Alembert, eds. *Encyclopédie, ou Dictionnaire raisonné des sciences, des arts et des métiers*. 28 vols. Paris: Briasson, 1751–72; six-vol. supplement, 1776–77.

DiGaetani, John Louis. *Puccini the Thinker: The Composer's Intellectual and Dramatic Development*. New York: Peter Lang, 1987.

———. "Puccini's *Tosca* and the Necessity of Agnosticism." *Opera Quarterly* 2:1 (Spring 1984): 76–84.

Di Giacomo, Calvatore. "Paisiello e i suoi contemporanei." *Musica e musicisti* 2 (1905): 762–68.

Divertimento e penitenza nella vita popolare romana (sec. XVII–XIX). Catalogue of an exhibit at the Braschi Palace (Museo di Roma) 1–31 October 1975. Rome, 1978.

Döhring, Sieghart. "Musikalischer Realismus in Puccinis *Tosca*." *Analecta musicologica* 22 (1984): 249–96.

Donakowski, Conrad L. *A Muse for the Masses: Ritual and Music in an Age of Democratic Revolution, 1770–1870*. Chicago and London: University of Chicago Press, 1972.

D'Onofrio, Cesare. *Castel S. Angelo: Images and History*. Rome: D'Onofrio, 1984.

Dowd, David Lloyd. *Pageant-Master of the Republic: Jacques-Louis David and the French Revolution*. Lincoln, Nebr.: University of Nebraska, 1948.

Drot, Jean-Marie. *L'Accademia di Francia a Roma: Villa Medici*. Translated by Annalisa Cicerchia. Rome: Fratelli Palombi, 1991.

Ducloux, Walter. "A Tale of Three *Toscas*." *Opera Quarterly* 2 (Autumn 1984): 183–87.

Dumas, Alessandro [Alexandre Dumas]. *I Borboni di Napoli*. Naples: Tipografica Universale, 1862.

Dupaty, Charles Mercier. *Lettres sur l'Italie écrites en 1785*. Paris: 1785. Republished Paris: A. Payen, 1824.

Duppa, Richard, *A Journal of the Most Remarkable Occurrences that Took Place in Rome upon the Subversion of the Ecclesiastical Government in 1798*. London: G. G. and J. Robinson, 1799.

Durante, Sergio. "Vizi privati e virtù pubbliche del polemista teatrale da Muratori à Marcello." In *Benedetto Marcello: La sua opera e il suo tempo*, ed. Claudio Madricardo and Franco Rossi, 415–24. Atti del Convegno Internazionale Venice 15–17 December 1986. Florence: Olschki, 1988.

Ellis, B. *Rousseau's Venetian Story: An Essay upon Art and Truth in "Les Confessions."* Baltimore: Johns Hopkins Press, 1966.

Enciclopedia dello spettacolo. 9 vols. and index vol. (1968). Rome: Casa Editrice Le Maschere, 1954–62.

Escudier, Marie, and Léon Escudier. *Vie et aventures des cantatrices célèbres*. Paris: Dentu, 1856.

Fei, Idalberto. *Burattini a Roma: Teatro minimo dal Petrarca a Podrecca.* Rome: Palombi, 1992.

Ferris, John. "A Holy Terror." *Opera News* (15 Feb. 1969): 6–7.

Fétis, François-Joseph. *Biographie universelle des musiciens, et bibliographie générale de la musique,* 8 vols. Paris: Firmin-Didot, 1860–65.

Fiorelli, Pietro. *La tortura giudiziaria nel diritto comune.* 2 vols. Varese: Giuffrè, 1953–54.

Fischer-Williams, Barbara. "Gigi." *Opera News* (1 Jan. 1977): 22–23.

Fraccaroli, Arnaldo. *Giacomo Puccini si confida e racconta.* Milan: Sonzogno, 1957.

Franchi, Anna. *Fra' Diavolo.* Milan: Vir, 1945.

Fraser, Flora. *Beloved Emma: The Life of Emma, Lady Hamilton.* London: Weidenfeld and Nicolson, 1986.

Fratta Cavalcabò, Claudio. *Mascagni e Puccini: Battaglie, vittorie e distrazioni.* Parma: La Giovane Montagna, 1942.

Fritz, Hans. *Kastratengesang: Hormonelle, konstitutionelle, und pädagogische Aspekte.* Tutzing: H. Schneider, 1994.

Fusco di Ravello, Anna. "Tra conservazione e ratione: La tortura giudiziaria nello stato pontificio del '700." *Archivio della Società Romana di Storia Patria* 107 (1984): 307–24.

Gachot, Edouard. *Histoire militaire de Massena: La troisième campagne d'Italie (1805–1806).* Paris: Librarie Plon, 1911.

Gara, Eugenio, ed. *Carteggi Pucciniani.* Milan: Ricordi, 1958.

Gasbarri, Carlo, and Vittorio Emanuele Giuntella, eds. *Due diari della Repubblica Romana del 1798–1799.* Rome: Istituto di Studi Romani Editore, 1958.

Gavoty, André. *La Grassini, première cantatrice de S. M. l'Empereur et Roi.* Paris: Graset, 1947.

Gay, Peter. *The Enlightenment: A Comprehensive Anthology.* New York: Simon and Schuster, 1973.

———. *The Enlightenment: An Interpretation.* Vol. 1: *The Rise of Modern Paganism.* New York and London: W. W. Norton and Co., 1966. Vol. 2: *The Science of Freedom.* New York and London: W. W. Norton and Co., 1969.

Gérard, François. *Correspondance.* Rome, 1790.

Gerlini, Elsa. *Piazza Navona, catalogo della mostra omonima.* Rome: 1943.

Giazotto, Remo. *Puccini in casa Puccini.* Lucca: Akademos, 1992.

Gigli, Beniamino. *The Memoirs of Beniamino Gigli.* Translated by Darina Silone. London: Cassell and Company, 1957.

Giovannoni, G. "Il Settecento." In *Topografia e urbanistica di Roma.* Bologna, 1958.

Girardi, Michele. *Giacomo Puccini: L'arte internazionale d'un musicista italiano.* Venice: Marsilio, 1995. Forthcoming in English translation: Chicago: University of Chicago Press.

———. "La rappresentazione musicale dell'atmosfera settecentesca nel secondo atto di *Manon Lescaut.*" In Maehder, ed., *Esotismo e colore locale nell'opera di Puccini,* 65–82.

———. "*Turandot:* Il futuro interrotto del melodramma italiano." *Rivista italiana di musicologia* 17 (1982): 155–81.

Giuffrè, Antonino. "The Supporting Structure." In *The Angel and Rome,* 117–58.

Giuntella, Vittorio Emanuele. "Le classe sociali della Roma giacobina." *Rassegna storica del Risorgimento* 38, fasc. iii–iv (July–Dec. 1951): 432 et seq.

———. "I Cosacchi a San Pietro e i turchi al Laterano." *Urbe,* Year 13, n.s., 3 (1950): 19–23.

———. "Documenti sull'istruzione popolare in Roma durante il Settecento." *Studi romani* 9:5 (1961): 553 et seq.

———. "La giacobina repubblica romana (1798–1899): Aspetti e momenti." *Archivio della Società Romana di Storia Patria* 73 (1950): fasc. i–iv.

———. *La religione amica della democrazia: I cattolici democratici del triennio rivoluzionario (1796–1799).* Rome: Edizioni Studium, 1990.

———. "Ricerche per una storia religiosa di Roma nel Settecento." *Studi Romani* 8:3 (1960): 302 et seq.

———. *Roma nel Settecento*. Bologna: Cappelli, 1971.

———. "Roma nel Settecento: La capitale e i problemi dello stato," *Studi romani* 14 (1966): 269–91.

———. "Scuola e cultura nella Roma settecentesca." *Studi romani* 11:5 (1963): 528 et seq.

———. "Studi sul Settecento romano: La cultura e la società." *Studi romani* 10:6 (1962): 679 et seq.

———, ed. *Le dolci catene: Testi della controrivoluzione cattolica in Italia*. Istituto per la Storia del Risorgimento Italiano, Serie II: Fonti, 75. Rome: Alpha Press, 1988.

Glover, Michael. *A Very Slippery Fellow: The Life of Sir Robert Wilson, (1777–1849)*. Oxford and New York: Oxford University Press, 1978.

Goethe, Johann Wolfgang von. *Italian Journey (1786–1788)*. Translated by W. H. Auden and Elizabeth Mayer. London: Penguin, 1970. Published in Italian as *Viaggio in Italia* (Rome: Paravia, 1925).

Gold, Robert, and Robert Fitzdale. *The Divine Sarah: A Life of Sarah Bernhardt*. New York: Alfred A. Knopf, 1991.

Gonzáles-Palacios, Alvar. *David e la pittura Napoleonica*. Milan: Fratelli Fabbri, 1967.

Gori Sassoli, Mario. *Della chinea e di altre "Macchine di gioia": Apparati architettonici per fuochi d'artificio a Roma nel Settecento*. Roma: Charta, 1994.

Graff, Yveta Synek. "Tosca Talks: Fifteen Divas Discuss the Role and Their Lives." *Opera News* (18 Jan. 1986): 18–23.

Grancourt, Pierre-Jacques Bergeret de, and Jean-Honoré Fragonard. *Journal inédit d'un voyage en Italie 1773–1774*. Paris: Lib. impr. réunies, 1895. Translated by Felice Piemontese under the title *I tesori di Roma*. Naples: Guida, 1993.

Greco, Franco Carmelo. "Pulcinella a Roma." In *Pulcinella: Una maschera tra gli specchi*, 363–69. Naples: Edizioni Scientifiche Italiane, 1990.

Greenblatt, Steven. "Fiction and Friction." In *Reconstructing Individualism: Autonomy, Individuality, and Self in Western Thought*, ed. Thomas C. Teller, Morton Sosna, and David Wellbury, 66–93. Stanford: Stanford University Press, 1983.

———. *Learning to Curse: Essays in Early Modern Culture*. New York: Routledge, 1990.

———. *Shakespearean Negotiations: The Circulation of Social Energy in Renaissance England*. Berkeley: University of California Press, 1988.

———. "Towards a Poetics of Culture." In Veeser, ed., *The New Historicism Reader*, 1–14.

Greenwald, Helen. "Recent Puccini Research." *Acta musicologica* 65 (1993): 23–50.

Groos, Arthur, and Roger Parker. *La Bohème*. Cambridge: Cambridge University Press, 1986.

———, eds. *Reading Opera*. Princeton: Princeton University Press, 1988.

Gross, Hanns. *Rome in the Age of Enlightenment: The Post-Tridentine Syndrome and the Ancien Régime*. Cambridge: Cambridge University Press, 1990.

Grunchec, Philippe. *Le Grand Prix de peinture: Les concours des Prix de Rome de 1797 à 1863*. École Nationale Supérieur des Beaux-Arts. Paris: Marchand, 1983. In English as *The Grand Prix de Rome: Paintings from the École des Beaux-Arts, 1797–1863*. Washington, D.C.: International Exhibitions Foundation, 1984.

Guidotti, Fabrizio. "La musica per strumenti a tastiera di Domenico Puccini (1772–1815)." *Nuova rivista musicale italiana* 24 (1990): 335–60.

Gutteridge, Harold Cook. *Nelson and the Neapolitan Jacobins: Documents Relating to the Suppression of the Jacobin Revolution at Naples, June 1799*. London: Navy Records Society, 1903.

Hales, E. E. Y. *Revolution and Papacy*. London: Eyre & Spottiswoode, 1960.

Hansell, Kathleen Kuzmick. "Il ballo teatrale e l'opera italiana." In Bianconi and Pestelli, eds., *Storia dell'opera italiana* 5: 177–306.

Hart, Jerome A. *Sardou and the Sardou Plays*. Philadelphia and London: J. B. Lippincott, 1913.

Heartz, Daniel. "Farinelli Revisited." *Early Music* 18 (Aug. 1990): 430–43.

———. "From Garrick to Gluck: The Reform of Theater and Opera in the Mid-Eighteenth Century." *Proceedings of the Royal Musical Association* 94 (1967–68), 111–27.

Heger, Robert. *Lady Hamilton: Oper in drei Akten*. Vienna: Universal Edition, 1941.

Heinsheimer, Hans. "Great Publishing Houses II: Casa Ricordi." *Opera News* (19 Jan. 1980): 9–13.

Heriot, Angus. *The Castrati in Opera*. London: Martin Secker and Warburg, 1956.

———. *The French in Italy (1796–1799)*. London: Chatto and Windus, 1957.

Hersant, Yves. *Italies: Anthologie des voyageurs français aux XVIIIᵉ et XIX siècles*. Paris: Robert Laffont, 1988.

Hibbert, Christopher. *Rome, the Biography of a City*. New York and London: Norton, 1985.

Hind, Arthur M. *Giovanni Battista Piranesi: A Critical Study with a List of his Published Works and Detailed Catalogues of the Prisons and the Views of Rome*. London: 1922. Repr. London: Holland Press, 1978.

Holtman, Robert B. *The Napoleonic Revolution*. Philadelphia and New York: Lippincott, 1967.

Howgrave, Walter. "The Tragedy of La Tosca." London: Dranes Ltd., 1925.

Hughes, Spike. *Famous Puccini Operas: An Analytical Guide for the Opera-goer and Armchair Listener*. London: Hale, 1959.

Hughes, Steven. "Fear and Loathing in Bologna and Rome: The Papal Police in Perspective." *Journal of Social History* 21:1 (1987): 97–116.

Hunt, J. L., *Giovanni Paisiello: His Life as an Opera Composer*. [New York]: National Opera Association, 1975.

Hunt, Lynn. *The New Cultural History*. Berkeley: University of California Press, 1989.

Huppert, George. *After the Black Death: A Social History of Early Modern Europe*. Bloomington: Indiana University Press, 1986.

Isherwood, Robert. *Farce and Fantasy: Popular Entertainment in the Paris Fairs*. New York: Oxford University Press, 1986.

Jackson, Stanley. *Monsieur Butterfly: The Story of Giacomo Puccini*. New York: Stein and Day, 1974.

Jallonghi, Ernesto. *Fra' Diavolo nella storia e nell'arte*. Città di Castello: 1910.

Jellinek, George. *History through the Opera Glass: From the Rise of Caesar to the Fall of Napoleon*. London: Kahn and Averill, 1994. White Plains, N.Y.: Pro/Am Music Resources, 1994.

———. "Napoleon and the Prima Donna." *Opera News* (8 Feb. 1975): 14–15.

John, Nicholas, ed. *Tosca: Giacomo Puccini*. Opera Guide Series 16. London: John Calder; New York: Riverrun Press, 1980.

Katz, Robert. *Death in Rome*. London: Macmillan, 1967.

Keefe, Bernard. "The Music of Puccini's *Tosca*." In John, ed. *Giacomo Puccini: Tosca*, 13–22.

Kerman, Joseph. *Opera as Drama*. New York: Knopf, 1952. Rev. ed. Berkeley: University of California Press, 1988.

Kleine-Ahlbrandt, Laird. "The Hero as Revolutionary." *Opera News* (15 Feb. 1969): 24–25.

Kubler-Ross, Elisabeth. *On Death and Dying*. New York and London: Macmillan, 1969.

La Guardia, Rina. *Il fondo d'archivio Zanetti-Bellati nelle civiche raccolte numsimatiche di Milano*. Bibliotheca archeologica, vol. 15. Milan: Comune di Milan, Settore Cultura e Spettacolo, 1992.

Lais, Giuseppe. "Memorie e scritti di Mons. Filippo Luigi Gilii, direttore della Specola Vaticana ed insigne naturalista del secolo xviii." *Memorie della Pontificia Accademia dei Nuovi Lincei* 6. Roma: Tip. della Pace, 1890.

Lalande, C. de. *Voyage en Italie*. Paris: De Saint, n.d. Originally published as *Voyage d'un français en Italie* (Paris: De Saint, 1769).

Langbein, John H. *Torture and the Law of Proof: Europe and England in the Ancien Regime.* Chicago and London: University of Chicago Press, 1977.

La Pauze, Henri. *Histoire de l'Académie de France à Rome.* Paris: Plon, 1924.

Larousse, Pierre. *Grande Dictionnaire universel du XIXᵉᵐᵉ siècle.* 17 vols. Paris: Librairie classique Larousse et Boyer, 1866–90.

Law, Joe K. "Alessandro Moreschi Reconsidered: A Castrato on Records." *Opera Quarterly* 2:1 (1986): 1–12.

Lawrence, Robert. "The Connoisseur's Tosca." *Opera News* (17 Apr. 1965): 24–25.

———. "On Conducting Tosca in Italy." *Opera News* (4 Feb. 1946): 7–12.

Lentricchia, Frank. "Foucault's Legacy: A New Historicism." In Veeser, ed., *The New Historicism Reader*, 231–42.

Levi, Anthony. *Guide to French Literature.* Chicago and London: St. James Press, 1992.

Lingg, Ann. "Meet Angelotti." *Opera News* (6 Apr. 1959): 10–11.

Lippmann, Friedrich. "Un'opera per onorare le vittime della repressione borbonica del 1799 e per glorificare Napoleone: *I Pittagorici* di Vincenzo Monti e Giovanni Paisiello." In Bianconi and Bossa, eds., *Musica e cultura a Napoli dal XV al XIX Secolo*, 231–306.

"Litanie di Pasquino." *Monitore di Roma*, suppl. al numero LX. 13 Sept. 1798.

Londei, Luigi, and Neri Scerni. "Giustizia, politica e paternalismo nello stato pontificio: Nuove ricerche sul processo contro Cagliostro." *Rassegna storica del Risorgimento* 74:4 (1987): 411–40.

Lorenzi, Giambattista. "Notes on *Nina, or the Girl Grazy with Love.*" Liner notes for Bongiovanni recording GB 2054155-Z, recorded 22 November 1987.

Maehder, Jürgen, ed. *Esotismo e colore locale nell'opera di Puccini. Atti del convegno internazionale sull'opera di Giacomo Puccini.* Pisa: Giardini, 1985.

Mahler, Alma. *Gustav Mahler: Memories and Letters.* Edited by Donald Mitchell; translated by Basil Creighton. 3d ed. Seattle: University of Washington Press, 1975.

Mahon, Denis. "A Note on the Staging of *Tosca.*" *Opera* (London) 2 (1951): 162–67.

Malipiero, Gian Francesco. "La musica dopo la decadenza della cappella ducale." In *Sensibilità e ragionamento nel '700*, 475–479. Venice: Sansoni, 1967.

Mancini, Giovanni Battista. *Pensieri e riflessioni pratiche sopra il canto figurato.* Vienna, 1774. Repr. Bologna: Arnaldo Forni, 1970.

Manie, Sylvie. *Les Grands Castrats napolitains à Venise au xviiiᵉ siècle.* Liège: Mardaga, 1994.

Marchetti, Arnaldo, ed. *Puccini com'era.* Milan: Curci, 1973.

Marek, George R. *Puccini: A Biography.* New York: Simon and Schuster, 1951.

———. "The Well-Made Play." *Opera News* (30 Mar. 1985): 36–37.

Martinori, Edoardo. *La Moneta: Vocabolario generale.* Perugia, 1915.

Masson, Georgina. *The Companion Guide to Rome.* London: Wm. Collins and Son, 1965.

McBrien, Richard P. *Lives of the Popes: The Pontiffs from St. Peter to John Paul II.* San Francisco: Harper-San Francisco, 1997.

Memes, John Smythe. *Memoirs of Antonio Canova: A Critical Analysis of His Works, and a Historical View of Modern Sculpture.* Edinburgh: Constable and Co., 1825.

Messina, Costantino, ed. *Sogni e favole io fingo: Teatro pubblico e melodramma a Roma all'epoca di Metastasio.* Rome: Tip. Ed. Romana, 1985.

Michelet, Jules. *Le Prêtre, la femme, et la famille.* Paris, 1845.

Miller, Anna, *Letters from Italy.* Dublin, 1776.

Miller, Jonathan. *The Don Giovanni Book: Myths of Seduction and Betrayal.* Faber and Faber: London and Boston, 1990.

Milnes, Rodney. "What Does the Orchestra Scream?" *Opera* (London) 38 (Jan. 1987): 11–13.

Moindroit, Isabelle. *L'Opera seria, ou, Le règne des castrats.* Paris: Rayard, 1993.

Monnier, Marco. *Notizie storiche documentate sul brigantaggio nelle provincie napolitane.* Naples: Berisco, 1965. Trans. of *Histoire du brigandage dans l'Italie méridionale.*

Monnier, Philippe. *Venice in the Eighteenth Century.* London: Chatto and Windus, 1910.

Monson, Craig. *Disembodied Voices: Music and Culture in an Early Modern Italian Convent.* Berkeley and Los Angeles: University of California Press, 1995.

Moore, John. *A View of Society and Manners in Italy.* London: Stratham, 1781.

Morandi, L. *Le annotazioni di Mastro Tita, carnefice romano. Supplizi e suppliziati. Giustizie eseguite da Giovanni Battista Bugati e dal suo successore (1796–1870).* Città di Castello, 1886.

Morini, Mario. "La Tosca all'anagrafe della storia." *La Scala* (Mar. 1963). Reprinted in 49th Maggio Musicale Fiorentino, 1986.

Morini, Mario. "Illica e Fontana". *La Martinella* (Jan. 1958).

Mouly, George, ed. *Les Papiers de Victorien Sardou.* Paris: Albin Michel, 1934.

Murata, Margaret. *Operas for the Papal Court, 1631–1638.* Ann Arbor: UMI Research Press, 1981.

Muratori, Ludovico A. *Della perfetta poesia italiana* (Modena: Soliani, 1706); ed. Ada Ruschioni (Milan: Marzorati, 1971–72).

Nardi, Pietro. *Vita e tempo di Giuseppe Giacosa.* Milan: Mondadori, 1949.

Navenne, Ferdinand de. *Rome e le palais Farnèse pendant les trois derniers siècles.* Paris: Librairie Ancienne Honoré Champion, 1923.

New Grove Dictionary of Music and Musicians. Edited by Stanley Sadie. 20 vols. London: Macmillan, 1980.

New Grove Dictionary of Opera. Edited by Stanley Sadie. New York: Grove's Dictionaries of Music, 1992.

New Harvard Dictionary of Music. Edited by Don Michael Randel. Cambridge, Mass.: Harvard University Press, 1986.

New Oxford Companion to Music. Edited by Denis Arnold. Oxford: Oxford University Press, 1983. (Based on Percy Scholes, *Oxford Companion to Music,* 10th ed., 1970.)

Newton, Judith Lowder. "History as Usual? Feminism and the 'New Historicism'." In Veeser, ed., *The New Historicism Reader,* 152–67.

Nicassio, Susan V. "'The Pain Doesn't Matter': *Tosca* and the Law." *The Opera Quarterly* 8:1 (1991): 30–45.

Nicola, Carlo. *Diario napoletano, 1798–1825.* Naples: Società Napoletana di Storia Patria, 1906.

Nicoletti, Gianni, "La macchina Sadista," Saggio introdottivo [introductory essay]. In D. A. F. de Sade, *Juliette, ovvero la prosperità del vizio,* ed. Paolo Guzzi, 7–26. Rome: Newton, 1993.

Noether, Emiliana. *Seeds of Italian Nationalism (1700–1815).* New York: Columbia University Press, 1951.

Nolli, Giambattista. *La nuova topografia di Roma.* Rome: 1748.

Norci Cagiano de Azevedo, Letizia. "Un teatro tutto di legno: Il teatro Valle e il dramma giocoso a Roma attraverso i resoconti di viaggiatori francese del Settecento." *Nuova rivista musicale italiana* 24 (1990): 305–34.

———. "I viaggiatori francesi: De Brosses spettatore a Roma." In *Le Muse galanti,* ed. Cagli, 89–100.

Norwich, John Julius. *A History of Venice.* New York: Knopf, distributed by Random House, 1982.

Nouvelle biographie générale depuis les temps les plus reculés jusqu'à 1850–60. 46 vols. Paris: Firmin-Didot, 1853–66.

Nussdorfer, Laurie. *Civil Politics in the Rome of Urban VIII.* Princeton: Princeton University Press, 1992

Odell, George C. D. *Annals of the New York Stage.* New York: Columbia University Press, 1945.

Opdycke, Leonard. "The Topography of *Tosca*." *Opera News* (2 Jan. 1986): 4–7, 29.

Orlandi, Giuseppe. *La fede al vaglio: Quietismo, satanismo, e massoneria nel Ducato di Modena tra Sette e Ottocento.* Modena: Aedes Muratoriana, 1988.

Ortkemper, Hubert. *Engel wider Willen: Die Welt der Kastraten.* Berlin: Henschel, 1993.

Ortolani, S. *Sant'Andrea della Valle.* Chiese di Roma illustrate 4. Rome: Edizioni Roma, ca. 1965.

Osborne, Charles, *The Complete Operas of Puccini: A Critical Guide.* London: Gollancz, 1981.

Ovid, *The Technique of Love, and Remedies for Love.* Translated by Paul Turner. London: Panther, 1968.

Oxford Companion to Music, ed. Percy Scholes. 10th ed. Revised by John Owen Ward. London: Oxford University Press, 1975.

Paglia, Vincenzo. *La pietà dei carcerati: Confraternite e società a Roma nei secoli XVI–XVIII.* Rome: Edizioni di storia e letteratura, 1980.

Panichelli, Pietro. *Il "pretino" di Giacomo Puccini racconta.* 3d ed. Pisa: Nistri-Lischi, 1949.

Parker, Roger. "Analysis: Act I in Perspective." In *Giacomo Puccini: Tosca,* ed. Mosco Carner, 117–42. London: Cambridge University Press, 1985.

——, ed. *Giacomo Puccini, "Tosca."* Reduction for voice and piano of the revised edition of the full score based on the original sources. Milan: Ricordi, 1995.

Pastor, Ludwig von. *Storia dei papi dalla fine del Medio Evo,* ed. Angelo Mercati and Pio Cenci. Rome: Desclée et C., 1925–63.

Pastura, Maria Grazia. "Legislazione pontificia sui teatri e spettacoli a Roma." In Antolini et al., *La musica a Roma attraverso le fonti d'archivio,* 167–76.

Pavan, Giuseppe, "Il teatro Capranica: Saggio cronologico delle opere rappresentate nel XVIII secolo." *Rivista musicale italiana* 29:3 (Sept. 1922): 425–44.

Pencak, William. "Cherubini Stages a Revolution." *Opera Quarterly* 8:1 (Spring, 1991): 8–27.

Perusse, Lyle F. "*Tosca* and Piranesi." *Musical Times* (Nov. 1981): 743–45.

Peschel, Enid, and Richard Peschel. "Medicine and Music: The Castrati in Opera." *Opera Quarterly* 44 (Winter 1986–87): 21–37.

Petrobelli, Pierluigi. *Music in the Theater: Essays on Verdi and Other Composers.* Princeton Studies in Opera. Princeton: Princeton University Press, 1994.

Petrocchi, Giorgio, ed. *Orfeo in Arcadia: Studi sul teatro a Roma nel Settecento.* Rome: Istituto della Enciclopedia Italiana, 1984.

Peyre, Henri. "The Belle Epoque." *Opera News* (12 Dec. 1970): 9–13.

Piazza, Carlo Bartolomeo. *Eusevologio romano, ossia Delle opere pie di Roma.* Rome, 1698.

Picca, Paolo. *La tortura in Roma: Vicende storiche e abolizione.* Rome: Centenari, 1908.

Piozzi, Hester. *Observations and Reflections Made in the Course of a Journey through France, Italy and Germany* (1789), ed. Herbert Barrows. Ann Arbor: University of Michigan Press, 1967.

Plaut, Eric. *Grand Opera: Mirror of the Western Mind.* Chicago: Ivan R. Dee, 1993.

Porter, Roy. "Libertinism and Promiscuity." In Miller, ed., *The Don Giovanni Book,* 1–19.

Puccini, Giacomo. *276 lettere inedite,* ed. Giuseppe Pintorno. Milan: Nuove Edizioni, 1974.

——. *Lettere a Riccardo Schnabl,* ed. Simonetta Puccini. Milan: Emme Edizioni, 1982.

——. *Tosca.* Revision based on the original sources, ed. Roger Parker. Ricordi Opera Vocal Score Series. Milan: Ricordi, 1995.

The Puccini Companion, ed. William Weaver and Simonetta Puccini. New York: Norton, 1994.

Quirini, L. *Della beneficenza romana: Saggio storico statistico.* Rome: Tipografia Elzeviriano, 1878.

Rachleff, Owen. "Saturday [*sic*], June 14, 1800." *Opera News* (13 Jan. 1968): 24–25.

Rava, Arnaldo. *I teatri di Roma.* Rome: Palombi, 1953.

Rémy, Pierre-Jean. *La Mort de Floria Tosca.* Paris: Mercure de France, 1964.

Rescigno, Eduardo. *Giacomo Puccini: Tosca.* Milan: G. Ricordi, 1985.

Riccardi, Cesare. *La ristorazione del 1799, ossia I martiri di Napoli.* Milan: Visaj, 1860.

Ricci, Luigi. *Puccini interprete di se stesso*. Milan: Ricordi, 1980.

Richard, Jean. *Description historique et critique sur l'Italie*. 6 vols. Paris, 1766. Repr. as *Nouveau Guide du voyageur en Italie*. 2 vols. Paris, 1829.

Rinaldi, Mario. *Due secoli di musica al teatro Argentina*. 3 vols. Florence: Olschki, 1978.

Riti, cerimonie, feste, e vita di popolo nella Roma dei papi. Bologna: 1970.

Rivoluzione francese e Roma. Rome: Associazione Cattolica Artistico-Operaia, 1990.

Robinson, Michael F. "A Deconstructive Postscript: Reading Libretti and Misreading Opera." In Groos and Parker, eds., *Reading Opera*, 328–46.

———. "Paisiello e la cappella reale di Napoli." In Bianconi and Bossa, eds., *Musica e Cultura a Napoli dal XV al XIX secolo*, 267–80.

Rodocanachi, Emanuel. *Le Château Saint-Ange*. Paris: Hachette, 1909.

Romano, Pietro, and Peppino Partini. *Piazza di Spagna nella storia e nell'arte*. Rome: Palombi, n.d.

Roosevelt, Blanche. *Victorien Sardou: A Personal Study*. London: Keegan Paul, 1892.

Rosa, Mario. *Cattolicesimo e lumi nel Settecento italiano*. Rome: Herder, 1981.

Rosselli, John. "The Castrati as a Professional Group and a Social Phenomenon, 1550–1850." *Acta musicologica* 60 (1988): 143–79.

———. "Italy: The Decline of a Tradition." In Samson, ed., *The Late Romantic Era*, 126–50.

———. *Music and Musicians in Nineteenth-Century Italy*. Portland, Ore.: Amadeus, 1991.

———. *The Opera Industry from Cimarosa to Verdi: The Role of the Impresario*. Cambridge and New York: Cambridge University Press, 1984.

———. *Singers of Italian Opera: The History of a Profession*. Cambridge and New York: Cambridge University Press, 1992.

———. "I teatri di dipendenza della famiglia Capranica." In Antolini et al., *La musica a Roma attraverso le fonti d'archivio*, 177–82.

Rossi, L. "L'occupazione napoletana di Roma (1799–1801)." *Rassegna storica del Risorgimento* 19 (1932): 693–732.

Rousseau, Jean-Jacques. *Profession de foi du vicaire savoyard*. Paris: J. Vrin, 1978. First published ca. 1776.

———. *The Confessions*. Hanover: Dartmouth College, 1995.

Russell, Jack. *Nelson and the Hamiltons*. New York: Simon and Schuster, 1969.

Sade, Donatien A. F., Marquis de. *Florence, Rome et Naples*. In *Voyage d'Italie*. Oeuvres complètes, vol. 7. Paris: Jean-Jacques Pauvert, 1965.

———. *L'Histoire de Juliette . . . ou les prospérités du vice*. 6 vols. Translated into Italian as *Juliette, ovvero la prosperità del vizio*, ed. Paolo Guzzi. Opere complete. Rome: Newton, 1993.

———. *Justine, ou les malheurs de la vertu*. 2 vols. Paris: Girouard, 1791. Translated into Italian as *Le sventure della virtù*, ed. Claudio Rendina. Opere complete. Rome: Newton, 1978.

Salmon, J. *An Historical Description of Ancient and Modern Rome*. London, 1800.

Samson, Jim, ed. *The Late Romantic Era from the Mid-19th century to World War I*. Music and Society. Englewood Cliffs, N.J.: Prentice Hall, 1991.

Santi, Pietro. "Tempo e spazio ossia colore locale in *Bohème, Tosca*, e *Madama Butterfly*." In Maehder, ed., *Esotismo e colore locale nell'opera di Puccini*, 83–97.

Sardou, Victorien. *Patrie! An Historical Drama in Five Acts (Eight Scenes)*, ed. Barrett Harper Clark. Garden City, N.Y.: Doubleday, 1915.

———. *La Tosca*. In *L'Illustration théâtrale* 121 (19 June 1909): 1–33.

———. *La Tosca (The Drama Behind the Opera)*. Edited and translated by W. Laird Kleine-Ahlbrandt. Studies in the History and Interpretation of Music 19. Lewiston, N.Y.: The Edwin Mellen Press, 1990.

Schama, Simon. *Citizens: A Chronicle of the French Revolution*. New York: Knopf, 1989.

Scherer, Barrymore Laurence. "The Purloined Plot." *Opera News* (16 Dec. 1978): 11–14.

Schickling, Dieter. *Giacomo Puccini: Biografie.* Stuttgart: Deutsche Verlags-Anstalt, 1989.

———. "Giacomos kleiner Bruder: Fremde Spuren im Katalog der Werke Puccinis." *Studi Pucciniani* 1 (1998), 81–92.

Schoffman, Nachum. "Puccini's *Tosca:* An Essay in Wagnerism." *Music Review* 35 (1992), 268–90.

Seligman, Vincent. *Puccini Among Friends.* London: MacMillan, 1938.

Il Settecento a Roma. Catalogue of an exhibit 19 March–31 May 1959. Rome: De Luca, 1959.

Severi, Stefania. *I teatri di Roma.* Rome: Newton Compton, 1989.

Shaw, George Bernard. "Sardoodledom." In *Saturday Review*, 1 June 1895.

———. *Bernard Shaw: The Drama Observed, Vol. II (1895–1897),* ed. Bernard F. Dukore. University Park, Pa.: Pennsylvania State University Press, 1993.

Silvagni, David. *La corte pontificia e la società romana nei secoli XVIII e XIX.* Naples: Berisio, 1967.

Simoni, Antonio, and Adolfo Cano. "La pistola a semi-ricarica, un interessante caso giudiziario." *Armi antiche: Bollettino dell'Accademia di S. Marchiano-Torino* 2 (1955): 87 et seq.

Smith, Kay Nolte. "Sarah." *Opera News* (1 Jan. 1977): 15–17.

Smith, Patrick J. *The Tenth Muse: A Historical Study of the Opera Libretto.* New York: Knopf, 1970.

Smollett, Tobias. *Travels through France and Italy.* London: R. Baldwin, 1776.

Smoot, J. Edward. *Marshal Ney Before and After Execution.* Charlotte, N.C.: Queen City Publishing, 1929.

Solomon, Nicholas. "Signs of the Times: A Look at Late 18th-Century Gesturing." *Early Music* 17 (Nov. 1989): 551–62.

Sontag, Susan. *The Volcano Lover: A Romance.* New York: Farrar, Strauss, Giroux, 1992.

Specht, Richard. *Giacomo Puccini: The Man, His Life, His Work.* Translated by Catherine A. Phillips. London: Dent; New York: Knopf, 1933. Repr. Westport, Conn.: Greenwood Press, 1970. Translation of *Giacomo Puccini: Das Leben, der Mensch, das Werk* (Berlin, 1931).

Spreti, Vittorio, ed. *Enciclopedia storico-nobiliare italiana: Famiglie nobili e titolate viventi . . .* Milan: Edizioni Enciclopedia Storico-Nobiliare Italiana, 1929. Repr. Bologna: Arnaldo Forni, 1968–69.

Staël, Madame de [Anne-Louise Germaine]. *Corinne, or Italy.* Translated by Avriel H. Goldberger. New Brunswick, N.J., and London: Rutgers University Press, 1991.

Stark, Marianna. *Letters from Italy, 1792–1798.* London: R. Phillips, 1799.

Stendhal [Marie Henri Beyle]. *Promenades dans Rome.* Paris, 1829. Edited and translated by Haakon Chevalier, under the title *A Roman Journal.* New York: Orion Press, 1957.

———. *Rome, Naples et Florence,* ed. V. del Litto and Ernest Abravanel, annoted by Daniel Muller. Geneva: Edito-Service, 1968.

———. *Voyages en Italie,* ed. V. del Litto. Paris: Gallimard, 1973.

Stevenson, Florence. "The Day of the Premiere." *Opera News* (6 Apr. 1959): 6–7.

———. "Sant'Angelo's Ladies." *Opera News* (8 Apr. 1978): 32–33.

———. "She was Tosca." *Opera News* (18 Apr. 1964): 24–25.

Story, William W. *Roba di Roma.* 2 vols. Boston: Houghton, Mifflin and Co., 1887.

———. *Castel St. Angelo and the Evil Eye: Being Additional Chapters to "Roba di Roma."* London: Chapman and Hall, 1877.

Tackett, Timothy. *Priest and Parish in Eighteenth-Century France: A Social and Political Study of the Curés in a Diocese of Dauphiné, 1750–1790.* Princeton: Princeton University Press, 1977.

————. *Religion, Revolution, and Regional Culture in Eighteenth-Century France: The Ecclesiastical Oath of 1791*. Princeton: Princeton University Press, 1986.

Il teatro a Roma nel Settecento. Papers of an international conference held in Rome, 15–20 November 1982. Rome: Istituto della Enciclopedia Italiana, 1989.

Il teatro e la festa: Lo spettacolo a Roma tra papato e rivoluzione. Rome, 1989.

Tirincanti, Giulio. *Il teatro Argentina*. Roma: Palombi, 1971.

Titone, Antonino. *Vissi d'arte: Puccini e il disfacimento del melodramma*. Milan: Feltrinelli, 1972.

Tivarone, Carlo. *L'Italia durante il dominio francese (1789–1815)*. Turin: L. Roux, 1889.

Tomaselli, Sylvana, and Roy Porter, eds. *Rape*. Oxford: Oxford University Press, 1986.

Tosi, Pietro Francesco. *Observations on the Florid Song*. Translated by John Ernest Galliard (1680–1749). Edited by Paul Henry Lang. New York and London: Johnson Reprint Co., 1968.

Trasselli, C. "Processi politici romani dal 1792 al 1798." *Rassegna storica del Risorgimento* 25: 11–12 (1938): 1495–1613.

Trozzi, M. *Il boia si confessa: memorie di carnefice*. Rome, 1932.

Valesio, Francesco. *Diario di Roma, 1700–1742*, ed. Gaetano Scano. 6 vols. Milan: Longanesi, 1977–79.

Vannucci, Atto. *I martiri della libertà italiana dal 1794 al 1848*. Milan: Prato, 1848.

Vaussard, Maurice. *Daily Life in Eighteenth-Century Italy*. Translated by Michael Heron. London: George, Allen and Unwin, 1962. Originally published as *La Vie quotidienne en Italie au XVIIIᵉ siècle* (Paris: Hachette, 1959).

Veeser, Harold Aram, ed. *The New Historicism*. New York: Routledge, 1989.

————. *The New Historicism Reader*. New York: Routledge, 1994.

Venuti, Ridolfino. *Accurata e succinta descrizione topografica e istorica di Roma moderna*. Rome: Barbiellini, 1766. Repr. Rome: Multigrafica, 1977.

Venturi, Franco. *La chiesa e la repubblica dentro i loro limiti, 1758–1774*. Settecento riformatore 2. Turin: Einaudi, 1976.

————. *Da Muratori a Beccaria*. Settecento riformatore 1. Turin: Einaudi, 1969.

————. *The End of the Old Regime in Europe, 1768–1776: The First Crisis*. Translated by R. Burr Litchfield. Princeton: Princeton University Press, 1989. (Translation of *La prima crisi dell'Antico Regime*. Settecento riformatore 3.)

————. *The End of the Old Regime in Europe, 1776–1789*. Translated by R. Burr Litchfield. Princeton: Princeton University Press, 1991. (Translation of *Caduta dell'Antico Regime, 1776–1789*.)

————. *L'Italia dei Lumi (1764–1790)*. Settecento riformatore 5. Turin: Einaudi, 1987.

————. *Italy and the Enlightenment: Studies in a Cosmopolitan Century*. London: Longman, 1972.

————. *Utopia and Reform in the Enlightenment*. Cambridge: Cambridge University Press, 1971.

Verdone, Mario. *Spettacolo romano*. Rome: Golem, 1970.

Verri, Alessandro. *Le notti romane*. Florence and Paris: Samson figlio, 1823.

Verri, Pietro. *Osservazioni sulla tortura*, ed. Giulio Carnazzi. Milan: Rizzoli, 1988.

Vicchi, Leone, *Les Français à Rome pendant la Convention*. Rome: 1892.

Vigée-Lebrun, Elisabeth. *Memoirs of Vigée-Lebrun: Member of the Royal Academy of Paris, Rouen, Saint-Luke of Rome, Parma, Bologna, Saint-Petersburg, Berlin, Geneva and Avignon*. Translated by Sian Evans. Bloomington and Indianapolis: Indiana University Press, 1989.

Villa Medici: L'Accademia di Francia a Roma. Rome: Fratelli Palombi, 1991.

Weaver, William. "A Drama of Rome." *Opera News* (5 Dec. 1987): 24–25.

Weber, Eugen. "About *Thermidor:* The Oblique Uses of a Scandal." *French Historical Studies* 17:2 (1991): 330–42.

White, Hayden. "New Historicism: A Comment." In Veeser, ed., *The New Historicism Reader,* 293–302.

Williams, Alan. *The Police of Paris 1718–1789.* Baton Rouge: Louisiana State University Press, 1979.

Williams, Bernard. "Manifest Artifice." In John, ed., *Giacomo Puccini: Tosca,* 7–13.

Wilson, Robert Thomas. *The Life of General Sir Robert Thomas Wilson 1777–1849.* Translated by Herbert Randolph as *Vita del Generale Sir Robert Wilson.* Milan: Cento Libri, 1972.

Winterhoff, Hans-Jürgen. *Analytische Untersuchungen zu Puccinis "Tosca."* Regensburg: Gustav Bosse Verlag, 1973.

Woolf, Stuart. "Historical Perspectives on *Tosca.*" In John, ed., *Giacomo Puccini: Tosca,* 25–29.

Zanazzo, Luigi. *Tradizioni popolari romane: Usi, costumi e pregiudizi del popolo di Roma.* Rome: La Bancarella Romana, 1907–10.

Zeldin, Theodore. *Conflicts in French Society: Anticlericalism, Education and Morals in Nineteenth-Century Society.* London: George, Allen and Unwin, 1970.

———. *France, 1848–1945.* 3 vols. Oxford: Clarendon Press, 1973–77.

Index

Abbondi, Crispino, 197

Acton, Lord, 98

Adua, Italian defeat at, 24

Alembert, Jean le Rond d', 66, 67

Alexander VI, and Farnese family, 181

Alexander, Tsar: and Knights of Malta, 281n.47; plan to rescue pope, 46; and Alliance, 72

Alfieri, Vittorio, *La congiura dei Pazzi*, 42

Alibert, Count Jacques d', 81

Alibert theater: carnival balls at, 72; gala at, 76; financial problems of, 78; among Roman theaters, 81; Luigi Marchesi at, 88; Teresa Bertinotti at, 93; as official theater, 98; open in 1800, 82; *Roma liberata* at, 99

Allies: and amnesty, 110, 278n.1; caricatured, 45; disorderly troops of, 71–72; executions under, 39, 51; policies in Rome, 71; treaty terms with, 48

Altieri, Monsignor, 111

"Amaro sol per te," text of, 241, 243–44, 301n.51

American Academy in Rome, xiv

Ancona, as border of Papal States, 23

angel (on Castel Sant'Angelo): and Benedict XIV, 222; as the "Genius of Liberty," 43, 222; and Gregory the Great, 221; by Francesco Giardoni, 222; by Peter Anton Verschffelt, 222

Angeletti, Nicola Antonio: as model for Angelotti, 35; whipped in Naples, 104f

Angelotti, Cesare (character): alternative model for, xvi; and Cavaradossi, 54, 139–41; costume design for, 125f; flees Naples, 279n.22; in *La Tosca*, 126; models for, 35, 54, 104, 117; and Parthenopean Republic, 2; in plot summary, 6, 54; suicide and hanging of, 214; and Scarpia, 256; and well, 9

Angelotti motif: first appearance of, 123; illustrated, 124; in Scarpia's Plan, 180; in Te Deum scene, 161

Angelucci, Liborio: corruption charges against, 36; freed from prison, 35; friends arrested, 171; as model for Angelotti, 35; as model for Scarpia, xvi; and palace of Order of Malta, 37; returns to Rome, 37, 44

Angelus: described, 132–33; and Madonna, 144; and Sacristan, 131; sets time for Act I, 2; signal for escape, 127

anti-clericalism: in French law, 276n.10; and occupation of Rome by Napoleon III, 284n.4; and Puccini, 18; and Sacristan, 133; Sardou's use of, 16; shocks New York, 251; in Te Deum scene, 161; and Third Republic, 15

Apollo theater. *See* Tordinona

Apostolic Camera, 78

Appian Way: Neapolitan troops enter Rome by, 48; and prostitutes, 296n.5; and tomb of Scipios, 174; villa on, 48, 70, 172

Arcadian academy, 83

Ardeatine caves, massacre in, 25, 256

Argentina theater: and Alibert theater, 98; Angelica Catalani at, 90; *Artaserse* at, 89; financial problems at, 78; and *La congiura dei Pazzi*, 42; Luigi Marchesi at, 88; origin of name, 285n.17; owner of, 72; Paisiello's *Barber of Seville* at, 97; and Pannini, 83f; performers under suspicion, 171–72; and Roman theaters, 81–2; shows described, 287n.32

Attavanti, Marchesa (character): and Cavaradossi 138–39; fan and crest of, 8, 147, 152, 154, 293n.38, 294n.51; portrait of, 54, 150, 152; property at Frascati 147, 171; and Scarpia 147

Attavanti motif, 135